AF328529

War along the Border

NUMBER SIX: University of Houston Series in Mexican American Studies
Sponsored by the Center for Mexican American Studies
Tatcho Mindiola, Director and General Editor

A list of titles in this series appears at the back of the book.

WINNER OF THE 2011 ROBERT A. CALVERT BOOK PRIZE

WAR ALONG THE BORDER
THE MEXICAN REVOLUTION AND TEJANO COMMUNITIES

Edited by Arnoldo De León

TEXAS A&M UNIVERSITY PRESS | COLLEGE STATION

This paper meets the requirements of ANSI/NISO Z39.48-1992 (Permanence of Paper).
Binding materials have been chosen for durability.

Library of Congress Cataloging-in-Publication Data

War along the border : the Mexican Revolution and Tejano communities / edited by Arnoldo
De León. — 1st ed.
    p. cm. — (University of Houston series in Mexican American studies ; no. 6)
    "Several of the papers in this collection were read . . . [at] a symposium held in September
2010 by the University of Houston's Center for Mexican American Studies."—Introd.
    Includes bibliographical references and index.
    ISBN-13: 978-1-60344-524-5 (cloth : alk. paper)
    ISBN-10: 1-60344-524-2 (cloth : alk. paper)
    ISBN-13: 978-1-60344-525-2 (pbk. : alk. paper)
    ISBN-10: 1-60344-525-0 (pbk. : alk. paper)
    e-ISBN-13: 978-1-60344-569-6
    e-ISBN-10: 1-60344-569-2
    e-ISBN-13: 978-1-60344-570-2
    e-ISBN-10: 1-60344-570-6
    1. Mexican Americans—Texas—History—20th century—Congresses. 2. Mexico—
History—Revolution, 1910–1920—Mexican Americans—Congresses. 3. Mexico—History—
Revolution, 1910–1920—Social aspects—Congresses. 4. Mexican American women—
Texas—History—20th century—Congresses. 5. Texas—History—1846–1950—Congresses.
6. Mexican-American Border Region—History—20th century—Congresses. 7. Mexico—
History—Revolution, 1910–1920—African Americans—Congresses. 8. Mexico—History—
Revolution, 1910–1920—Refugees—Texas—Congresses. I. De León, Arnoldo, 1945–
II. University of Houston. Center for Mexican American Studies. III. Series: University of
Houston series in Mexican American studies; no. 6.
    F395.M5W37 2011
    972.08'16—dc23
                                                                          2011018192

Contents

Mexican American communities in the United States owe much to *la frontera*. The Texas–Mexico border has given people on both its sides the distinctive style of music known as *conjunto,* led to the making of delectable Tex-Mex dishes, kept popular the *vaquero* style of dress, acted as an arena where Spanish and English blend, and ultimately has created a syncretic Chicano identity. Due to cultural and historic influences, Mexican American communities throughout the United States annually observe some of Mexico's epochal events, among them the day on which the *Virgen de Guadalupe* appeared to Juan Diego (December 12), the day on which Mexico declared independence from Spain (the *Diez y Seis de Septiembre*), and the day in 1862 when Mexican forces inflicted a defeat on the French army at Puebla (the *Cinco de Mayo*). In the year 2010, numerous Mexican American communities in Texas, and indeed nationally, commemorated the hundredth anniversary of the Mexican Revolution. Unfortunately, scholarship at times does not give deserved attention to aspects of these historic episodes. To our knowledge, for instance, *War along the Border: The Mexican Revolution and Tejano Communities* represents the first treatment of how the Mexican Revolution of 1910 affected the economic, cultural, and political climate of Mexican Americans in Texas. What the essays in the collection reveal is that during the 1910s there was a war on the Texas–Mexico border, Mexico seemed on the brink, and anti-Mexican sentiment in Texas was high. A hundred years later, in 2010, there is a war on the Texas–Mexico border, Mexico seems on the brink, and anti-Mexican sentiment is high. Clichés abound. Have we not learned anything from history? Does history repeat itself? Does history move in circles? To be sure the circumstances between 1910 and 2010 are very different, but can it be that the more things change, the more they stay the same? One major difference is that Mexican Americans in Texas today are larger in number (close to 10 million by some estimates) and possess more political and economic power than they did in 1910. Our power, however, like our scholarship, is still nascent, and much more remains to be accomplished. It is our hope that the essays presented here will stimulate more research on how the Mexican Revolution affected Mexican Americans specifically and on Mexico–Mexican American relations in general. The Center for Mexican American Studies at the University of Houston is pleased to have participated in this discussion and contributed to bringing new knowledge to the public through its Monograph Series.

Tatcho Mindiola, Director
Center for Mexican American Studies
University of Houston

War along the Border

Introduction

ARNOLDO DE LEÓN

In late 1910, a fateful revolution burst forth in Mexico. Today, some observers tout the uprising as matching in scope the Russian Revolution of 1917, the Chinese Revolution of 1949, the Cuban Revolution of 1959, and the Iranian Revolution of 1979. The Revolution of 1910, now a century past, continues to fascinate scholars, attract history majors to courses on the subject, and take up much shelf space in university libraries across the globe.

The basic facts of the Revolution are fairly well-known. Its origins lay in the massive discontent existing throughout the land against the dictator Porfirio Díaz (1876–1911). Landless *campesinos* felt angered with land theft, *peones* with hacienda life, laborers with industrial conditions in factories, the literati with intellectual suppression, political dissenters with disfranchisement, educators with illiteracy, and so on. It was an unlikely figure by the name of Francisco I. Madero who galvanized the many restive elements throughout Mexico and started the Revolution from his place of exile in San Antonio. From Texas he issued the *Plan de San Luis Potosí,* calling for a nationwide uprising of his compatriots against Díaz to occur on the 20th day of November 1910.

Those familiar with the history of the Revolution know that Díaz submitted to revolutionary forces, resigning his office in May 1911, that Madero assumed the presidency in November 1911, only to face assassination in February 1913, and that Victoriano Huerta, who coordinated the plan leading to Madero's murder, succeeded to the presidency (only to be forcibly removed from the executive by insurgent armies in August 1914). Known also is that Mexico, shortly after Madero took over the reins of government, slipped into internecine fighting and that subsequently leaders in command of this or that revolutionary faction were Francisco (Pancho) Villa, Emiliano Zapata, Pascual Orozco, and Venustiano Carranza, among others. Of equal understanding is that those who fought in the Revolution did so for different purposes, among them to achieve land reform, hold free elections, require separation of church and state, bring an end to foreign domination of Mexico's infrastructure, introduce unionization, and the like. They did so fiercely, and the Revolution quickly deteriorated into forced conscription, disruption of homes and communities, sustained violence, chaotic economic conditions, widespread hunger, and much misery.

In the year 2010, the nation of Mexico commemorated the one-hundredth anniversary of the Revolution. Citizens rightfully celebrated the ousting of Díaz the dictator, the decline of peonage as a feudal system, gains made by labor union members, land reform, anticlericalism, and the termination of foreign ownership of the nation's natural resources. They observed the relative calm that had reigned over the country during the course of a century.

Throughout the United States, Mexican American communities in 2010 also paid homage to the Mexican Revolution. It seemed fitting that Mexican Americans too observe the many principles embodied in the rebellion, which, after all, represented universal ideals. But the Revolution could not have had the same meaning for Mexicans in the United States in the year 2010 as it did for citizens of Mexico. Common folks in Texas had no more than curiosity about the protagonists in the Revolution, such as Villa and Zapata! Nor would many have debated whether the Revolution ended in success or disappointment. Rather, any interest in the Revolution after one hundred years would have revolved around questions such as these: "How did the Mexican Revolution affect communities across the border in the United States?" and "Did the Revolution have any relevance to the Mexican American experience?"

Addressing such questions was the intent of a symposium held in September 2010 by the University of Houston's Center for Mexican American Studies. There, several of the papers in this collection were read. For the purpose of disseminating their scholarly findings to a wider audience, they have been assembled under the title *War along the Border: The Mexican Revolution and Tejano Communities.*

As a unit, the book has two objectives. Mainly, it aims to explain the nexus between the Revolution and the Mexican American experience in Texas. The first essay in the collection lays the stage for making that link. Professor Paul Hart lists the many causes that sparked the massive display of discontent that produced the Mexican Revolution of 1910. He explains the varied meanings the Revolution held for its many participants—for some it represented a fight for democracy; for peasants, a struggle for land distribution; and for still others, a crusade for workers' rights. Then, Hart details the impact of the Revolution, focusing on such monumental events as the displacement of Mexico's large population from the war zones and their trek to safer parts of the nation, as well as to the United States. Last, he identifies a lesson from the Revolution that indicates forces destined to remake Texas and the greater United States in this century: to wit, economic interaction between the United States and Mexico determines oscillating patterns of migration. During the era circa the 1930s to the 1970s, when Mexico pursued a policy of economic autonomy, outward migration to the United States slowed. But when the United States (or other foreign powers, for that matter) have influenced Mexico's economy, as in the years of the Revolution or more especially in more recent decades, increased outward migration (much of it to the United States) followed.

Certainly, the 1910 tumult did not confine itself to Mexico; it spread past international borders and touched Texas-Mexican communities (positively and adversely) along a line from Brownsville to El Paso. On the one hand, *colonias* in Texas that played host to fleeing refugees experienced demographic expansion and cultural invigoration. Ethnic enclaves became settings for nationalist activity as refugees and exiles sought to extend moral, financial, and even military aid to their favorite faction from afar. In *barrios,* women (whether immigrant or native born) influenced by the rhetoric of the conflict in Mexico, took up strategies for improving women's status and workers' rights. On the other hand, death visited many Mexicans having the misfortune of living close to the Rio Grande where raiders from Mexico and ranchers from Texas clashed over livestock and property. Such is only a sampling of the manner by which the Mexican Revolution weighed on Spanish-speaking communities in Texas. The essays that follow elaborate on this impact.

A second objective is to draw attention to the vast possibilities available for investigation on this subject too long slighted by the academic establishment. Our several contributors single out some potential topics. Richard Henry Ribb, for instance, brings attention to a rampage that during the 1915 era Tejanos called "*la rinchada.*" The campaign, a derivation of "*los rinches*"—a derogatory term for "Rangers" used by many South Texans—resulted in the killing of hundreds, if not thousands, of Tejanos, the displacement of thousands more, and a wide-ranging, determined resistance to unjust authority. Simultaneously, key Texas Ranger figures participated in illegal and extralegal activities designed to undermine the Revolution in Mexico: *la rinchada* in this context represented a counterrevolutionary strategy to restore a Díaz-style regime in Mexico.

Trinidad Gonzales brings light to an indigenous Tejano movement in 1915, which Gonzales believes has previously been confused with the *Plan de San Diego.* For Gonzales, the Mexican Revolution created an environment for what he terms the "*revolución de Texas.*" During this offensive to overturn colonial rule in the Lower Rio Grande Valley, México Texanos and Mexicanos utilized the weakly policed southern side of the border set by the chaos of the factional fighting to launch and retreat from their military operations against the U.S. military. In the process, however, many innocent Mexicans suspected of supporting the *revolución* were killed out of frustration. Gonzales refers to this retaliatory campaign as the "*matanza*" (massacre).

The lacuna in the scholarship exploring the ramifications of the Mexican Revolution on Tejano communities also suggests the necessity for inquiry into how white society judged Tejanos who got involved in the Revolution, directly or otherwise. Miguel A. Levario asserts that during the 1910s whites came to consider Mexicans of El Paso guilty of treachery (even if only by association) and thus unworthy of equal consideration before the law. International militarization, especially in 1916 as Pancho Villa increasingly threatened U.S. interests, he concludes, contributed to the definition of Mexicans as an "enemy other." For most of the twentieth century in the U.S. Southwest, "American" generally meant white, while the word "Mexican" stood for race and not citizenship.

Suggestive to scholars as well is the subject of Tejanas and how the Revolution affected them, or alternatively, how women (both foreign and native born) engaged in the life of their immediate communities during the 1910s and after. For Juanita Luna Lawhn, *rico* (rich) women exiles (some of them relatives of powerful political figures ousted by the Revolution) asserted their presence within the Mexican *colonia* during their stay in San Antonio. They set examples of courage while living in the city and contributed to humanitarian causes. *México de Afuera* women, for example, participated within the San Antonio Round Table and volunteered and carried out charitable work within the city's *Cruz Azul* into the 1920s. Sonia Hernández explains that immigrant women and Tejanas used the rhetoric of the Revolution to address gender inequalities and unfavorable labor conditions. This revolutionary-inspired activism further shaped the larger conversation about labor in Texas. Although the Revolution did not overturn gender inequalities with regard to labor issues, the contributions of women workers and their efforts to improve their socioeconomic conditions accentuated their active roles in the building of the greater Texas–Mexico borderlands.

Other authors present solid evidence validating the assumption most scholars have long held that the refugees, either as individuals, families, or groups, made constructive (yet unappreciated) contributions to both the state of Texas and to Tejano communities. For Roberto R. Treviño, the expulsion of thousands of poor and working-class Mexicans by the Revolution of 1910 redounded to the benefit of both the Texas economy and the Tejano community. Mexicano common people formed the backbone of the Texas agricultural boom of the early twentieth century even as their burgeoning numbers and community building breathed a new vitality and permanency into Mexican American communities throughout the state.

Down and out, the refugees sought vigorously to reassemble their lives in their new environment, and although some found they had simply exchanged one barrio for another, others effectively made a fresh start. There must be hundreds such success cases for scholars to consider, among them the subject of Thomas H. Kreneck's essay. According to Professor Kreneck, the Mexican Revolution produced more than workers for a cheap labor pool; it contributed to the emerging middle class as well. Felix Tijerina was one such case; he came to the United States as a humble immigrant in 1915 and achieved success beyond his greatest expectations, becoming Houston's first Mexican American millionaire and a role model for an entire generation of Mexican Americans before 1965. In doing so, however, Tijerina had to grapple mightily with his immigrant status, the particulars of which biographer Thomas H. Kreneck reveals through painstaking, creative research.

Although it is well-known that Tejanos participated to different degrees in the Revolution, further investigation regarding motives behind their involvement is needed. For John Eusebio Klingemann, patriotism moved Tejanos along the Big Bend country to support rebels opposing the dictator Porfirio Díaz in 1910–1911, and after 1913, to give aid to the *Villistas* (followers of Pancho Villa). Sympathy for revolutionaries in the north lay in the historic connection between the people of northern Chihuahua and those in counties like Brewster and Presidio. Tejanos thus aided and abetted the struggle with money, weapons, and necessary supplies. Certainly, opportunists and selfish characters sought profit in the contraband of arms and supplies, and such an element merits examination, a task assumed here by George T. Díaz. According to Díaz, entrepreneurial and sympathetic border people disregarded U.S. law, to trade illicit arms and rationed foodstuffs to revolutionary Mexico. Support for the Revolution and a desire for personal gain led most Tejanos to accept the practice of revolutionary smuggling across the border.

The Mexican Revolution had effects on communities in Texas other than those of Mexicans, as indicated in the coauthored essay by Professors Gerald Horn and Margaret Stevens. For African Americans who sought to challenge the seemingly hegemonic strictures of the "Jim Crow" United States, these two authors conclude, the Mexican Revolution stood as a beacon of inspiration; at times its proponents from both south and north of the border were even allies in the movement to overturn the American empire.

This volume published in commemoration of the one-hundredth anniversary of the Mexican Revolution, then, can well serve as a template for further study on the question of the Mexican Revolution's place in Chicano history (or African American history for that matter). It identifies the multifarious ways in which the Revolution touched Mexicans in Texas, whether native or foreign born. It suggests alternatives for looking at this watershed moment in Mexican American history. Most significantly, the collection stands as another affirmation that the history of Mexicans in Texas is transnational in scope, as Raúl A. Ramos emphasizes in his concluding essay.

For Ramos, writing Tejano history must take into account events that might occur south of the Rio Grande, for at times (as in the instance of the Revolution) they shape ethnic experiences in the United States. Furthermore, Ramos counsels, to fully comprehend violence, migrations, and constraints on state authority, scholars need to place these forces in broader geographic planes. Upon so doing, they can discern ideologies, identity, culture, and economics transcending boundaries and influencing international currents. What unfurls in one nation can likely spill over into an adjacent land, as in the example of the violence that accompanied the

Revolution and in the case of people escaping the war zone into Texas. In Ramos's judgment, the violence, state authority, and migration that persisted during the subsequent one hundred years impacted (and continues to affect) Mexican American ethnicity in the United States. A transnational paradigm thus helps us see border areas as zones of engagement and not ones obstructing human interaction.

Those who write Mexican American history employ a wide range of terms (whether to avoid repeatedly using the same label or because the context calls for a different name), and such is the case in this book. The word "Mexican" is herein utilized to identify people born in Mexico, though many of the authors apply it generically to Mexican Americans as a group. The words "of Mexican origin or Mexican descent," as is obvious, refer to those of Mexican ancestry. Some writers turn to the phrase "ethnic Mexican" when they cannot specifically determine their subject's (or subjects') country of birth. *Tejanos* would be Mexican-origin people who reside in the state of Texas, whereas "México Texano" was a self-referent used by Tejanos during the time period covered in this collection. The term "Mexican American" is utilized frequently in the several essays to mean U.S. citizens of Mexican heritage. Modern-day terms such as "Chicano," "Hispanic," or "Latino" slip into the writing here and there; where found, they substitute for "Mexican American." When referring to Euro-Americans, authors employ terms like "white" and "Anglo-American"; "African Americans" is the commonly accepted term for black Americans.

Beyond Borders Causes and Consequences of the Mexican Revolution

PAUL HART

The Mexican Revolution of 1910–1920 was the first successful revolution of the twentieth century. It was also the most enigmatic. It overthrew a dictatorship, but unlike other major revolutions such as the Russian, Chinese, or Cuban, no unified ideology directed it. No vanguard party seized power and implemented clearly articulated reforms designed to create an idealized society. Instead, the ruling party that emerged in Mexico coalesced after the Revolution and rested on a delicate alliance of often competing groups whose visions of what revolutionary Mexico should look like had differed violently.

The outcome of that struggle defined the future of modern Mexico and transcended its borders, impacting society in the United States, especially in border states like Texas. Revolutionaries, reactionaries, migrant workers, labor organizers, and refugees, found their way to the state. From the increased ethnic violence and initial civil rights activism of early twentieth century Texas, to immigration and the politics of ethnicity today, the results of the Mexican Revolution reached beyond the border.[1]

Three main struggles defined Mexico's Revolution. First, the agrarian revolution of peasants and landless laborers sought the redistribution of land and wealth in the countryside. They lost the war but won significant concessions from the new revolutionary government. Second, the workers' revolt of urban and industrial labor included anarchist-inspired revolutionary demands for worker control of production, distribution, and profits. The workers were too few and too weak for victory, but they too won important guarantees. Third, the nationalist bourgeois rebellion desired a greater political voice through representative democracy, and modernization through government support of Mexican businesses versus powerful, and previously privileged, foreign capital. Their goals did not include a radical social transformation through the redistribution of wealth to peasants or labor. In the end, they won the war, but not decisively enough to impose their vision on the rest of the nation. They had to accommodate the peasants and workers, at least to a degree. That accommodation anchored the ruling party of the Revolution (eventually known as the *Partido Revolucionario Institucional,* PRI) and gave it enough cross-class legitimacy to maintain control for most of the twentieth century. However, over time, peasants and workers were sufficiently co-opted, and then marginalized, so that by 1968 revolutionary change neared a halt, and by the mid-1980s it had slipped into reverse. Since then, many of the major social reforms of the Revolution designed to protect workers, peasants, and the national economy have been dismantled. Today, the results, especially increased immigration, make headlines in Texas almost every week.

The Revolution overthrew the thirty-five-year-long dictatorship of Porfirio Díaz (the *Porfiriato,* 1876–1910) when people from different social classes joined together in 1910–1911 to demand fair elections and an end to the reelection of the President. However, different social groups voiced their demands for very different reasons. Once they drove Díaz from power, the real fight began, as the revolutionary factions turned on each other in a brutal decade-long war.

The Revolution of 1910 had many causes, some ancient, and some coming about during the reign of Díaz. Defeated multiple times in elections for the presidency, first by Benito Juárez and then by Sebastián Lerdo de Tejada, General Díaz launched a rebellion and seized power in 1876. His revolt, called the "Revolution of Tuxtepec," took its name from a town in his home state of Oaxaca, but actually, powerful Americans interested in economic opportunities in Mexico in part funded it, and the *Plan* had San Antonio, Texas, as its inaugural point. Some Americans backed Díaz because President Lerdo's nationalistic policies impeded their desires to build railroads and gain access to Mexico's vast natural resources. Reflecting his protectionist attitude, Lerdo is supposed to have said "between strength and weakness, the desert." Others, like rancher Richard King in Texas, supported Díaz for local reasons. Most importantly for King and his allies in South Texas, Díaz promised to restrain General Juan N. Cortina and end the so-called Cortina Wars, which involved Mexicans and Tejanos "rustling" cattle and interfering with the operation of Anglo ranchers whom they felt had acquired the land from Mexicans in fraudulent and illegal ways. Cortina's family had lost their land, and he supported the raids and gave safe haven to Mexicans and Tejanos whom Anglo ranchers considered "bandits." Cortina and many border Mexicans, however, thought the Anglo ranchers to be the actual perpetrators. Díaz's assurances to reign in Cortina, therefore, made him an appealing alternative for some Texas ranchers.[2]

Díaz also looked good to American banking, railroad, agribusiness, timber, and mining interests, because he promised to open Mexico to foreign investment. The General wanted to modernize Mexico, but he felt that to join the ranks of modern industrializing countries, the country, like all poor nations, needed foreign capital, technological expertise, and markets. Therefore, he opened the doors to Mexico and enticed foreign capital with land concessions, tax breaks, cheap labor, and the promise of a secure social climate for investment. Capital flowed in and his policies spurred impressive economic growth for a time. The problem, though, was that Díaz failed to ensure that the benefits reached enough Mexicans.

The Porfirian model of economic growth and modernization came with a high human cost. Hoping to modernize farming beyond the ox and the plow, Díaz and his associates promoted large-scale commercial agriculture and the greater privatization of landholding. That decision came at the expense of subsistence-oriented communal villages and self-sufficient small landholders across the country. Taking sides in a longstanding struggle between *hacendados* and *pueblos,* Díaz allowed *hacendados* and local authorities to strip *pueblos* of communal land and water rights. When *pueblo* leaders protested, he often had them arrested, conscripted into the army, or sent to labor camps in Yucatán.

Díaz's approach was not entirely new. Mexican elites pursuing modernization had tried to privatize and commercialize the land of the communalist Indian and *mestizo pueblos* since the mid-nineteenth century. Liberal ideas of progress included the belief that communal landholding retarded Mexican national development and needed to be turned into private property, with individuals producing for a profit. Even though it was a foreign concept derived from outside experiences from other countries and represented a doctrine totally antithetical to the historical development of rural Mexico, the Liberals imagined that private property would stimulate a productive class of independent yeoman farmers that would provide the basis for individual initiative and the new mentality they believed necessary for national progress. Laws were passed creating the mechanisms necessary to carry out the transformation, including opening up communal pastures and woodlands and declaring them vacant lands. Díaz intensified the process. First, he followed through on a land law of 1875 that allowed surveying companies to survey "vacant" lands and granted the companies one-third of the land surveyed as payment. Another law, passed in 1883, followed when Díaz's associate, General Manuel González, served as President of Mexico. The law forced people to prove legal title to the land on which they lived. Small landholders and communal *pueblos* often lacked documentation, though, or could not afford drawn-out legal proceedings and lost their land. As a result, foreign surveying, railroad, timber and mining companies, wealthy landowners with good lawyers, and Díaz's political allies and associates came into possession of vast amounts of territory, much of it claimed by others and some of it already occupied.

During the *Porfiriato,* land became concentrated in fewer and fewer hands so that by 1910, the amount held by communal villages had shrunk from 25 percent of landholdings to only 2 percent. It was a dismal statistic that reflected not only changes in land ownership, but a concerted assault on a way of life. Communal landholding provided the foundation on which a self-sufficient, locally controlled agricultural lifestyle had been built in Mexico. The communal *pueblo* provided the main social unit for centuries, and the Spanish Crown had recognized indigenous rights to their *pueblos* through *fundo legal,* a concept and tradition which provided common access to land, water, woods, and pasture in order to provide for the survival and natural growth of a community. The assault on what remained of community lands was especially noteworthy in areas producing cash crops, such as Emiliano Zapata's home state of Morelos, the heart of the Mexican sugar industry at the time. Much of the more wide-open North, where Francisco (Pancho) Villa recruited his famous *División del Norte,* was simply declared vacant, and the government began to sell and give away large chunks of it as "*terrenos baldios*" (uncultivated land). Like other modernizing Mexican elites before him, Díaz hoped the land privatization program would lead to greater productivity based on export-led growth. The approach worked for a time, and it led to fantastic profits for a few Mexicans and foreigners, but it caused widespread resentment in the countryside.

While the government failed to address the needs of Mexico's impoverished and politically excluded rural population, workers objected to the lopsided benefits of industrialization. Mexicans working in foreign-owned enterprises chafed at living in segregated company towns, receiving lower wages than foreign workers, and being excluded from positions in management. Widespread child labor helped keep wages low. Making matters worse, Díaz repressed independent labor unions, and many felt he allowed foreign companies to treat Mexicans like second-class citizens in their own country.[3]

Beyond worker and peasant resentment, which is common in the harsh early phases of industrialization no matter where it occurs, Díaz had another problem. Some Mexican businessmen began to feel that foreign capital received preferential treatment over domestic firms. Díaz lavished tax breaks on foreign companies and offered massive land grants to an array of American companies that, amazingly, often also included the subsoil rights. Responding to those inducements, foreigners, mainly Americans, came to acquire over 25 percent of the land in the country. Foreign interests also owned much of the best agricultural, timber, and mineral-rich land, and all of the oil by 1910; this alienated elements of the bourgeoisie, who felt they were being disadvantaged by their own government favoring foreign firms. But because the Díaz regime amounted to a dictatorship, limited opportunities existed to effect change. Eventually, disgruntled citizens of all classes began to object to the antidemocratic nature of their government. Foreign investors, on the other hand, who profited from low-wage Mexican labor, minimal taxes, government grants, and a labor movement under the dictator's control, held up Porfirian Mexico as a model for other developing nations to follow.

Enticed by the land concessions from the Mexican government and the vast mineral wealth of Mexico, American railroad companies built tracks that stretched from the Pacific port of Guaymas, Sonora, to Nogales, Arizona, and another from El Paso, Texas, to Mexico City. British and French investors financed a line from Laredo, Texas, to the Mexican capital. These railroads provided access to the natural resources of the Mexican interior and linked them to American markets. Land values near the railroads shot up as a result, and as the land along the rail lines became more valuable, foreigners and wealthy Mexicans acquired it, diverting water from streams and rivers and setting off a series of community revolts against the land usurpations.[4]

Invited in by Díaz, foreign mining companies drilled, dug, and blasted out Mexico's mineral wealth and shipped it to American smelters in Texas, Arizona, and Colorado on the newly laid rail network. The advent of electricity made copper increasingly valuable, and American copper companies made fortunes while boomtowns teeming with Mexican miners rose out of the desert. One of the largest copper mining concerns was the American-owned Cananea Consolidated Copper Company in Sonora, which employed about four thousand Mexican workers and ran a segregated company town. Along the Gulf Coast, discoveries in Mexican oil fields attracted American and British capitalists who took over the Mexican oil industry just as petroleum became the world's most important source of energy. French capital led the way in textile production. Americans dominated the railroads and extractive industries, while Mexican capitalists invested in new soap, cement, beer, and cigarette factories, especially in Mexico City and Monterrey. Taken together, all these new industries fed a major process of internal migration within Mexico as they attracted newly landless laborers driven from the countryside. Manufactured American imports arriving from the United States by train further dislodged skilled artisans from their livelihoods. The uprooted and occupationally displaced became industrial workers in modernizing Mexico. Once on the move, many crossed the border seeking seasonal work and higher wages in Texas and other border states.[5]

Across the country, but especially in the North, agricultural production shifted to provide crops and beef to feed workers in the mines, railheads, and industrial centers and the cities growing around them. Cotton production increased to feed the textile mills. The railroad, irrigation projects, and a dramatic increase in cotton production transformed the Laguna area of north-central Mexico. Well-funded enterprises took over the best and most well-watered land as locals relocated to scratch out a living on the margins. The rise in cotton production created a migrant, floating rural population as forty thousand cotton pickers looking for work descended on the Laguna area with each harvest.[6]

The cattle industry in Chihuahua grew with the railroad, sending cattle to the expanding cities of northern Mexico and to the United States. In the South, the sugar industry in Morelos exploded as well, as *haciendas* encroached onto *pueblo* lands as profits from sugar soared. By 1910, large agribusinesses accounted for 70 percent of all landholdings in Mexico. The rapid commercialization of agriculture came at the expense of a wide array of rural people, including Indian and *mestizo* villagers, communal landholders, and small-scale farmers. The census of 1910 recorded between nine and ten million landless peasants out of a population of about fifteen million people. It was not just an economic process. The Mexican army violently removed the Yaqui Indians from the Yaqui River valley to make way for commercial agriculture and firms such as the Richardson Construction Company of Los Angeles, which acquired 993,650 acres in the valley, and the Wheeler Land Company from Phoenix, which bought 1,450,000 next to it. Powerful northern elites allied with Díaz also created vast empires. The most obvious came to be that of the Luis Terrazas family of Chihuahua, who controlled millions of acres, employed over eight thousand people on their many *haciendas,* and had 40 percent of the industrial workers in the state working for their businesses. Needless to say, that kind of control limited competition, and those not allied with Terrazas and Díaz faced an unfair situation.[7]

Traditional communities resisted the rapid change underway because it threatened their economic and cultural independence. Many did not wish to trade in their lives as *pueblo* citizens with guaranteed rights to communal land inherited from their ancestors for the uncertainties of wage labor. The new agricultural enterprises needed workers though, and they resorted to a variety of machinations to get them. One of the most common was the "*enganche,*" or forwarding of cash and transportation costs to a worker to get him to go to an *hacienda* or mine. Once on site, however, people found themselves having to pay exorbitant prices to rent shabby lodging, and then got gouged at company stores for food and tools as they became tied to the employer by debt. Tying labor down through debt, especially on *haciendas* in parts of the underpopulated and removed North, became one tactic for maintaining a labor supply. Another method of securing workers in mines and to pick crops at harvest time involved the promise of high pay. *Haciendas* in Morelos kept impoverished permanent workers year around, housing them in dirt-floored huts of thatch and wood, and then hired seasonal workers at good wages when the sugar harvest depended on an intense period of around-the-clock labor. But because of its seasonal nature, the system offered little security and left people scrounging for work half of the year.

Workers displaced from the security of their communities became vulnerable to things outside their control. By 1910, foreign investors controlled 90 percent of the incorporated value of Mexican industry, and Americans alone controlled 70 percent. Global market demand produced in the North a new landless and migratory population following the rail lines in states like Coahuila, Durango, Sonora, and Chihuahua. Once they became accustomed to seasonal migrations within Mexico, many people headed across the border into Texas and to other parts of the American Southwest offering higher wages. Between 1900 and 1910, the Mexican and Mexican American population in the United States grew from 400,000 to 640,000. Immigration from Mexico to the United States during the *Porfiriato* displayed the economic transformation American capital helped produce in Mexico.[8]

The economic penetration of Mexico by American capital led to the rapid rise of mining, railroads, oil, timber, and export agriculture, and that caused a major internal migration as many Mexicans took leave of their struggling rural communities in search of work in booming mining towns, railheads, and agricultural centers in northern Mexico. The pattern increased immigration into the United States by uprooted peasants and farmers seeking work. The process began long before the Revolution broke out, as Mexicans found jobs in Texas and California agriculture, Arizona mining, and in railroad construction across the Southwest. Between 1902 and 1907, for example, about sixty thousand Mexicans a year crossed the border at El Paso, Texas, and other border towns witnessed a similar influx. Many of the same kinds of industrial and agricultural enterprises that made use of Mexican labor in Mexico recruited that labor north of the border as well. Phelps Dodge, for example, hired hundreds of Mexican workers for its smelting operations in El Paso and housed them in the Mexican section of their company town. Mexican labor both in Mexico and in the United States became another of the natural resources put at the disposal of U.S. economic expansion.[9]

Theoretically, the Porfirian model of economic growth could have worked had the new economy been able to absorb the displaced peasantry, provide enough well-paying jobs, and avoid dependency on foreign capital and foreign markets. Reality proved different. Industry in Mexico only employed about 11 percent of the workforce. That was not enough to employ those driven off their land. Meanwhile, domestic food production suffered because of the emphasis on export crops. During the *Porfiriato,* the amount of land devoted to the traditional Mexican staples of corn and beans shrunk. As a result, prices for food soared. Corn production dropped 50 percent from 1877 to 1907. With the land turned over to cotton and other crops for export, corn had to be imported to fend off famine in otherwise rich agricultural zones of the North. Food riots broke out across the region as desperate people stormed warehouses and stores. The concentration of land ownership meant that peasants and small farmers who had been turned into workers had no place to find security.

The initial prosperity of the Díaz model of economic growth faded as the benefits failed to trickle down to the rural and industrial working classes. Despite government hostility, and efforts by the Catholic Church to offer more moderate labor organizations, workers began to organize independent, sometimes militant, unions. Backed by the government, employers felt little need to bargain. As a result, the most developed industries saw the greatest unrest, as textile workers, railroad workers, and miners turned to the strike to make their demands for better pay, shorter hours, and decent working conditions heard.

Two labor conflicts stand out because they revealed some of the causes of labor unrest and they anticipated the Revolution. First, miners at the American-owned Cananea Consolidated Copper Company in Sonora went out on strike on June 1, 1906, when American management refused to negotiate and address worker grievances including American workers paid double what Mexicans got for the same job; Mexicans assigned the worst jobs; and Mexicans denied any technical or managerial positions, regardless of skill and competence. The confrontation turned violent as management attempted to disperse the crowd. Company guards shot dozens of Mexican employees, and workers killed two American managers. The alarmed governor of Sonora allowed over two hundred Arizona Rangers to cross the border and take up positions outside the general offices of the Cananea Company. The Mexican *rurales* arrived later, rounded up suspected labor leaders, and either arrested them or killed them on the outskirts of town. The episode stood out as a stark example of the Díaz regime favoring foreign capital over Mexican workers.

The other major episode occurred at the French-owned textile mill at Río Blanco, Veracruz, in January 1907. Conditions at the mill were harsh, with long hours, low pay, child labor, and aloof foreign French ownership. When workers sought to negotiate for improved conditions, ownership locked them out of the factory. Díaz stepped in to arbitrate, and he took the side of ownership on all the major issues. Management then ordered workers back to the line, but a stone-throwing riot broke out in the early morning hours of January 7th. Along with other slogans could be heard chants of "Death to Porfirio Díaz!" and "Death to the Dictator!" Troops were called in and opened fire on the crowd, slaughtering men, women and children. The army killed almost two hundred people at Río Blanco.

Once again, the Díaz regime put the interests of foreign businesses above those of Mexican workers. Instead of recognizing the widespread dissatisfaction in the country, the government blamed "outside agitators," "anarchists," and "communists" for the unrest.

Vocal groups had indeed begun to criticize the Díaz regime, and antigovernment underground newspapers proliferated. The most important anti-Díaz group was the *Partido Liberal Mexicano,* or PLM. Initiated by an educated collection of lawyers, engineers, and journalists, they put out a periodical called *Regeneración,* later renamed *Revolución,* and Liberal clubs sprang up in various cities. Initially, the PLM attracted support from some important members of the northern professional class. They were not just against Díaz, however, but for a deep social revolution. The anarchist-inspired radicalism of their newspaper and of their main spokesman, Ricardo Flores Magón, alienated more moderate opponents of the Díaz regime and forced the leadership of the PLM to flee into exile in the United States. Flores Magón went first to Laredo, Texas, in 1904, where he was received by Sara Estela Ramírez, editor of *La Corregidora,* and one of a group of exiled female journalists advocating for greater women's rights as part of the change needed in Mexico. So, Díaz correctly guessed when he blamed PLM literature and activists for labor unrest, because they did play a role in affecting public opinion, organizing labor, and inspiring worker action. PLM organizers were at both Cananea and Río Blanco. The PLM did not create labor radicalism, of course, but they helped give expression to radical social alternatives to dictatorship and capitalism from both sides of the border. Important PLM operative Praxedis Guerrero used San Antonio, Texas, as a base to raise arms and ammunition for an assault on the dictator. Guerrero's writings from El Paso, Texas, circulated in Mexico and caused the Foreign Relations office in Mexico City to complain that his work had "sold profusely" and "increased agitation" in the capital.[10]

When the world silver market bottomed out and copper production in other nations rose, driving prices down, the Northern economy went into deep crisis as Mexican mining collapsed. Naturally, mining companies responded by limiting production, throwing thousands of men out of work. A global recession in 1907 created a serious social crisis in Mexico. Demand for Mexico's cash crops, cattle, and mineral exports plummeted. The displaced and unemployed searched for work, as real desperation gripped much of the North. People found themselves struggling to feed their families and, because of the situation's human-created origins, anger and resentment seethed.

A similar process unfolded in the South. The state of Morelos, lying across the mountains south of Mexico City, served as the hub of the Mexican sugar industry. More heavily populated than the North, and with a deep preconquest history, many communal *pueblos* traced their existence to Aztec rule. People there revered the land as their just inheritance and as a guarantee of local autonomy and economic independence. During the *Porfiriato,* railroads, urban and foreign demand for sugar, and new technology made sugar production extremely profitable. Consistent with its general model for growth, the Díaz regime promoted the expansion of the sugar industry at the expense of communal landholding. Villagers resisted *hacendado* assaults on their land and water through the courts, but *hacendados,* backed by corrupt local officials and in accordance with the larger Porfirian plan of privatization, seized *pueblo* lands with impunity.

Sugar production soared as *hacendados* began to monopolize the land and water. *Pueblos* lost much of their land, and many citizens became dependent peons on the estates, undergoing the painful transition from peasant into worker. But because of the proximity of the mills and the seasonal nature of sugar work, many of the workers on the plantations continued to live in their *pueblos,* which allowed the structure of their communal villages to survive. So, while other uprooted workers migrated to cities and mining centers and turned to new organizations like mutual aid societies or labor unions, people in Morelos relied on established social structures of local self-government and the communal use of resources offered by their *pueblos* as a source of mutual defense. The example of the *municipio libre,* or free landholding village, with guaranteed rights to land, water, and woods, and local autonomy, provided an important alternative to the process of industrialization taking place around them. The political meaning of the *municipio libre* basically meant local rule based on local representation and leadership. Materially, it meant collective labor, shared resources, and shared expenses at the local level. Those communal values allowed villagers to articulate their own ideas about how to divide resources, structure work, and live in a condition that challenged the demands being imposed by State builders and industrialists promoting sink-or-swim individualism. That alternative vision resonated with people elsewhere and would play a defining role in the Revolution.

The aspirations of peasants or workers gave the Revolution its depth and meaning, but they burst forth when Francisco Madero called for the overthrow of Díaz and set November 20, 1910, as the date for a general uprising. Madero came from a large and powerful family in Coahuila that owned extensive land as well as mining, industrial, and banking interests throughout the North. Madero's concerns reflected those of some regional elites, especially in the North. Madero felt Mexican businesses received fewer benefits from the federal government than did foreign ones. Madero family interests competed directly with far wealthier American companies, such as the Guggenheim-controlled American Smelting and Refining Company, ASARCO. Between Phelps Dodge and the Guggenheims, the Madero family lost control over smelting. The government also facilitated the arrival of other competitors from both the United States and Mexico City in the production and marketing of coal for the railroads. At the same time, the Madero estate's rubber-producing companies suffered when Díaz licensed the Continental Rubber Company to arrive on the scene, with a board of directors that included John D. Rockefeller, Bernard Baruch, and Daniel Guggenheim.[11]

Madero wrote a book called *La sucesión presidencial de 1910* that called for an end to the reelection of the President. Madero then ran for the office. He gained support from various sectors of society, including the PLM. Díaz, realizing the threat, had him arrested until the election took place. Madero then fled to San Antonio, Texas, where Díaz had financed his own rebellion thirty-five years earlier. Madero issued the *Plan de San Luis Potosí* from San Antonio. The plan offered representative democracy, less central control, expanded workers rights, and a statement about restoring lands that had been illegally taken from their rightful owners.

The statement about restoring lands to their rightful owners caught the attention of Emiliano Zapata in Morelos. The sugar *haciendas* had expanded, taken over the land, displaced people, driven them from being independent producers to dependent workers, and then sugar collapsed. People were landless and only marginally employed. The *hacendados* destroyed one system without replacing it with a secure, stable alternative. Dependents on the sugar estates confronted degrading working conditions and abusive administrators, and felt totally unprotected by the State. Villagers and *hacienda* workers joined Zapata, who announced in favor of Madero. They attacked the *haciendas,* drove off or killed the administrators, and began seizing the sugar estates and giving the land back to the *pueblos.*

In northwestern Chihuahua, an army of miners, small landholders, rural workers, and ranch hands, including Pancho Villa, rebelled in favor of Madero and seized Ciudad Juárez. Control of Juárez gave the rebels access to arms and ammunition from American arms dealers. With a rebellion on two fronts, Díaz resigned and sailed into exile in France, offering the observation, "Madero has unleashed a tiger; let us see if he can control it." Madero had let loose popular forces with social goals far more radical than his own. He quickly let down many of his supporters, especially Zapata. Rather than carry out any land reform, Madero left most of the Porfirian army intact and ordered Zapata to disarm. Dismayed, Zapata, realizing Madero would not restore the land to the communal *pueblos* unless forced to, issued the famous *Plan de Ayala* on November 25, 1911. It accused Madero of treason and called for local autonomy and land redistribution from the *haciendas* to the *pueblos.* Madero sent in an army to neutralize Zapata and formed a commission to study the land question.

Other rebellions broke out, including a predictable effort by reactionaries led by Félix Díaz, a nephew of the old dictator, and Bernardo Reyes, the influential former Porfirian governor of Nuevo León, who, like so many other Mexicans dissatisfied with their government, had launched a rebellion against Madero that was planned and financed in San Antonio, Texas. He had basically hoped to return Mexico to the days of the *Porfiriato,* with himself in control. Díaz and Reyes attacked the National Palace only to be repulsed and Reyes killed. Díaz retreated to an old fortress called the Ciudadela, and Madero sent general Victoriano Huerta to put down the revolt. Instead, Huerta made an agreement with Félix Díaz; then followed the *Decena Trágica,* where the two sides did not really fight one another but instead fired artillery shells into the surrounding neighborhoods, killing scores of civilians. To the foreign community in Mexico, the episode demonstrated Madero's inability to provide security, even in Mexico City. Huerta then met with U.S. ambassador Henry Lane Wilson, who arranged the *Pacto de la Embajada,* designed to overthrow Madero. Wilson thought Madero incompetent and unable to provide the stability American interests desired. Madero also represented a more assertive Mexican bourgeoisie, which made him lose the support of foreign investors in Mexico. With Wilson's backing, Huerta sent troops to the National Palace to arrest Madero. Others assassinated Madero's brother, Gustavo, at a nearby restaurant as he ate lunch. Huerta subordinates then arrested Madero and his Vice President, José María Pino Suárez, and shot them after forcing the two executives to resign their positions. Huerta seized control and had himself named President. Madero had made two colossal blunders. He failed to reward those who had helped put him in power, like Zapata, and he retained too much of the Porfirian army and officer corps rather than developing a loyal force of his own.

Because foreigners in Mexico facilitated Huerta's coup, it met with a violent response from Mexicans throughout the country, especially Madero supporters like Pancho Villa. Villa's role in the seizure of Ciudad Juárez had helped put Madero in power and Villa remained loyal to Madero. Villa, who ran mule trains supplying remote mining centers in Chihuahua, knew the countryside well. He fought to overthrow Huerta, whom he viewed as Madero's assassin. Villa recruited an army of miners, cowboys, ranch hands, landless *hacienda* workers, and lumberjacks, and threw his support behind the powerful regional elites who had backed Madero, especially Venustiano Carranza, the governor of Coahuila. He had his own vision for a better Mexico though, one based on an end to debt peonage, improved wages, and land reform. Villa's army grew to several thousand and he took Ciudad Juárez at the end of 1913, securing access to weapons from the United States. He became the provisional governor of Chihuahua, and confiscated the *haciendas* of his enemies and created some of the first *ejidos* (communal lands). Villa attracted to his ranks agrarian radicals fighting for the restitution of their lands. That gave him and Zapata something in common. The *Zapatistas* and *Villistas* formed an alliance, which existed more in spirit than in military coordination. For his part, Zapata rejected Huerta totally as a reactionary trying to recreate the conditions of the *Porfiriato*. Huerta resolved to hunt down and kill Zapata, and the war against the *pueblos* of Morelos grew even more savage. From 1910 to 1921, the population of the state went from about 170,000 to about 105,000, as people fled and died.[12]

Villa won a series of smashing victories against the federal army, gained control of the North, and prepared to take Mexico City. Americans who had supported Huerta expressed disappointment with his inability to crush Zapata, while Villa's victories convinced the U.S. government that Huerta could not provide the security it sought. With the writing on the wall, Huerta stepped down in the summer of 1914. Among the many revolutionaries that had united in the war against the usurper Huerta were Carranza in Coahuila and Alvaro Obregón in Sonora. Men of wealth and prestige compared to Villa and Zapata, Obregón and Carranza were the core of the group calling themselves the Constitutionalists. They positioned themselves as the heirs to Madero and offered a similar program, calling for political democracy, Mexican control of its resources, and greater workers' rights. Initially, they did not offer a program of land reform, and that precluded any alliance with Zapata.

After the experience with Madero, the *Zapatistas* did not trust the Constitutionalists. With Huerta gone, Carranza proclaimed himself "First

Chief" of the Revolution and prepared to take the presidency. Zapata demanded that the Constitutionalists accept the *Plan de Ayala* and the redistribution of land, in which case he would support them. If not, he would fight them too. Villa urged Carranza to agree to recognize an agrarian reform program. Carranza refused. Carranza's vision of the Revolution did not call for righting social and economic inequalities. He hardly presented himself as a revolutionary looking forward to a new, more egalitarian Mexico. He harked backward to the restoration of the Constitution of 1857, which Porfirio Díaz had violated.[13]

The several revolutionary factions called a convention at Aguascalientes in September 1914 in order to resolve their differences and create a new government. Instead of creating an accord, it led to a violent split, with Villa and Zapata on one side and Obregón and Carranza on the other. The *Villistas,* who had the best army in the Revolution, and the *Zapatistas,* whose home state bordered the capital, took Mexico City without a fight. The Constitutionalists retreated to Veracruz. At Veracruz, the United States supplied the Constitutionalist army, which proved decisive. Prior to the Constitutionalists having received arms from the Americans, the *Villistas* had not lost any major battles. After that, they did not win any.[14]

The radicalism of the Zapata-and-Villa–led wing of the Revolution alarmed American interests in Mexico, as well as those in control of the U.S. government. The *Zapatista* and *Villista* demands for land reform represented a direct threat to private property, and with over 25 percent of Mexico in the hands of U.S. citizens and businesses, that was a threat the U.S. government did not ignore. The American leadership saw two choices. The elite, educated Carranza and the upper-middle-class and educated Obregón, and their basically reformist political agendas recognizing the sanctity of private property, represented one possibility. The other option was the confiscation and redistribution of large land holdings being carried out by the *Zapatistas* in Morelos and supported by Villa. Zapata put the *campesino* vision into practice in what historian Adolfo Gilly has called the Morelos commune, where the rulings of village elders and municipal councils now determined the partitioning of land. Local decisions then went to *Zapatista* headquarters, not the other way around. The *Zapatistas* planned to create agricultural credit banks to assist the *pueblos,* and associations of *pueblos* were to act like producers' cooperatives. The American political leadership could wait and see who won the Revolution or intervene on behalf of private American interests in Mexico. They chose intervention. Having supported Díaz for years, questions of political democracy were not the issue.

After having their army outfitted by the Americans in late 1914, the Constitutionalists moved out of Veracruz and engaged the *Villistas* in the major showdown battles of the Revolution in the late spring of 1915. Using World War I battle tactics of barbed wire and machine gun nests, Obregón's armies obliterated the repeated *Villista* cavalry charges. Modern tactics and weaponry gave Obregón's armies victory at Celaya, León, and Aguascalientes. The *Villistas* scattered in disarray. Later in the year, remnants of the *División del Norte* regrouped and over six thousand *Villistas* attacked Agua Prieta on the border in an effort to regain access to weapons from U.S. dealers and rearm. President Woodrow Wilson prevented a *Villista* victory by moving Constitutionalist troops and artillery by rail across New Mexico and getting them to Agua Prieta in time to repulse the *Villista* attack. The stunned *Villistas* suffered a devastating rout and the *División del Norte* dissolved.

Villa reacted by turning on Americans in Mexico. *Villistas* stopped a train in Chihuahua, took off a group of between sixteen and eighteen American mine workers and engineers and killed them. Then Villa attacked Columbus, New Mexico. That provoked Wilson into sending in an army of twelve thousand, commanded by John Pershing, to capture or kill Villa. The so-called "Punitive Expedition" did not do much punishing, but it did march around northern Mexico for several months. The Americans never saw Villa, much less captured or killed him. The episode did embarrass Carranza's government, though, and turned Villa into an even larger figure than he had been before.

The Revolution made an impact north of the border, especially in Texas. Díaz plotted his overthrow of Lerdo in San Antonio. Madero's planned his ousting of Díaz in San Antonio. The PLM and Praxedis Guerrero agitated from both San Antonio and Laredo, and served as a conduit for radical ideas from Mexico, on the one hand, and labor-organizing tactics from the United States that could be used in Mexico, on the other. Reyes plotted against Madero from San Antonio, and Huerta had lived in El Paso. Throughout the Revolution, members of defeated groups found their way to Texas, mixing in with Mexican Americans already there. Reactionaries and revolutionaries, anarchists and Porfirians settled in the state, and exiles from all political persuasions published newspapers in Texas, hoping to influence events in Mexico and sentiments in the United States.

Luther T. Ellsworth, American consul along the border on the eve of the Revolution, informed his superiors that the editorializing of Mexicans in Texas and the generally radical ideas on open display in Mexico influenced the Mexican American population of the State and inclined them toward socialism. Ellsworth also reflected a widely held worry about the numbers of Mexican Americans in South Texas and their sympathies with the PLM.

The Revolution exacerbated existing ethnic tension in Texas, especially when refugees came across in large numbers, as five thousand did in Brownsville during the summer of 1913. The violence in Mexico caused some Anglos to fear ethnically driven social unrest in South Texas and along the border in general. The Revolution heightened racist ideas about Mexican banditry and untrustworthiness already in currency. Texas Governor Oscar B. Colquitt informed Secretary of State William J. Bryan in 1913 that large numbers of former Porfirians supporting Huerta were in Eagle Pass, whereas the local population of "American Mexicans who live here are strongly against the Huerta government." One of the most sensitive periods came during the American attack and occupation of Veracruz, when fear of a Mexican American uprising was expressed in some border communities.[15]

The most recognized way in which the Mexican Revolution affected Texas was the *Plan de San Diego* (PSD) of 1915. It called for a rebellion of oppressed races in Texas. The appearance of the *Plan* followed Obregón's victories over Villa, as Carranza sought recognition from Washington. The actual events associated with the *Plan de San Diego* began with a series of attacks by Mexican Americans and Mexican nationals on symbols of Anglo domination in South Texas, including the King Ranch. Repression followed swiftly and brutally as both Mexicans and Mexican Americans became generally suspect and Texas Rangers, other "lawmen," and civilian vigilantes terrorized the Mexican American population. Anglos shot hundreds and lynched many in extralegal actions.

The violence associated with the PSD had its roots in a deeper and enduring tension along the border. One of the most flagrant episodes of ethnic hostility took place in January 1918, at the tiny ranch community of Porvenir, just up the Rio Grande from Pilares, Chihuahua. Local Anglo ranchers considered the place a squatter settlement of undesirable Mexican and Mexican American squatters. Recent bandit-type raids from Mexico had put the area on edge, and U.S. Army troops and Texas Rangers had been called in. Responding to a recent raid that left some American ranchers dead, Texas Rangers arrived at Porvenir in the dark of night, rousted the inhabitants, picked out fifteen men, took them to the edge of the settlement, and executed them. Most of the dead were poor tenant farmers. Events like the one at Porvenir caused thousands of Mexicans to leave the border region and caused others to live in fear.[16]

The Revolution also had an indirect impact on Mexican American identity formation. Mexican Americans and Mexican nationals living in Texas met in Laredo in 1911 and held *El Primer Congreso Mexicanista* conference in response to a call by Clemente Idar, the editor of the Spanish-language Laredo newspaper, *La Crónica*. The event intended to bring together delegates of Mexican descent from across Texas, regardless of their citizenship, to discuss how to combat discrimination and segregation of ethnic Mexicans in Texas. The Revolution helped doom the effort to create ethnic unity regardless of nationality as a way to pursue civil rights for Mexicans in South Texas, as many Mexican Americans, especially the educated professional class, began to try and distance themselves from being associated with the violence in Mexico and the border raids of the Revolution. Thereafter, they pursued a civil rights position based mainly on Americanism.[17]

As tensions in South Texas smoldered, Carranza and Obregón moved to turn their military victories into political control. Obregón went to Mexico City and won support for the Constitutionalists by making promises to the urban labor movement and enlisting their armed support in the fight against Villa and Zapata. Later, when labor leaders, organized under the anarchist-inspired *Casa del Obrero Mundial,* led a series of strikes, the Constitutionalist government moved against them, disbanded the radical unions, and began the process of replacing them with more compliant, official government-sponsored ones, starting with the *Confederación Regional Obrera Mexicana* (CROM).

Importantly, the Constitutionalists wrote a new Constitution in 1917. Two articles stand out because they represent some of the core struggles of the Revolution. Article 27 called for a redistribution of land to *pueblos,* the granting of additional land and water as necessary, and the creation of new *ejidos.* It passed in part out of conviction and in part out of necessity in order to take away the reason the *Zapatistas* had for fighting. A deep significant difference separated the two approaches, however. Article 27 put the federal government and the president at the center of reforms, making the highest offices in the land the makers of decisions and granters of favors, as opposed to merely legitimating prior actions carried out by citizens at the local level, as the *Zapatistas* did. Article 27 also restored

Mexican control over its borders, coasts, land, and natural resources. The delegates to the Constitutional Convention declared that all subsoil resources belonged to the nation and asserted the government's right to nationalize foreign property. The other main article was 123, which granted workers the eight-hour day and the right to organize and strike, but only with government approval. By addressing the central concerns of the *pueblos* and the rural and urban working classes, the Constitutionalists astutely absorbed those elements into the new revolutionary regime. Meanwhile, Villa's once popular movement had turned into guerrilla war in Chihuahua, and his stature, even among many former supporters, declined markedly due to forced loans, arbitrary actions, and other abuses.

Zapata, however, remained in rebellion because the Constitutionalists carried out no real land reform. Faithful to his cause to the very end, Zapata fought all regimes that refused to carry out his ideals. Carranza had him assassinated in April 1919. That weakened, but did not end, *Zapatismo*. Carranza then maneuvered to select his own successor (one unacceptable to Obregón), whereupon Obregón rebelled against the president.

Obregón held a more inclusive vision of government than Carranza. Obregón represented the aspirations of the middle and upper middle classes, including the possibility of upward mobility, a more open and more inclusive political process, greater access to participation in national government, and a society based more on a meritocracy than favoritism. Importantly, Obregón gained the support of the remaining *Zapatista* leadership by promising to carry out the land reform that Madero and Carranza had refused to implement. Obregón, having defeated Villa, also enjoyed the support of most of the Constitutionalist army. Carranza fled Mexico City in 1920 for Veracruz but was assassinated on the way. Obregón took office, incorporated the *Zapatista* "Liberating Army of the South" as the "Division of the South," and immediately began to implement the agrarian reform in Morelos. That ended the war there. Villa had retired and no longer represented a threat in the North, but he too met death by assassination.

The Mexican Revolution overthrew a dictatorship, reclaimed its natural resources from powerful foreign interests, brought basic worker guarantees, and broadened political participation. It also guaranteed people born into historically recognized *pueblos* access to land as a birthright for most of the twentieth century; no other society in the western hemisphere pursued such a course. The Revolution brought important psychological changes as well, as the public that brought the government into being now believed that government had an obligation to provide for social needs through programs like land redistribution and policies such as sympathetic labor arbitration. Whether the government lived up to that remains another matter, but many people expected it.

The Revolution offers some lessons for understanding processes that will reshape Texas and the greater southwest in the twenty-first century. Dramatic episodes of defined duration like the U.S. Mexican War of 1846–1848, or the Mexican Revolution of 1910–1920, had important impacts on the Mexican-born population of the United States, but the larger, longer processes of interplay between the U.S. and Mexican economies better explains the forces behind Mexican immigration and its ebbs and flows over time. It is during the periods of most intense economic interaction between the two nations, when economic borders are open and free trade pursued, that the greatest immigration has occurred. The Revolution temporarily contributed to that immigration. Between 1911 and 1920, the Immigration and Naturalization Service recorded about 220,000 Mexicans coming into the United States. That figure, however, is much smaller than the approximately 460,000 who came from 1921–1930, when the fighting had ended, but the reconstruction of the nation still threatened life throughout Mexico. During the Great Depression, fewer than twenty-five thousand Mexicans immigrants were recorded. These numbers do not reflect the people who simply avoided registering, but they still offer a sense of the larger pattern. So, the turmoil of the Revolution and its aftermath created special, temporary conditions for many to immigrate to the United States, and it caused some, especially the more economically secure who would probably not have immigrated otherwise, to make that choice. The larger story of Mexican immigration, however, is not to be found in internal disorder, but in the prevailing economic conditions in Mexico, and understanding the historical forces at work that cause those conditions informs our contemporary experience.

The Mexican Revolution was enigmatic. Revolutionaries overthrew a dictatorship and called for democracy but ended up with one-party rule for most of the twentieth century. Some revolutionaries also demanded more economic equality. They achieved it for a time, yet today Mexico stands as one of the most unequal societies on earth, with millions of landless rural laborers and staggering unemployment. Mexico's Revolution included economic nationalism. Under the call of "Mexico for the Mexicans," the revolutionary government reclaimed the nation's natural resources, including oil and mineral rights, and land from mainly American corporations who had dominated the most important parts of the Mexican economy. They implemented moderate protections that required that a Mexican, or the Mexican government, have a 51 percent share of foreign ventures. Meanwhile, State-run industrial concerns proliferated, providing inexpensive Mexican-made goods to the public rather than imported ones from global industrial centers. An extensive agrarian reform that provided land and mitigated rural-to-urban migration and unemployment accompanied such nationalistic approaches. All of these efforts had their flaws, but from World War II until the mid-1970s the results were called the "Mexican Miracle" as Mexico enjoyed sustained economic growth rates over 5 percent. That held down Mexican immigration to the United States for decades. For example, in 1960 there resided fewer than one million foreign-born Mexicans in the United States, legal or illegal.[18]

Today, at a time of increased economic intercourse between the two countries, Mexico is more dependent on the U.S. market and on U.S. investment than ever. Over 90 percent of Mexico's exports go to the United States, and 75 percent of Mexican imports come from the United States. Sadly, three of the four largest parts of the Mexican economy, illegal drugs, tourism, and dollars sent home by Mexicans abroad, depend on the United States. Oil, which Mexico nationalized in 1938, constitutes the fourth part, but it too is compromised as collateral on the national debt. These contradictions have had an historic impact on the development of Mexican society and directly affect immigration and the changing face of Texas and the greater Southwest.

The bourgeoisie won the Revolution, and after placating peasants and labor long enough to incorporate, then co-opt and demobilize them, they reversed the course of the Revolution, implementing policies reminiscent of the *Porfiriato*. The end of the Agrarian Reform carried out by President Carlos Salinas in 1992, intended to open up the *ejidos* to commercial agribusiness, was a prerequisite for entry into the North American Free Trade Agreement (NAFTA) of 1994. NAFTA allowed U.S. government–subsidized corn to flood the Mexican market and invited U.S. agribusiness to move back into Mexico. The combination destroyed small-scale Mexican producers. As a result, millions of small farmers have been displaced from the land. They migrate to places like Mexico City or other cities already overflowing with slums and unemployment, and try to find work there. When unable to subsist, many go to the United States. Meanwhile, the elimination of trade protections has driven many smaller and medium-sized businesses under in Mexico. Previously independent small business owners struggle to find work. Mexico needs to create one million new jobs annually just to absorb the new people entering the labor force every year, but it creates only half that, so it should be no surprise that the number of undocumented Mexican immigrants a year approximates 450,000. Today, having given up many of the gains of the Revolution through a reversal of policy, Mexico has sunk to compete with other third-world countries desperate to attract foreign investment through low-wage labor. Mexico's control over its own economy is totally compromised. Foreign countries generate an estimated 40 percent of private sector jobs, and Wal-Mart thrives as Mexico's largest private employer. It is difficult to imagine a solution under current policies. As long as the contradictions of open borders for capital and closed borders for labor persist, so will "illegal" immigration.

Notes

Author's note: As this is a synthetic piece, with much of the information common knowledge to the field, I offer the endnotes (sans page numbers) as a guide for non-specialists who wish to find the best scholarship on the point under discussion. In particular cases, I list sources that advance new knowledge on the Mexican Revolution.

1. Roderic A. Camp, *Politics in Mexico: The Democratic Consolidation* (New York and Oxford: Oxford University Press, 2007).

2. John Mason Hart, *Revolutionary Mexico: The Coming and Process of the Mexican Revolution* (Berkeley: University of California Press, 1987).

3. Rodney Anderson, *Outcasts in Their Own Land: Mexican Industrial Workers, 1906–1911* (Dekalb, Ill.: Northern Illinois University Press, 1976).

4. John Coatsworth, *Growth Against Development: The Economic Impact of Railroads in Profirian Mexico* (Dekalb, Ill.: Northern Illinois University Press, 1981).

5. William K. Meyers, *Forge of Progress, Crucible of Revolt: Origins of the Mexican Revolution in La Comarca Lagunera, 1880–1911* (Albuquerque: University of New Mexico Press, 1994).

6. Some important books on the Mexican Revolution are Hart, *Revolutionary Mexico;* Friedrich Katz, *The Secret War in Mexico: Europe, the United States and the Mexican Revolution* (Chicago: University of Chicago Press, 1981); Alan Knight, *The Mexican Revolution,* 2 vols. (Cambridge: Cambridge University Press, 1986); and Ramón Eduardo Ruiz, *The Great Rebellion: Mexico, 1905–1924* (New York: Norton, 1980).

7. Mark Wasserman, *Capitalists, Caciques, and Revolution: The Native Elite and Foreign Enterprise in Chihuahua, Mexico, 1854–1911* (Chapel Hill: University of North Carolina Press, 1984).

8. Hart, *Revolutionary Mexico;* Juan Torres-Mora, "The "First Mexican Immigrants," in *Beyond the Border: The History of Mexico–U.S. Migration,* ed. Mark Overmeyer-Velásquez (Oxford: Oxford University Press, forthcoming).

9. Gilbert González, *Culture of Empire: American Writers, Mexico and Mexican Immigrants, 1880–1930* (Austin: University of Texas Press, 2004).

10. Ward S. Albro, *To Die on Your Feet: The Life, Times, and Writings of Praxedis G. Guerrero* (Fort Worth: Texas Christian University, 1996); and W. Dirk Raat, *Revoltosos: Mexico's Rebels in the United States, 1913–1923* (College Station: Texas A&M University Press, 1981).

11. Hart, *Revolutionary Mexico.*

12. Friedrich Katz, *The Life and Times of Pancho Villa* (Stanford: Stanford University Press, 1998); Samuel Brunk, *¡Emiliano Zapata!: Revolution and Betrayal in Mexico* (Albuquerque: University of New Mexico Press, 1995); and John Womack, *Zapata and the Mexican Revolution* (New York: Knopf, 1968).

13. Douglas Richmond, *Venustiano Carranza's Nationalist Struggle, 1893–1920* (Lincoln: University of Nebraska Press, 1983).

14. Hart, *Revolutionary Mexico.*

15. Rodolfo Rocha, "The Influence of the Mexican Revolution on the Texas–Mexico Border, 1910–1916" (Ph.D. diss., Texas Tech University, 1981).

16. Glenn Justice, *Revolution on the Rio Grande: Mexican Raids and Army Pursuits, 1916–1919* (El Paso: Texas Western Press, 1992); Rocha, "The Influence of the Mexican Revolution on the Texas–Mexico Border"; and James A. Sandos, *Rebellion in the Borderlands: Anarchism and the Plan of San Diego, 1904–1923* (Norman: University of Oklahoma Press, 1992).

17. José E. Limón, "El Primer Congreso Mexicanista de 1911: A Precursor to Contemporary Chicanismo," *Aztlán* 5 (Spring/Fall, 1974): 85–117; and Jeffrey Lambert, "Decade of Change: Origins of a Mexican American Identity in Texas, 1910–1920" (M.A. thesis, Texas State University, 2009).

18. Roger Hansen, *The Politics of Mexican Development* (Baltimore: The Johns Hopkins University Press, 1971).

The Mexican Revolution's Impact on Tejano
Communities The Historiographic Record

ARNOLDO DE LEÓN

Works on the topic of the Mexican Revolution and how it affected communities on the Texas side of the Rio Grande do not occupy much space in Tejano history bibliographies today. Several reasons might explain this lacuna. For one thing, the time span seems too narrow for historians to study, extending for slightly less than a decade. Most affected by the Revolution, furthermore, were border communities along the Rio Grande

Many uprooted by the turmoil of the Revolution crossed into Texas to augment established communities or to found new ones. Courtesy Williwood Meador Collection, West Texas Collection, Angelo State University

(though not strictly confined thus), a factor that consigns the topic to regional history. Further, historians judge many other events in the history of Tejanos as more important than the Mexican Revolution. Generally speaking, scholars prefer studying topics that extend over a larger time frame, cover wider geographic areas, and contain monumental significance. Such reasons might explain the inattention, at least for the moment.

It cannot be said, however, that scholars have completely passed over that ten-year period and the events that unfolded along the border from Brownsville to El Paso. There exist, for instance, creative works that have as part of their subplot the Revolution and how it played out among people living in southern Texas.[1] A number of theses, dissertations, books, and articles have Texas as a setting of revolutionary activity, but not Tejanos as their subjects. Some of these studies cover the intrigues undertaken in Texas by Mexican Revolution luminaries such as Francisco Madero, Bernardo Reyes, and Pascual Orozco. Historians have also launched serious investigations of the extensive spying, strategizing, and gunrunning undertaken by revolutionary plotters inside border towns and even in interior cities such as San Antonio. Others have further researched the manner in which rich exiles (*ricos*) who took refuge in Texas marked time as they waited out the Revolution.[2]

More relevant to Mexican American history is the body of works that does place Tejanos in center position during the period of the 1910s. Some of these publications, however, tend to be broad surveys of the Tejano experience and only provide a snapshot of events surrounding the Revolution. Related studies may be categorized as urban/rural history. For the most part, these are overviews of life in cities such as El Paso, San Antonio, Houston, and Fort Worth or specialized treatments of agricultural labor.[3] In other words, few of these titles seek to determine how the Mexican Revolution affected Tejano communities.

Still, the Mexican Revolution and its implications for Texas Mexican communities is not a completely neglected subject. The several books and articles on the topic act as the corpus for this essay and a more complete listing may be found in the bibliography included in the Appendix (to this collection). Most writings on the Mexican Revolution and Tejano communities are of recent vintage, although here and there can be encountered an older study tracking the fate of immigrants in Texas after 1920. During the 1960s, a few historians began reflecting upon the episode and its consequences for the Lone Star State, although a main concern was with the *Plan de San Diego* (PSD) in one form or another. Attraction to the Revolution and any Texas connections increased during the 1970s with the ascendancy of Chicano history, and that interest has accelerated since. These modern-day studies can be sorted into several categories, though the ones to receive more coverage seem to be immigration, the *Plan de San Diego,* violence upon border communities, and Tejano identity. This essay is accordingly divided into these four identifiable classifications.

Immigration

Any historiographic discussion of the Mexican Revolution's impact on Mexican-descent communities in Texas begins with immigration. In response to the chaos in Mexico, a massive flight of Mexicans into Texas (as well as other parts of the United States) unfurled. No one has ever been able to accurately establish the number of immigrants that headed for the Lone Star State; the most reliable calculations put the number of immigrants living in Texas in 1910 at 125,016 and in 1920 at 251,827.[4]

What occurred as a result of the influx into Texas was community building, and historians have taken a close interest in this development, albeit only since the early 1970s, when Mexican American history gained credence. To be sure, early observers (among them journalists, educators, and various social scientists) expressed concern over the impact of immigration on communities, both urban and rural, in the state. In the considered judgment of Paul S. Taylor (the famed economist who would later write much on Mexican Americans), the refugees arriving in mid-year 1916 and congregating in El Paso's *Chihuahuita,* "homeless, poverty stricken, chronically hungry, alien in speech, manners, habits and ideas, have proved a heavy burden for so young a community as El Paso to carry." For those witnessing the flood of immigrant humanity, the newcomers foreboded a heavy weight on society because they would exacerbate unemployment, spread contagious diseases such as typhus or tuberculosis, and contribute to city blight.[5] The legacy of the immigrants into the 1920s (and after), in the view of these partisan commentators, was manifest in poverty, hunger, illiteracy, and fatalism, if not physical and mental illness. Immigration spawned problems, some declared in alarm, as the newcomers often became social parasites, refusing to assimilate and fostering racial discord.[6]

More recent scholarship by trained historians sees the refugees' arrival in Texas as having a salutary effect on *colonia* development. For those advancing this position, existing ethnic quarters eased the immigrants' transition into a culture zone that somewhat resembled the one left in haste. Studies that focus on urban areas (the scholarship on rural villages and settlements for this time period lags) note how the immigrants fortified ethnic cohesiveness in towns and, upon finding jobs, expanded barrio perimeters.[7] They did so not solely by means of sheer numbers, but through initiatives undertaken by the those better-off among them. In the *colonias* of the large cities, some refugees of the *rico* class established enterprises such as grocery stores, theaters, bars, funeral parlors, restaurants, pharmacies, barbershops, and even real estate companies.[8]

Immigration shaped *colonias* not only structurally, but ideologically, influencing nationalist sentiments. With the arrival of the refugees, scholars have noted recently, some Texas barrios became bases for revolutionary activity as operatives (both Mexican American and Mexican) of many sorts labored to advance one cause or another in the country to which they still attached themselves.[9] Along the border (and even far into the interior of the state), for instance, barrios functioned as havens where sympathizers plotted forays into Mexico. The most notable of these invasion plans involved Tejanos Francisco A. Chapa (newspaper publisher of San Antonio's *El Imparcial de Texas*) and Webb County Sheriff Amador Sánchez, who conspired in the fall of 1911 with the Mexican exile Bernardo Reyes to restore a Díaz-type government. The courts in 1912 convicted both Chapa and Sánchez of violating U.S. neutrality laws (the federal government pardoned both), but the episode did not figure as the last effort hatched from Texas to influence the course of the Revolution.[10]

Immigrant enclaves served the Revolution's sympathizers in numerous other capacities. Within the *colonia,* parties wanting to aid or abet a particular warring army in Mexico circulated about, soliciting contributions almost unimpeded. Both the well-to-do in exile and some Tejanos with available resources lent money to agents dispatched to Texas in fund-raising missions by the revolutionaries. Ordinary folks held benefit events or organized dances in order to assist in the war campaign.[11] Recruiting stations surfaced in barrios, especially those along the border (such as ones in El Paso), set on enlisting volunteers. Recruiters included not solely agents from Mexico, but Mexican Americans.[12] The historians Charles H. Harris and Louis R. Sadler describe one such venture under the direction of Deodoro Guerra of Hidalgo County thusly:

> [B]eginning in late 1914 and accelerating into January 1915, Guerra
> and his associates assisted [Villa representative Dr. Andrés] Villarreal in
> recruiting local Hispanics and refugees from the Revolution. As a result
> of their cooperation, Villarreal successfully recruited, equipped, and dis-
> patched from Hidalgo County at least five armed expeditions, each
> numbering from seventeen to fifty men, across the river to attack car-
> rancista units attempting to defend Matamoros against an approaching
> *Villista* army.[13]

The Mexican quarter further operated as a conduit for smuggling supplies and (after 1917) war provisions to the revolutionaries. Both sympathizers and profiteers in Texas engaged in this kind of illicit commerce.[14]

The barrio also functioned as a sanctuary where Mexican American residents tendered charitable assistance to fleeing civilians or injured rebels. Barrio residents provided refugees with surpluses of food and clothing as well as with shelter. Humanitarians might also have played a more direct role in the Revolution, as did Laredo resident Jovita Idar, who crossed the border into Mexico in 1913 to assume nursing duties in the Revolution as a civilian volunteer and later as a member of *La Cruz Blanca*.[15]

Mexican American neighborhoods sheltered journalists engaged in editorializing for a preferred revolutionary faction. Some Tejano newspapers supported the government of Francisco Madero until his assassination in 1913, whereas others favored Venustiano Carranza. During the mid-1910s, one journalist from the small town of San Diego (Duval County) promised a campaign to sway public opinion in behalf of U.S. diplomatic recognition of Carranza's Constitutionalists. As of the late 1910s, the aforementioned Francisco A. Chapa still used his newspaper, *El Imparcial de Texas,* to denounce revolutionary politics and to promote a Díaz-type administration. The exile press also took advantage of U.S. freedoms, and from the barrios the *ricos* agitated for a regime favorable to their politics. *La Prensa* (San Antonio), among the most prominent of newspapers managed by an exile, sided with Huerta and after his removal from the presidency in 1914, critiqued the many factions responsible for the bloodbath in the homeland.[16]

Aside from the wide effects it had on barrio sentiments, the massive influx reinforced pervasive Mexican cultural tenets and outlooks already entrenched in segregated Tejano communities dispersed throughout the state. One scholar notes of the situation in El Paso: "The influx of impoverished Mexicans was staggering; it changed the El Paso area, for the time being, from a city whose population was composed of about equal numbers of Anglos and Mexicans into a much more Mexicanized locale."[17] Culturally and philosophically, the immigrants in segregated Mexican *colonias* throughout the state came to compose what some historians dub "The Immigrant Generation."

What specifically did the immigrants add to those urban and rural communities of Texas they infiltrated? They preserved historical memory but also superimposed fully developed cultural institutions and community traditions. Because the refugees generally came in families (if the men folk had not been impressed into the many fighting outfits), they tended to respect long-standing beliefs about the family unit, including the patriarchal ideal and the deference of children, while looking upon divorce as an unacceptable option for women. Raised in the Catholic faith, they bolstered Tejano loyalty to the Church. Foreign-born Mexicans joined native-born Tejanos in observing holy days such as December 12 (the day of *la virgen de Guadalupe*), celebrating the many saints' days in the Catholic calendar, and working with parish societies. The immigrants either introduced new leisure pursuits or buttressed those present. Ethnic activities consisted of enjoying Spanish-language stage performances, Mexican music, and attending Mexican dances. Reinforced were the celebrations of *fiestas patrias*, actually a long-standing observation in Texas of the famous Mexican historic episodes: the *Cinco de Mayo* and the *Diez y Seis de Septiembre*.

Although the immigrants felt acculturating pressures while in Texas, these several influences were never so intense as to cause a complete psychological and cultural conversion: the newcomers still perceived themselves as "Mexicans." Moreover, they seldom severed ties with the motherland, and they even entertained thoughts of returning home once the Revolution ended. According to historian Mario T. García and other proponents of the generational model, the immigrants lived in *"México de afuera"* (Mexico outside the homeland) and sought to create a social and cultural environment that replicated the one they had hastily abandoned. For the majority of the immigrants, their stay in Texas amounted to not much more than a temporary hiatus.[18]

The consequence of immigration for Tejano communities that during the nineteenth century had been undergoing acculturation to U.S. institutions, therefore, was a temporary disruption of that process, at least for some sectors of the *colonia*. For García, Mexican communities receiving the immigrants between 1900 and 1920:

now became predominantly immigrant ones. At no other time in Chicano history have Mexican immigrants and refugees so totally dominated the Spanish-speaking Mexican condition in the Southwest and elsewhere.[19]

The *Plan de San Diego*

By far, the *Plan de San Diego* has intrigued scholars more than any other topic that links the Mexican Revolution. The episode, as historians know it, came to light on January 24, 1915, when authorities in McAllen, Texas (Hidalgo County), apprehended one Basilio Ramos and found on his person a proclamation called the *Plan de San Diego*. The *Plan* (a manifesto) called for Texas Mexicans on the border region to rise up in arms (a subsequent revision of the declaration called for launching a social revolution and establishing a republic that would include Texas and the U.S. Southwest) against Anglos on February 20, 1915. Between February and July, authorities believed, PSD agents took to activism in South Texas, simultaneous with an upsurge in raiding from Mexico into Texas (though invasions had been occurring since 1911, when hostilities in Mexico escalated). Strikes by paramilitary units on South Texas intensified beginning in early July, with swift retaliation wreaked upon Texas Mexicans implicated in the forays. On August 3, 1915, a posse looking for horse thieves advanced upon the ranch (Cameron County) of a Tejano named Aniceto Pizaña, causing grave hurt and damage to those defending the property. Pizaña at this point assumed leadership of the *sediciosos* (Seditionists), alongside a close friend named Luis De la Rosa, their purpose to inflict injury and death on Anglo-Americans for past offenses (among them cases of discrimination, violence, humiliation, cultural disparagement, abuse of agricultural workers, and land dispossession) upon Mexican Americans. From then until October, there followed what some scholars call the "Bandit War," a race conflict between Anglos and Mexicans, with no quarter considered by either side.[20]

Scholars over the years have debated much about the *Plan de San Diego,* with firm conclusions still elusive. Although the *Plan* bears the place name of San Diego, historians remain skeptical that this small town in the chaparral of South Texas (Duval County) could have been the place of its fabrication. As well, its authorship continues to be in dispute. Nonetheless, a school of thought, traceable to the 1950s, when historians first began studying the episode, detects ties between opposition forces in the

Mexican Revolution and PSD activities in Texas. For these writers, any number of revolutionary factions could have been involved in the intrigue, among them sympathizers of the exiled Victoriano Huerta, of the Constitutionalist Venustiano Carranza, or of Ricardo and Enrique Flores Magón and the *Partido Liberal Mexico* (PLM). Even Germany might have played a part in the drama, using the PSD movement to distract the United States from affairs occurring in Europe during World War I.[21]

A complement to this interpretation finds the PSD movement as being of Texas provenance but determines that Venustiano Carranza and the Constitutionalists used its ranks (both Tejanos and Mexican nationals participated in the movement) for selfish ends. For these historians, PSD action did not occur until Carranza sought diplomatic acceptance from the United States in early 1915 (about the time the PSD was issued) and then ended within days after President Woodrow Wilson recognized the Carranza government. On achieving his objective, Carranza stopped permitting the *guerrillas* to use Mexican soil for raids into Texas, and PSD troubles ceased (Carranza toyed with resurrecting the PSD once again in 1916 in an effort get the John J. Pershing expedition to leave Mexico but never followed up on this strategy).[22]

A more recent point of view questions a direct link between Mexican revolutionary factions and the PSD Texas movement. Mainly advanced by students of U.S. history (as opposed to Latin Americanists) this interpretation finds simmering discontent among Tejanos as begetting the PSD movement. Hatred toward the *gringos* for their many outrages lay behind the proclamation and a vendetta against the white population could have exploded at any time, but the Mexican Revolution and the disorder it created furnished a fortuitous opportunity for reprisals. Tejano *guerrilleros* used Mexico as a base (with the acquiescence of sympathetic military leaders in Mexico) to attack symbols of domination in Texas (ranches, railroads, telegraph lines, water towers, and irrigation pumps), and then easily retreated into Mexico.[23] A corollary to this thesis concurs that insufferable conditions in the Rio Grande Valley, together with Mexican Revolution influences, produced an armed uprising. But that insurgency, which they label the "Tejano Revolt," erupted and gained momentum independent of the PSD movement. According to this explanation, attacks by Tejanos with revenge and retaliation in mind and raids by PSD followers frequently overlapped. Further, both received surreptitious backing from the Constitutionalists. But the Tejano Revolt did not necessarily consist of social revolutionaries advocating notions of a grand republic (as did the PSD).

Instead, its leaders were primarily Tejanos who found the scene created by the Mexican Revolution in South Texas ripe for settling old scores and harming (even ousting from the Valley) those responsible for their down-trodden state.[24]

Most historians would agree that Mexico played roles in the PSD movement in ways beyond those referenced above. Certainly, refugees streaming across the border into Texas before 1915 helped politicize the Tejano community, shaping people's thoughts and hastening their will-ingness to join the *sediciosos.* According to one Tejano in 1915, the refu-gees were "almost generally revolutionary inclined at all times and [had] great influence with their countrymen already here prior to them." Refu-gees and exiles closely monitored the course of their revolution, natu-rally shared information and opinions on developments with sympathizers, whether Tejanos or emigrants, and persuaded friends and neighbors that lofty ideals existed worth a fight. Certainly, the ranks of the *sediciosos* came from both foreign and native-born members of the Tejano community.[25]

As well, people in Mexico sympathized with the PSD movement be-cause the conflict in Texas paralleled the struggle astir in Mexico. Indeed, the PSD mantra of "*igualdad e independencia*" (equality and independence) was borrowed from revolutionary language employed by the warring camps in Mexico. The *Plan's* plebian groundings transcended borders and appealed to Mexicans whether they lived on the Texas or Mexico side of the border. Masses of people in the motherland identified with (and backed) what appeared to be another armed struggle of beleaguered and downtrodden poor folks everywhere.[26]

The ideology of the Mexican Revolution, especially the brand pro-pounded by the PLM, induced Tejanos to rethink their proletariat con-dition. An early generation of historians paid only cursory attention to this association,[27] but in recent years historians have been more mind-ful of it. In 1992, one scholar asserted boldly that the Flores Magón news organ *Regeneración* "helped to mobilize marginalized Americans and Mexi-cans for political action against the governments of the United States and Mexico."[28] Current scholarship concurs that many Tejanos, by the early years of the Revolution, knew of *Regeneración* and had knowledge of the PLM's advocacy for the powerless masses, for land redistribution, and for improved wages for exploited laborers. In the pages of *Regeneración,* the Flores Magón team condemned lynching, segregation, prejudice, and other forms of discrimination, whether in Mexico or Texas. Motivated by the party's message, PLM enthusiasts in South Texas (and in fact in towns as far away as the state's Panhandle) formed PLM chapters and stayed abreast of PLM discourses as well as events transpiring in Mexico. Among such followers was Aniceto Pizaña, the Tejano who struck back when Anglos invaded his ranch on August 3, 1915.[29]

In the end, events along the border affected Tejano communities adversely. Almost all historians, past and present, have acknowledged consequences for Tejanos. First, that Mexican residents of Texas should in any manner align themselves with the Revolution immediately cast questions of loyalty on an entire people (Texans came to suspect the allegiance of even those Tejanos living deep in the interior of the state). Certainly the discovery of PLM literature (upon searching Aniceto Pizaña's home during the incursion of August 3) convinced Anglos of ties existing between the PSD and *magonismo* and anarchism. Anglos hunting *sedicioso* participants did so convinced that anyone behind the Texas troubles was no patriot. From Rio Grande City, an army officer observed: "The population of the county is more than 95 percent Mexican birth and a very large proportion of this element is in sympathy with raiders or bandits, now apparently trying to get together."[30]

A second immediate consequence deriving from suspected connections between the Revolution in Mexico and Tejano PSD rebels was a war of annihilation against Tejanos. Anglo-Americans united behind the rubric of race in a brutal campaign of retaliation for the mayhem (of murder and destruction of property) kindled by the PSD movement. Historians have given much attention to the "Bandit War," but only a brief overview need be offered here, and that for the purpose of illustrating how the PSD hysteria impacted Mexican American communities along the lower border. Anglo-American accomplices in the vendetta against Tejanos included vigilante groups (posses), civilian militias, deputies, masked men, and farmers, with the most notorious being *los rinches* (the Texas Rangers, discussed in greater detail later in the essay). Victims of this campaign of no quarter included suspected raiders, citizens thought guilty due to some loose association with the rebels, property owners whose land Anglos coveted, and a wide circle of innocent bystanders who knew of the rebellion only from what they heard of it. No one knows the number of Mexicans who perished during the "Bandit War"—figures run anywhere from 102 to 5,000 deaths—though the tendency lately has been to set the fatalities in the hundreds.[31]

Recent monographs (in contradistinction to older studies more preoccupied with ascertaining who instigated the *sediciosos*) document a third immediate effect of the Mexican Revolution on Tejanos: the mass departure of Texas Mexicans toward Mexico, a flight ironically brought on by forces inciting the PSD from Mexico and indirectly eliciting the war of terror against Tejanos. The exodus started around August 1915 (it did not ease until about December) and included an array of terrified residents, from common working-class folks to middle-class property owners forsaking their homes, ranches, and businesses establishments. One newspaper account had more than seven thousand Texas Mexicans having left for Mexico from Cameron and Hidalgo Counties in September and October, a quantity that amounted to some 40 percent of the Hispanic population there. Many returned to Texas to find their ranch property now claimed by Anglos, their homes in tumbledown condition, their allegiance in doubt, and their future uncertain. One historian speculates that some time passed after military troubles waned before the population (both Mexican and Anglo) in the Valley returned to its prewar levels.[32]

Still another immediate outcome historians identify as stemming from the Mexican Revolution was fragmentation within the Tejano community. Political splits surfaced, most demonstrably between the *sediciosos* (and their supporters) and those lining up against their cause. PSD adherents blasted members of the Mexican American community who by 1910 had thrown in their lot with malicious elements that included Anglos who hated Mexicans, land swindlers, segregationists, and farmers who unconscionably exploited their field hands. Such "opportunists" included Texas Mexican ranch owners and business people who had fared materially well under the Anglo regime. Other such "race traitors" included Tejano law officials engaged in tracking down the marauders. Also targeted were the Tejano Progressives, an emerging class of middling standing who before the Revolution had envisioned for themselves (as well as for fellow Tejanos) a place in an Anglo world of peace, progress, and prosperity, if not in a nation tolerant of racial and cultural diversity.[33]

Violence

As noted briefly above, the Mexican Revolution brought terrible times to border Mexicans as a consequence of the murder of Anglos and the destruction of their properties. Whether because Anglos suspected Tejanos of aiding and abetting the revolutionaries fighting in Mexico or of allegedly colluding with raiders who crossed into Texas to round up livestock or steal supplies, Tejano communities too often found themselves under violent attacks from white men and law enforcement authorities. So did barrios and ranch settlements in other parts of Texas, though due to factors unconnected to the PSD. Still, the primary cause for violence targeted at communities outside South Texas was the Revolution; the casualties, deaths, and the destruction of property the Revolution wrought upon U.S. citizens, whether on the Texas side or the Mexican side of the border, implicated Mexican American people in transnational misdeeds.

The extent of violence along the border has preoccupied scholars since the 1950s, though a newer generation of border historians during the last two decades has taken it up as a topic for more serious scrutiny. Although the subject presents broad possibilities for study, scholars have generally focused on the causes behind the bloodlust, the forms of violence employed by the several antagonists, and the group most generally associated with barbarities against Mexicans, the Texas Rangers.

Behind almost every act of cruelty committed upon Tejanos (at least between 1915 and 1918, the highpoint of the border war) lurked the shadow of the Mexican Revolution. For Anglos who felt the brunt of attacks from Mexican raiders and marauders, violence seemed a necessary means to defend their lives and property. Ranch owners, businessmen, and law officials saw no alternative but to take the offensive in the crisis of the moment. Few modern-day historians, of course, would attempt to justify their criminality.

Embedded racial and cultural distaste for Mexicans powered the violent impulse that erupted during the mid-1910s, some scholars maintain. Scorn toward and loathing of Mexicans throughout Texas was manifest long before the 1910 Revolution, apparent in the entrenched practice of discrimination, a system of justice unfair to Mexicans, and the practice of lynching without fear of legal castigation. The turmoil of the decade, therefore, presented an opportune moment for Anglos (including newly arriving farmers who made no distinctions between ranch-owning and landless Mexicans) to spew feelings of hatred and to exact violent havoc upon the "greaser" element.[34]

Economic motives, according to a leading interpretation, drove Anglos to join in a campaign of no quarter against Tejanos. Generally advanced by those trained in Mexican American history (this line of analysis seldom resonates with traditional Latin Americanists), the argument has newly arriving farm owners from out of state using the Mexican Revolution as a pretext to enfeeble the very element—Mexican Americans—that undergirded the ranch society obstructing agricultural growth in South Texas.

In the Revolution, farmers saw a window conducive to foisting conditions upon the Lower Rio Grande Valley wherein Mexicans would serve as seasonal field hands in a predominant farm society.[35] David Montejano, a foremost proponent of this thesis, quotes Emilio Forto, a Cameron County businessman and politico, who in 1918 assessed the motives behind the violence of 1915 thusly:

> From all reports (some from army officers whose testimony is probably available) a campaign of extermination seemed to have begun in those days. The cry was often "we have to make this a white man's country!!" It would not be difficult to establish the fact that many well-to-do natives of Texas, of Mexican origin, were driven away by Rangers, who told them "If you are found here in the next five days you will be dead." They were in this way forced to abandon their property, which they sold at almost any price.[36]

Whatever lay behind their motives, Anglo-Americans used numerous means to attack Tejanos, and historians have yet to devise a schema for chronicling that bloodshed; a simple listing of the horrors suffices for them at the moment. Physical intimidation, some note, surfaced as a successful tactic to acquiring coveted South Texas ranch properties. Anglo land buyers in collaboration with law authorities forcefully drove out Tejano rancheros, threatening property owners and their families with homicide if they were found to be shielding revolutionaries. Retribution for suspected complicity in the raids or involvement in the PSD movement produced burnings of private residences (when considered meeting places for the *guerrilleros*). Vigilante wrath, often taking the form of cold-blooded slayings or merciless hangings of Tejanos, intensified during the era, but according to contemporary reports, taking the lives of Mexicans believed involved in the border troubles hardly roused notice from the general populace.[37] Lynching became commonplace, and condoned by some, as the *Lyford Courant* (August 1915) editorialized: "Lynch law is never a pleasant thing to contemplate, but it is not to be denied that it is sometimes the only means of administering justice."[38]

Violence directed at Tejanos in the form of rioting occurred only in El Paso, but historians have taken a close look at this particular outbreak, and the scholarship explaining it appears to be expanding (there is one article on the episode included in this volume). The catalyst for the incident was the execution of several American mining employees by *Villista* followers at Santa Ysabel (state of Chihuahua) on January 10, 1916. Although historians have correctly seen frustration with an ineffective federal policy toward border depredations, as well as anger over Mexico's inability to contain border troubles, as factors fueling tempers that ignited the violence in El Paso, they also find racism stoking emotions. For Americans, the Santa Ysabel executions appeared a blatant example of reverse racism, as the Mexican soldiers had selected only Anglos for death. Newspaper reports immediately following the murders excited readers with the horrific nature of the slaughter, as if sadism were innate to the Mexican character. On the evening of January 13, 1916, therefore, an aroused crowd of some five hundred to fifteen hundred townspeople and soldiers hit the streets with the intended purpose of inflicting bloody harm on Mexicans in the city and driving them out of *El Segundo barrio.* The spontaneous rioting involved every kind of physical assault with knives and guns upon Mexicans; military force ended the tumult around midnight. Though brief, the El Paso race riot stands as another example of how the Mexican Revolution touched Tejano communities.[39]

A third area of interest involving violence leveled against Tejanos due to the turbulence created by the Mexican Revolution is the role of the Texas Rangers. No credible study today would likely excuse the Rangers for their actions; about all admirers can do is explain the problems involved in distinguishing between atrocities committed by the Rangers and others attributable to posses, vigilantes, farmers, and their accessories.[40] But the list implicating the Rangers in the killing of Mexicans, both raiders and innocent Tejano civilians, is extensive and can be found in contemporary news accounts, government investigative reports, oral histories, the Ranger Force Investigation (the Canales Ranger investigation of 1919), the Rangers Records, and much more.

It would be redundant here to list the litany of wrongs attributed to *"los rinches"*; the recent study by Richard Henry Ribb documents their "reign of terror" and "the killing fields" that implicate them in the carnage. The persecution of Tejanos included *"la rinchada"* (to be "rangered," or to be killed by Rangers in a murderous spree). *La rinchada* involved mass lynching, cold-blooded executions in front of relatives, demolition of Tejano homes and ranchos, and a callous disrespect for the deceased (the Rangers left bodies decomposing alongside roads).[41]

Given such indifference toward the lives of Mexicans, a massacre of Tejanos by Rangers seemed possible, and it occurred in the village of Porvenir in Presidio County (the Big Bend country of Texas). Almost all historians writing on the episode agree on its particulars, with no one absolving the main culprits of the atrocity. According to this well-known account, the Rangers ostensibly received reports that some residents of Porvenir had participated in the December 25, 1917, attack by presumed *Villista* raiders on the nearby Brite Ranch. On a cold January 28, 1918, around midnight, Rangers burst into Tejano *jacales* (shacks) at Porvenir, took some fifteen men of different ages behind a small hill there at the settlement, administered upon them a severe beating, then slaughtered them. Women found their loved ones' (husbands', grandfathers', and grandsons') bodies piled up in a heap that dawn and transported them to Mexico for burial. A Ranger cover-up followed, but five accomplices were made to face charges. All escaped sentences, however.[42]

Other historians, of course, do not see the Rangers as vicious racists bent on a campaign of mass murder. Professors Harris and Sadler, authors of the most comprehensive work on the Rangers for that time period, commit themselves "neither to justify nor to condemn but rather to paint as accurately as possible a portrait of the Rangers, warts and all."[43] For them, the Ranger presence along the border corresponded more to government directives: they were to protect the border and its population (both Anglo and Mexican) from raiders and other disturbances that might spring from the Mexican Revolution. Once there, however, the Rangers fell to defying the laws they swore to uphold, perhaps because they did hate Mexicans or felt the need to take extreme measures in order to clean the region of banditry, or because they followed the example of their own officers who waged a war of torture and assassination. Robert M. Utley, author of the most recent monograph on the Rangers, believes that exempting the years of the Mexican Revolution, the myth of the Rangers holds up well to scrutiny.[44]

Identity

There exists an incipient historiographic debate regarding the Revolution and the exact philosophical and cultural implications it had for Tejano communities. As noted earlier, proponents of the generational model maintain that the refugees escaping north transformed Mexican American communities into Mexican enclaves that culturally and philosophically now looked south to Mexico. But several recent works dispute such a conclusion. According to this counterargument, the immigrants augmented the size of Tejano communities, but their number did not necessarily alter the social and psychological identity of many longtime inhabitants of *colonias.* Living in Texas barrios long before the Revolution were Mexican-descent Texans—some of them members of a fledgling middle class—who had adjusted to American life; they saw themselves as being of Mexican heritage, but they had staked their future on life in Texas. Members of this cohort (whether of poor or middling status) went by many labels, among them the self-referent México Texanos.[45]

Such a binational identity persisted despite the presence of so many immigrants entering Tejano communities. The Mexican Revolution, therefore, instead of converting *colonias* into immigrant camps, had another and opposite outcome. For one, it advanced the consciousness of those middle-class México Tejanos who, in response to the immigrants (who to them were not "Americans"!) and PSD troubles (as well as other historical currents unfolding during the decade and into the 1920s), increasingly distinguished themselves as "Mexican Americans."[46] Then, the Revolution sent north parents who would help broaden the ranks (through their children) of México Texanos, the cohort that by the 1920s emerged as the voice of the barrios and subsequently as spokespersons during the 1930s through the 1950s. The children of immigrants (if not the immigrants themselves) faced too many pressures in Texas not to change. Daily life during the 1910s and 1920s (and after, of course) included exposure to the English language, consumer goods, sports, American moving pictures, Spanish-language newspapers carrying American advertisements, schools, and much more.[47] Many began looking to their land of birth instead of the land of revolution and cast their lot with those coming to think of themselves as Mexican Americans.

Among the strongest supporters of the thesis that the Revolution's impact was "turning Mexicans into Americans" is Benjamin H. Johnson. His primary focus, however, is on the PSD and not on how the immigrants' presence swayed the barrios. As noted earlier in the essay, PSD members had marked for attacks what Johnson calls the Tejano Progressives. For this circle of middle-class individuals wanting to be part of the Valley's economic modernization, the PSD was an abomination. They detested the state of virtual anarchy that the *sediciosos* (with the aid of revolutionary factions in Mexico) had wrought, and they abhorred the raiders' disruption of the economic and social world they had hoped to join and sought to advance. The Revolution only made them greater admirers of the ideology and values of the nation they inhabited. For them, American democracy (instead of revolutionary turmoil) offered the ideal of justice and equality; economic modernization gave them hope for prosperity; and the U.S. military provided security against the PSD marauders as well as the despised Texas Rangers.[48]

It was to the American standard, then, that Progressives turned to deal with the aftermath of the PSD disorder. They placed genuine trust in the American system to help them in dealing with lynching, violence, land loss, segregation, disfranchisement and all else stemming from the "Bandit War" of 1915. For Johnson, then, a link exists between the PSD and the statewide civic organizations that the Progressives organized in the 1920s, with names such as the Order of Sons of America, the Order of Knights of America, and the League of United Latin American Citizens (LULAC). Thus had the PSD turned Mexicans into Americans; indeed these fledgling organizations represented the concerns of the native born, not of immigrants.[49]

Conclusions

Although historians heretofore have not given deserved attention to the Mexican Revolution and its effects on Tejano communities, enough writings exist on the general subject to categorize the present scholarship. The miscellany of works may be broken down into four major (though not exclusive) groupings: immigration, the PSD, violence, and identity. This essay has focused on those four categories and finds that despite neglect, a healthy and fruitful historiographic debate does exist apropos to the impact that the Revolution had on Tejano communities.

Although contemporaries and social scientists writing in the aftermath of the Revolution viewed immigration with apprehension, that consideration took a turn when Chicano history came to center stage in the 1970s. For those belonging to this interpretive school, immigration during the 1910s (and after) actually proved salubrious for the many Texas Mexican settlements throughout Texas, as it led to population increases, politicized *colonias,* and reinforced "*lo mexicano.*" Some Chicano historians find the immigrants such a force in community building that they label the era between 1900 and 1930 as that of the "Immigrant Generation."

Scholarly studies of the *Plan de San Diego* go back to the 1950s, although more in-depth investigations began only during the 1970s. In their earliest probes, historians sought to determine the connection existing between the PSD and the Revolution in Mexico, focusing on the involvement of various personalities or interest groups, among them Venustiano

Carranza, Victoriano Huerta, and Germany. Explanations regarding such a connection today are more nuanced; historians since the 1970s have offered various interpretations: that the PSD was of Texas origins but used by Carranza for political reasons; that the PSD was of Texas origins but abetted by revolutionaries in Mexico (not necessarily affiliated with *Carrancistas*); that the PSD was of Texas origins, but the Revolution offered a historical opening for Tejanos to retaliate against malicious gringos; or that the PSD was inspired by the PLM. Almost all scholars agree that Texas Mexican involvement in PSD activities produced ugly results for Tejano communities. In the short term, Tejanos suffered through the "Bandit War" and other forms of violence in parts of the border that included rioting and massacres. Long-term consequences included disfranchisement, segregation, and angst under white supremacy.

The extensive violence experienced by Tejanos during the years between 1915 and 1918 takes up considerable space in some of the writings spotlighting the period. Though hardly any significant disputes divide historians on the extent of the bloodshed, different interpretations do exist on the causes behind the violence: some find its wellspring in the instinct for retaliation induced by the damage and murders that accompanied the border raids; others, in racism; and still others, in economic interests. Few excuse those most culpable for atrocities upon Tejanos, namely the Texas Rangers. Long portrayed in legendary proportions in Texas history, recent writings see them as tarnishing the Texas escutcheon, certainly for the years of the Revolution.

The literature on Tejanos of the 1910s era has also inquired into the matter of identity formation, or how the Mexican Revolution shaped Tejano consciousness. Writings in the 1970s and 1980s posited that the newly arriving immigrants influenced Tejano identity profoundly, turning communities into predominantly immigrant enclaves (at least into the latter 1920s). Recently, historians have reconsidered such a proposition, detecting the presence of different philosophical attitudes in barrios and rural hamlets. Among such inclinations would have been the one affirmed by México Texanos, a cohort traceable to the nineteenth century. Notwithstanding the problems of race they faced and despite the impact of the Mexican Revolution on their communities, this class persisted in its allegiance to Texas and the United States (and not to Mexico as with the immigrants fleeing the Revolution), maintaining the notion that state and country had room for native-born people of Mexican descent.

What does a review of discourses on the Mexican Revolution and its impact of Tejano communities yield? First, that the 1910s indeed represent watershed years during which the Revolution forced thousands of people into Texas, not only reinforcing communities founded in the nineteenth century and earlier but supplying corporations and agribusiness enterprises with the cheap labor they coveted. Also, it casts light onto the sustained interest historians have in the PSD; one writer in this collection regards the event as the last great revolt (previous ones would be the Cortina War of 1859 and the Garza War of 1891) against nineteenth-century colonialism. In this same context, current writings unrelentingly underscore the trauma that visited Tejano communities as a consequence of the turmoil in Mexico. Last, recent literature demonstrates that the rise of the Mexican American civil rights movement, generally seen as a post-1920s occurrence, actually had its foundations earlier in the development of a Mexican American mentality at the turn of the century and was then hastened by the Mexican Revolution and PSD troubles.

Conversely, appraising the scholarship on the Mexican Revolution's impact on Tejanos exposes gaps in the research. Certainly, there are subjects beyond the four arrangements identified in this essay that require investigation. For instance, how did the Revolution affect settlements beyond the Rio Grande border? Much of what has been discussed herein transpired in the Rio Grande Valley counties of South Texas, the Big Bend, and El Paso. What of interior cities such as Corpus Christi, Victoria, Houston, Temple, Amarillo, San Angelo, Fort Stockton, or Alpine?

A most important but neglected topic is that of women; to date, less than a handful of unpublished theses and dissertations address gender, and these works study the subject only tangentially (see Selected Bibliography). The Master's thesis by Michelle Margot Espinoza suggests some possible areas of focus. The participation of South Texas Tejanas in helping or otherwise abetting revolutionaries in Mexico and PSD followers through such exploits as espionage begs attention. So do actions taken by Tejanas who bravely protected family property and their male loved ones from either revolutionary forces who crossed into Texas looking for conscripts or from PSD activists with the same intention; women faced down such recruiters by hiding fathers, sons, and grandsons or by simply lying to them. Historians should also look more closely at the way in which immigrant women restructured their lives upon arriving in Texas. Those of high social standing and who had lost everything in the Revolution, for example, now faced the daunting task of beginning anew.[50]

Epochal, then, were the implications of the Mexican Revolution for

Tejano communities. While suffering untold turbulence, Mexican-descent people withstood the convulsion and persisted to face down future crises, ones associated with poverty, infant mortality, migration, deportation, job exploitation, Jim Crow, and much more. Future scholarship can only elaborate upon these travails and triumphs.

Notes

1. The most prominent example would be Américo Paredes, *George Washington Gómez: A Mexicotexan Novel* (Houston: Arte Público Press, 1990), pt. 1, 9–34.

2. David Nathan Johnson, *Madero in Texas: Prelude to a Revolution, 1910–1911,* ed. Félix D. Almaráz Jr. (San Antonio: Corona Publishing, 2001); Don M. Coerver and Linda B. Hall, *Texas and the Mexican Revolution: A Study in State and National Border Policy* (San Antonio: Trinity University Press, 1984); Michelle Lorraine Gomilla, "*Los Refugiados y los Comerciantes:* Mexican Refugees and Businessmen in Downtown El Paso, 1910–1920" (M.A. thesis, University of Texas at El Paso, 1990); Charles H. Harris and Louis R. Sadler, *The Secret War in El Paso: Mexican Revolutionary Intrigue, 1906–1920* (Albuquerque: University of New Mexico Press, 2009); Charles H. Harris III and Louis R. Sadler, "The 1911 Reyes Conspiracy: The Texas Side," *Southwestern Historical Quarterly* 83 (April 1980): 325–348; Peter V. N. Henderson, *Mexican Exiles in the Borderlands, 1910–1913* (El Paso: Texas Western Press, 1979); Mary Ester Hernández, "Some Connections between San Antonio and the Mexican Revolution" (M.A. thesis, University of Texas at Austin, 1973); Victor M. Macías-González, "Mexicans of the Better Class: The Exile of Chihuahuan Upper Classes in El Paso, 1913–1930," *Password* 45 (Winter 2000): 175–195; W. Dirk Raat, *Revoltosos: Mexico's Rebels in the United States, 1903–1923* (College Station: Texas A&M University Press, 1981); Douglas W. Richmond, "*La guerra en Tejas se renova:* Mexican Insurrection and Carrancista Ambitions, 1900–1920," *Aztlán* 11 (Spring 1980): 5–9; and David D. Romo, *Ringside to a Revolution: An Underground Cultural History of El Paso and Juárez, 1893–1923* (El Paso: Cinco Puntos Press, 2005).

3. Shannon E. Barker, "*Los Tejanos de San Antonio:* Mexican Immigrant Family Acculturation, 1880–1929" (Ph.D. diss., University of Texas at Austin, 2006); Carlos Eliseo Cuéllar, *Stories from the Barrio: A History of Mexican Fort Worth* (Fort Worth: Texas Christian University Press, 2003); Arnoldo De León, *Ethnicity in the Sunbelt: Mexican Americans in Houston* (Houston: Mexican American Studies Program, 1989); Mario T. García, *Desert Immigrants: The Mexicans of El Paso, 1880–1920* (New Haven, Conn.: Yale University Press, 1981); Richard A. García, *The Rise of the Mexican American Middle Class in San Antonio, 1929–1941* (College Station: Texas A&M University Press, 1991); Gabriela González, "Two Flags Entwined: Transborder Activities and the Politics of

Race, Ethnicity, Class and Gender in South Texas, 1900–1950" (Ph.D. diss., Stanford University, 2005); Cynthia Orozco, *No Mexicans, Women, or Dogs Allowed: The Rise of the Mexican American Civil Rights Movement* (Austin: University of Texas Press, 2009); and Emilio Zamora, *The World of the Mexican Worker in Texas* (College Station: Texas A&M University Press, 1993).

4. Arnoldo De León, *Mexican Americans in Texas: A Brief History,* 3rd ed. (Wheeling, Ill., Harlan Davidson, 2009), 74. Figures close to these are provided in E. E. Davis, "King Cotton Leads Mexicans into Texas," *The Texas Outlook* (April 1925): 7.

5. Paul S. Taylor, "The Mexican 'Invaders' of El Paso," *The Survey* (July 8, 1916): 380–382.

6. Davis, "King Cotton Leads Mexicans into Texas," 7–8; Max Sylvius Handman, "The Mexican Immigrant in Texas," *The Southwestern Political and Social Science Quarterly* 7 (June 1926): 37–38, 40; Emory S. Bogardus, "The Mexican Immigrant and Segregation," *The American Journal of Sociology* 36 (July 1930): 76–77; and Flora Lowrey, "Night-School in Little Mexico," *Southwest Review* 16 (October 1930): 37.

7. See García, *Desert Immigrants,* chapter 10; De León, *Ethnicity in the Sunbelt,* 11–18; García, *Rise of the Mexican American Middle Class,* 44–46; and Cuéller, *Stories from the Barrio,* 7–16.

8. Gomilla, "*Los Refugiados y Los Comerciantes,* 67–110.

9. Actually, support in Texas barrios for revolutionary ideals preceded the breakout of hostilities in November 1910. Among sources referencing such activity would be Johnson, *Madero in Texas,* 105, 120–121; Ana Luisa Martínez, "Frontier of Dissent: *El Regidor,* The Regime of Porfirio Díaz, and the Transborder Community," *Southwestern Historical Quarterly* 112 (April 2009): 389–408; and Romo, *Ringside Seat to a Revolution,* 18–75.

10. Coerver and Hall, *Texas and the Mexican Revolution,* 36–37; and Richard Henry Ribb, "José Tomás Canales and the Texas Rangers: Myth, Identity, and Power in South Texas, 1900–1920" (Ph.D. diss., University of Texas at Austin, 2001), 137–138. The full story of Chapa and Sánchez and their involvement with Reyes is told in Harris and Sadler, "The 1911 Reyes Conspiracy," 325–348.

11. Richard Estrada, "The Mexican Revolution in the Ciudad Juárez-El Paso Area, 1910–1920," *Password* (Summer 1979): 62; García, *Desert Immigrants,* 181; and De León, *Ethnicity in the Sunbelt,* 14.

12. García, *Desert Immigrants,* 184; and Rodolfo Rocha, "The Influence of the Mexican Revolution on the Mexico–Texas Border, 1910–1916" (Ph.D. diss., Texas Tech University, 1981), 63–65, 104.

13. Charles H. Harris and Louis R. Sadler, *The Texas Rangers and the Mexican Revolution: The Bloodiest Decade, 1910–1920* (Albuquerque: University of New Mexico Press, 2004), 214.

14. Rocha, "The Influence of the Mexican Revolution on the Mexico–Texas Border," 192; James Alex Garza, "On the Edge of the Storm: Laredo and the Mexican Revolution, 1910–1917" (M.A. thesis, Texas A&M International University, 1996), 36, 38, 46–47, 51, 75; Orozco, *No Mexicans, Women, or Dogs Allowed,* 42; Romo, *Ringside Seat to a Revolution,* 109–111; and Harris and Sadler, *The Texas Rangers and the Mexican Revolution,* 214.

15. Rocha, "The Influence of the Mexican Revolution on the Mexico–Texas Border," 178, 190–191; and Nancy Baker Jones, "Jovita Idar," in *The New Handbook of Texas,* 6 vols., eds. Ron Tyler et al. (Austin: Texas State Historical Association, 1996): vol. 3, 815. For the work of the Cruz Blanca in Laredo during the Revolution, see Leonor Villegas de Magnón, in *The Rebel,* ed. Clara Lomas (Houston: Arte Público Press, 1993), 70–105.

16. Ribb, "José Tomás Canales and the Texas Rangers," 84, 137; and Richard Griswold del Castillo, "The Mexican Revolution and the Spanish-Language Press in the Borderlands," *Journalism History* 4 (Summer 1977): 43.

17. Quoted in Jason T. Darrah, "Anglos, Mexicans, and the San Ysabel Massacre: A Study of Changing Ethnic Relations in El Paso, Texas, 1910–1916" (M.A. thesis, Texas Tech University, 2003), 6, citing Richard Medina Estrada, "Border Revolution: The Mexican Revolution in the Ciudad Juárez-El Paso Area, 1906–1915" (M.A. thesis, University of Texas at El Paso, 1975), 132.

18. García, *Desert Immigrants,* chapter 10; Mario T. García, *Mexican Americans: Leadership, Ideology & Identity, 1930–1960* (New Haven, Conn.: Yale University Press, 1989), 13–15; and De León, *Ethnicity in the Sunbelt,* 11, 18. A critique of the generational model is found in Louis Gerard Mendoza, *Historia: The Literary Making of Chicana & Chicano History* (College Station: Texas A&M University Press, 2001), 16, 61, 67–69, 128, 129.

19. García, *Mexican Americans,* 14. See further, García, *Desert Immigrants,* 122; and García, *Rise of the Mexican American Middle Class,* 28.

20. Scholarship on the PSD is extensive and grows yearly. The most significant studies include Evan Anders, *Boss Rule in South Texas: The Progressive Era* (Austin: University of Texas Press, 1982); Coerver and Hall, *Texas and the Mexican Revolution;* Charles C. Cumberland, "Border Raids in the Lower Rio Grande Valley 1915," *Southwestern Historical Quarterly* 57 (January 1954): 285–311; Ciro R. De la Garza-Treviño, *El Plan de San Diego* (Ciudad Victoria, Tamp.: Universidad de Tamaulipas, 1970); Allen Gerlach, "Conditions Along the Border—1915: The Plan de San Diego," *New Mexico Historical Review* 43 (July 1968): 195–212; Juan Gómez-Quiñones, "The Plan of San Diego Reviewed," *Aztlán* 1 (Spring 1970): 124–132; Trinidad Gonzales, "The World of México Texanos, Mexicanos and México Americanos: Transnational and National Identities in the Lower Rio Grande Valley during the Last Phase of United States Colonization, 1900–1930" (Ph.D. diss., University of Houston, 2008); William A.

Hager, "The Plan of San Diego: Unrest on the Texas Border in 1915," *Arizona and the West* 5 (Winter 1963): 327–336; Charles H. Harris and Louis R. Sadler, "The Plan of San Diego and the Mexican–United States War Crisis of 1916: A Reexamination," *Hispanic American Historical Review* 58 (August 1978): 381–408; Harris and Sadler, *The Texas Rangers and the Mexican Revolution;* Benjamin H. Johnson, *Revolution in Texas: How a Forgotten Rebellion and Its Bloody Suppression Turned Mexicans into Americans* (New Haven, Conn.: Yale University Press, 2003); Douglas Meed, *Bloody Border: Riots, Battles, and Adventures Along the Turbulent U.S.–Mexican Borderlands* (Tucson: Westernlore Press, 1992); Michael Meyer, "The Mexican-German Conspiracy of 1915," *The Americas* 23 (July 1966): 381–408; Richmond, "*La guerra en Tejas se renova*"; Ribb, "José Tomás Canales and the Texas Rangers"; Rocha, "The Influence of the Mexican Revolution on the Mexico–Texas Border"; Rodolfo Rocha, "The Tejano Revolt of 1915," in *Mexican Americans in Texas History,* eds. Emilio Zamora, Cynthia Orozco, and Rodolfo Rocha (Austin: Texas State Historical Association, 2000); Frank N. Samponaro, and Paul J. Vanderwood, *War Scare on the Rio Grande: Robert Runyon's Photographs of the Border Conflict, 1913–1916* (Austin: Texas State Historical Association, 1992); James A. Sandos, *Rebellion in the Borderlands: Anarchism and the Plan of San Diego, 1904–1923* (Norman: University of Oklahoma Press, 1992); James A. Sandos, "The Plan of San Diego: War and Diplomacy on the Texas Border, 1915–1916," *Arizona and the West* 14 (Spring 1972): 5–24; Robert M. Utley, *Lone Star Lawmen: The Second Century of the Texas Rangers* (Oxford: Oxford University Press, 2007); Jake Watts, "The Plan of San Diego and the Lower Rio Grande Valley," in *More Studies in Brownsville History,* ed. Milo Kearney (Brownsville, Tex.: Pan American University at Brownsville, 1989); L. H. Warburton, "The Plan de San Diego: Background and Selected Documents," *Journal of South Texas* 12 (1999): 125–155; and William V. Wilkinson, "The Mexican Revolution and the Bandit Wars: The Lower Rio Grande Valley in 1915," in *Still More Studies in Brownsville History,* ed. Milo Kearney (Brownsville, Tex.: Pan American University at Brownsville, 1991). Among the best of the most current treatments are Harris and Sadler's *The Texas Rangers and the Mexican Revolution* (chapters 8–11); Johnson's *Revolution in Texas;* and Sandos, *Rebellion in the Borderlands,* 72–75.

21. Studies connecting the PSD to Carranza include Cumberland, "Border Raids in the Lower Rio Grande Valley," 308–309; Harris and Sadler, *The Texas Rangers and the Mexican Revolution,* 252–253, 280, 290, 295–297, 322; Utley, *Lone Star Lawmen,* 43–45; and Coerver and Hall, *Texas and the Mexican Revolution,* 90–91, 97–101. The major work tying the PSD to the PLM is Sandos, *Rebellion in the Borderlands,* xv. Those seeing Germany and Huerta behind the PSD include Meyer, "The Mexican-German Conspiracy of 1915," 76–89; Gerlach, "Conditions Along the Border," 198, 201, 204; and Virgil Lott and Virginia M. Fenwick, *People and Plots on the Rio Grande* (San Antonio: Naylor Company, 1957), 46–47.

22. The foremost advocates of this position are Harris and Sadler, *The Texas Rangers and the Mexican Revolution,* chapter 11.

23. This argument may be found in David Montejano, *Anglos and Mexicans in the Making of Texas, 1836–1986* (Austin: University of Texas Press, 1987); 123; Watts, "The Plan of San Diego and the Lower Rio Grande Valley," 333; Sandos, "The Plan of San Diego," 10, 24; Johnson, *Revolution in Texas,* 99–101; and Juan Gómez-Quiñones, "The Plan de San Diego Reviewed," 124–132.

24. Rodolfo Rocha, "The Tejano Revolt," 103, 105, 109, 111, 113, 119. This argument is more fully advanced in Rocha's, "The Influence of the Mexican Revolution on the Mexico–Texas Border," chapter 6, and especially 256–257, 300–301, 331–333.

25. Johnson, *Revolution in Texas,* 59–60; quote is from p. 60.

26. Montejano, *Anglos and Mexicans in the Making of Texas,* 119; Johnson, *Revolution in Texas* 79; and Anders, *Boss Rule in South Texas,* 227.

27. Cumberland, in "Border Raids in the Lower Rio Grande Valley," discusses this on 286–287.

28. Sandos, *Rebellion in the Borderlands,* 174–175.

29. Johnson, *Revolution in Texas,* 60–62. The strongest advocate for a PLM connection is Sandos, *Rebellion in the Borderlands,* 72–75, 77–78. See also Ribb, "José Tomás Canales and the Texas Rangers," 87–88.

30. Sandos, *Rebellion in the Borderlands,* 88. The quote is from Johnson, *Revolution in Texas,* 96.

31. Full coverage of the "Bandit War" may be found in Harris and Sadler, *The Texas Rangers and the Mexican Revolution,* chapters 9–10; Utley, *Lone Star Lawmen,* 26–47; Johnson, *Revolution in Texas,* 85–88, 113–120; and Sandos, *Rebellion in the Borderlands,* 87–109. Estimates of death come from Harris and Sadler, *The Texas Rangers and the Mexican Revolution,* 296.

32. Rocha, "The Influence of the Mexican Revolution on the Mexico–Texas Border," 316–318; Sandos, *Rebellion in the Borderlands,* 109–110; Johnson, *Revolution in Texas,* 120–124, 134–135; Harris and Sadler, *The Texas Rangers and the Mexican Revolution,* 285; Utley, *Lone Star Lawmen,* 38; and Cumberland, "Border Raids in the Lower Rio Grande Valley," 302.

33. Johnson, *Revolution in Texas,* 41, 42, 70, 79, 84, 85, 124, 125, 126.

34. Montejano, *Anglos and Mexicans in the Making of Texas,* 118; and Anders, *Boss Rule in South Texas,* 221.

35. Ribb, "José Tomás Canales and the Texas Rangers," 331.

36. Montejano, *Anglos and Mexicans in the Making of Texas,* 125–127, citing Emilio C. Forto, "Actual Situation on the River Rio Grande: Information Rendered to Colonel

H.J. Slocum of the American Forces at Brownsville," *Pan American Labor Press,* September 11, 1918.

37. Cumberland, "Border Raids in the Lower Rio Grande Valley," 301; Johnson, *Revolution in Texas,* 114, 115; and Sandos, *Rebellion in the Borderlands,* 87, 89, 98.

38. Cited in Johnson, *Revolution in Texas,* 86–87.

39. Raúl R. Reyes, "The Santa Isabel Episode, January 10, 1916: Ethnic Repercussions in El Paso and Ciudad Juárez," *Password,* 42 (Summer 1997): 55–75; Darrah, "Anglos, Mexicans, and the San Ysabel Massacre," 81–99, 109; and Shawn Lay, *War, Revolution and the Ku Klux Klan: A Study of Intolerance in a Border City* (El Paso: Texas Western Press, 1985), 16–17, 25.

40. Harris and Sadler, *The Texas Rangers and the Mexican Revolution,* 289–290.

41. Ribb, "José Tomás Canales and the Texas Rangers," chapter 7, 301.

42. Glenn Justice, *Revolution on the Rio Grande: Mexican Raids and Army Pursuits, 1916–1919* (El Paso: University of Texas at El Paso Press, 1992), 21–47; Meed, *Bloody Border,* 129–131; and Ribb, "José Tomás Canales and the Texas Rangers," 333–348.

43. Harris and Sadler, *The Texas Rangers and the Mexican Revolution,* 8.

44. Harris and Sadler, *The Texas Rangers and the Mexican Revolution,* 255–256, 259, 292; and Utley, *Lone Star Lawmen,* 47.

45. Orozco, *No Mexicans, Women, or Dogs Allowed,* 41; Ana Luisa Martínez, "Pablo Cruz and *El Regidor:* The Emergence of a Bicultural Identity in San Antonio, 1888–1910," *Journal of the West* 45 (Fall 2006): 22, 27; and Arnoldo De León, "Tejanos of Middling Status on the Chaparral, 1880–1900," in *Tejano Epic: Essays in Honor of Félix D. Almaráz, Jr.,* ed. Arnoldo De León (Austin: Texas State Historical Association, 2005): 59–60, 70.

46. Orozco, *No Mexicans, Women, or Dogs Allowed,* 40–41.

47. García, *Mexican Americans,* pp. 13–14; and García, *Desert Immigrants,* 197, 211, 231.

48. Johnson, *Revolution in Texas,* 5, 39, 126–128, 185, 189; Gonzales, "The World of México Texanos, Mexicanos, and México Americanos," 216, 275–276.

49. Johnson, *Revolution in Texas,* 182, 184.

50. Michelle Margot Espinosa, "*Las Mexicanas del Valle*": Revolution, Power and Identity, 1910–1920 (M.A. thesis, University of Texas at El Paso, 1994), 9, 21–22, 33–37, 41, 42–43.

La Rinchada Revolution, Revenge, and the Rangers, 1910–1920

RICHARD RIBB

The Mexican Revolution spilled violently into Texas in 1915 with the Plan de San Diego. The Plan drew from a common well of revolutionary ideology and involved uniformed officers from Mexico's revolutionary factions. The Plan mobilized hundreds, if not thousands, of Tejanos in a swirling war of resistance and reform that Anglo contemporaries called "the Bandit War." Like Emiliano Zapata—indeed, like all Mexican revolutionary leaders, including Pancho Villa and Venustiano Carranza—Tejano participants drew from local experiences and sources while they employed site-specific tactics; they too met violent opposition from counterrevolutionary forces. For Tejanos, the counterrevolution came in the form of the Texas Rangers. And while many Tejanos fought for social justice, others, notably Francisco Chapa and his Anglo ally William Hanson, leader of the Rangers, orchestrated a fierce "orgy of bloodshed" that left thousands of Tejanos homeless or dead.

The role of the Texas Rangers as a counterrevolutionary force to the threats of the Plan—and of Chapa and Hanson in shaping this force's activities—provides a crucial explanation for understanding the effects of the Mexican Revolution on Tejanos between 1910 and 1920. The violence inflicted by the Rangers in the wake of the Plan constitutes the single most significant effect of the Mexican Revolution on Tejanos.

The Texas Rangers destabilized the border region during the period of the Mexican Revolution in Texas. The Rangers and the vigilantes they mobilized killed hundreds, if not thousands, of innocent border Mexicans; drove off tens of thousands of Tejanos; fueled prejudices against mejicanos; and increased resistance to authority by border Mexicans and abuse of authority by Anglo authorities. The violent tactics of suppression and aggression, in short, exacerbated the troubling conditions the Rangers were sent to address.[1]

The Rangers' tactics of violence were part of a larger strategy to reverse the Revolution in Mexico carried out by gubernatorial advisors Col. Francisco Chapa and Ranger Inspector William Hanson. Chapa and Hanson, two of the most influential characters in the deployment of the Rangers during the decade, directly undermined legitimate Mexican leaders and managed Ranger efforts in a manner that promoted antipathy toward mejicanos as symbols of revolutionary Mexico.

Rangers did not shoot unarmed citizens solely to realize Chapa and Hanson's aspirations for a neo-Díaz regime. Rangers had their own reasons. Historically, Rangers had acted harshly toward mejicanos in times of change since the Alamo. Anglo-Texas society, generally speaking, provided a supportive atmosphere for treating Tejanos as second-class citizens. The threats of violence against Anglos (and mejicanos) during the decade of the Mexican Revolution heightened ethnic tensions considerably. The Rangers' responses fed from and fed the often hysterical Anglo response.

Chapa and Hanson used the growing antipathy in support of their mission to overturn the Revolution in Mexico. In both their personal, tactical use of the Rangers for specific purposes and in their consistent counsel to governors about Ranger policy generally, Chapa and Hanson provided the ideological and strategic framework for la rinchada in Texas. La rinchada, a derivation of "los rinches" (a derogatory term for "Rangers" used by many South Texans) was the sustained use of terror by the Rangers and their proxies that resulted in the killing of hundreds, if not thousands, of Tejanos; the displacement of thousands more; and a wide-ranging, determined resistance to unjust authority.

The Politics of the Rangers: Revolution and Revenge

San Antonio's Francisco Chapa was the most politically powerful Tejano for the first quarter of the twentieth century. Merchant, newspaper publisher, and advisor to Texas governors, Chapa shaped public policy and molded public opinion, especially that of Tejanos. Governors Oscar Colquitt, James Ferguson, and William Hobby sought Chapa's counsel on a host of sensitive political matters, including the issuance of pardons and the operations of the Rangers.[2]

Chapa's family, business, and political ties assured his prominence in Texas.[3] Born in Matamoros, Tamaulipas, Mexico, in 1870, Chapa left the border to pursue academic interests. After earning a degree in pharmacy from Tulane University in New Orleans, Chapa settled in San Antonio, where he soon opened a thriving pharmacy and general retail operation.[4]

Chapa edited and published *El Imparcial de Texas*, a Spanish-language weekly newspaper that gained widespread attention for a decade when it championed folk hero Gregorio Cortez.[5] In 1910, Chapa delivered the pivotal anti-Prohibition Tejano vote to gubernatorial candidate Oscar B. Colquitt, who quickly commissioned him a lieutenant colonel on his personal staff.[6] Chapa printed a rousing defense of Cortez in pamphlet form, widely circulated, that helped to secure support from Governor Colquitt for a pardon.[7]

Chapa's views on the course of the Revolution appeared frequently and unambiguously. He consistently denounced the revolutionary impulse and passionately championed ousted dictator Porfirio Díaz.[8] The combination of social prominence, high-level access to Texas politicians, and a fervent desire to overturn the Revolution led Chapa into criminal activity that eventually involved the use of the Texas Rangers.

In the fall of 1911, Chapa traveled back to New Orleans, this time to concoct a deadly mixture of intrigue and insurrection. He returned to San Antonio with General Bernardo Reyes, Mexico's minister of war under President Porfirio Díaz before Francisco Madero's ascension the year before. Together, Chapa and Reyes plotted an armed invasion of Mexico.[9] Reyes settled in the palatial home of Miguel Quiroga, Chapa's ally and business partner. For more than a month Reyes met with fellow conspirators, quite often with Chapa in attendance, to develop a plan for simultaneous incursions through Brownsville and El Paso. Chapa used the presses of *El Imparcial* to print three manifestoes advocating the armed invasion and overthrow of the U.S.-recognized regime in Mexico.[10]

Chapa provided the counterrevolutionary junta with apparent legitimacy when he conducted a meeting between Reyes and Governor Colquitt. Chapa sought to protect the invasion scheme by securing appointment of Rangers who supported the *reyista* cause and, failing that, by convincing Colquitt not to deploy Rangers against the invaders. Colquitt, on his own, already had appointed his captains, men who showed no sympathy with the revolutionary regimes of the decade.[11] In the weeks following the meeting, Colquitt made no effort to use the Rangers to disrupt the plans for the armed group acting to overthrow the government of a neighboring nation.[12] The federal government, on the other hand, after six weeks of surveillance, finally moved to quash the junta. In mid-November 1911, the federal government indicted Reyes, Chapa, Quiroga, and thirty-five others. Soon found guilty of conspiring to take military action against a friendly nation in violation of neutrality acts, Chapa was fined $1,500, which he paid on the spot.[13]

With the help of Colquitt, Chapa received an unconditional pardon from President Taft in May 1912, just six months after his arrest, then immediately rejoined Colquitt's private staff. For the rest of the decade, Chapa continued to provide assistance to accused violators of the neutrality acts who supported Mexican military leaders, like ex-President Victoriano Huerta, bent on reversing the revolutionary movement in Mexico.[14] Not surprisingly, on "repeated occasions" he advised Governors Colquitt, Ferguson, and Hobby in the deployment of the Texas Rangers.[15]

While Chapa used his influence toward his aim of a "stable" Mexico under a new strongman, another counterrevolutionary operative was active as well: William Mangum Hanson. Like Chapa, Hanson used his influence for personal revenge against the revolutionary impulse.

Hanson was born in 1866 in Gonzales County, Texas, into a family mildly prospering from farming and mercantile holdings.[16] After a brief stint as a deputy sheriff, young Hanson turned his interest to the local railroad, climbing to a director's position before the railway failed and was sold at foreclosure the following year.[17] In 1898, Hanson moved to Laredo after appointment as U.S. marshal for the western district of Texas. In 1902, Hanson received an appointment from President Roosevelt as U.S. marshal for the southern district of Texas, headquartered in Houston but with jurisdiction for the Rio Grande Valley. While in South Texas, Hanson became acquainted with political boss James B. Wells and further developed his relationship with the prominent lawyer and legislator J. T. Canales. Hanson was reappointed marshal in 1906 but resigned to organize and operate huge agricultural, ranching, and petroleum operations in Mexico.

Hanson began his operations in Mexico in 1906 with the thirty-thousand-acre Hacienda de Conejo (Rabbit Manor) located about eighty miles northwest of the port city of Tampico, Tamaulipas, Mexico.[18] "Friends" from St. Paul, Minnesota, provided the capital for the project, a sum that reached $400,000 by 1914.[19] Hanson quickly developed his own interests in the area as well. Soon, Hanson and his associates were the largest citrus growers in Mexico.[20]

In addition to his agricultural pursuits, Hanson served as an officer for oil companies that controlled thirteen thousand acres in the rich Tampico field. Some "gushers" produced seventy-five barrels a day of 93 percent pure, ready-for-use asphalt, while another area produced more than nine hundred barrels a day of superior crude oil.[21] According to Hanson, the American oil companies, like the Anglo farmers, were considered "saviors" by the Mexican laborer, who, "while he may appear ever so ignorant" was "quick to catch on," that is, was a great "imitator."[22]

Francisco Madero's challenge to Porfirio Díaz's dictatorship, beginning in the fall of 1910, interrupted the steady growth in Hanson's fortunes. Hanson believed his holdings were safe under Díaz and quickly moved to thwart Madero. Claiming Díaz's support, he proposed to Enrique Ornelas, Mexico's consul in San Antonio, the creation of a "permanent secret service on the border" to prevent the introduction of weapons into Mexico, a maneuver designed to choke Madero. In a telegram to Enrique Creel, Mexico's Secretary of Foreign Affairs, Ornelas related that Hanson wanted to begin spying within the week and lacked only expense money and the assurance of $100 monthly salaries for him and five others he had selected for the cabal. Creel replied that he accepted Hanson's proposal for one month and was awaiting results before deciding on further commitments.[23] Former U.S. Marshal and future Ranger Inspector Hanson had sought and secured a position as paid agent of President Díaz.

Files in the Secretaría of Relaciones Exteriores, Mexico's Department of Foreign Relations, show that Hanson's "*Fuerza Secreta*" (Secret Force) operated for at least several months in the spring of 1911. Hanson appointed J. D. Womack to serve as "Jefe" with responsibility for overseeing the other spies "in service to" the Mexican consulate. With Madero's power growing, Hanson's spy ring soon shifted from their original purpose of preventing all arms shipments, to supporting shipments intended for anti-Maderista factions.[24] Hanson himself carried out surveillance of a warehouse believed to contain arms, while others followed up tips concerning a band of "revoltosos" near Falfurrias, comprised of African Americans and Tejanos, or tailed Madero's representatives in San Antonio.[25] In mid-May 1911, Hanson returned to Hacienda de Conejo near Tampico, which he used as his "new station" in his antirevolutionary secret force.[26] Soon Madero reigned in Mexico, and Hanson's friend Chapa courted Reyes to carry out his counterrevolutionary intervention scheme.

With General Huerta's assassination of President Madero in February 1913 and ascension to power, another Díaz-style strongman ruled Mexico, much to Hanson's delight. In April, he asked J. A. Fernández, Mexico's Consul in San Antonio, to make public an open letter addressed "To my Texas friends," which soon appeared in a local newspaper. Hanson assured readers that "good" Americans living in Mexico were "perfectly satisfied" with the government "as constituted at this time." Hanson and his ilk received "the best of treatment" by the Huertistas, and he emphasized that "our lives and our property seem perfectly safe."

Hanson then justified taking lives without regard for legal process in a defense of the Huerta regime against the "howling" U.S. press, which gave too much coverage to so-called "outrages," he argued. Regarding killing of citizens, he wrote,

> It is the same attitude taken by the northern press, when a black brute "rapes" a southern woman, and is hung or burnt at the stake for his crime. We all know that generally speaking, it is not right, but if the same people who condemn it, had one of their relatives treated the same way, they would not decry it as they do. I plead for justice for [Mexico].

Continuing his defense of Huerta, Hanson asked Americans to stop the shipments of arms to anti-Huerta leaders, such as Venustiano Carranza, remain open-minded, and let Mexico sort itself out.

Consul Fernández amplified Hanson's remarks in his own cover letter to the *San Antonio Express*, which had published Hanson's treatise. The Huerta regime was "capable, strong and respectable," Fernández contended, and was "the product of . . . and absolutely in accord with" Mexico's constitution. Calling Carranza's claim of constitutionality "amusing if not ludicrous," he too implored Americans to stop supporting additional "insurectos" so that the fighting could stop.[27]

Hanson's dream of a benevolent empire shattered in late 1913, however, when the fighting attendant to the Mexican Revolution forced his operations to cease. The U.S. consul ordered all American citizens in the area to convene in Tampico, under the safety of the U.S. fleet in the harbor. In January 1914, Hanson visited his citrus haciendas for what turned out to be the last time. The intense fighting between Huertistas and Carrancistas had destroyed Hacienda de Conejo. Various factions had wrecked the huge, elegantly appointed main house; appropriated or slaughtered the several thousand head of livestock; and torched the tens of thousands of citrus trees.[28] The Carranza factions, in Hanson's eyes, "rose by loot, by theft, and by murder to the high places," and "encouraged their followers to do the same."[29]

Hanson traveled to Ciudad Victoria, capital of Tamaulipas, to obtain a "receipt" from the Carrancista governor for the damages to the haciendas. Instead of recognizing Hanson's claim, the governor charged Hanson with being in favor of American intervention and a "Huerta spy." Hanson later admitted sending U.S. congressmen reports from Mexico concerning outrages perpetrated during the Revolution.[30] Several knowledgeable observers knew of Hanson's activities during this time, among them Canales and Chapa, who noted that Hanson often carried out "errands" for the ousted Díaz.[31] Hanson, sentenced to die after a ten-day court-martial proceeding, escaped the firing squad only through the last-minute intercession of Mexican friends and the American consul. Deported, he was sent by auto to Matamoros, where he was released after additional wrangling between U.S. and Mexican representatives.[32] He eventually went to Washington to press his demands for reparations, to no avail.[33] Although he and his investors had lost everything in Mexico in 1914, Hanson retained hope of recovering and avenging his losses.

Hanson insisted that he had only "temporarily suspended" the oil and farming operations because of the fighting along Mexico's Gulf Coast. K. H. Merren, proprietor of Hacienda La Victoria and fellow citrus grower, interceded on Hanson's behalf in an effort to lift the ban on his return to Mexico. Carranza's government refused to allow Hanson to return because he had accepted terms of expulsion that included an admission of spying for Huerta in Mexico and a vow not to interfere further in the internal affairs of Mexico. In essence, Hanson had traded his life for a promise not to return but now wanted to renege.[34]

While appealing to the Carranza regime for a change of heart and policy, Hanson took a job as "special agent" for a Texas railway with headquarters in San Antonio, the incubation site for several revolutionary and counterrevolutionary figures of the era, such as Francisco Madero and Bernardo Reyes, respectively.[35] During the summer of 1915, as matters were heating to a boil in South Texas, Hanson coolly sought suppliers for five million rounds of ammunition for Porfirio Díaz's nephew and heir apparent, Félix.[36] He continued his private investigations during the Border War to follow.[37]

When Hanson assumed the Inspector position in 1918, he was still waiting both for indemnification from Mexico to cover his financial losses and for wholesale occupation by the United States to provide what he considered the requisite stability for resumption of his projects. Hanson believed that in Mexico only a "firm government" could respect "law and the rights of property and human life," and then, only with "outside help."[38]

The Rangers: Prelude, 1910–1914

After a decade of decline, by 1910 the moribund Texas Rangers force numbered only "three tiny companies," twelve men total. In 1911, federal funds increased the force to forty-two men for the year, but the number dropped to only thirteen the next, and rose only to eighteen by 1915.[39] In 1910, John Hughes and John Rogers, two of the "four great captains" of Ranger lore, still commanded companies, but Rogers left within a year, leaving Hughes "to watch sadly," writes esteemed Ranger historian Robert Utley, "as the Ranger Force declined in numbers, proficiency, and public respect," before he retired a couple of years later himself.[40]

One year after Huerta's ascension following the assassination of Madero, newly appointed Ranger Captain J. J. Sanders managed to create an uproar that echoed from Mexico City, through Austin, and on to Washington, D.C. It almost brought the United States and Mexico into direct conflict. The incident involved stolen horses, Huerta forces, and Rangers.

Texas rancher Clemente Vergara kept horses on a small island just off the north bank of the Rio Grande, some miles downstream from Laredo. In early February 1914, a neighbor informed him that several Huertista soldiers had crossed eleven of his horses to Hidalgo, Mexico, a small village opposite the Vergara ranch. Vergara crossed to demand compensation for or return of his stock but was told that the commanding officer was not available for negotiation. The next day, Vergara received word to come back across to settle matters and rowed across in a skiff with his nephew.

On arrival, three men seized Vergara, chased the boy into the chaparral, and departed for Hidalgo with Vergara. The following day, Vergara's wife and daughter visited him in a crude holding cell, where they found him bleeding but alive. They unsuccessfully worked for his release, left, and never saw him alive again.[41]

Gov. Oscar Colquitt solicited from Secretary of State William Jennings Bryan two pertinent opinions: With whom should he negotiate to bring back Vergara? and Could the Rangers cross the river to apprehend the horse thieves? Bryan, like everyone else in Washington in 1914, had no clue as to who could speak with authority regarding Mexican border matters, but he did respond without reservation that the Rangers could not enter Mexico for any reason. An official stalemate ensued until the appearance of Vergara's body on the Texas bank late in the evening of March 7.

Sanders sent Colquitt a short telegram, long on significance: "Have just returned from Hidalgo. Have the body of Clemente Vergara on Texas soil." Colquitt, unobservant or unrepentant, published the telegram, and Washington immediately howled with displeasure. Sanders began to feel the need to change his hasty report and found a willing ally in T. A. Garrett, U.S. Consul in Nuevo Laredo, whose jurisdiction included Hidalgo. The men concocted a story about how fatigue had caused Garrett and Sanders to report "from Hidalgo" instead of "to Laredo" in their respective reports, and thus the problem lay in poor transcription and not transgression of stated international policy. Perhaps no one believed the amended explanation, but it stood. One newspaper reported much later what many believed at the time: a Ranger had claimed success for something he did not deserve.

The report asserted that Garrett and Sanders did cross the river, then watched Tejano vaqueros exhume Vergara from the Hidalgo cemetery, return with the body, and present it for identification to Vergara's family, before reburying it in a Catholic cemetery in Laredo. A newspaper account revealed that Sanders "stood by prepared for eventualities" while the "cowboys under orders from Consul Garrett" recovered the body.[42] The Vergara affair and Sanders's "correction" gained national attention and raised questions about the danger of Rangers along the border.

The Army's commanding officer in Texas, Brig. Gen. Tasker Bliss, concluded that even one Ranger along the border "could become a source of international danger" because "the Texas Rangers naturally take advantage of the present conditions to aggrandize themselves."[43] As Ranger historian Walter Webb correctly observes, "Every teller of the [Vergara] tale is convinced that the episode, which occurred at a time when relations were strained, came near to causing trouble between the United States and Mexico."[44]

Because Governor Colquitt had allowed the trouble, he and Texas would have incurred federal wrath, with implications for funding of border activities, including the Rangers. And with Huerta's regime the target of American retaliation, chances for counterrevolutionary success would have been in danger.

The Rangers: La Rinchada, 1915–16

If the Rangers exerted relatively minor influence on events in Texas during the early years of the Mexican Revolution there, the situation changed dramatically—for the worse—during the middle years. The years 1915 and 1916 witnessed "la rinchada" in the Tejano communities along the border during the Revolution. It resulted in the killing of hundreds, if not thousands, of Tejanos; the displacement of thousands more; and a wide-ranging, determined resistance to unjust authority.

Hundreds, if not thousands, of border Mexicans responded to conditions in 1915 with armed resistance and insurrection.[45] Many fought as social revolutionaries, or sediciosos, most notably in varying degrees of allegiance to the ambitious Plan de San Diego, which called for a massive uprising and establishment of a new republic in the American Southwest. In response to widespread raiding and violence in South Texas, the U.S. Army militarized the border in 1915 and 1916 with all available regular troops and National Guard units, placing more than fifty thousand troops in the Lower Rio Grande Valley alone. Many contemporary observers, especially Anglo ones, termed the period of conflict in 1915 and 1916 the "Bandit War." A more fitting term, however, is "Border War," in recognition of the instrumental roles played not only by border Mexicans, but also by the U.S. Army, civilians, and particularly the Texas Rangers in a volatile situation that many called a "reign of terror."[46] Confirming the notion of a serious regional struggle, not simply a wave of lawlessness, the Texas Court of Criminal Appeals found South Texas to be in a "state of war" in a 1916 ruling, still cited today, that recognized the existence of limited war regardless of its formal declaration.[47]

In his annual report of June 1916, U.S. Army General Frederick Funston, commanding officer of the Brownsville District, reported to the Secretary of War that border Mexican raiders had killed twenty-one civilians and soldiers the previous year.[48] The actual number of border Mexicans killed by Rangers and their allies is unknowable—contemporary estimates ranged from three hundred to five thousand—because, as one newspaper reported in 1915, "it is likely that many more have bit the dust that have never been reported."[49]

Activity attributed to the Plan de San Diego finally began on the Fourth of July, 1915, when a group of twenty to forty men entered northern Cameron County on a two-week supply mission. The group forced one rural merchant to supply them with food and ammunition, demanded three horses from one ranchero and a rifle from another, and bought from an old Tejano farmer the savory main course for the traditional meal of cabrito, or young goat. Before they left the area, they probably killed Bernard Boley, an Anglo teenager, in a case of mistaken identity near Raymondville, then skirmished with a posse, losing two of their men.[50] The band returned a few days later to continue their mission and this time reduced the chances of interception by burning a trestle of the St. Louis, Brownsville, and Mexican Railway near Sebastian and cutting all telegraph lines north of Harlingen.[51] Authorities, both lawful and otherwise, did not, however, respond immediately.

Adj. Gen. Henry Hutchings and Gov. James Ferguson waited several weeks to respond to the raid. Six months had passed since the discovery of the Plan; besides, raiding had characterized the border for a century. The Ranger Force stood at eighteen men in March 1915, with only a handful of Company A stationed within 100 miles of the Valley, despite reports by Capt. John Sanders that border residents viewed shipments of "large quantities" of weapons as a "menace to welfare."[52] Adjutant General Hutchings replied that no action was necessary because the arms embargo was no longer in place.[53] Hutchings did send two Rangers to guard the State Comptroller, or at least his financial instruments, when he traveled to Brownsville, and instructed them to meet at the designated safe place, J. T. Canales's law office.[54]

As spring 1915 continued with no hint of Plan activity, Hutchings and Governor Ferguson were concerned not with revolutionaries but with goat rustlers on the border, specifically on the ranch of State Senator Claude Hudspeth of West Texas. In April, Ferguson not only sent him two Rangers to apprehend the culprits but also allowed Hudspeth to select his own Special Ranger to pay, Nat Jones.[55] The ability to pay for a Ranger helped that year because the Rangers, as usual, had overspent their allocation.[56] Help was on the way, however, in the form of an emergency allocation of $10,000 to expand the force to meet "disturbed conditions on the border, resulting in enormous losses to the livestock industries." The measure, passed with few dissenting votes, authorized the expenditure during the period ending March 1, 1916.[57] The governor instructed Hutchings to hold down Ranger expenses because he had a special solution in mind for the border troubles.[58] Two weeks after the killing of Boley, Ferguson made the most fateful, and fatal, appointment of his career, selecting Henry Ransom of Houston to serve as captain of a new Ranger company, Company C.

Henry Ransom received a Ranger commission on July 20, 1915, for his third tour of duty on the force.[59] Besides two years with the Rangers, Ransom had gained law enforcement experience as a guard on state prison farms, from which he stocked his Ranger company, and as chief of police in Houston. He had left his police chief's position after killing a prominent defense attorney, for which he was free on appeal.[60] One observer asserted that "it took a man of his disposition to get along" during the "strenuous" times on the border.[61] Clarifying the necessary qualities, he said that Ransom "would kill and kill quick."[62] W. W. Sterling—rancher, Ranger, and eventually adjutant general—who worked with Ransom, listened one night to his swapping of stories about service in the Philippines, finding that the "tales they told about executing Filipinos made the Bandit War look like a minor purge."[63]

Ferguson sent Ransom to act as an assassin. W. W. Sterling believed that Ransom saw himself as "an instrument of justice" with a "definite mission to perform." He quotes Ransom about that mission: "A bad disease calls for bitter medicine. The Governor sent me down here to stop this trouble, and I am going to carry out his orders. There is only one way to do it. President Diaz [sic] proved that."[64] Elaborating on Ransom's mission, E. A. Sterling, W. W.'s father, said Ferguson had sent Captain Ransom to clean up "that nest down there" or Ferguson would "put a man down there that would."[65] Ferguson was prepared for Ransom "to kill every damned man connected with" the trouble, swore E. A. Sterling. Ferguson promised to end the violence, using any means at hand, and to pardon Ransom and others if necessary—and Ferguson made a career of pardoning.[66]

Protests erupted at the news of the appointment. Sheriff W. T. Vann of Cameron County travelled to Austin to plead with Ferguson to send Ransom somewhere else, after his effort by telegram had failed.[67] He told the governor he did not like Ransom's "style," based on the "good deal" he had heard about him. "I don't want him down there," he declared to Ferguson, but to no avail.[68] Ransom soon arrived, and Ferguson cleared out the two captains already in the area.

Captain Sanders later told James B. Wells explicitly that "he was ordered not to interfere or go into Ransom's territory."[69] Ferguson also shipped Capt. Monroe Fox back to Marfa in West Texas from Brownsville, just a few miles from the initial raid.[70] The reasons for isolating Ransom and his company became clear soon after their arrival in the Valley during the last week in July. Meanwhile, other Rangers were responding on their own.

On July 23, two officers in Hidalgo County, including J. D. White, who was between appointments as a Ranger, killed the two Manríquez brothers in separate incidents near Mercedes. Frank Pierce, longtime Brownsville attorney and advisor to the U.S. Consul in Matamoros, noted in his 1917 work on the region that "It is alleged they resisted arrest" and that no investigation took place of the two killers known to act out of racial prejudice.[71]

According to Canales, Daniel Hinojosa and his partner's killing of Rodolfo Muñiz, coming on the heels of the other officers' killing of the Manríquez brothers in nearby Mercedes, ignited the Border War, "the spark that fired the flame."[72] After that incident, Canales argued, border Mexicans charged with crimes or pursued as suspects refused to submit to authorities "because they did not believe that the officers of the law would give them the protection guaranteed to them by the Constitution and the laws of the State."[73] The rule of law had ended, he believed.

Lawlessness soon produced one of the leaders of the sediciosos, Aniceto Pizaña, who, together with Luis De la Rosa, would respond to violence with violence in turn. In a fruitless search for the raiders who killed Boley, the Rangers and their posse created the conditions they ostensibly sought to quell. The story illustrates the counterproductive elements of the Rangers in the Border War: increased violence, especially by vigilantes; radicalization of Tejanos; displacement of Tejanos; and lack of cooperation between federal and Ranger forces.

In 1915, Aniceto Pizaña Dávila was "as honorable, and a high-class and straight a Mexican as there was," whose ranching practices had left him "unusually well-fixed," according to Lon Hill, who had known him for years.[74] Pizaña was born in 1877 on March 2, Texas Independence Day, and spent his early years on farms and ranches near Brownsville and Matamoros.[75] By the time he was an adult, Pizaña knew Cameron County very well, was an excellent horseman, and had experienced a range of economic activity.

Pizaña became a follower of floresmagonismo after he met the Magón brothers, internationally known promoters of anarchism, in Laredo in 1904. He soon began subscribing to the anarchist periodical *Regeneración*, a practice he maintained for the next ten years, and in 1908 founded his own floresmagonismo group, "*Solidaridad Perpetua.*" Writing years later, Pizaña claimed he still held the ideals formed in those days: "I pursued the struggle ... for the emancipation of the proletariat of the world and especially for the proletariat of Mexican peoples."[76] In the years just previous to 1915, Pizaña had distributed floresmagonismo literature, read *Regeneración* to his illiterate friends, and written a good deal of poetry in support of reformist and radical causes.[77] In his attachment to floresmagonismo, Pizaña shared the radical ideology of other early leaders of the Revolution.

At dawn the morning of August 3, 1915, a posse led by Jeff Scrivener, Pizaña's jealous neighbor, consisting of Rangers, deputies, federal officers, and private citizens—some thirty-five men in all—made a sedicioso of the front-porch radical Pizaña. As the Anglo raiders drew guns and dismounted, shots killed Army Private McGuire, on furlough but an eager volunteer, and wounded three others. In the heavy gunfire, Aniceto Pizaña and five others escaped from the ranch house.[78] The posse then stormed the house and captured Ramón Pizaña, Aniceto's brother, and José Buenrostro, a citizen of Mexico, along with Manuela Pizaña, Aniceto's wife, and their twelve-year-old son, Guadalupe, who had sustained a gunshot wound to his right leg that led to its amputation. No ties to the killers of Boley or to other crimes materialized.

In December 1916, the state district court in Brownsville found Ramón Pizaña guilty of murder in the death of Private McGuire and sentenced him to fifteen years in the penitentiary. Canales and a team of attorneys appealed the conviction to the Court of Criminal Appeals in Austin, the state's highest court for criminal cases, where in March 1917 they won a reversal on the grounds that the killing resulted from self-defense.[79] Clearly the raid was ill conceived and basically illegal, the court ruled.

The raid on Los Tulitos brought several changes to the situation in the Valley. Federal officials began to withhold prisoners from some local authorities, a practice that became a policy within weeks. The commanding officer of Troop A, 12th Cavalry, assumed control of Ramón Pizaña and

José Buenrostro from the posse because some law-abiding citizens on the scene convinced him that the prisoners certainly would be killed "while trying to escape." The officer told the posse, according to his official report, "I would personally take the prisoners to San Benito, and would use every power at my disposal to protect them." With custody settled, the officer, "two picked men," and the prisoners sped by car to Harlingen, not San Benito, home of Carr and Hinojosa.[80]

The making of a sedicioso out of Pizaña was the most important result of the raid on Los Tulitos. For ten years, he had lived his radical political views within legal bounds, nonviolently. Just before the assault, in fact, two friends had brought him a letter from his old friend De la Rosa, urging him to join him in the raiding. As he had five years before to another friend, Pizaña declined to use violence against the state.[81] With the raid on his house, however, believing as he and many others did that the posse intended to shoot them then or later, Pizaña turned to armed resistance. He and his fellow escapees joined De la Rosa to fight in Cameron, Hidalgo, and Starr counties, where, in his words, "we will be able to defend against the gringo son-of-a-bitches."[82] Incensed about the attack and especially the wounding of his son, Pizaña also fought to avenge the deaths of friends, he later wrote, such as the Flores family, Felipe Falcón, and Norberto Pesina, "and others that are murdered that I don't know about."[83] Once pushed into war, Pizaña responded by assuming control of activity in the southern part of the tri-county area of the Rio Grande Valley, ceding the northern section to De la Rosa.[84]

The hunt for Aniceto Pizaña and his friends began the day after the raid on Los Tulitos, led by Captain Ransom, just arrived. Frustrated by dense undergrowth, reluctant federal officials, and uncooperative residents, Rangers and deputies descended upon the ranch of Desidiero Flores and his two sons near the Paso Real. No suspects escaped from this encounter as all three rancheros were dead within minutes.[85] The Flores men, unarmed according to witness Sheriff Vann, were being interrogated by the posse when one of the posse grew "hot-headed and fired the first shot."[86]

Officers—federal, state, local, or self-appointed—managed to gather little reliable information, if any at all, from local Tejanos after the Ranger raids on Los Tulitos and Paso Real. One cavalry officer complained that the troop hunted for the raiders, or at least information about them, for days, but "without avail."[87] Of the handful of pursuits by officials that actually resulted in armed encounters with sediciosos, not one instance resulted from specific information provided by a party not serving as a scout.[88] Language barriers prevented full communication in many instances, no doubt, but locals' anger over what many considered unprovoked attacks on fellow Tejanos and fear of being considered traitors by the sediciosos accounted for a much larger part of the impasse. The "natives," as one officer saw the Tejanos, "seemed to be much frightened and disinclined to talk."[89]

Tejanos were caught in the middle between the sediciosos and the officers. One astute Anglo resident observed, "There are a number of well-known Mexicans who are law abiding and good citizens, whose condition is worse at present than that of the Americans." Tejanos were "at the mercy of the lawless element," continued the writer, yet were "afraid to talk freely to the Americans."[90] Valley merchant W. S. Spears clearly stated the dilemma of those with knowledge of activities in cooperating with authorities: "The better class of [border] Mexicans are willing to co-operate with the better class of [Anglo-]Americans, if this co-operation will bring relief, but if it should not, their condition would be worse than it is now. *As it is, only their property is in jeopardy, but if they should tell what they know, their lives will also be endangered*" [emphasis added].[91] Evidence of punishment for cooperating with Anglo authorities abounded. In a single week, within miles of one another, two men lost their lives to Plan raiders, one because he "had allied himself with the Americans" and the other for being "too friendly to the Americans," according to the local paper.[92] Longtime Brownsville attorney Harbert Davenport asked two clients, Pablo Falcón and Chon Cuéllar, to procure information about the Plan, and the men soon reported a bit of information. A few days later, they were shot to death at a *baile*, or dance.[93] Unwittingly displaying another polarization that the Border War brought about, an Army officer noted that "even the loyal Mexicans are now so timid and secretive as to make it very hard for officers and men in uniform to get information of value from them"— and impossible for the Rangers and other Anglo posses.[94]

Canales, who represented the area in the state legislature, believed the violent responses by Rangers and other authorities had escalated the unstable situation into an all-out armed conflict. Instead of quieting matters, the Rangers pushed more residents into complicity if not active participation with the sediciosos, and he could point to Pizaña as evidence for his view. Federal officers confirmed the counterproductive nature of Ranger raids, finding vaqueros "openly" expressing a desire "to join the bandits or followers of the Plan de San Diego" in light of Ranger behavior.[95] Once set in motion, the horrifying cycle of violent attacks and reprisals by the sediciosos and Rangers polarized the area. Most of the sediciosos raids in August and early September 1915 did not follow through on the genocidal rhetoric of the Plan de San Diego, but instead were targeted attacks on representations of the Anglo domination of South Texas.

A few days after the assaults on Pizaña at Los Tulitos and on Flores at Paso Real, De la Rosa retaliated with direct attacks on civilian targets, actions that filled the Valley with hysteria. On August 6, De la Rosa and about a dozen other sediciosos rode to the principal site of the area's economic activity, a corn-shelling facility, where several men remained, while others took food and a saddle from a "Mexican" store nearby.[96] Having obtained available provisions, the sediciosos turned to their primary task, exacting revenge on the facility's operators, the Austins.

Vermont natives A. L. Austin, sixty, and son Charlie, thirty-six, had moved to the Valley a few years before as expectant capitalists in the developing agricultural market, after a stint as labor bosses on the Panama Canal project.[97] A. L. served as leader of the Sebastian Law and Order League, founded in 1913 for "mutual protection," presumably for Anglos against others. In this position, A. L. "had given notice to a number of Mexicans [sic] of dubious reputation, to leave the country," according to a local newspaper.[98] Charles Pierce verified reports that Austin had earned a reputation for treating border Mexicans harshly.[99] In one instance, county officers had arrested one "undesirable" Tejano on suspicion of plotting to rob a nearby bank and started off for Brownsville the same night with the man. "Somewhere between Sebastian and Harlingen," however, masked men seized the prisoner and hung him from a mesquite tree just off the road. Anglo residents did not dispute Tejano charges that the killers belonged to the Law and Order League.[100]

On the morning of August 6, A. L. and Charlie stood before their accusers. The Plan raiders ordered Elmer Millard, an Austin employee, to drive a cart holding the Austins back to the Austin home. Once there, the raiders gathered guns and ammunition, then ordered Millard to drive away. A short distance down the lane, the sediciosos ordered the three men out of the cart. After one bandit established that Millard was not Louie Austin, another son who was expected to have arrived in the Valley, Millard boarded the wagon and rolled off.[101] Within seconds the raiders executed the Austin men. The raiders then seized the horse pulling Millard's cart, fit it with the stolen saddle, and rode off, each man finally with his own mount.[102] Before they left the area, the band destroyed two railroad bridges and fired shots at trains.[103] Most observers realized that De la Rosa's activity was retaliation for the injustices of the vigilantes perpetrated against local Tejanos.[104] A Raymondville banker noted, "The news of this bloody outrage spread like wildfire and stirred the entire [Rio Grande] Delta."[105]

Two days after the raid on the Austins, De la Rosa shocked South Texas again when he led seventy-five to one hundred men on a frontal assault against the King Ranch station house at Norias.[106] One of his officers was Ricardo Gómez Pizaña, Aniceto's cousin and survivor of the Los Tulitos raid, who sought heavy tools to effect a train derailing. The site also attracted the sediciosos because they believed it held a large cache of weapons. Norias symbolized the vast King Ranch empire. It served both as a major cattle shipping point for the huge King Ranch herds, considered by many South Texans to be comprised of cattle assembled by suspicious means, and as a transportation nexus for its Anglo owners, identified most readily as practitioners of the commercial ranching transformation that had displaced many Tejanos. Though De la Rosa's raiders suffered high casualty rates and failed in their assault, they demonstrated great audacity in extending the conflict seventy-five miles north of the river, before escaping from their pursuers.[107] The large size of the attacking party, the presence of officers and men from Carranza's army, the use of a Plan-inspired flag, and the finding of pamphlets containing a copy of the Plan de San Diego combined to escalate both the violence on the part of the authorities and the fears of the Anglo residents and their allies.[108] Effects of the killings of the Austins and the Norias attack appeared immediately.

Actually, Ransom already was very busy carrying out his orders to clean up the Valley by any means necessary. According to W. W. Sterling, who acted as his guide for a while, Ransom looked to kill anyone who had "guilty knowledge" of crimes or who "harbored bandits." On one occasion, Ransom targeted some vaqueros on the Santa Anita Ranch, saying, "we ought to get rid of them." Sterling vouched for the men, claiming that they were "only ranch hands," and the men were spared. He reported making "similar pleas" on "several" other occasions, as well.[109]

Many other suspects did not have an Anglo to save them. One of Ransom's Rangers, Private Roy Aldrich, later Quartermaster, described the murder of less fortunate suspects in the wake of the Austin slayings by sediciosos: "The two men responsible for this crime we afterwards apprehended, and met the fate they so well deserved. They were taken to the scene of the murder and summarily executed."[110] Pierce, in his murder list provided to the State Department, noted, "Immediately following the Las Norias Raid, on August 8, 1915 ... the Rangers began a systematic manhunt and killed, according to a verified list [I compiled], 102 [border] Mexicans. It is claimed by citizens and army officers who saw many of the bodies, that at least 300 Mexicans were so killed."[111] The *Brownsville Herald* cited one specific incident in late August in which Rangers killed a "Mexican, an alleged participant" near Raymondville. "He attempted to resist arrest," or flee, as Canales had said suspects would, " and was shot and killed."[112]

The circle of violence spawned by German intrigue, the Mexican Revolution, social unrest, and the brutality of the Rangers closed one afternoon in October 1915 around the symbol of the new era, the St. Louis, Brownsville & Mexico Railroad. De la Rosa and about sixty men, including Ricardo Gómez Pizaña, sabotaged the St. Louis, Brownsville & Mexico track about six miles north of Brownsville near the settlement of Olmito. The sediciosos removed the spikes and fishplates from the rails, then attached a heavy wire to the freed end of the rail pointing north. With the wire wrapped around a crowbar for leverage, and one end of the crowbar buried in the ground, the raiders created a lever to pull apart the rails. As the southbound passenger train steamed close at nearly its top speed of thirty miles an hour, the saboteurs pulled back the crowbar, immediately sending the locomotive and tender into a nearby ditch, and the baggage and mail cars onto their sides as well. Engineer H. H. Kendall died instantly, hand on the throttle, and Fireman B. B. Woodall lay screaming from extensive scalding. The attackers hailed their effort with shouts of "¡Viva Carranza! ¡Viva De la Rosa! ¡Viva Pizaña!" and peppered the tottering two passenger cars with bullets. De la Rosa and others entered the smoker first, the car that they knew held the men, and immediately shot three soldiers and an ex-Ranger. The raiders demanded valuables from most passengers as they continued down the aisle, then shot a local physician when he locked himself in a washroom. The sediciosos killed three Anglos, wounded two seriously, and left several families grieving. The raiders assured a mejicano couple that they, like others on the train, had no reason to worry: "¡Mexicanos no, gringos no más!" The sediciosos, as in other raids, spared people they considered German.[113] After ten minutes on the train, the raiders disappeared into the dense chaparral.[114]

In separating the train rails, the raiders risked causing the deaths of the engineer, fireman, and many others unknown to them. The Olmito derailing represented one of a very few instances in which sediciosos injured or killed civilians at random, though terrified and vengeful residents, understandably, did not discern that pattern at the time. Despite the highly charged racial rhetoric of the Plan de San Diego itself and of subsequent manifestos in support of it, the sediciosos usually targeted people they believed guilty of oppression, such as the Austins, or obvious enemies of their cause, like soldiers, as well as railroads, pumping stations, and other manifestations of the new order in South Texas. The raiders never randomly assaulted settlements as a whole, shooting and burning at will, nor did they attack residents on isolated and virtually defenseless farms or ranches, of which hundreds dotted the Valley. In fact, the sediciosos spared the lives of many other innocent Anglos who got caught up in raids: Nils Peterson (Lyford); Elmer Millard and Jud Deyo (Sebastian); Stanley Dodd (Los Fresnos); John Kleiber, Morris Edelstein, L. I. Henninger, and several others (Olmito); and a Mr. Tremble (Progreso).[115] Sediciosos spared neutral Tejanos, as well, in their selective violence.[116] Many Rangers, however, showed little discrimination in choosing their targets.

The day after the train derailment, Ransom arrested four suspects. He told Sheriff Vann that he was going to kill them and asked Vann to join in. When Vann declined to shoot the men whose hands were tied behind their backs, Ransom replied, "[I]f you haven't got guts enough to do it, I will do it myself." Vann left to investigate another area but found on his return that Ransom had marched the four suspects into the brush and executed them. Ransom then tried to gain control of two prisoners under Vann's authority, but Vann sent them off with a deputy.[117]

Canales recognized that many citizens were replicating the Rangers' summary executions: "[Y]ou will always find if your officer does a bad thing, there are other citizens that will follow."[118] Robert Utley, from a vantage point seventy years later concurs: "Allied with the Texas Rangers—if not actually led by them—citizens responded with the worst retaliation of which Texas was capable."[119] "Thousand Avengers on Manhunt" screamed a Brownsville headline after the Olmito train wreck.[120] The avengers scoured the chaparral to teach the ingrates a lesson—"one not soon forgotten"—that South Texas "is white man's country."[121] What commenced in such circumstances was a violent free-for-all on the part of the authorities that developed into an open season on mejicanos. "Hunting bandits is more like hunting coyotes than organized warfare," suggested one avenger.[122] "Hunting Mexican bandits in this mesquite brush is worse than hunting rats in a hay stack and far more expensive," complained another writer.[123] In the poisonous atmosphere developing in South Texas, vigilantism thrived. The news of a "necktie party" was met with "relief" by the public for removing a "menace to the security" of the area. A local writer placed the event in the context of a haphazard judicial system: "Lynch law is never a pleasant thing to contemplate, but . . . is sometimes the only means of administering justice." Furthermore, intoned the writer, future apprehensions called for similar solutions because "It is now time for vigorous action and it should not stop until the community is cleared of the criminal element."[124] In the context of the Border War, Rangers and their allies indiscriminately considered all mejicanos to be "bandits." Thus, the Mexican Revolution in Texas became a nightmarish all-out assault on Tejanos by Rangers and their allies. Chapa and Hanson had long held the motive—counterrevolutionary revenge; had secured the means—the Rangers; and now had their opportunity—the "Bandit War."

One of the largest mass executions of the Border War occurred in September 1915 near the railroad station at Alamo, formerly Ebenezer Station, a few miles west of Donna on the spur line linking Hidalgo County to the main rail line at Harlingen. According to witness Cosme Casares Muñoz, a large group of riders hung fifteen border Mexicans in trees on either side of the railroad track.[125] Other Valley residents who saw the corpses afterward commented that they "were all laying all in a row," charred by fire, each with a bullet in its head.[126] James B. Wells described the bullet holes in the skulls as big enough to poke a finger in.[127]

Eyewitness Victor Berrones, a field worker, identified the assailants as Rangers. Asked why the Rangers killed the men, he replied simply, "The Rangers killed them because they were mejicanos, I believe."[128] Adam Medvecky, a U.S. soldier at the time of the lynchings, acknowledged that "rumor" held the Rangers responsible, though he personally had not been present for the event.[129] Other sources attributed the atrocity to a posse run by Hidalgo County Sheriff A. Y. Baker.[130] Medvecky had earlier witnessed Baker shoot three border Mexicans "in cold blood" and described a "cruel, heartless" Baker as routinely "killing Mexicans on sight." Baker's deputy Tom Mayfield held a similar reputation. According to John Peavey, a deputy in Cameron County at the time and federal law enforcement officer for thirty years after, Mayfield was a "brute of a man. If he arrested a man he'd beat him all to death with a gun before he put him in jail."[131] More likely than a posse comprised solely of Rangers or deputies was one led by a Ranger or two, with several deputies and civilians riding as well. The identifications by the witnesses and general public reaction to the lynching placed them as part of la rinchada. Even if no active Rangers participated, the witnesses were not off the mark: Baker had served for years in the Rangers just prior to assuming the sheriff's role, and Mayfield held Special Ranger authority periodically as well.[132]

Frustrated by the raiders who consistently eluded them, authorities and vigilantes solved their problem by reclassifying most mejicanos as "bandits." The result, testified one longtime observer, was that "90 percent" of the people killed by the Anglos and allies were "innocent" of insurrection or brigandage.[133]

The number of casualties inflicted during the "orgy of bloodshed" conducted by the authorities cannot be known, given the popular methods of handling the dead.[134] Killers often left the bodies where they fell, dragged them into the chaparral, or left them swinging from branches, like the ones Miriam Swann remembered seeing, where the harsh climate quickly decomposed bodies that the animals had not devoured.[135] Further, hundreds, if not thousands, of residents simply "evaporated," in the terminology of the Anglos, some departing for Mexico, others for good. The huge range in estimates for the number of mejicanos killed in the Border War—three hundred to five thousand—reflects the indiscrimination in the killings as well as the difficulty in accounting for the bodies and identifying them afterward. One witness, attempting to defend the Rangers, suggested that they killed no more of the total than did the citizenry. In any case, dead bodies littered the countryside. One San Antonio newspaper reported that "The finding of dead bodies of Mexicans . . . has reached the point where it creates little or no interest."[136]

In anticipation of escalating reprisals, border Mexicans evacuated the Valley. During August and September 1915, more than 40 percent of border Mexican residents departed Cameron and Hidalgo counties, the areas most affected by the Border War, for the war-wracked northern border of Mexico, a move that suggests, in and of itself, a sense of danger about remaining where officers and posses could reach them.[137] Official reports from the border succinctly described the exodus: "Unusually large number of [border] Mexicans moving with household effects from Texas to Mexico, none returning."[138] As one Valley resident described the process of depopulation in South Texas that involved perhaps thirty thousand residents, the border Mexicans went "that way," pointing south toward Mexico, while the "Americans" went "the other way," hooking his thumb north.[139] Authorities forced some Tejano families to relocate in towns where, like those already there, "they were followed about by armed men who kept a constant watch" on them.[140]

Although the war against border Mexicans continued for much longer, raiding by De la Rosa and Pizaña stopped within weeks of the Olmito derailment, though individuals and small bands continued to steal livestock and pester residents, as always. The Army officer in command at Mercedes reported on November 12, 1915, that the "Situation is better here now than at any time since bandit [sic] troubles started last July and steadily improving all the time."[141] A few large-scale raids in June 1916 were the last Plan-inspired ones of the Border War.

The reasons the sediciosos ceased hostilities varied as greatly as the reasons that began them. Carranza had begun to back away from support for De la Rosa and Pizaña before Wilson's formal recognition of him in October and instituted the shift in policy by replacing the pro-Plan General Nafarrate in the Matamoros sector with Gen. Alfredo Ricault, who cooperated more fully both with Carranza and the United States.[142] Thus, the arc of the Revolution in Texas bent according to the larger developments in Mexico.

In addition to Carranza's Constitutionalist efforts, an intensifying militarization of the border made raiding more problematic. By October 1915, more than four thousand soldiers patrolled Cameron and Hidalgo counties, especially along the river, a situation that made entering and leaving the United States—much less staying there—a great deal more dangerous for sediciosos.[143] By the summer of 1916, the political atmosphere, heated by Villa's raid on Columbus, New Mexico, in March and Pershing's pursuit soon thereafter, suddenly provided support for U.S. forces to regularly cross the river in "hot pursuit" of offending parties, sometimes with success.[144] On June 18, 1916, Wilson delivered the final blow to sedicioso plans: he mobilized essentially all state guards and ordered them to join the entire Regular Army on the border, some fifty thousand all told.[145]

La rinchada succeeded fully in one respect: it increased antipathy toward mejicanos and, by extension, against the Mexican Revolution. Anglos, especially, and their counterrevolutionary Tejano allies, used the chaos of the Border War as evidence of the need for subjugation of a dangerously unstable "people." By conflating "revolutionaries," "sediciosos," "bandits," and "Mexicans," Chapa, Hanson, and the Rangers were able to mobilize—and justify—a brutal counterrevolutionary response as a strategy of perceived national security.

Chapa and Hanson must have been pleased with the growing cry for revenge and retaliation against any resistance to firm rule in the presumed source of the violence, a revolutionary Mexico. Chapa, of course, sat on Governor Ferguson's staff during the bloodiest years, and no doubt counseled an already rabid Ferguson on the need for swift, brutal action to push back the Revolution across the river, if not beyond. Documentary evidence of Chapa's day-to-day role in la rinchada has not been found—if it exists—but his counterrevolutionary goals, well established before the Border War, surfaced again under William Hobby, Ferguson's successor.

Hanson settled into a role as railroad special agent during the Border War and continued his work against Carrancistas. His role in the Ponce-Morín Affair elucidates the interconnectivity of the Rangers and counterrevolution.

"The Best Ranger Captain That Ever Saw Texas"

In May 1916 near Kingsville, Hanson was present at the arrest by a federal officer of José Morín, a suspected Carrancista agent whom Hanson had been tracking for some time. Swept up by the local sheriff was Morín's presumed coconspirator, Victorino Ponce. Two weeks later, Ranger Captain Sanders, Ranger Joe Brooks, and Special Ranger W. T. Moseley removed the federal prisoners from a nearby jail, ostensibly so they could be taken around the area to be identified as active sediciosos in earlier raids. Sanders then sent Ponce and Morín with Brooks and Moseley for further investigation. When Brooks and Moseley arrived in Raymondville, they were alone. The prisoners had "evaporated," in the parlance of South Texas.

Sanders continually denied any knowledge of the prisoners' whereabouts. U.S. Assistant Attorney General C. M. Cureton, after reading Sanders' Scouting Reports, reached the common conclusion regarding Rangers and prisoners: Brooks and Moseley had killed the prisoners and left the bodies for the coyotes. Sanders' highly incriminating Scout Reports disappeared from the Adjutant General's files.[146]

During the investigation of the Rangers in 1919, the story surfaced that in the wake of the incident, Sanders pistol-whipped attorney Thomas Hook outside a Kingsville courtroom in hopes of provoking a shootout, because Hook had intervened for local Tejanos in calling for federal protection from the Rangers' practice of having prisoners disappear.[147] When Hook offered the investigating committee the reply to the petition he had sent to President Woodrow Wilson, Chairman Bledsoe refused to consider it, saying, "We don't care anything about those [replies]."[148]

President Wilson had initiated an investigation immediately and responded to Hook on behalf of the signatories one month after receiving the petition in June 1916. An investigation of the prisoners' disappearance by the Justice Department under supervision of the U.S. Attorney General produced few consoling findings. Despite an extensive inquiry, Wilson explained to the petitioners, federal agents did not uncover the bodies of the missing men. His men "had not been able to ascertain definitely exactly what happened except that officers of the State of Texas," whom other documents established as Ranger Joe Brooks and Special Ranger Tom Moseley, "took these men from jail for the alleged purpose of identifying them as participants in certain other crimes, and that they have not since been heard from." Wilson, acknowledging the petitioners' concern, wrote, "If it is true that these men have been killed, it is a source of great regret to me."[149]

Wilson stated it was "clear that no federal officer was in any degree responsible" for the transfer of the prisoners, and, in fact, "state officers," referring to Sheriff Scarborough, ignored specific instructions in the matter.[150] Thus, Wilson explained, he had little authority to rectify unlawful behavior that threatened the petitioners' lives and presumably had cost the prisoners theirs. All Wilson could do was to ask then-Governor James Ferguson to cooperate with federal efforts to respect the rights of citizens generally. Wilson did forbid the transfer of federal prisoners to state or county officers in the future.[151]

The disappearance of the two prisoners produced several unforeseen consequences. Besides leading to the presumed deaths of the two alleged sediciosos, explained Wilson, the loss of the prisoners also was a "serious detriment" to developing a sound case against their alleged associates in a conspiracy to renew the Plan de San Diego. Loss of their testimony could lead to additional, unnecessary violence.[152]

Sanders interfered with a federal prosecution by snatching the prisoners; facilitated their murder; lied about his role; threatened officers of the court who dared to expose his behavior; and heightened the mistrust between Tejanos and the Rangers. Quite a feat. Hanson undoubtedly was pleased by the Rangers' tactics in the promotion of chaos and by another, larger result: an increased need, as he saw it, for a counterrevolution from within or from the United States. Sanders—Hanson's lifelong friend and "the best Ranger Captain that ever saw Texas" according to Hanson—accomplished the strategic aims of Hanson and Chapa.[153]

New Regime, New Promises of Ranger Reform

When the special session of the Texas legislature convened in Austin in March 1918, J. T. Canales arranged a meeting to discuss the Rangers with the Hobby regime's Ranger team: Francisco Chapa, who served as advisor to Hobby; Adj. Gen. James A. Harley; and newly appointed Ranger Inspector William Hanson. At the meeting, Canales described "terrible conditions" in South Texas "by reason of the Ranger outrages." The men listened "very patiently" to Canales, then "congratulated" him on being "frank" with them, according to Canales. Hanson, the first Ranger to hold "Inspector" rank, a position that called for him to investigate and monitor the Rangers, promised to "do his duty" and to "correct all those evils."[154] Canales, in essence, was briefed on a reform program that Hobby had outlined to Chapa just weeks before, when Hobby solicited his advice even before Ferguson had been impeached.[155]

Governor Hobby earlier had conceded to Chapa that the Rangers had created much of the tension and destruction along the border, not reduced it. "Nothing ... will go further," wrote Hobby to Chapa, "to cement the friendly relations" between the United States and Mexico "and to guarantee protection and safety to Mexicans living" in Texas than to select Rangers "who are concerned more about preserving peace and order than about spreading fear and terror" through resorting to "rough and odious tactics." Harley, his new adjutant general, "is cooperating" in reforming the Ranger Force "on the highest plane possible," continued Hobby. His regime, Hobby assured Chapa, would offer a different Ranger than had served before: "That type of old time ranger known as the 'gunman' will be eliminated under my administration, and only those men who are peaceful and law abiding, and yet who are firm, will be employed in the [Ranger] service."[156] Reform was coming to the Rangers, Hobby assured Chapa, who must have been surprised, if not alarmed.

More detrimental than Chapa's private war against revolutionaries or even his counsel to a string of governors, however, was his support for Hanson as a Ranger. In 1917, he had helped Hanson secure a Special Ranger commission.[157] In January 1918, he nominated Hanson to the new position of "Inspector" of the Rangers. Chapa publicly explained why Hanson was well suited for the position: He spoke Spanish "as well as the natives" and from his "many years" on the border, knew "everyone there— merchants, business men, lawyers, cotton men." Basically, Chapa confessed,

"I was glad to see a man that was humane ... at the head of the Ranger force."[158]

Canales had heard it all before—just the year before, in fact, when Canales had received Ferguson's "word of honor" that he would reform the Rangers if Canales supported an increase in the Ranger Force to emergency levels.[159] From the meeting with the Ranger leaders, nevertheless, Canales accepted the assurances that the Hobby administration "would correct the faults of the old" and hoped that Hanson's "intelligence and shrewdness" would be used "for the purpose of weeding out bad men."[160] Inspired by the promise of a progressive regime, Canales joined the others in ensuring a Hobby victory in the coming elections and in securing political allegiance afterward.

That the attitude of Chapa's nominee Hanson was "humane," of course, was not clear. Hanson's attitude led W. W. Sterling, Ranger Captain and Adjutant General in the 1920s, to suggest, erroneously, that Hanson, "eager for revenge," had written the Plan de San Diego in order to provoke armed invasion of Mexico.[161] The point, however, was valid: Hanson certainly capitalized on the Plan's existence as a pretext for retaliation. Regarding the Border War, Hanson argued that raiding "Mexicans" destroyed ranches and killed "American citizens" in Texas until "the people, the citizens themselves, rose en masse" in a general "uprising." Hanson admitted that "rangers and citizens"—even though they were "very careful"— killed "a good many Mexicans." Hanson did not lament the dead, even the innocent ones, because the "majority" of those killed by the Rangers and their vigilantes "were either raiders, sympathizers, or harborers of the people from the other side."[162] Hanson had provided similar arguments about the necessity for murder on the part of the Huerta regime. His defense then eerily foretold his reasoning about the Rangers' atrocities later.

Let those persons with a direct stake decide the course of events, Hanson had argued in his public letter in 1913, and he maintained that attitude back in Texas. Until the day he could join a formal retaliation against Mexico, Hanson decided to pursue his goal by serving as commander of the Rangers in their war along the border.

Hanson's first official assignment for the new regime foretold his responsibility as Inspector, as he saw it: to manage political crises for Hobby, not to address legal or moral outrages on the part of the Rangers. He left ostensibly to investigate reports of a massacre conducted by Rangers in Porvenir, Spanish for "future," an isolated community on the Rio Grande in the arid Big Bend region of far West Texas. Instead, he sought to cover up the killings and thus ensure border support for Hobby's election.

Just after midnight on January 29, 1918, after the departure of U.S. cavalry troops, Rangers and local ranchers separated out fifteen men, ages sixteen to seventy-two, then released the rest of the gathered villagers. Masedonia Huerta watched the Rangers escort her husband Masedonio and the others around a little hill on the edge of the village, not more than a three-minute walk from home. About thirty minutes later, she and the other villagers began hearing gunshots as the Rangers started executing the men.[163] The Rangers and ranchers shot the victims in the body and the head, each skull hollowed by a bullet hole. The Rangers left the bodies in parallel lines, with no pretense of burying the corpses. Dead were Manuel Morales, Antonio Casteñeda, Pedro Herrera, Hiviana Herrera, Siberiano Herrera, Román Nieves, Longinas Flores, Tiburcio Jáquez, Alberto García, Masedonio Huerta, Ambrocio Hernández, Serapio Jimínez, Juan Hermanez, Pedro Jimínez, and Eutemio González. The Rangers orphaned forty children that frigid January night;[164] then they and their accomplices whooped and hollered as they rode into the night.[165]

Adjutant General Harley and Governor Hobby responded to a developing public relations crisis by sending "special investigator" William Hanson, hired the week of the massacre, to Big Bend.[166] Hanson traveled to Marfa to investigate not so much the killings as the political support for Hobby in his Democratic primary battle with Ferguson. What made Hanson "special" to Hobby's regime was his undercover campaign work in the guise of carrying out Ranger investigations. In a long report to Harley following the trip to West Texas, Hanson revealed the Hobby regime's priorities that guided its handling of the Porvenir massacre.

On February 6, Hanson went to Marfa to investigate rumors that Captain Fox had distributed campaign literature for Ferguson, not that Fox's company had executed fifteen citizens. Upon arrival he checked in with banker H. M. Fennel, who declared himself a friend of Hobby "personally and politically," to discuss the matter "in strict confidence." Fennel assured Hanson that if Fox had been working against Hobby, he would have heard about it. Although Hanson discussed the campaign in general conversation with the dozens of men he met in Marfa, he assured Harley that "Mr. Fennel was the only man in Marfa that really knew what I was there for."

Content with his quick gauge of political support for Hobby, Hanson concluded his "investigation" of the Porvenir massacre by stating, "I believe Cpt. Fox is loyal to the core and that he is doing his full duty, and giving entire satisfaction to the good people of that section." A single day in Marfa—a hundred miles from Porvenir and the survivors, no discussion with Army officers or enlisted men, no independent research of any sort, and Hanson's first of many special investigations ended in fulfilling only his duty to Harley and Hobby—"always with a view of serving your best interest," he signed off in his report from Big Bend.[167]

Eventually, the culpability of the Rangers surfaced in a series of investigations by the U.S. Army that the Ranger team could not ignore. Still, Army Colonel Langhorne moved to maintain a joint cover-up by contacting Hanson regarding the Army's intentions. Langhorne asked Hanson whether he wanted the affidavits collected in an officer's inquiry. He also wondered whether Hanson wanted to be present when principal investigator Col. W. J. Glascow conducted his review of the matter: "If so, I will try to warn you in time."[168] Hanson again placed the Porvenir massacre in terms of politics, not justice. He passed the note from Langhorne to Assistant Adjutant General Woodul with a warning: "I think some action must be taken to keep our Department from getting the worst of it from the U.S. government." Such attention, he continued, "would ruin the Ranger force and the General [Harley] if he does not take action." He instructed Woodul to "call his attention to it."[169] Hanson recognized that Hobby would sacrifice anyone, even the adjutant general, to limit political damage from the ongoing fiasco.

Eventually, Hobby reprimanded the murderers: Fox, reassigned, resigned; the other Rangers were dismissed, their discharge orders backdated to Hanson's visit. But the Rangers, and Harley and Hanson, carried on.

J. T. Canales experienced firsthand Hanson's duplicity in overseeing the Rangers: professing to ensure their appropriate behavior but actually covering up their crimes. After working toward Hobby's successful primary election with Hanson for several months, Canales approached Hanson about the killing of Lisandro Muñoz by Ranger John Edds. Despite what Canales considered a clear case of manslaughter, if not murder, Hanson maintained Edds's innocence and refused to reconsider his finding. Incensed about the Edds case and others he had brought to Hanson, Canales wrote Chapa that Hanson was "double-crossing" them because he was not conducting proper investigations "as he promised you . . . and me." Not surprisingly, Canales never heard from Chapa regarding the allegation.[170] Instead, he soon was threatened by Ranger Frank Hamer on the streets of Brownsville for complaining about the Rangers. Canales immediately wrote Governor Hobby that the "corrupt Republican intrigeur [sic]" Hanson was "inciting the Rangers to commit unlawful acts under the promise that he is the only one provided by the department to investigate the outrages and that he will see to it that nothing be done."[171]

Events in 1918 ended Canales's hopes for Rangers to reform themselves. Where Canales's February meeting with Chapa, Harley, and Hanson had concluded with credible-sounding promises to address Ranger misbehavior and to reconstitute the force itself, by year's end Canales believed that the citizens of South Texas faced a resurgence of Ranger brutality with the close of the political campaign. The very border Mexicans he had reassured about reformed Rangers under the Hobby regime once again became the targets for Rangers. Already Rangers had resumed the practices that threatened the safety and property of the citizens, as in the incidents involving his cousin, brothers, and sister, not to mention the confrontation by Hamer. Canales had predicted a dramatic increase in violence because Hanson desired to provoke general bloodshed along the border as a pretext for U.S. intervention in Mexico. Indeed, Canales had known Hanson since Hanson's arrival in South Texas at the turn of the century, and Canales often voiced accurate assessments of Hanson's activities as a counterrevolutionary in Mexico and Texas. Canales's view was valid, and Hanson later confirmed it in his efforts with the Fall Committee in 1920.

Canales met with Harley and Chapa soon after arriving in Austin in January 1919 for the coming legislative session, but not before Hamer intersected him again. In the meeting, Chapa and Harley provided no concrete steps to reign in the Rangers or their Inspector, so Canales, exasperated, notified them of his intent to file reform legislation. On his way across town, Hamer appeared a third time.

Shorn of hope for the Rangers to police themselves; incensed by his yearlong manipulation by Hanson, Harley, and Chapa; and livid over the intimidating tactics of Hamer, Canales the following morning wrote out in longhand House Bill 5, "An Act reorganizing the State Ranger force, prescribing the pay, qualifications and duties of State Rangers."[172]

The original Canales bill called for a Ranger Force consisting of four companies, each with a captain, sergeant, and four privates, or twenty-four men "in time of peace."[173] All Rangers would receive a substantial increase in salary. Also, "in time of emergency," companies could consist of a captain with two sergeants and seventeen privates, for a total of eighty men.[174] The binding legislation in place since 1901 allowed up to eighty-nine regular Rangers in four companies, each consisting of a captain, sergeant, and up to twenty privates at any time, as well as for a quartermaster. The Ranger Force never reached that figure, however, until the summer of 1917, after the end of the Border War. Significantly, the bill also called for the setting of a bond for Rangers, as for all other peace officers of the state.[175]

Reaction to the proposed bill was swift and decisive. Ranger staff and legislative supporters quickly maneuvered to have a joint committee investigate the Rangers. During the twelve days of the hearings, eighty witnesses generated fourteen hundred pages of testimony, and the advocates entered more than two hundred pages of documents into the record. Reporters from the Associated Press and newspapers across the state reported the developments.[176]

Canales wanted to show that the Rangers committed illegal and violent acts against citizens of the state and that Harley and Inspector Hanson overlooked or blindly justified them. The Ranger team sought to make the hearings a referendum on the continued existence of the fabled force and an inquiry into the trustworthiness of Canales. Everyone believed that the fate of HB 5 and reform of the Rangers depended on the outcome of the hearings. The Rangers won despite considerable testimony and evidence detailing Ranger outrages and their cover-ups.

Chairman William Bledsoe presented the investigating committee's report to the House on Wednesday, February 19, five days after the hearings ended.[177] Bledsoe implored the members to study Canales's charges, Harley's exceptions to them, and the transcript of the hearing, copies of which he would file soon, in connection with the report—though he never did. A "unanimous opinion" of the committee held that "conditions" along the border necessitated the maintenance of an "adequate" Ranger Force with "just compensation." The report provided judgment on the veracity of most charges, though it contained the names of no Rangers except Inspector Hanson.

The report found that the evidence supporting charges against Adjutant General Harley for "improper conduct" was "wholly insufficient," and, to the contrary, that an "intelligent" and "conscientious" Harley had operated "in the best manner possible."[178] To substantiate this finding, the committee cited Harley's claim that he had fired more than one hundred Rangers because of "incompetency, and other reasons." Instead of "condemnation," wrote the committee, Harley deserved "commendation" for the "able, efficient, impartial and fearless" manner in which he had overseen the Rangers, though the committee had forbidden direct consideration of Harley's actions.

As to the charges alleging Inspector Hanson's "inefficiency, partiality and unfairness," the report countered that he had been "efficient, prompt and fair" in his actions "at all times." The committee rushed to "acquit" Hanson of all charges.

Regarding the Rangers in general, the committee expressed its "appreciation" for the "great service" rendered under "trying conditions." The Rangers could not receive "too much credit" for the "faithful" discharge of their responsibilities.

The Rangers were ecstatic with the report. Inspector Hanson immediately wired Ranger C. J. Blackwell of his Headquarters company that the "committee report was all we could hope for. Vindication complete." Harley sent telegrams carrying the identical message to his defense counsels, Dayton Moses and R. E. L. Knight.[179] Hanson rejoiced at having survived the "cowardly attacks" by Canales.[180]

A bill passed under the direction of Investigating Chairman Bledsoe. As for his original reform bill that started the whole episode, Canales lamented, "I do not recognize my child." The Rangers had received an inoculation against the disease of reform.

After the hearings ended, Chapa continued his influence with Hobby.[181] He pointedly used Rangers to pursue a private foreign policy regarding Mexico. For two years, Chapa controlled Ranger Fred Marks in an unsuccessful attempt to capture Luís De la Rosa, the Tejano leader of the Plan de San Diego of 1915 and later a Mexican Army officer with credentials from President Venustiano Carranza.[182] Marks, who joined the Rangers on the basis of a special "understanding" among Harley, Hanson, and Chapa in 1918, spied for Chapa into 1920.[183] Marks filed his "confidential" reports to Captain Hanson, codename "Samson," who stationed his Headquarters Company in San Antonio, not Austin.[184] Hanson regularly relayed the intelligence from the border to Chapa.[185] When Harley's successor, W. D. Cope, tried to end Chapa's private war, Chapa wired Hobby to reiterate the "special mission" that Marks was on.[186] Hobby overturned Cope's housecleaning efforts and reinstated Marks.[187] No one overrode Chapa regarding the Rangers in South Texas—not Hanson, not an adjutant general, not even Hobby.[188]

Hanson too experienced a resurgence. Investigating committee members provided strong support for Inspector William Hanson's reappointment in the wake of the hearings. Rep. Sam Lackey, incredibly, claimed that "there was not one sentence of evidence" presented against him.[189] Hanson soon resigned, however, to accept a role as chief investigator for Albert Fall's U.S. Senate investigation into Mexico's affairs.[190] He signed on "to run down and check up" on "propaganda along the river" and to "examine witnesses and take evidence" regarding the taking of property and other actions against Americans in Mexico.[191] The move reflected his still-simmering intent to return to Mexico either as hacendado or conqueror, or both. The Fall Committee strove from the outset to stir up interventionist sentiment that would lead to control of Mexico's immense oil fields.

The empowering S. Res. 106 charged Fall's subcommittee to "investigate the matter of outrages on citizens of the United States in Mexico," though the subcommittee interpreted the charge broadly enough to include all forms of anti-Mexican interpretations and pro-intervention sentiments. Fall, soon of Teapot Dome infamy, chaired the committee, with Frank Brandegee and Marcus A. Smith serving as members. The hearings were conducted in Washington, D.C., Brownsville, Laredo, San Antonio, El Paso, Tucson, Nogales, San Diego, and Los Angeles, from September 8, 1919, to May 20, 1920. The hearings and examinations produced more than five thousand pages of testimony from 257 witnesses. Hanson, whose testimony lasted two and one-half hours, longer than any except one other, was the last witness to testify.[192] The virtual absence of discussion in his testimony about his landholdings in Mexico or his oil interests contributed to the "pioneer" image he invoked and, more telling, minimized charges that "oil interests" were behind the interventionist intentions of Hanson and Fall. In other words, the lead "witness" in the hearings failed to provide any context for his views—that he had been a hacendado who had lost a fortune and nearly his life for spying for counterrevolutionary forces during the early days of the Revolution or that as a U.S. citizen he had been paid by Mexican officials to continue spying in Texas.

Fall believed his committee could provide the answer to one plaintive question: "Where has the voice been lifted in behalf of the common, everyday, housemaking, honest, industrious American with his family, teaching the Mexican modern methods of agriculture and handicraft, who has, while tied to a tree, seen his daughter raped and his wife disemboweled in his presence?"[193] In his preliminary report, Fall announced that the United States should send in a "police force" to keep open communication lines and to protect U.S. citizens.[194] Hanson saw the opportunity to provoke military intervention in Mexico that superseded the low-level warfare he had encouraged as leader of the Rangers.

The hearings led to neither a glorious intervention nor restoration of his hacienda, so Hanson returned to San Antonio to work in politics. In 1921, he was president of the "Republican Club of the 14th District" in San Antonio while his friend Col. Frank Chapa served as vice-president.[195] In the Congressional race that year, they successfully touted Harry Wurzbach, the first native Texan elected from the Republican Party. Wurzbach served ten of the next twelve years as representative from the San Antonio area.[196]

Hanson wrote ex-Ranger "Honey" Hunnicutt that he was disappointed that Hamer was set to replace Brooks as Senior Captain. He was still "afraid that such men as Canales will have too much to say about it's [sic] management," though he need not have worried that Hamer would listen to Canales or vice versa. Hanson had hired on with a "very wealthy company" primed to conduct "much business" with Central and South America, so did not ask "anything" from the government—"[I] have a much better lay than anything [the Rangers] could offer me."[197]

The new opportunity did not last long, as he shortly accepted a patronage post as District Director of the Immigration Service for the Department of Labor. His jurisdiction again included South Texas and Big Bend, and border Mexicans were still his enemies. In 1925, the Rangers were target of a high-profile suit challenging their jurisdiction along the border, and Hanson suggested to his friend Ranger Quartermaster Aldrich that they again rally pro-Ranger forces in a statewide show of support, with "say, a thousand petitions." The suit failed, as Hanson believed it would.[198]

Franciso Chapa, perennial advisor to Texas governors, and William Hanson, man of intrigue and Ranger Inspector, had much in common. Both men had been convicted for violation of neutrality acts in support of counterrevolutionaries—Hanson in Mexico, Chapa in the United States. Both looked at the Porfiriato with longing akin to the "moonlight and magnolia" memorialists of the Old South. Both Chapa and Hanson orchestrated spy networks to pursue their foreign policy goal of reversing the revolution in Mexico and Texas.

They succeeded in portraying the Plan de San Diego as the only Texas variant of a dangerously unstable Mexican Revolution, in large part by casting all mejicanos, especially Tejanos, as avatars of mayhem and by energizing the Rangers to attack them. In this context, la rinchada became their counterrevolution against the Revolution in its northernmost theater. And Texans, Tejanos especially, suffered as a result.

Notes

1. A note on terminology: I use "mejicanos" when referring to citizens of Mexican ethnicity, regardless of residency; "Tejanos" when referring to Texas citizens of Mexican ethnicity; and "border Mexicans" when referring to ethnic Mexicans living on either side of, but near, the Rio Grande.

2. For examples of Hobby's requests for political advice from Chapa, see Hobby to Chapa, January 8, 1918, Letter Book 7 [hereafter, LB]; November 8, 1918, LB "October 18–November 15"; and May 16 and 20, 1919, Texas State Archives [hereafter, TSA].

3. Biographical information derives from various issues of *El Imparcial de Texas* (San Antonio), his newspaper; his testimony in Transcript, Joint Committee of the Senate and House in the Investigation of the State Ranger Force, January 31, 1919, 3 vols., 36th Legislature, Regular Session, 1919; 208–20 [hereafter, RFI]; clippings from the *Dallas Morning News* (February 19, 1924), and the *Texas Pythian Banner-Knight* (April 1915), in "F.A. Chapa," Vertical File, Center for American History, University of Texas at Austin [hereafter, CAH]; Teresa Palomo Acosta, "Francisco A. Chapa," in *New Handbook of Texas* 42 [hereafter, Acosta, "Chapa" for the document, and NHBTX for the book]; and Frank Carter Adams, ed., *Texas Democracy: A Centennial History of Politics and Personalities of the Democratic Party, 1836–1936*, 4 vols. (Austin: Democratic Historical Assoc., 1937), a publication for which his son, Frank, served on the Advisory Board. The only Spanish-surnamed figures profiled in the *Centennial History* were Francisco Chapa; Antonio V. Navarro, descendant of one of the signers of the Texas Declaration of Independence; H. P. Guerra Sr. and Jr.; and two Guerra associates, all of Starr County.

4. Chapa worked as a druggist for four years before opening his own store, "La Bótica del León, La Grán Droguería y Bótica" at 816 West Commerce St. Chapa ran the pharmacy and adjoining "Chapa Mercantile Co." until his death in 1924, at which time control passed to his son, who operated the store for another fifty years. The stores sold items intriguing to recent arrivals from Mexico, such as *molinas para nixtamal* (a mill to grind maize for tortillas) and traditional herbs, dyes, and dry goods, as well as items of more general appeal, such as furniture, Liberty Bonds, and books, including a selection of fourteen "Novelas de Buffalo Bill, a buc. cada una" (Novels of Buffalo Bill, a buck each); *El Imparcial* (January 23, 1919): 2.

5. Gregorio Cortez drew immense attention in Texas and beyond. Seen by many in Texas as a twentieth-century Robin Hood who stood against the abuse of power

and by others as nothing more than a bandit "terrorist," Cortez became a polarizing figure in American history. The classic account of his story and influence remains Américo Paredes's *"With His Pistol in His Hand": A Border Ballad and Its Hero* (Austin: University of Texas Press, 1958).

The best source of political information about Chapa, besides the newspaper itself, is his correspondence with Governors Oscar B. Colquitt and William P. Hobby; also, Charles H. Harris III and Louis R. Sadler, "The 1911 Reyes Conspiracy: The Texas Side," *Southwestern Historical Quarterly* 83 (April 1980): 325–48. Chapa's partner in the newspaper was Miguel Quiroga; 330.

6. See Harris and Sadler, "1911 Reyes Conspiracy," 330; and for background, see Gould, *Progressives*, 28–57, 88. Colquitt remained friends with Chapa and served as pallbearer at his funeral; Acosta, "Chapa," 42. See also Chapa's self-promotion regarding his appointment to Hobby's "Estado Mayor" in *El Imparcial* (January 23, 1919): 1.

7. For the importance of the forty-eight-page "Chapa pamphlet," see Américo Paredes, *"With His Pistol in His Hand": A Border Ballad and Its Hero* (Austin: University of Texas Press, 1958), 87, 97–8, 101, 112.

8. See, e.g., the editorial of January 16, 1919, "El gobierno mexicano debe sofocar el terrorismo" ("The Government of Mexico Ought to Suffocate Terrorism"), which contrasted the perceived weaknesses of the current regime with the effective suppressions by Díaz.

9. Harris and Sadler, "1911 Reyes Conspiracy," 327. The two authors supplement previous work with extensive use of U.S. Bureau of Investigation files regarding the Mexican Revolution.

10. Harris and Sadler, "1911 Reyes Conspiracy," 336, draws primarily on Bureau of Intelligence reports.

11. See discussion of Capts. John Sanders and Monroe Fox in Richard H. Ribb, "José Tomás Canales and the Texas Rangers: Myth, Ideology, and Power, 1910–1920" (Ph.D. diss., The University of Texas at Austin, 2001), chapter 6. Both Sanders and Fox committed outrages against Tejanos along the border.

12. Harris and Sadler, "1911 Reyes Conspiracy," 332–33, 336.

13. *Brownsville Daily Herald* (January 11, 1912), in Harris and Sadler, "1911 Reyes Conspiracy," 336–37. See discussion in Harris and Sadler, "1911 Reyes Conspiracy," passim, of *U.S. v. Miguel Quiroga Sr. et al.*, U.S. Commissioner, San Antonio; U.S. v. Bernardo Reyes et al., District Court, Laredo; and for Chapa, *U.S. v. Ishmael* [sic] *Reyes Retana et al.*, District Court, Brownsville. Quiroga and the others pled guilty soon after the trial opened in January 1912. Only Chapa remained to face the charges of insurrection, ably defended by Jacob F. Wolters, a fellow personal staff member and previous campaign manager for Governor Colquitt (335–36). Reyes, arrested on November 18, 1911, fled immediately to Mexico after payment of his $5,000 bond

by Chapa. On Christmas Day, Reyes surrendered to Madero's troops and was jailed in Mexico City. In February 1912, Reyes led a revolt that quickly toppled Madero, though Reyes died in the first day of fighting (335, 344).

14. Harris and Sadler, "1911 Reyes Conspiracy," 341, 346, describe his standing bond for individuals accused of further violations of the neutrality acts.

15. Charles H. Harris III and Louis R. Sadler, *The Texas Rangers and the Mexican Revolution: The Bloodiest Decade, 1910–1920* (Albuquerque: University of New Mexico Press, 2004), 503.

16. Hanson was the only child of Susan L. Mangum, an Alabama native, and Englishman Cornelius James Hanson. Biographical information derives from "Capt. William M. Hanson," in Frank W. Johnson, *A History of Texas and Texans* (Chicago and New York: American Historical Society, 1916), vol. 3, ed. and rev. by Eugene C. Barker and Ernest W. Winkler, 1229–30; [n.a.] . . . Record of Southwest Texas . . . (Chicago: Goodspeed Bros., 1894), 369–70; and *Testimony of William M. Hanson, Investigation of Mexican Affairs*, Sen. Doc. No. 285; 2 vols., 66th Cong., 2nd sess., Washington, D.C: Government Printing Office, 1920), 3223–47.

17. Nancy Beck Young, "San Antonio & Gulf Shore Railway," *NHBTX*, 5, 798.

18. Johnson, *A History of Texas and Texans*, 1229; and *Hanson Testimony, Investigation of Mexican Affairs*, 3223–24, 3226.

19. *Hanson Testimony, Investigation of Mexican Affairs*, 3224, 3226. Hanson envisioned a citrus empire, fed by a massive irrigation system and serviced by the Mexican national railway, that would allow each of the one million grapefruit and orange trees in his nursery to yield within a few years fruit worth $40 million annually, "American gold, f.o.b. Tampico"; 3224, 3226, 3238.

20. He served as president of the Buena Vista Land and Irrigation Company, owner of Hacienda San Procopio with its eight thousand acres of irrigated land, and he was the sole owner of the nearby Hacienda Guadalupe, an irrigated citrus farm of three thousand acres. In addition, he served as president of the regional growers' association that sought, with some early success, to sell citrus fruit in Europe and in the United States, especially in Minnesota.

21. Johnson, *Texas and Texans*, 1230. Hanson served as secretary and general manager of the Tamesi Petroleum and Asphalt Company and of the Standard Petroleum Company. Oil production in the Tampico field began in 1901 and reached 13 million barrels by 1910; Manuel G. Gonzales, *Mexicanos: A History of Mexicans in the United States* (Bloomington: University of Indiana Press, 1999), 116.

22. *Hanson Testimony, Investigation of Mexican Affairs*, 3244–45,

23. Ornelas to Creel, February 18, 1911; Creel to Ornelas, February 22, 1911; Creel to [? Comptroller], February 22, 1911, authorizing expenditures; all in L–E–633R, Leg

37, Revolución Mexicana series, Archivos de la Secretaría de Relaciones Exteriores de México (Secretariat of Foreign Relations), Mexico, D.F [hereafter, RM and SRE].

24. All of the following discussion derives from a series of documents found in L-E 685R, Leg 5, RM, SRE. Serving with Hanson and Womack were Frank Mathews, J. Wallis, J. J. Allen, and [?] Clyett. For Womack's general duties "en la vigilancia y persecusión de revoltosos," see San Antonio Consul M. E. Diebold to Secretary of Foreign Relations [Enrique Creel], May 13, 1911. For the selective approval of weapons smuggling, see Womack to Hanson, May 12, 1911.

25. Hanson writes of receiving "instructions" (instrucciones) at "the office" to continue his work "on the street," but he does not reveal who issued them; Hanson to Womack and Enrique Ornelas, May 1, 1911. Diebold replaced Ornelas sometime in early May, and Hanson may have received orders from Diebold on May 1. On May 11, Ornelas left the country; Womack to Hanson, May 12, 1911.

26. Womack to Hanson, May 12, 1911.

27. Hanson to "My friends in Texas," April 1, 1913, provided by J. A. Fernández, Mexican Consul to San Antonio, with a cover letter, April 11, 1913, to the *San Antonio Express*. A copy of the letters and related documents are in L-E-762R, Leg 44(1), RM, SRE.

28. *Hanson Testimony, Investigation of Mexican Affairs*, 3228.

29. *Hanson Testimony, Investigation of Mexican Affairs*, 3240. Hanson claimed he never had heard of violence against Americans or the Mexican government during the long reign of autocrat Porfirio Díaz, but with the ascent of the "ignorant" revolutionaries under Madero in 1910, he had watched with dismay a complete breakdown in stability. Hanson commented that he never "knew" of a bank or train robbery, slept with doors unlocked, and never lost an animal under Díaz. For a different interpretation of the Díaz regime, see Paul Vanderwood, *Disorder and Progress: Bandits, Police, and Mexican Development*, rev. ed. (Wilmington, DE: Scholarly Resources, 1992 [1981]), passim. Vanderwood shows quite convincingly that under Díaz, order and disorder constantly overlapped and blended to create the violent regime itself. In important ways, though not avowedly, Vanderwood applies development theory to intranational affairs. On development theory, see Gunther Frank's prolific writings.

30. *Hanson Testimony, Investigation of Mexican Affairs*, 3230.

31. *Chapa Testimony, RFI*, 208; and *Canales Testimony, RFI*, 893.

32. *Hanson Testimony, Investigation of Mexican Affairs*, 3229–30.

33. President Wilson did not advocate intervening to wring reparations from chaotic Mexico. One War Department spokesman, a "Mr. Daniels," pointedly asked Hanson "whether or not ... [the Wilson Administration] thought a lot of filibusters, schemers, and adventurers, who had gone to Mexico to exploit the Mexican people"

deserved federal assistance. "That brought on a kind of a scrap," Hanson recalled, "and things got a little personal and we left"; *Hanson Testimony, Investigation of Mexican Affairs*, 3234.

34. The discussion derives from a series of letters concerning Hanson's return to Mexico in entry 9–4–212, Archivo Histórico Diplomático Mexicano, SRE [hereafter, AHDM]. See Gen. Luís Caballero, the original arresting officer, to K.H. Merren May 25, 1917; Merren to Subsecretary of State, June 17, 1917; Gov. [Tamaulipas] and Gen. Gregorio Osuna to Subsecretary of State, July 12, 1917.

35. *Hanson Testimony, Investigation of Mexican Affairs*, 3240. Madero, Reyes, and Díaz's nephew all launched military movements from San Antonio between 1910 and 1916. Hanson's intention to return to Mexico when "settled conditions" allowed was apparent in his inclusion in a contemporary biographical sketch of his Mexican post office address and a description of his operations. Further indicating his plans to resume operations was the sketch's highlighting of the careers of two of his four sons, one a doctor and another a Texas A&M–trained farmer, both of whom had "been educated especially for association with their father's interests in Mexico"; Johnson, *Texas and Texans*, 1230.

36. Agent Joe H. Grimes to War Department, June 15, 1915, quoted in Harris and Sadler, *The Texas Rangers*, 384.

37. *Canales Testimony*, RFI, 893.

38. *Hanson Testimony, Investigation of Mexican Affairs*, 3244.

39. Robert M. Utley, *Lone Star Lawmen: The Second Century of the Texas Rangers* (Oxford and New York: Oxford University Press, 2007), 8–14. In chapter 1, Utley reviews the Rangers during the first part of the decade.

40. Utley, *Lone Star Lawmen*, 9.

41. Utley, *Lone Star Lawmen*, 23–4; Walter P. Webb, *The Texas Rangers: A Century of Frontier Defense* (Austin: University of Texas Press, 1993 [1935]), 488–90; and *San Antonio Express* (February 8, 1924): 3.

42. *San Antonio Express* (February 8, 1924): 3.

43. Quoted in Utley, *Lone Star Lawmen*, 24.

44. Webb, *Texas Rangers*, 488–90.

45. Secretary of War to the Secretary of State, September 11, 1916, cited in Don M. Coerver and Linda B. Hall, *Texas and the Mexican Revolution: A Study in State and National Border Policy, 1910–1920* (San Antonio: Trinity University Press, 1984), 106.

46. Commentators from opposite camps used the term "reign of terror" to describe the bloody days along the river. In 1919, Virginia Yeager noted, "It was and still is a reign of terror" because of Ranger activities; "Exhibit A," RFI, 6A. W. W. Sterling, representing the camp that attributed the cause and perpetuation of violence solely to the border Mexicans, used the term freely in his memoir *Trails and Trials of a Texas*

Ranger. Governor James Ferguson, ever the politician, referred to the situation as "almost a reign of terror"; in James Sandos, *Rebellion in the Borderlands: Anarchism and the Plan de San Diego, 1904–1923* (Norman: University of Oklahoma Press, 1992), 86 (emphasis added).

47. See *José Antonio Arce et al. v. State of Texas*, 202 S. W. Tex. Crim. Rep. 951 (April 17, 1918 [1916]). The invaluable, extensive district court records concerning the case, which include jury lists, motions, evidence, and newspaper accounts, are housed at the South Texas Archives, University of Texas–Pan American, Edinburg [hereafter, Pan Am]; see "Webb County: District Clerk's Criminal Court Case Papers, 1915–16," MSS., Group 5–27 of Texas State Library, Regional Depository, Pan Am. The ruling found the United States and Mexico to be in a state of war, despite the lack of formal declarations, and has been cited repeatedly to establish criteria for undeclared wars. See, e.g., *Western Reserve Life Insurance Co. v. Meadows*, 261 S. W. 554 (Texas 1953).

48. The most original and nuanced interpretation of the period is Benjamin H. Johnson, *Revolution in Texas: How a Forgotten Rebellion and Its Bloody Suppression Turned Mexicans into Americans* (New Haven, Conn.: Yale University Press, 2003), passim. See also Frank C. Pierce, *Brief History of the Lower Rio Grande Valley* (Menasha, Wis: George Banta, 1917), 89–103, which provides a convenient, if incomplete, calendar of conflicts for the Lower Rio Grande Valley only. See also the "Weekly Reports" for examples of feuds and thievery not connected to the insurrection; e.g., report of November 6, 1915, 16803, in U.S. State Department, Records Relating to the Internal Affairs of Mexico, 1910–1920, Record Group 59, microfilm, Nettie Lee Benson Library, University of Texas at Austin. My estimate of fifty raids by border Mexicans derives from General Funston, in Secretary of War to the Secretary of State, September 11, 1916, cited in Coerver and Hall, *Texas and the Mexican Revolution*, 106; James Sandos, "The Plan of San Diego: War & Diplomacy on the Texas Border, 1915–1916," *Arizona and the West* 14 (Spring 1972), 5–24; Charles C. Cumberland, "Border Raids in the Lower Rio Grande Valley–1915," *Southwestern Historical Quarterly* 57 (January 1954), 301–324; and the author's research in the Papers of the Adjutant General (Texas), Texas State Library (TSL). For a visual interpretation of the killings, see "Murder Map of Mexico," in U.S. Congress, Senate, Investigation of Mexican Affairs, 1: 845. Note that the estimate does not include the many incidents in the Big Bend region from 1916–18, of which about six resulted in the loss of many lives there. Though these raids also contributed to the general notion of a "Border War" and occasionally sprung from deep feelings of social injustice, they did not draw on the Plan nor did they develop out of reaction to a wholesale social and economic transformation, as in South Texas. For a fuller discussion of the issues surrounding conflict in the western theatre theater of the Border War, see Ribb, "José Tomás Canales," chapter 7, "*La Rinchada?*"

49. The *Lyford Courant* (August 20, 1915), typescript, Harding Collection, Raymondville (Texas) Public Library (quotation) [hereafter, RPL].

50. "Weekly Report," July 10, 1915, 15517, State. See also, Pierce, *Brief History*, 89–90, and Sandos, *Rebellion in the Borderlands*, 87. In the slaying of Bernard Boley, one source suggests that the killing was a case of mistaken identity: Raiders may have assumed Boley was W. P. Gano, owner of San Francisco Ranch, who "always stopped at the gate at about the same time" that Boley was shot; transcript of interview with Mrs. E. M. Sorenson, longtime Sebastian resident, by [?] Harding, August 23, 1971, RPL. Also, Sandos, *Rebellion in the Borderlands*, 87, and 188, n.37, cites the *Corpus Christi Caller* (July 6, 1915), as a source for the raiders' killing of two Anglo farmers near Lyford, but neither the *Brownsville Herald* nor Pierce, *Brief History*, two sources very attuned to Cameron County matters, mention the killings. Plan-driven raiders rarely, if ever, engaged in random killings; Pierce noted that the boy was killed "supposedly by members of the [raiding] party which had been reported [earlier that month]"; *Brief History*, 89. See also *Mercedes* (Texas) *Tribune*, August 19, 1915, clipping, which states that the Austins were the first civilians killed by Plan adherents. See later in this chapter the fuller discussion of the sparing of lives by Plan raiders and the selective violence they usually employed in their attacks.

51. "Weekly Report," July 31, 1915, 15730, State.

52. Ranger Deployment, March 28, 1915, and quotation in Sanders to Hutchings (teleg.) March 24, 1915, 549/3, Adjutant Generals' Records, General Correspondence, [hereafter, AGGC].

53. Hutchings to Sanders (teleg.), March 24, 1915, 549/3, AGGC.

54. Hutchings to Rangers Felps and Davenport (teleg.), March 27, 1915, 549/3, AGGC.

55. Sheriff John Almond to Hutchings, April 19, 1915, 549/11; Hutchings to Hon. R. H. Martin, April 28, 1915, 549/13; Hudspeth to Ferguson, April 24, 1915, 549/14; Hutchings to Hudspeth, April 28, 1915, 549/14; Hutchings to Martin, April 28, 1915: "Nat B. Jones is appointed to Ranger Force by direction of Governor," 549/14, all AGGC.

56. For shortfalls, see Ribb, "José Tomás Canales," chapter 8.

57. General Laws, 34th Leg., Reg. Sess. (January 12–April 20, 1915), 151.

58. Hutchings to Fox, to Sanders, July 17, 1915, ordering the captains to cut back on scouting, expenses, and to abstain from new enlistments; 550/14, AGGC.

59. He had served in Company A under Capt. James Brooks in 1905 and 1909, Adjutant Generals' Records, Service Records [hereafter, AGSR].

60. Biographical information derives from W. W. Sterling, *Trails and Trials*, 47–8, Testimony of "Captain [sic]" W. T. Vann. RFI, 574, and Testimony of A. G. Crawford, RFI, 39–42.

61. Crawford Testimony, RFI, 39–42. Crawford mentioned that Ransom was polite to women; RFI, 41.

62. *Crawford Testimony*, RFI, 43.

63. Sterling, *Trails and Trials*, 47.

64. Sterling, *Trails and Trials*, 47

65. RFI, 1502–03.

66. RFI, 1502–04.

67. See Vann to Hutchings (teleg.), July 26, 1915, and Hutchings to Vann July 27, 1915, 550/14, AGGC.

68. Vann Testimony, RFI, 574.

69. Testimony of James B. Wells, RFI, 694.

70. See Hutchings to Fox, July 10, 1915, 550/13, AGGC.

71. *Brief History*, 90. Sheriff Stocke Chaddick, who killed Lorenzo Manríquez, gained a reputation while mayor of Mercedes as intolerant: "obró con toda presión en contra de los mexicanos" and "es reconocido su animadversión" (acted with all force against mejicanos and was well-known for his hatred). J. D. White killed Gorgonio; "Lista."

72. See Testimony of W. G. B. Morrison, RFI, 33, for the cause-and-effect analysis regarding Ranger violence and counterviolence. Pierce wrote "En este caso hay que mencionar que la opinión general asegua que esa maniobra fué preparada de antemano por Carr e Hinojosa" (In this case it must be mentioned that the general opinion holds that there had been no interception, only that the "handiwork" had been prepared beforehand by Carr and Hinojosa); "Lista detallada de los mexicanos que fueron asesinados por los Rangers y empleados del gobierno de Texas, desde junio 1 hasta noviembre 30 de 1915," [3], (Detailed List of [border] Mexicans Killed by the Rangers and State Employees of Texas, from June 1 to November 30, 1915) enclosed with letter from Matamoros Consul Jesse Johnson to Secretary of State Robert Lansing, January 26, 1916, in Entry no. 17186, State [hereafter, "Lista"].

73. RFI, 859.

74. *Mexican Affairs*, 1263. According to Hill, Pizaña had lived on Los Tulitos for twelve to fifteen years.

75. Biographical information derives from various documents, particularly the memoir "Apuntes viográficos de un Revolucionario del Año de 1915" (Biographical Notes of a Revolutionary for the Year 1915) in Aniceto Pizaña Papers, José Canales Collection, Carlos Larralde Private Library, used by permission [hereafter, "Apuntes," CLL]. Spellings and colloquialisms in the "Apuntes" match other usages in South Texas in this era. Special thanks to Ben Johnson for extending the range of this information. Incidents in the sketch accord with information found during the raid on Los Tulitos; see, e.g., Sandos, *Rebellion in the Borderlands*, 88, on the literature in the ranch house. Additional information is from Sandos, *Rebellion in the Borderlands*, 72–3 and 87–8,

which draws on documents from the Justice Department, various claims commissions, and other federal agencies. In further irony of his life as putative liberator, Pizaña also died on Texas Independence Day–March 2, 1957; see *Sol de Tampico*, March 3, 1957, clipping, CLL. Still another, more tragic irony attended the death of his mother, Adela García de Pizaña, in March 1916. Her "mettlesome" horse became frightened by a locomotive—emblem of the new order in South Texas—and threw her to the ground, a fall which resulted in a punctured lung and life-ending pneumonia. She was buried in Matamoros; *Brownsville Daily Herald*, March 11, 1916.

76. "Seguí luchando y seguiré luchando por la emancipación del proleteriado mundial y más por el proleteriado mexicano."

77. "Apuntes," 39, CLL.

78. Details derive from the records in *Ramón Pizaña v. The State [Texas]*, No. 4404, as found in the Attorney General's Case File, Records of the Court of Criminal Appeals, TSL. See also "Apuntes," 39, CLL; "Weekly Report," July 31, 1915, 15730, State, establishes that Troop A arrived after the fighting, a distinction that Pierce, *Brief History*, 90, uncharacteristically missed. Joe Taylor, a Customs Inspector at the time of the clash, was a once and future Ranger; see his testimony in this case, in the Ranger investigation of 1919, and before the Fall Committee in 1920 [*Mexican Affairs*, 1317]. One of the wounded, Mike Monohan, a deputy sheriff, apparently was shot by a posse member or soldier as he fled the shooting. The civilians and deputies abandoned the fight to the soldiers; Case File 4404, TSL.

79. District court case no. 3613, Cameron Co., December 1, 1915. For appellate case, see *Ramón Pizaña v. The State [Texas]*, No. 4404, 81 Tex. Crim. Rep. 81 (1917), 193 SW 71 (Texas, 1917).

80. "Weekly Report," July 31, 1915, 15730, State.

81. "Apuntes," 47, CLL.

82. "nos podremos defender de los sonafaviches gringos"; "Apuntes," 52, CLL.

83. "y otros que están matado y yo no sé"; "Apuntes," 58, CLL.

84. "Apuntes," 55, CLL; "Weekly Reports" also confirm the rough division of authority, passim, State.

85. Both Pierce, *Brief History*, 90, and Sandos, *Rebellion in the Borderlands*, 89, draw on Cameron County Sheriff's eyewitness account given to the *Brownsville Herald*, August 6 and 7, 1915. "Lista" claims that at least one of the three was shot fleeing, not struggling.

86. Testimony of "Captain [sic]" W. T. Vann. RFI, 561 and 568 (quotation). Ranger J. L. Anders and other Rangers returned the following day to discover the surviving brother hidden beneath a bed by the women of the family. Anders claimed that after the suspect fired at him point blank, he returned fire, killing the man; RFI, 561, 568. During the investigation, Canales did not raise the possibility that the burn marks on Anders's face may have been caused by his own pistol's discharge.

87. "Weekly Report," August 7, 1915, 15812, State.

88. A conclusion based on my extensive research

89. "Weekly Report," July 10, 1915, 15517, State.

90. Samuel Spears to T. W. Gregory, U.S. Postmaster, c/o Justice Department, in "Weekly Report," August 1915, 15814, State.

91. Spears to Gregory, in "Weekly Report," August 10, 1915, 15814, State (emphasis added).

92. *Lyford Courant*, September 17, 1915, typescript, RPL.

93. "Lone Star and Four Others Were to be 'Freed' in 1915 Plot," n.d., San Antonio [?], transcript of newspaper article, RPL.

94. "Weekly Report," October 23, 1915, 16667, State (emphasis added).

95. Border Reports, August 28, 1915, 16011. See also October 30, 1915, 16752; and January 8, 1916, 17112, State.

96. *Courant*, August 13, 1915; Sandos, *Rebellion in the Borderlands*, 88–9, provides information on Beda Schultz, the proprietor, who sustained injuries in her frantic flee from the men and soon left the Valley for good.

97. Information by transcribed interview of Mrs. E. M. Sorensen, Sebastian resident, by [?] Harding, August 23, 1971, RPL.

98. *Courant*, August 13, 1915, calls Austin "secretary" of the organization; Sandos, *Rebellion in the Borderlands*, 89, refers to him as "president"; and the *Delta Irrigation News*, March 17, 1926, describes him simply as "leader," clipping, RPL.

99. "Lista."

100. *Delta Irrigation News*, March 17, 1926.

101. Information from transcribed interview of Mrs. E. M. Sorensen (by Harding August 23, 1971), RPL.

102. *Courant*, August 13, 1915.

103. "Weekly Reports," August 10, 1915, 15814, State.

104. *Courant*, August 13, 1915; and *Delta Irrigation News*, March 17, 1926. The men did not hide their faces and released Millard, two actions that lend credibility to the notion of selective retaliatory violence by the Plan's adherents.

105. *Delta Irrigation News*, March 17, 1926; C. H. Pease, the banker, wrote a memoir of the "Bandit War" in four installments in the *Delta Irrigation News*, March 3, 10, and 17, and April 14, 1926, RPL.

106. See Ribb, "José Tomás Canales," chapter 7, "*La Rinchada?*" for a fuller discussion of the significance of the Norias raid in revealing attitudes and tactics of the Texas Rangers in South Texas.

107. See "Statement of Manuel Rincones," August 12, 1915, in *Testimony of Caesar Kleberg, Mexican Affairs*, 1282–86. The sediciosos took Rincones hostage to serve as a guide to the border after the raid. Five raiders and two soldiers died in the battle, San-

dos, *Rebellion in the Borderlands*, 90–1. Chapter 7 of Ribb, Canales, "*La Rinchada?*" discusses the incident in detail.

108. For an example of the rhetoric that fed the attack on Norias, see translation of a circular in "Weekly Report," August 7, 1915, 15812, State: "Mexicans, we have to fulfill a sacred duty. The revolution in Texas in a few days will have acquired a gigantic proportion. We should unite with our [Tejano] brothers there and take the same chances that they are taking, for this is the solemn moment for the vindication of right and justice lost for us so long a time. Help us in this combat [with] all possible aid in order that our efforts may be crowned with success. Rest assured that this movement started in Texas will, as a consequence, bring a blessed peace so justly to be desired." Sandos, *Rebellion in the Borderlands*, 92, notes the presence of a copy of the Plan left behind by the raiders, and various photographs discussed in chapter 7 establish the presence of an insurrection flag at Norias.

109. *Trails and Trials*, 48.

110. Aldrich, "The Texas Rangers," July 21, 1937, typescript, 3P159/3, Aldrich Papers, CAH.

111. The quotation is from Pierce, *Brief History*, 114; In "Weekly Report," January 26, 1916, accompanying "Lista," the Consul noted that Pierce "informs me that he will be able to get many more [names] soon." The Consul also realized that "[t]here were many [men] killed whose names will never be known," and, hence, would not qualify for the "verified" list. The U.S. immigration agent for the Hidalgo area reported that "31 bandits [sic] had been killed in that vicinity by the rangers during the past 24 hours"; Inspector David Warren to Supervising Inspector, August 12, 1915, quoted in Sandos, *Rebellion in the Borderlands*, 94. The agent's report included several victims that Pierce did not verify for his list, for whatever reasons; see dates and sites on Pierce's "Lista." My research substantiates both that any list in any given time period always undercounted the dead and that many, many more "unverifiable" deaths occurred than verifiable ones, given the rampant, usually clandestine vigilantism by authorities and citizens alike—bodies turned up all the time; see below and also Ribb, "José Tomás Canales," chapter 7, "*La Rinchada?*"

112. August 27, 1915, 1.

113. See Testimony of John Kleiber, 1270–74, and of Henry Wallis, 1342–44, in *Mexican Affairs*; Pierce, *Brief History*, 96–7; Sandos, *Rebellion in the Borderlands*, 101–03.

114. "Weekly Report," October 23, 1915, 16667, State.

115. See August 13, September 10, and October 22, 1915, *Lyford Courant*, RPL; Pierce, *Brief History*, 89; and September 30, 1915, *Mercedes Tribune*, RPL.

116. Sediciosos sometimes warned Tejanos about impending raids; see, e.g., "Weekly Report," October 30, 1915, 16752, State.

117. Vann Testimony, RFI, 574–75. Regarding the four dead men, Vann noted that

their fate was sealed when "they were arrested—they were unfortunate by living that close to the wreck"; RFI, 589. Ransom's report for the week did not mention the incident: "A number of trails were followed east from the place of the wreck to Mexican shacks & into the brush going in the direction of Brownsville. Returned to Harlingen"; entry for 19 October 1915, "Scout Reports—Co. D," Adjutant Generals' Records, Ranger Records, TSA.

118. RFI, 955.

119. Utley, *Lone Star Lawmen*, 16.

120. *Brownsville Sentinel*, 20Oct15, cited in Tony Ramírez, "The Olmito Raid," *The Junior Historian* 16 (March 1956), 31.

121. *Lyford Courant*, August 20, 1915, typescript, RPL.

122. C. H. Pease, *Lyford Courant*, August 6, 1915, clipping, RPL.

123. B. D. Stevenson, *Lyford Courant* [?], n.d. (summer 1918), clipping, RPL.

124. *Lyford Courant*, August 6, 1915, RPL.

125. Interview no. 2796 (by Leticia Miroslava Gamboa, June 25, 1987), Oral History Collection, Lower Rio Grande Valley Historical Collection, Pan Am.

126. James Franklin Ewers, no. 1638 (by Hubert J. Miller, December 12, 1982), Pan Am. Some sources apparently looked on only one side of the rail line. Ranger Investigation Chairman William Bledsoe asked A. G. Crawford about "seven Mesicans [sic] being strung up at Ebenezer Station." See also Victor Berrones, no. 0933 (interviewer, date unkown), Pan Am: "I saw six men killed by the Rangers" (seis hombres que mataron los rinches [sic]). Frank C. Pierce learned that one of the victims had been a waiter, another a shopkeeper, and a third worked for a local farmer; "Lista."

127. RFI, 677. Wells counted eleven bodies.

128. [Los rinches los mataron por que eran mexicanos, yo creo], Pan Am.

129. No. 2741 (by Armando Rubén Ramos, September 22, 1978), Pan Am.

130. Medvecky, no. 2741, and James Franklin Ewers, no. 1638 (by Hubert J. Miller, December 12, 1982), Pan Am. When confronted for his murders, Baker allegedly replied, "We are the law here."

131. Jon Peavey, interviewed by Hubert J. Miller, Pan Am.

132. AGSR, TSA and his testimony in *Mexican Affairs*. In light of the probable role of the two men in lynchings, consider W. W. Sterling's remark that Baker and Mayfield "contributed most to the suppression of the trouble"; *Trails and Trials*, 51.

133. Testimony of R. B. Creager, RFI, 355; see also Webb, who noted "the death of hundreds of Mexicans, many of them innocent, at the hands of the local posses, peace officers, and Texas Rangers," *Texas Rangers*, 478.

134. Webb, *Texas Rangers*, 478.

135. Miriam Swann saw "charred" bodies and also ones hanging from trees; Valley Home, 70. See discussion surrounding the Flores case (Vann says the bodies were left

where they dropped); Florencio García (body not identifiable); and Wells Testimony (the smell of rotten bodies), RFI.

136. *Daily Express*, September 11, 1915. The Anglos and their allies conducted a campaign of violence that mirrored the indiscriminate retaliation on the part of slaveholders in the wake of slave rebellions such as the one planned by Denmark Vesey in 1822 and the one carried out by Nat Turner in 1831. As in the antebellum South, authorities suspended legal process and actively participated in the murder of innocent residents in a response based on denial, fear, and hysteria that far exceeded the known threat. Also like the planters, the Anglos and their allies were confident in their presumed benevolence and the intellectual shortcomings of their presumed inferiors, thus could not believe that "their" people could or would revolt in the first place.

137. *Brownsville Herald*, November 3, 1915, cites Immigration Service figures, which hardly were exhaustive, given the porous nature of the Texas–Mexican border. For daily assessments of the out migration, see, e.g., "Weekly Report," August 21, 1915, 15985; September 4, 1915, 16175; and September 11, 1915, 16256, State.

138. "Weekly Report," August 21, 1915, 15985, State.

139. David Montejano, *Anglos and Mexicans in the Making of Texas, 1836–1986* (Austin: University of Texas Press, 1987), 122, provides the figure, while Lon Hill provides the visual representation, *Mexican Affairs*, 1312; [hereafter, *Anglos and Mexicans*]

140. Pease, March 17, 1926, *Delta Irrigation News*, RPL; "Weekly Report," September 11, 1915, 16216; Montejano, *Anglos and Mexicans*, 122.

141. "Weekly Report," November 13, 1915, 16842, State.

142. Canales Testimony, 868, RFI; Pierce, *Brief History*, 100, 102. Sandos, *Rebellion in the Borderlands*, xvi, writes regarding Carranza's motivations for a shift in policy regarding the sediciosos: "In short, the faction that could deliver to Wilson security on America's southern border would win Wilson's permission to govern Mexico." Pierce, writing in 1917, was moved to exclaim that since June 18, 1916, "peace has reigned supreme" in the Lower Rio Grande Valley, 102.

Carranza's role in the Border War remains disputed among historians. Agreement does reign, however, in acknowledging his vacillating attempts to use various factions nominally under his control to tactical advantage along the border, whether against rivals or U.S. forces. I conclude that he had neither the willingness nor the resources to control, much less direct, the insurgency of the Border War.

143. Pierce, *Brief History*, 100–02.

144. See especially Ronnie C. Tyler, "The Little Punitive Expedition in the Big Bend," *Southwestern Historical Quarterly* 73 (January 1975), 271–91, passim.

145. In Pierce, *Brief History*, 103.

146. Wilson to Hook, July 8, 1916, Wilson Papers, PCL; and Charles Warren to L. S. Rowe, August 29, 1916, Gray-Lane Files, Dept. of State, doc. no. 56, RG 43, U.S.

National Archives. For an in-depth account, see Harris and Sadler, *The Texas Rangers,* 303–8.

147. See Ribb, "José Tomás Canales," chapter 6 for relevant testimony.

148. RFI, 243.

149. Wilson to Hook, July 8, 1916, Wilson Papers, PCL; and Charles Warren to L.S. Rowe, August 29, 1916, Gray-Lane Files, Dept. of State, doc. no. 56, RG 43, USNA.

150. Wilson to Hook, July 8, 1916, Wilson Papers, PCL.

151. After June 16, 1916, just days after receiving the petition, Wilson ordered all federal prisoners to be housed in Army facilities. See Sandos, *Rebellion in the Borderlands,* 202, note 30, citing Secretary of War to Attorney General, July 17 and 19, 1916, Records of the Adjutant General's Office, 1780s–1917, no. 2377632, RG 94, USNA.

152. Wilson to Hook, July 8, 1916, Wilson Papers, PCL.

153. For the assessment of "Saunders [sic]" by Hanson, see Hanson to Asst. Adj. Gen. Walter F. Woodul, December 24, 1917, in his service record, AGSR; and Hanson to "James E. Furguson [sic]," April 19, 1917, 561/15, AGGC.

154. *Canales Testimony,* RFI, 877–88. Canales remembered the meeting taking place in February, but was incorrect. He did not reach Austin, or did not appear on the daily roll calls of the House, until 1 March; House Journal. The meeting apparently took place before the session ended on March 27.

155. "Acting Governor" Hobby to Col. F.A. Chapa, September 1, 1917, [unnumbered] LB, 82, Hobby Papers, TSA.

156. Hobby to Chapa, January 5, 1918, Letter Book 6, Governors' Papers–William P. Hobby Papers, TSA.

157. Harris and Sadler, *The Texas Rangers,* 384–85.

158. *Chapa Testimony,* RFI, 219.

159. *Canales Testimony,* RFI, 869.

160. *Canales Testimony,* RFI, 870, 877–88.

161. W.W. Sterling, *Trails and Trials,* 28.

162. *Hanson Testimony, Investigation of Mexican Affairs,* 3243.

163. For detailed histories of the protracted, sordid affair, see Ribb, "José Tomás Canales," especially 329–43; Utley, *Lone Star Lawmen,* 58–64; and Glenn Justice, *Revolution on the Rio Grande: Mexican Raids and Army Pursuits, 1916–1919* (El Paso: University of Texas at El Paso, 1992). For the widows' view of the massacre, see Depositions of Masedoni[a] Huerta, Francisc[a] Hernández Morale[s], Librada Montoya Jáquez, Felipa Méndez Casteñerda, Estefana Jaso Morale[s], Alejandra Larez Nieves, and Eulalia Gonzales Hernández, April 5, 1918, before Lieut. Patrick Kelly, Summary Court, in RFI, 841–48 [hereafter, "Women's Depositions"].

164. Juan Méndez to General J.C. Muguía, January 28[29], 1918, in RFI, 1605.

165. See Keil's correspondence used in Justice, *Revolution,* 39.

166. For Hanson's rise to Ranger power, see Ribb, "José Tomás Canales," chapter 4. For the title, see, e.g., Harley to Robert Lansing, Secretary of State, January 31, 1918, requesting a diplomat's passport for Hanson; 573/18, AGGC. On February 4, 1918, Harley had asked simply, "Please come to Austin"; 573/23, AGGC.

167. Hanson to Harley, February 8, 1918, 573/26, AGGC. Document features title, "Distribution Literature." Pencil notation on the document indicates that Harley passed it to Hobby: "Return to adj't genl's office."

168. Langhorne to Hanson, May 22, 1918, "Adjutant General's Records—1918," Walter P. Webb Papers, CAH.

169. Pencil notation signed "Hanson" on Langhorne to Hanson, May 22, 1918, 2R290; "Adjutant General's Records—1918," Webb Papers, CAH.

170. For the Edds-Muñoz affair, see Ribb, "José Tomás Canales," 162–71.

171. Canales to Hobby, December 12, 1918, in RFI, 888–890.

172. The text of the bill as slightly amended by committee appears in House Journal, 163–64.

173. The information for the original HB 5 and amendments derives from "Bill File," 36th Leg., Reg. Sess. (1919), Legislative Papers, TSL [hereafter, HB 5 and BF]. The bill called for the following raises: captain, from $125 to $150; sergeant, $60 to $100; and private, $50 to $75. For current salaries, see General and Special Laws of Texas, 35th Leg., First Called Sess. (1917) (Austin: A.C. Baldwin, 1917), Chap. 36, 57, (based on SB 28) [hereafter, 1917 Law].

174. HB 5; see also, *House Journal*, 36th Leg., Reg. Sess., (1919), 163, 168, and 199.

175. The legislation governing the Ranger Force was HB 52, 27th Leg., Reg. Sess. (1901), or Chap. 34, Gammel, *Laws of Texas*, vol. 9, 745–47 [hereafter, 1901 Law]. The force strength hovered around sixteen men from 1911 until 1915, and then grew to no more than forty regular Rangers at any given time between July 1915 and July 1916, the most violent period along the border. Emergency legislation creating a "Home Guard" in May 1917 authorized the governor to appoint up to one thousand additional Rangers to serve with all the duties and benefits of the regular Rangers. Between September 1917, when he assumed office, and December 1918, Hobby tripled the number of paid Rangers to 127, all of whom operated as regular Rangers. In setting reduced levels for the force, Canales attempted to return the force to its level before the Border War and World War I.

176. Three reporters from the *Dallas Morning News*, three from the *San Antonio Express*, two from the *Austin Statesman*, and an unknown number from the *Brownsville Daily Herald, La Prensa* (San Antonio), *El Imparcial* (San Antonio), and other newspapers covered HB 5 and the hearings; see *Austin Statesman*, January 14, 1919, 3.

177. All references are from the report as printed in the *House Journal*, 36th Leg., Reg. Sess., 536–39.

178. The report did not mention that the committee had ruled early in the proceedings that it had no jurisdiction regarding the adjutant general's behavior.

179. Hanson to Blackwell (emphasis added), Harley to Knight, and Harley to Moses (telegs.), February 19, 1919, AGGC.

180. Hanson to J. J. Thornham, February 14, 1919. Thornham, County Judge of Willacy, received thanks for sending unspecified "files" to Hanson during the hearings, AGGC.

181. Chapa testified that Ranger W. B. Bentley, who had just attempted to pistol-whip his waiter in a San Antonio restaurant, was drunk when he threatened him at his drugstore near the scene. Again, Harley discharged the Ranger after learning of an incident from a prominent supporter, Chapa Testimony, RFI, 216–17. Bentley's attack on a waiter was the basis for Canales's Charge Eight. The only defense the Rangers offered was that Bentley had been discharged the week before.

182. See Ribb, "José Tomás Canales," chapter 3.

183. Adj. Gen. W. D. Cope to Fred Marks, March 13, 1920, AGGC, refers to the "understanding." Cope followed Harley as Adjutant General in September 1919. This letter is marked "X F. A. Chapa," which probably indicates that a copy was sent to Chapa. One aspect of the agreement was that Marks lived and worked out of San Antonio, where Chapa lived and Hanson kept his office. For Mark's Ranger career, see his Service Record, Adjutant General's Papers, TSA. Marks enlisted as a Loyalty Ranger; see below for details of this service, on July 11, 1918. The "Special Ranger" Enlistment Oath carries the notation "OK WMH [William M. Hanson]" on the front. On the back appears the notation "Cancelled Mr. Marks now in the Regular Force 10/23/18 Hanson." He joined the regular Force on October 21, 1918, according to his second Enlistment Oath, where he listed his residence as 618 Frost Building, San Antonio, Hanson's office address. Marks reenlisted on June 20, 1919, but his termination date does not appear in the records.

184. See telegram Marks to "Samson" at the "Adjutant General's Dept.," October 7, 1918, in Hobby Papers, TSA, and Hanson to Harley, October 10, 1918, recounting the message, Webb Papers, CAH.

185. Chapa frequently visited Hanson's office to update his information and strategy; see his testimony in RFI, 209. As De la Rosa continued to evade Marks, Chapa provided new incentive for his capture. Marks wrote "confidentially" to W. D. Cope, the new adjutant general, that "a friend of mine" (almost certainly Chapa) had offered to pay $500 for the delivery of De la Rosa—alive in Texas. Marks was "very anxious" to proceed with his plan of using a Mexican informant from the other side to bring De la Rosa across; Marks to Cope, January 5, 1920, AGGC.

186. Chapa to Hobby (teleg.), April 2, 1920, AGGC.

187. Marks, ebullient, informed Ranger Quartermaster R. W. Aldrich that he was

returning to Rio Grande City in search of the elusive De la Rosa, whom he never captured despite tailing him deep into Mexico; Marks to Aldrich, April 14, 1920, AGGC.

188. In December 1918, for instance, Chapa, after hearing that De la Rosa was living in Camargo, opposite Rio Grande City, notified Hobby that Marks should go at once to try to lure De la Rosa back across the river; December 30, 1918, AGGC.

189. Lackey to Hobby, May 2, 1919, 579/19. See also, Sen. Edgar C. Witt to Hobby, April 30, 1919, 579/16, AGGC.

190. *Hanson testimony, Investigation of Mexican Affairs,* 3223–47.

191. *Hanson testimony, Investigation of Mexican Affairs,* 3308. For his service to Mexico as a spy, see chapter 4.

192. *Hanson testimony, Investigation of Mexican Affairs,* 3223–49.

193. Albert Fall, "Partial Report," in *Mexican Affairs,* 3325.

194. Fall, "Partial Report," in *Mexican Affairs,* 3373.

195. Hanson to John Hunnicutt, March 30, 1921, 2–22/673/"Personal correspondence, 1921," J. R. Hunnicutt Papers, TSA.

196. Jeannette H. Flachmeier, "Harry McCleod Wurzbach," NHBTX, 6, 1095.

197. Hanson to John Hunnicutt, March 30, 1921, 2–22/673/"Personal correspondence, 1921," J. R. Hunnicutt Papers, TSA.

198. Hanson to Aldrich, January 28, 1925, 3P157/3, Aldrich, CAH.

The Mexican Revolution, *Revolución de Texas,* and *Matanza de 1915*

TRINIDAD GONZALES

The headline in the *Brownsville Herald* for October 18, 1915, announced the U.S. government's intention to recognize Venustiano Carranza, the First Chief of the Mexican Constitutional forces, as Mexico's legitimate leader the following day. At 10:45 P.M. that night, a band of México Texano and Mexicano revolutionaries in a well-organized military operation derailed the St. Louis, Brownsville & Mexico 101 six-and-a-half miles outside of Brownsville.[1] Luis De la Rosa, chief military leader of the *revolución de Texas,* led the raid. Three people were killed by the attack. Engineer H. H. Kendall was pinned under the train's engine, while raiders shot and killed Corporal McBee, 3rd Cavalry, and Dr. E. S. McCain, deputy state health officer. Rebels targeted U.S. military personal in particular and shouted, "*¡Viva Pizaña, Viva Carranza!*" as they robbed ethnic white passengers.[2] The following day, local and state law enforcement along with civilian paramilitary killed nine Mexicans in retaliation for the attack. Cameron County Sheriff W. T. Vann reported that five of the nine men killed were from a village twenty miles away from the location of the train derailment, suggesting they were not involved with the raid. Five other men were arrested and held in the Cameron County jail after being interrogated by U.S. Marshal, E. T. Herring.[3]

There is no better example of the Mexican Revolution directly affecting the lives of Mexicans living in Texas than the events surrounding the *revolución de Texas* of 1915. However, questions concerning the nature and origins of the *revolución* and the *matanza* (massacre) that resulted as a backlash from the revolt in the Lower Rio Grande Valley continue. Contemporaries labeled rebels as "bandits" or "Plan-de-San Diegoistas." These were English language labels. Spanish language labels likewise included the term *bandidos,* but also *sediciosos* (seditionists). Both *sedicioso* and *San Diegoistas* indicated a political motive for the attacks. The different labels reflected both the confusion of what was occurring and the biases of those that utilized them. The use of "bandit" reflected both a misunderstanding of rebel activities and the desire to deny such activities as political acts. The use of *sedicioso* and *San Diegoistas* reflected an understanding of rebel activities as politically motivated. Two conspiracy theories for rebel activities were circulated at the time. First, some suggested that the motive was a capitalist cabal's effort to force a U.S. invasion of Mexico by linking Carranza to the raids, or at the least to deny Carranza's recognition. An explanation that developed during World War I was that German agents caused the revolt in an effort to distract the United States from the war in Europe. Some contemporaries actually viewed the *revolución de Texas* as what it purported to be, a rebellion against the United States.[4]

The purpose of this essay is to examine the relationship between the Mexican Revolution and the *revolución de Texas.* The two primary historiographic debates concerning the revolt rest on whether it was external or indigenous, and whether it was a political movement or a simple reactionary response to a harsher environment. Charles H. Harris III and Louis R. Sadler are the primary proponents for the view that Carranza supported the revolt for the purpose of forcing U.S. recognition—that is, external effort. However, most historians of the topic generally agree that the revolt was an indigenous campaign. All but one historian agree that the revolt was reactionary in nature. Those that believe the revolt represented a reactionary response tend to view Mexicans as pastoral people with underdeveloped politically ideologies. James Sandos is the only historian among this group to examine the ideological reasons for the revolt—a political movement. He argues that the *revolución* was anarchist inspired. Instead, I argue the revolt was an indigenous liberal movement to reclaim a part of *México perdido* (lost Mexico) by *México Texanos* and *Mexicanos* whose lives straddled the Rio Grande/*río bravo,* a river that became an international boundary as a result of U.S. conquest.[5]

There are two primary factors that historians exempt from the discussion of the *revolución de Texas.* First, Mexicans who lived in the Lower Rio Grande Valley and northern Mexico from the nineteenth to early twentieth century predominantly embraced Mexican liberalism as a worldview. Minimal scholarship exists about the intellectual and ideological history of Mexicans of the Lower Rio Grande Valley, in particular the force with which liberalism was embraced and sustained through educational institutions.[6] Instead, historians operate from a pastoral paradigm for interpreting Mexican history for the area. Thus, the pastoral paradigm becomes the foundation for viewing the revolt as a reactionary effort by politically unaware and illiterate Mexicans.[7] Second, the Mexican Revolution is usually discussed as an inspirational factor for the revolt or, in the case of Harris and Sadler, as Carranza directly orchestrating it. The problem is that little or no clear military analysis of the Mexican Revolution's unfolding during 1915 has been undertaken for contextualizing its relationship to the *revolución de Texas.* In taking into account Mexicans embracing liberalism and their literacy rates, an understanding of the *revolución de Texas* as a political movement becomes clearer. A simultaneous military analysis of the unfolding of the Mexican Revolution and the *revolución de Texas* helps provide an understanding of the complex relationship between both.

Brief History of the Lower Rio Grande Valley from Spanish Settlements to Occupied Mexico

The Lower Rio Grande Valley currently consists of the four counties of Willacy, Cameron, Hidalgo and Starr along the southern tip of the Texas–Mexico border along the Rio Grande/*río bravo.* The Spanish settled both sides of the river during the 1740s. José de Escandón led the settlers, who founded the cities of Camargo, Reynosa, Matamoros, and Guerrero Viejo on the south side of the river, and San Ygnacio and Laredo on the north side. The communities were known as the *villas del norte* for Nuevo Santander.[8] After the War of Independence (1810–1821), the Mexican government renamed Nuevo Santander, Tamaulipas. The Texas War of Secession (1836) from Mexico did not disrupt the lives of people living along the river.[9] Although the Republic of Texas claimed the Nueces strip, the area between the Rio Grande/*río bravo* and the Nueces, it was too weak militarily to occupy it. Not until the United States invaded the disputed territory, causing the War of North American Aggression (1846), did the Nueces strip leave Mexico's control. The signing of the Treaty of Guadalupe Hidalgo (1848) ended the war but began U.S. colonization of conquered Mexicans. The colonization process lasted till the early twentieth century and was one of the primary structural factors that caused the *revolución de Texas*. Thus, the revolt should be understood as a colonial rebellion.

There were three primary phases to U.S. colonization of Mexicans from the Lower Rio Grande Valley from 1848 to 1930. The period from 1848 to 1904 represented a power sharing relationship between Mexicans and old-timers (ethnic whites who settled in the area prior to 1904) that David Montejano labeled as a peace structure. The period from 1904 to 1915 represented an acceleration of the colonization process as newcomers (ethnic whites who settled in the area after 1904) challenged the relationships between Mexicans and old-timers. By the 1910s, segregation and increased discrimination against Mexicans began replacing the peace structure. The *revolución de Texas* resulted in large part due to this structural change. The period from 1916 to 1930 represented the final incorporation of descendents of defeated Mexicans into the United States.

To understand the Mexican Revolution's effect on the Mexican community of the Lower Rio Grande Valley, it is important to take into account the socioeconomic and political history of the area. Nuevo Santander was settled by business interests. An early capitalist worldview imbued the mindset of colonists and further developed during the Bourbon Reforms. The people from the *villas del norte* later fully expressed this early capitalist worldview through liberalism both during and after the Mexican War of Independence (1810–1821). Liberalism is the view that individuals should be free economic players in a safe environment within a democratic form of limited government that respects the natural rights of individuals.[10] Mexican liberalism developed from both U.S. and French revolutionary ideals. A clear example of the continuance of Mexican liberal views during the early twentieth century is found within the speeches of *El Primer Congreso Mexicanista* (1911), when Mexicans discussed issues related to discrimination and violence against their community. Presenters advocated such solutions as increasing educational access, exhibiting a *gente decente* behavior, and organizing to lobby against discrimination. With the exception of one speaker, no presenter advocated a systemic dismantling of the democratic-capitalistic system found in the United States. Indeed, the overall theme was that Mexicans should be embraced as equals in such a world because they too were *gente decente* like ethnic whites.[11]

Educational institutions helped maintain Mexican liberalism and na tionalism within the community. The four primary educational institutions found in the Lower Rio Grande Valley during the early twentieth century included religious schools, ranch schools, the private Mexican schools, and public schools.[12] The first three institutions operated from a Mexican perspective, whereas the latter operated in a hybrid form, incorporating a U.S.-centered Americanism, in dealing with a predominantly Spanish-speaking student body. Both public and private educational efforts within the area are traceable to 1796. The importance of education within the community, in particular the ability to read and write, was not a late-nineteenth- or early-twentieth-century phenomenon.[13] By the turn of the twentieth century, religious schools, ranch schools, and private Mexican schools dominated the educational landscape, with Mexican nationalism as an important part of the curriculum.[14]

The census for 1900 and 1910 provides evidence of Spanish-language literacy rates for the Lower Rio Grande Valley.[15] These rates do not determine the ethnic breakdown for persons who were literate. However, the Mexican demographic dominance, the community's commitment to education, and wide circulation of Spanish-language newspapers, strengthens the accuracy of census data.[16] In 1900, the literacy rate for the total population of the Lower Rio Grande Valley was 61 percent, and 72 percent in 1910. The evidence leaves little doubt of the Mexican community's commitment to education, particularly literacy in Spanish.[17] Unfortunately, some historical studies continue the distortion of an illiterate and uneducated Mexican community.[18] Thus, it was a literate community committed to liberal ideals undergoing a harsher phase of U.S. colonization that shaped the lives of Mexicans during the early twentieth century. Mexican nationalism and a weakly policed southern border from which to launch and retreat from raids further help explain the sustained strength of the *revolución.*

The Complex Nexus among the *Plan de San Diego, Revolución de Texas,* and Carranza's Constitutionalists

One sentiment links the authors of the *Plan de San Diego,* insurgents of the *revolución de Texas,* and the Constitutionalists—anti-Yankeeism. The first two movements expressed a desire to return Mexico *perdido* to Mexico, and the Constitutionalists were motivated by the need for Mexico to belong once again to Mexicanos. However, although the leaders and followers of these three movements shared an anti-Yankeeism, that does not mean they always cooperated with each other or shared the same military or political objectives. At different times, their respective objectives coincided or conflicted.

The primary link that contemporaries and historians cite as connecting the *Plan de San Diego* to the *revolución de Texas* centers on Basilio Ramos Jr. Ramos was arrested in McAllen while recruiting members to join the *Plan de San Diego* during January 1915. Because insurgency attacks occurred six months after the Ramos arrest, the tendency has been to tie the *Plan de San Diego* with the *revolución de Texas*. However, the authors of the *Plan de San Diego* manifestos and the *revolución de Texas* manifesto are different. A link does develop between the leaders of these movements by November as a consequence of Carranza's forces clearing the Mexican side of *revolución de Texas* insurgents, according to U.S. military intelligence sources.[19] However, one document does exist tying the *Plan de San Diego* and the *revolución de Texas* movements together, but that evidence at this point needs further evaluation.[20]

The *Huertista* authors of the *Plan de San Diego* signed the manifesto while in a *Carrancista* jail in Monterrey during the early part of January 1915. The signers were released during the middle of January. Augustín S. de la Garza, one of the signers, was named commander of the Liberating Army for Races and People.[21] De la Garza is the person most associated with the *Plan de San Diego*. Ramos, a signer, went to Texas to find supporters. He was supposed to seek help from the *Carrancista* general in Matamoros, General Emiliano P. Nafarrate, as well.[22] While in McAllen, Ramos attempted to recruit Andrés Villarreal and Deodoro Guerra, *Villistas*. Instead, Villarreal and Guerra laid a trap for Ramos. Hidalgo County sheriff's officers arrested Ramos and turned him over to federal authorities. The plan called for a Mexican armed uprising to begin on February 20, but nothing happened. Ramos was eventually released from jail on bond in May, after which he fled to Mexico.[23]

While Ramos was in a Brownsville jail, a second *Plan de San Diego* manifesto, *¡A Los Pueblos Oprimidos de América!,* was signed on February 20, with aliases that helped hide the identity of the signers. With the exception of de la Garza, the signers of the second manifesto were not the same as the signers of the first manifesto.[24] Sandos argues that the authors of the *Plan de San Diego* manifestos organized the *revolución de Texas,* an anarchist revolt inspired by Ricardo Flores Magón's *Partido Liberal Mexicano.* However, there is no evidence to link de la Garza, the one constant person associated with the *Plan de San Diego* manifestos, to Magón or the *Partido*

Liberal Mexicano. De la Garza's link to Huerta is clear. When the United States occupied Veracruz, de la Garza offered to supply two hundred men to Huerta to fight against the occupying marines.[25] It is unlikely that de la Garza, a *Huertista,* was connected to Flores Magón, an anarchist.[26]

The self-proclaimed and widely accepted leaders of the *revolución de Texas,* Luis De la Rosa and Aniceto Pizaña, issued their signed manifesto, *A Nuestros Compatriotas, Los Mexicanos en Texas,* on August 26.[27] Fully aware of the *Plan de San Diego* manifestoes, De la Rosa and Pizaña did not refer to the earlier documents or to de la Garza. Although there is no evidence that De la Rosa and Pizaña worked with de la Garza during the beginning of military operations, evidence does exist that shows Pizaña and particularly De la Rosa later joined with de la Garza by November 1915. That alliance occurred as a result of *Carrancistas* securing the Mexican side of the border in late October; the accord eliminated insurgent safe havens and effectively ended the revolt. The coming together of De la Rosa, Pizaña, and de la Garza by late October occurred from necessity.

Sandos does substantiate a link between Pizaña and De la Rosa to Flores Magón and the *Partido Liberal Mexicano.* Pizaña received *Regeneración,* Flores Magón's anarchist newspaper, and corresponded with him and other *Partido Liberal Mexicano* leaders.[28] Américo Paredes also provides evidence of the two groups' connection. Paredes stated in an interview with Ramón Saldívar, his biographer, that his uncle Eduardo Manzano was contacted by the Flores Magón brothers to find out why Pizaña failed to begin an anarchist revolt in Mexico. The Flores Magóns apparently sent funds to Pizaña and De la Rosa for this purpose. According to Manzano, Pizaña instead used the funds slated for a Mexican anarchist revolt to fund the *revolución de Texas.*[29] Eventually, Flores Magón dismissed the *revolución de Texas* in an October issue of *Regeneración* as a reactionary response by exploited Mexicans.[30] Sandos argues that Flores Magón failed to recognize the *revolución de Texas* as an anarchist revolt because "it was not as beautiful as expected. Perhaps Ricardo could not recognize an anarchist struggle with which he had not personally been involved."[31] Another explanation for Flores Magón's dismissal is that he was probably disappointed in Pizaña and De la Rosa for failing to deliver an anarchist revolt in Mexico and because their manifesto cannot in any manner be construed as an anarchist document.

In their manifesto, Pizaña and De la Rosa asked, "How does one remain indifferent and accepting of such civil abuses (referring to Texas Ranger and ethnic white abuses against Mexicans)? How does one allow discriminatory offenses against our people? Or has our deep humanity and patriotism dissipated? No! It slumbers but it is easily wakened."[32] Clearly, the call to take up arms was based on the need to stop ethnic white abuses against Mexicans and not to begin an anarchist revolution. The manifesto continues, "Enough with patience, enough with suffering insults and disdain, we are men conscious of our acts, we know how to think just like them, 'the *gringos*,' we desire to be free and we will be free and we are sufficiently sophisticated and strong enough to choose our leaders and we will make it happen."[33] The call to action was a desire to be free like "*gringos*" and to choose their own leaders. Indeed, the point is that Mexicans and ethnic whites shared the same desires for freedom and abilities to govern themselves. To further illustrate the liberal nature of the revolt, the flag used by the revolutionaries utilized the symbol of a Mexican eagle with a French liberty cap atop its head. A burst of Enlightenment sun rays emanates from the cap. The tricolor Mexican flag was used with this image located in the center. The use of the French symbols on the rebels' flag was not merely an accident; it was a common symbol found on the tail's side of Mexican pesos during the early part of the twentieth century. Thus, the revolutionaries used French symbols of liberalism to connect their movement to such ideals and to tap into Mexican discursive awareness of liberalism so common that such symbols were found on their coins.[34]

The Carranza link to the *revolución de Texas* rests primarily with General Emiliano P. Nafarrate, commander of the *Carrancistas* in the Matamoros district. Nafarrate apparently granted Ramos a Constitutional safe pass that was seized by U.S. federal authorities. It was this pass that was used as evidence for linking him to the *Plan de San Diego*. De la Garza did advise Ramos to contact Nafarrate for support, but it is unclear if they met. Nafarrate vehemently denied supporting the *Plan* and stated publicly to the local press that he provided documented information to J. H. Johnson, U.S. consul in Matamoros, about a possible Mexican filibuster movement in the United States prior to Ramos's arrest in late January. The *Carrancista* general learned of this possible movement after Constitutionalists arrested Ramos, a known *Huertista*, sometime during the middle of January. However, Ramos was released at some point and entered the United States. There is no explanation provided concerning Ramos's release. Whatever happened, Ramos made his way to McAllen and was arrested. Johnson confirmed Nafarrate had nothing to do with the *Plan de San Diego* and supported his denial. Nafarrate also pointed out in his defense that those that arrested Ramos were *Villistas* and probably wanted to discredit him to U.S. authorities.[35]

The other argument linking Carranza to the revolt was Nafarrate's failure to clear his side of the border of insurgents and prevent some of his men from participating in the rebellion. Harris and Sadler argue that if Carranza had desired the raids to stop, he could have done so at will, but only chose to do so after U.S. recognition. It is clear that insurgents staged many of their operations from the Mexican side of the border and that Carranza officers and men participated in the *revolución de Texas* either by going on raids or through providing covering fire from the Mexican side of the Rio Grande/*río bravo* for insurgents retreating from the U.S. military. What is also clear is that Carranza probably did not sanction such activities because to do so would have been detrimental to his relationship to the United States, which was supplying him with arms and preventing arms from reaching his enemies. It is also clear that Constitutional forces in the Matamoros district were too small to secure the border. Even with four thousand troops supported by law enforcement and paramilitary groups, the insurgents at times seemed to operate freely on the U.S. side of the border.

Military Phase of the Mexican Revolution and the *Revolución de Texas*

The connection between the Mexican Revolution and the *revolución de Texas* cannot be understood without familiarity with U.S. relationships to the different warring factions in Mexico and how the Mexican Revolution progressed from 1914 through 1915. As already stated, the *revolución de Texas* originated from the process of U.S. colonization of Mexicans who shared the same liberal values as their conquerors. The sparks that led to the revolt were Mexicans' declining sociopolitical power and law enforcement officers killing them. The killings clearly were a direct violation of how the state was to act according to liberal understandings of a civil society, a breach the leaders of the *revolución de Texas* expressed in their manifesto as a reason to revolt.

There are three key factors for understanding the military circumstances of the *revoluctión de Texas*. First, the weakly policed southern side of the border as a result of the Mexican Revolution provided a location to launch and retreat from raids. This weakness developed from the fact that Carranza's forces did not completely control the Mexican side and his military organization did not operate in a U.S. disciplined manner of command and control. The loose exercise of control over Constitutional officers and men helps explain their participation or aid in raids despite Carranza's orders against such activity.[36] Second, insurgents found a support network among the predominant Mexican population on both sides of the border. This does not mean all Mexicans supported the revolt, but enough did so that military and law enforcement personal felt frustrated in their efforts to stop insurgents. Third, the physical environment, brush land, and a thorough knowledge of the area by rebels allowed for successfully evading capture on many occasions. Most Mexicans were not killed in battle but instead while they were in local, state, or civilian custody. Many killed were likely innocent, and such killings helped perpetuate the rebellion. Other factors that facilitated the insurgency included the arms trade that developed as a result of the Mexican Revolution and the participation of military-experienced México Texano and Mexicano soldiers who participated in that revolution.

The U.S. occupation of Veracruz on April 21, 1914, marked a turning point for the Mexican Revolution. Constitutional forces were already receiving arms, ammunition, and supplies secretly from the United States via Brownsville/Matamoros prior to the occupation. Despite this aid, Carranza's opponents pushed his forces to Veracruz. After taking the port city, the United States took control of the large stockpiles of arms, ammunition, and supplies stored there and diverted shipments of arms away from Carranza's opponents. Through the rest of 1914, Carranza and the Constitutionalists reorganized and rearmed under the guidance of the U.S. military at Vera Cruz. Carranza received this assistance from the United States based on his commitment to protecting private property rights, including those of foreigners. Eventually, the marines left Veracruz on November 23, 1914, leaving a vast arsenal to Carranza's Constitutionalists.[37]

Locally pro-*Villistas* in Hidalgo County were organizing a 150-man invasion force composed of former *Huertista* officers and men to take Reynosa during late November and early December. The Villa and Carranza alliance was already broken by late 1914. *Villistas* planned a campaign to take the cities of Mier, Reynosa, and Matamoros as a move toward controlling strategic points of entry from the United States. But the U.S. military prevented the invasion of Reynosa from Hidalgo County by arresting several *Villistas* as well as preventing them from receiving arms.[38] After these events occurred in November, Ramos was arrested in late January 1915, when he approached *Villistas* in McAllen. Constitutional forces captured Mexico City in January, though by early March they had retreated from the capital.

Although the *Villistas'* effort led by Mexicans in Hidalgo County failed to materialize in late 1914, *Villistas* took control of Mier and Reynosa by late March of 1915. Their early success rested on their larger numbers. When the *Villistas* launched their attack to capture Matamoros on March 27, their forces numbered four thousand versus thirteen hundred for the *Carrancistas.* However, the defenders utilized superior weapons and tactics to decimate the larger *Villista* force. The United States continued to prevent vital military supplies from reaching the *Villistas.* The Constitutionalists continued to receive a steady supply of arms from Brownsville, where Nafarrate was allowed to store them for safekeeping. Eventually, the *Villistas* retreated from the area, and the *Carrancistas* retook Reynosa and Mier with their limited numbers.[39]

During this period of warfare on the Mexican side, the anticipated *Plan de San Diego* uprising never materialized. Peace prevailed in the Lower Rio Grande Valley. However, newcomers increasingly became paranoid as a result of their demographic minority status and the military clashes occurring across the border. A U.S. military commander complained, "The apparently unwarranted uneasiness of the white people is the most annoying condition at the present time."[40] Ethnic white paranoia eventually exploded into the killing of Mexicans.

It was not until July that a band of either bandits or insurgents led a posse of law enforcement officers and some soldiers on a three-week chase through the brush country of Cameron County. It is unclear from both media reports and military dispatches whether this band was related to rebel activities. Even the number of the band and whether different units were being confused as a single band was not determined. In one case, the killing of an eighteen-year-old ethnic white male was originally reported as bandit activity, but the Cameron County sheriff later indicated that the killing was a personal matter. July was a confusing month for authorities concerning whether violent activities were banditry or the beginning of an organized military movement. The U.S. military commander's opinion was that it was banditry, whereas local ethnic whites viewed these activities with greater alarm. After three fruitless weeks, the posse eventually disbanded for a lack of success. The Mexican bandits or insurgents were never captured.

The inability to capture the band during July coupled with ethnic white paranoia contributed to the beginning process of killing suspected

Mexican criminals by law enforcement officers and vigilantes. Lorenzo Manríquez and Gregorio Manríquez were killed while in law enforcement custody on July 24. They were suspected of thievery. The *Brownsville Herald* stated in relation to these killings, "Stealing in this section has been going on for some time and now the farmers and town people are organized and will administer swift punishment to any thief caught."[41] On July 29, Rodolfo Muñiz, suspected of killing a San Benito ethnic white merchant, was being transported to Brownsville from San Benito at night by local law enforcement officers, when eight vigilantes seized and then lynched him.[42] These three killings represented the beginning of the *matanza* of 1915.

The first clear *revolución de Texas* activity, in retrospect, was the burning of a train bridge thirty-two miles north of Sebastian on July 26. The engineer of the St. Louis, Brownsville & Mexico train saw smoke coming from the burning bridge in time to stop and prevent a wreck. Insurgents cut telephone and telegraph wires in the area to disrupt communications as well, a clear sign of a thought-out military operation.[43] However, the local U.S. military commander did not believe there was a "political purpose" to this attack.[44] Railroad officials also dismissed the act as "malicious mischief" because the train lacked both money and passengers to rob.[45] By early August, though, a *Brownsville Herald* editorial presented speculation that the stealing of material such as horses, saddles, and weapons necessary for conducting military operations in the area and the burning of train bridges (a second was burned on August 2) pointed to a likely "filibuster movement."[46] The beginning of the *revolución de Texas* was underway, but the military did not recognize it. It is not clear to what extent Mexicans were aware of the beginning of the revolt, but a large segment of newcomers at this point generally suspected all Mexicans as bandits.

Meanwhile, Constitutional forces retook Mexico City in July, and Carranza entered the city on August 2. The *Carrancistas* defeated *Villistas* in the two battles of Celaya (April 4–10 and 13–15) and the battle of León (April–June 3). Villa's forces never regained their formidability because of the large casualties suffered from these losses. Carranza and the Constitutional forces became the dominant military power in Mexico by August, but this did not mean that Villa and Zapata were done. The Constitutional forces continued to conduct military operations against them during the rest of 1915 and 1916 in an effort to secure the nation. Carranza continued to have his hands full during the fall of 1915, and he still needed U.S. military supplies as well as the United States to continue its arms embargo against Villa and Zapata. To support the *revolución de Texas* would not have been in his interest at this point. The Mexican Revolution was not over for Carranza.

Revolución de Texas raids continued to increase during August, with the most famous attack occurring against the King Ranch's Norias division headquarters on August 8. The raid marked a turning point for Mexican public opinion, as they began to show increased signs of supporting the insurgency, particularly after the release of photos of dead insurgents from the raid. These photos displayed bodies of lassoed and mutilated Mexicans that Texas Rangers dragged through the brush. The Rangers sat mounted on their horses, posing as though they were exhibiting the carcasses of trophy animals recently killed.[47] The disrespect shown the slain insurgents coupled with the recent killings of Mexicans at the hands of law enforcement officers and others ignited the violence that followed.

Supervising immigration inspector F. W. Berkshire, who was sent to the Lower Rio Grande from Washington to investigate the revolt, pointed out both the photos' effect on the Mexican community and how law enforcement officers treated Mexicans. He stated in his report that "the civil officers in the disturbed territory may have over-stepped the bounds of propriety and perhaps have been unintentionally the indirect cause at least of the more critical situation which followed and exists at this time." He continued: "Photograph No. 2 (referring to the photo of Texas Rangers displaying dead Mexicans as trophies) was reduced to the size of a postal card and copies thereof distributed throughout that part of Mexico lying South [sic] of Brownsville and it appears that this did more perhaps than anything else to incite the Mexicans against the Americans."[48] By August 26, Luis De la Rosa and Aniceto Pizaña issued their manifesto, *A Nuestros Compatriotas, Los Mexicanos en Texas*. A ripe audience of angry Mexicans probably stood ready to listen and participate.

Insurgent attacks continued through September and early October, with several incidents of U.S. forces and *Carrancistas* engaging in cross-border firing at each other. By September 30, an additional fifteen hundred Constitutional troops were sent to Matamoros specifically to police the river's edge and to stop *revolución de Texas* rebels from launching raids. This was a reversal of policy. *Carrancista* General Alvaro Obregón ordered Nafarrate to move Constitutional forces away from the river to avoid further fire fights with U.S. troops, for Carranza awaited U.S. recognition. However, Obregón soon reordered troops to the river.[49] But because Nafarrate continued to be viewed with suspicion in regards to his relationship to the *revolución de Texas,* he was replaced by General Eugenio López, who arrived with an additional three hundred troops by October 3.[50] No insurgent attacks occurred from López's arrival until the train derailment on October 18, the day the *Brownsville Herald* announced that the United States planned to recognize Carranza the following day.[51]

The *revolución de Texas* came to an end about this point in time. De la Rosa and Pizaña fled from the Mexico border, and according to U.S. military reports, both were working with de la Garza by late October, following U.S. recognition of Carranza.[52] It is uncertain how many Mexicans supported the insurgency, but enough did so from both sides of the border to have sustained rebel activities for a few months. Between July and October, the military along with local and state law enforcement agencies responded to the movement. Newcomers organized themselves into paramilitary groups and lobbied different government representatives for increased law enforcement and military personal. There were various Mexican responses to the *revolución* and *matanza.* Many fled to the Mexican side of the border. Others engaged in distancing themselves from the insurgents either through public demonstrations of support for the suppression of the rebels or by actively patrolling the border to help track raiders for the U.S. military.[53] José T. Canales, the state representative who would head an investigation into Ranger atrocities by 1919, organized the local Mexican scouts. All these events occurred during the unfolding of the Mexican Revolution and while the United States continued to support Carranza.

Harris and Sadler argue that the *Plan de San Diego* and the *revolución de Texas* were the same movement, and that Carranza orchestrated the raids as an effort to force the United States to recognize him. They maintain that the raids stopped when the United States recognized Carranza with the exception of last train derailment and two other ambushes, and that *Carrancistas* partook in the *revolución.* The last three attacks they dismiss as "frustration" by insurgents because Carranza "pull(ed) the rug out from under them."[54] There are three problems with this position. First, the United States was already supporting Carranza seven to eight months prior to the beginning of the *revolución de Texas.* In essence, the United States gave de facto recognition to him not based on his militarily superior position in late 1914 (he was being pushed to the brink by Villa and Zapata), but because of his policy of protecting private property rights, including those of foreigners. Carranza certainly desired U.S. official recognition, but he did not need to begin an insurgency on American soil to achieve that end. Second, the *Carrancista* force at Matamoros was too small to effectively police its side of the border. Harris and Sadler assume Carranza could have ended the raids at any time. It was the arrival of more troops in early October 1915 that ended the raids. Certainly Carranza wanted to end the attacks to facilitate official recognition, but to portray that effort without acknowledging that the United States was already strongly supporting the Constitutional forces is problematic. Also, by October Carranza was in a better military position to assume the task of policing the border. Third, the Constitutionalist army was a revolutionary military force with the lack of discipline and order that usually accompany such units. That *Carrancistas* partook or supported the *revolución de Texas* should not be surprising. For instance, several soldiers that arrived with López were recruited for the last trail derailment and attacks. These soldiers went on the raids because they were paid, the motive many men of arms throughout history have followed.[55] Harris and Sadler operate from the assumption that Carranza had a command and control structure of his military forces that the current U.S. military enjoys. He did not. The Harris–Sadler thesis does not appear to hold up against the complexity of the events that surrounded the *revolución de Texas* and the Mexican Revolution.

Matanza

There is no accurate number concerning the killing of Mexicans during the period of the *revolución de Texas*. Estimates range from three hundred to five thousand. What is clear is that the *matanza* has not received the same attention by scholars as the revolt. In part, the reason for this lack of attention by scholars is the limited evidence that is available for research. Better attempts at uncovering the history of the *matanza* is needed not simply to advance the scholarship, but to provide a historical voice to those that were the victims of extra legal killings. What follows is an early effort to provide an analysis of the *matanza* based on the current evidence available.[56]

There are two extant lists of the names and locations of Mexicans killed. Frank C. Pierce, a son of a former U.S. Consul, kept one list, while Jesse Pérez, a Texas Ranger, kept another. Both cited seventy-six killings. Not listed in these two documents was the killing of thirty Mexicans in Alamo. The total number of Mexicans killed according to contemporary sources was 106 (see table). The height of the killings occurred during August and September, with seventy-six and thirty-six killed, respectively.

Table: Incomplete List of Names, Locations, and Dates of Mexicans Killed

		July 1915
Lorenzo Manríquez	Mercedes Canal	July 24, 1915
Gregorio Manríquez	Mercedes	July 24, 1915
Rodolfo Muñiz	near San Benito	July 29, 1915
		August 1915
Desiderio Flores (father)	Armendaiz Ranch	August 4, 1915
Desiderio Flores (son)	Armendaiz Ranch	August 4, 1915
Antonio Flores	Armendaiz Ranch	August 4, 1915
Jesús García	Norias Raid	August 8, 1915
Mauricio Gracía	Norias Raid	August 8, 1915
Amado Muñoz	Norias Raid	August 8, 1915
Muñoz's brother	Norias Raid	August 8, 1915
Ernesto Ramos	near Sebastian	August 10, 1915
Juan N. Rodríguez	near Sebastian	August 10, 1915
Guadalupe Treviño	Mercedes	August 15, 1915
Andrés Villanueva Zamora	Mercedes	August 16, 1915
Tomás Aguilar	near Lyford	August 19, 1915
José M. Cavazos	Lyford	August 1915
Thirty killed	Alamo	August 1915
		September 1915
Ventura Longoria	near San Benito	September 13, 1915
Daniel Longoria	near San Benito	September 13, 1915
Felipe Falcón	Cavazos Crossing	September 17, 1915
Refugio Pérez	Lyford	September 17, 1915
Alberto Cantú	Lyford	September 17, 1915
Martina Rivas (girl, 14 yrs)	near Los Fresnos	September 22, 1915[1]
Senovio Rivas (father)	near Los Frensos	September 22, 1915
Jesús Bazán	near Del Fina	September 1915
Antonio Longoria	near Del Fina	September 1915
Five killed	McAllen Ranch Raid	September 24, 1915[2]
Jesús Pérez	Ojo de Agua fight	September 1915
Margarita Buenrostro	near Lyford	September 1915
Alejos Vela	near Harlingen	September 1915
Angel Rincones	near Harlingen	September 1915
Ignacio Rivera	near Harlingen	September 1915
Fourteen killed	near Donna	September 1915
Catarine Rodríguez	Las Norias	September 1915

Table continued on next page

Juan Sánchez	Las Norias	September 1915
Franciscio Bocanegra	near Sebastian	September 1915[3]
		October 1915
Trinidad Ybarra	Olmito train raid	October 17, 1915
Manuel Ybarra	Olmito train raid	October 17, 1915
Severo García	Olmito train raid	October 17, 1915
Santiago Salas	Olmito train raid	October 17, 1915
Andrés León	Cavazos Crossing	October 20, 1915
Gregorio Cantú	Las Norias	October 1915
Norberto Pecina	near San Benito	October 1915
Alejandro Villareal	Lyford/Sebastian	October 1915
Juan Nieto	Las Norias	October 1915
Manuel Robles	Sebastian	November 1, 1915
No name	near Sebastian	November 10, 1915
Juan Tovar	Las Norias	November 1915
Jesús María Cantú	Mercedes	no date
Ygnacio Cavazos	Lyford	no date
Modesto Domínguez	near Sauz Ranch	no date
Manuel Estapa	Grangeno	no date
Manuel Flores	Tanquecitos	no date
Librado Garza	Monte Cristo	no date
Eusebio Hernández	El Sauz Ranch	no date
Pedro Longoria	Cavazos Crossing	no date
Francisco Loya	Texas/Mexico	no date
Pablo Pérez	Las Norias	no date
Abraham Salinas	near Lyford	no date
Juan de los Santos	Cavazos Crossing	no date

[1] In the Jesús Pérez memoir, this person is not listed as female, whereas in the "Partial List of Mexicans Killed" she is listed as a girl. F. Arutro Rosales details the account of the killing of both Martina Rivas (he identifies her as a girl) and her father Senovio Rivas by Texas Rangers in, *¡Pobre Raza!*, 89.

[2] James B. McAllen killed these five Mexicans, whereas Texas Rangers killed Bazán and Longoria. For a documentary of this incident, see *Border Bandits*, DVD, directed by Kirby Warnock (Dallas, Tex: Trans-Peco Productions, 2003).

[3] Jesús Pérez is cited as killing Bocanegra in the "Partial List of Mexicans Killed" document.

"Partial List of Mexicans Killed in Valley since July 1st, 1915," telegraph from American consul in Matamoros to Secretary of State, February 8, 1916, 812.00/17186, Roll 51, *Internal Affairs of Mexico*; and Jesús Pérez, "Memoirs of Jesse Pérez: 1870–1927," TS, Center for Center for American History, University of Texas at Austin, 57–58.

However, both these lists are partial, and as J. H. Johnson, American Consul in Matamoros, wrote in a letter to the secretary of state, "There were many killed whose names will never be known."[57]

The Harlingen commander stated, "The wide use of arms by white citizens and the extreme difficulty of the civil authorities supervising their use, leading to personal aggression, revenge and terrorism by white upon Mexican citizens, are certainly complicating the situation."[58] The killings of Mexicans became such a normal practice that E. P. Reynolds, immigration inspector in charge at Brownsville, failed to begin deportation proceedings for Pablo Diablo, a Mexican citizen, after Texas Rangers captured him in Pharr. Reynolds explained, "He will probably be kept in jail for some time, if he is not lynched; therefore it is inadvisable to institute deportation proceedings in his case at this time. The officers are making every effort to exterminate these bands of Mexican outlaws, as the only possible way of restoring law and order in this section." He also said that thirty-one Mexicans were killed in a twenty-four hour period as well, probably referring to the Alamo killings.[59] Cosme Casares Muñoz recalled this incident in an oral interview in 1987. He stated that Texas Rangers lynched fifteen Mexicans on one side of Alamo and another fifteen on the other side. One was taken into custody, who was probably Pablo Diablo.[60] Ethnic whites created black lists that targeted certain Mexicans for killings, which made the process more efficient.[61]

Although many Mexicans were killed in groups of two and three, there were several incidents where larger groups of Mexicans were killed in a single *matanza,* besides the Alamo incident already mentioned. In one incident, fourteen Mexicans were killed, and in another five. Other large group killings occurred at Ebenezer Station and Scrivener's Ranch and after the Olmito train derailment. The number of Mexicans reported killed at the Ebenezer Station ranges from four to twelve, according to different sources. A. G. Crawford of Mercedes claims to have seen seven Mexicans lynched at the station, whereas R. B. Creager stated that he saw five Mexicans killed, with empty beer bottles stuck in their mouths.[62] J. J. Busby said he saw four bodies. Seventeen to twenty bodies were found at Scrivener's Ranch, also known as "*Mata de Sandía*" (watermelon patch). Justice of the Peace 2, Cameron County, Henry J. Kirk reported he saw seventeen Mexicans killed at the Scrivener Ranch.[63] Ten other Mexicans were killed after the train derailment at Olmito on October 19, 1915, four of whom were killed while in Texas Ranger custody, according to Cameron County Sheriff W. T. Vann.[64]

Martha Minow in her study of genocide points out that the "most appalling goal of genocides, the massacres, systematic rapes, and tortures has been the destruction of the remembrance of individuals as well as of their lives and dignity...."[65] José T. Canales attempted to address the issue of injustice and loss of remembrance of those killed through the Joint Committee of the Texas Senate and House, which he formed in 1919 to investigate the Texas Rangers. However, his effort failed not only to force the re-formation of the Texas Rangers but also to make the official transcripts of the hearing available to the public.[66] The state of Texas kept silent the facts of the *matanza*.

Despite these efforts to cover up the *matanza,* the events of the revolt and *matanza* are remembered collectively through a contemporary *corrido* titled "*Los sediciosos,*" by families orally conveying stories about relatives killed, and more recently through scholarship, film, and literature. Although Benjamin Johnson labels the revolt as "forgotten"—and to an extent he is correct, the memories of these events continue to persist. Besides Johnson's book, a documentary, *Border Bandits,* has rekindled discussions of the *matanza* of 1915 by children and grandchildren of those killed.[67] Since releasing *Border Bandits,* Kirby Warnock, the director of the film, has received almost seventy calls from relatives whose family members were killed by the Texas Rangers.[68] Families who lost loved ones of course have not forgotten the time of the *matanza.* For instance, I grew up hearing about the *rinches* (derogatory term for Texas Rangers) who killed my great-grandfather, Paulino Serda. It should be noted that outside the Lower Rio Grande Valley the response to both Johnson's and Warnock's work centers on defending the Texas Rangers' reputation. The *matanza* outside of the Lower Rio Grande Valley is still ignored—silenced.[69] Hopefully, further studies of the killings will continue the effort to remember those killed.

Conclusion

A consequence of the defeat of the *revolución de Texas* by a combination of U.S. and Constitutional forces on both sides of the river led to the closing of a once open border. Between forty to sixty ferries operated from Brownsville and Roma during the early twentieth century. These ferries continued a 160-year-old practice of moving people and goods across the Rio Grande/*río bravo*. The U.S. military dismantled the ferries, and a Mounted Patrol began to police the border in 1915, to prevent insurgents from crossing the river. The patrol was eventually replaced with the Border Patrol by 1924. The final Mexican rebellion against U.S. colonialism ended as a result of Carranza's solidification of his superior position in the Mexican Revolution that resulted in large part from U.S. support. Its failure and the *matanza* ended the dream for many of returning Mexico *perdido* to Mexico. The Lower Rio Grande Valley was permanently American.

The final phase of U.S. colonization of Mexicans began after 1916. By the 1920s, some México Texanos began accepting the Lower Rio Grande Valley as no longer Mexico *perdido,* but as American. Some shifted their label of identification from *México Texano* to *México Americano* as an effort to emphasize their "Americanness." By this time, many were no longer arguing, "We are like the gringos"—*gente decente* who share the same liberal values—but argued, "We are American too." The descendents of conquered Mexicans began to embrace as their own the nation that had conquered their ancestors. This embrace, though, was not simple or smooth.

Context for analyzing the past events is important. An effort to examine the empirical data to understand a community's socioeconomic, political, and ideological world, and that community's relationship to larger world events, helps avoid flat or distorted presentations. In the case of the *revolución de Texas,* depictions failed to take into account the seriousness with which Mexicans held liberalism as a worldview and the impact of the U.S. military's support of Carranza during the Mexican Revolution. The Mexican Revolution, *revolución de Texas,* and *matanza* remind us that situations emanate from local relations that are shaped by larger structural forces such as colonization and revolution. México Texanos and Mexicanos in the Lower Rio Grande Valley both shaped and were shaped by these events.

Notes

1. "México Texano" and "Mexicano" were common terms of identification during this period. I use the former to indicate Mexicans who were U.S. citizens and the latter for Mexicans who were Mexican citizens. "Mexican" is used to refer to both groups regardless of citizenship status. For a discussion on the use of these terms as markers of group identity, see Trinidad Gonzales, "The World of México Texanos, Mexicanos and México Americanos: Transnational and National Identities in the Lower Rio Grande Valley during the Last the Phase of United States Colonization, 1900 to 1930" (Ph.D. diss., University of Houston, 2008); and "Conquest, Colonization, and Borderland

Identities: The World of Ethnic Mexicans in the Lower Rio Grande Valley, 1900–1930" in *Hybrid Identities: Theoretical and Empirical Examinations,* eds. Keri E. Iyall Smith and Patricia Leavy (Leiden, the Netherlands: Brill Academic Publishers, 2008), 179–196.

2. I use the term "ethnic white" to denote persons who were non-Mexicans instead of the term "Anglo-Saxon." There is a need to adjust our understanding of the diversity of cultural and ethnic backgrounds of non-Mexicans that lived in the Lower Rio Grande Valley. I use the term "Mexican" to denote all persons of Mexican cultural and ethnic backgrounds. I use the term "México Texano" to denote persons that were U.S. citizens, and "Mexicano" for Mexican citizens.

3. Two last attacks occurred after the train derailment. See *Brownsville Herald,* "3 Soldiers Killed, 8 Shot: Thrilling Early Morning Fight With 100 Bandits" (October 21, 1915), and "Bandits Attack American Soldiers Near Brownsville: 5 Minute Fight Results In Death of 1 American; Bandits All Elude Chase" (October 25, 1915).

4. The English-language labels were found in the *Brownsville Herald,* and the Spanish-language labels were found in various newspapers, including San Antonio's *La Prensa.* For the capitalists' cabal theory, see *Brownsville Herald,* "A Capitalistic Cabal?" (August 30, 1915). The German intrigue theory was put forward by various witnesses during the state's investigation of the Texas Rangers. See *Proceedings of the Joint Committee of the Senate and the House Investigation of the Texas Ranger Force* (Austin, Texas: 1919) [hereafter, *Investigation of the Texas Ranger Force*]. The notion that the events surrounding the attacks were a political movement is presented in different articles and editorials in the *Brownsville Herald* and other newspapers.

5. See Walter P. Webb, *The Texas Rangers: A Century of Frontier Defense* (Boston: Houghton Mifflin, 1935); Charles C. Cumberland, "Border Raids in the Lower Rio Grande Valley—1915," *Southwestern Historical Quarterly* 57 (January 1954): 301–324; Juan Gómez-Quiñones, "The Plan de San Diego Reviewed," *Aztlán* 1 (Spring 1970): 124–132; Charles H. Harris and Louis R. Sadler, "The Plan of San Diego and the Mexican–United States Crisis of 1916: A Reexamination," *Hispanic American Historical Review* 58 (August 1978): 381–408; Rodolfo Rocha, "The Influence of the Mexican Revolution on the Mexico–Texas Border, 1910–1916" (Ph.D. diss., Texas Tech University, 1981); James A. Sandos, *Rebellion in the Borderlands: Anarchism and the Plan of San Diego, 1904–1923* (Norman: University of Oklahoma Press, 1992); Rodolfo Rocha, "The Tejano Revolt of 1915," in *Mexican Americans in Texas History: Selected Essays,* ed. Emilio Zamora, Cynthia Orozco, and Rodolfo Rocha (Austin: Texas State Historical Association, 2000), 103–120; Benjamin H. Johnson, *Revolution in Texas: How a Forgotten Rebellion and Its Bloody Suppression Turned Mexicans into Americans* (New Haven, Conn.: Yale University Press, 2003); Charles H. Harris III and Louis R. Sadler, *The Texas Rangers and the Mexican Revolution: The Bloodiest Decade, 1910–1920* (Albuquerque: University of New Mexico Press, 2004); and Trinidad Gonzales, "World of México Texanos, Mexi-

canos, and México Americanos"; chapter 5 "The México Texano Revolt of 1915 and *La Matanza:* History, Memory and Identity, Construction at the Crossroads."

6. For works that examine liberalism in the area, see Joseph E. Chance, *José María de Jesús Carvajal: The Life and Times of a Mexican Revolutionary* (San Antonio, Tex.: Trinity University Press, 2006); and Elliott Young, *Catarino Garza's Revolution on the Texas–Mexican Border* (Durham, N.C.: Duke University Press, 2004).

7. For a recent discussion of this debate, see Gilbert G. Gonzalez and Raul A. Fernandez, *A Century of Chicano History: Empire, Nations, and Migration* (New York: Routledge, 2003), especially chapter 1. A similar debate is found for Latin American history; see the Steve J. Stern debate with Immanuel Wallerstein, "AHA Forum" in *American Historical Review* 93 (October 1988): 829–97. For a history of the uneven development of capitalism in Mexico, see Enrique Semo, *The History of Capitalism in Mexico: Its Origins, 1521–1763,* trans. Lidia Lozano (Austin: University of Texas Press, 1993).

8. The boundaries included the area encompassed by the Nueces River to the north; Laredo to the west on the north side of the Río Grande/*Río Bravo*; and the present boundaries of Coahuila, Nuevo León on the west, and Valles and Pánuco to the south. Armando C. Alonzo, *Tejano Legacy: Rancheros and Settlers in South Texas, 1734–1900* (Albuquerque: University of New Mexico Press, 1998), 17; and Omar Santiago Valerio-Jiménez, "'Indios Bárbaros,' Divorcées, and Flocks of Vampires: Identity and Nation on the Rio Grande, 1749–1894" (Ph.D. diss., University of California–Los Angeles 2001) 17.

9. Raúl A. Ramos was the first to label the Texas Revolution as the War of Texas Secession as an effort to recontextualize that conflict as a Mexican Centralist versus Federalist political struggle; see *Beyond the Alamo: Forging Mexican Ethnicity in San Antonio, 1821–1861* (Chapel Hill: University of North Carolina Press, 2008).

10. Natural rights is the concept of rights that developed from the eighteenth-century Enlightenment ideals that were expressed in the U.S. "Declaration of Independence" and the French "Declaration of the Rights of Man and of the Citizen."

11. See Gonzales, "The World of México Texanos, Mexicanos and México Americanos," 145–167.

12. Guadalupe San Miguel, Jr., *"Let All of Them Take Heed": Mexican Americans and the Campaign for Educational Equality in Texas, 1910–1981* (1987: repr., College Station: Texas A&M University Press, 2001), 8–13; and Jovita González, "Social Life in Cameron, Starr and Zapata Counties" (M.A. thesis, University of Texas, 1930), 69–82.

13. Milo Kearney et al., *A Brief History of Education in Brownsville and Matamoros* (Brownsville: The University of Texas–Pan American at Brownsville, 1989), 2; Alonzo, *Tejano Legacy,* 127; Oakah L. Jones Jr. states that the Spanish governments in the Southwest from 1790 to 1820 initiated early efforts at an educational system, *Los Paisanos:*

Spanish Settlers on the Northern Frontier of New Spain (Norman: University of Oklahoma Press, 1996), 249.

14. Roberto Ramón Calderón found that South Texas had 12.4 percent of the state's private schools and 2.9 percent of the state's public schools during the 1850s; see "Mexican Politics in the American Era, 1846–1900: Laredo, Texas" (Ph.D. diss., University of California–Los Angeles, 1993), 61–63. William E. Marsden has examined the effects of nationalism within institutions of education in Europe; see "'Poisoned history': A comparative study of nationalism, propaganda and the treatment of war and peace in the late nineteenth- and early twentieth-century school curriculum," *History of Education* 29 (2000): 29–47.

15. For census instructions stating that literacy can be measured in any language, see Jason G. Gauthier, *Measuring America: The Decennial Censuses from 1790 to 2000*, prepared for the U.S. Department of Commerce (Washington, D.C., 2002), 42, 54.

16. There were forty-two Spanish-language newspapers in circulation between 1900 and 1930. Nicolás Kanellos and Helvetia Martell, *Hispanic Periodicals in the United States, Origins to 1960: A Brief History and Comprehensive Bibliography* (Houston, Tex.: Arte Público Press, 2000).

17. Carlos Kevin Blanton, *The Strange Career of Bilingual Education in Texas, 1836–1981* (College Station: Texas A&M University Press, 2004), 50–51. Other studies related to Mexican literacy in Texas include Richard Griswold del Castillo, "Literacy in San Antonio, Texas, 1850–1860," *Latin American Research Review* 15 (1980): 180–185; Kenneth L. Stewart and Arnoldo De León, "Literacy Among *Inmigrantes* in Texas, 1850–1900," *Latin American Research Review* 20 (1985): 180–187; and Arnoldo De León and Kenneth L. Stewart, *Tejanos and the Numbers Game: A Socio-Historical Interpretation from the Federal Censuses, 1850–1900* (Albuquerque: University of New Mexico Press, 1989), 37–38, 85–86.

18. Lisbeth Haas uses the concept of "high oral residue" for understanding the Mexican community in California as both an oral and literate society. However, she emphasizes an oral paradigm over a literate paradigm even though her evidence of literacy rates for Mexicans is similar to those in Texas. See *Conquest and Historical Identities in California, 1769–1936* (Berkeley: University of California Press, 1995), 115–119. Evan Anders argues that political bosses existed in part because of the "illiterate Hispanic voters," *Boss Rule in South Texas: The Progressive Era* (Austin: University of Texas Press, 1982), 5.

19. See "Memorandum on certain conditions along the Mexican border and in Mexico, requested by the Secretary of the American and Mexican Joint Commission in letter of August 29, 1916, to Major General Hugh L. Scott, and referred by the Chief of Staff to the War College Division on August 30, 1916," August 30, 1916, 812.00/19219, Roll 56, Department of State, *Records of the Department of State Relating*

to Internal Affairs of Mexico, 1910–1929 RG 59, M 274 [hereafter, "Memorandum" for the document and *Internal Affairs of Mexico* for microfilm set].

20. I would like to thank Sonia Hernández for providing me with documents from the Archivo General del Estado de Nuevo León, Monterrey. These documents indicate that Luis De la Rosa and Basilio Ramos Jr. were the same person. However, this is probably unlikely as De la Rosa was a former Cameron County Deputy Sheriff. Ramos's interrogators certainly would have recognized a former law enforcement officer. See letter from Venustiano Carranza to General Pablo A. de la Garza, Governador del Estado de Nuevo León, January 20, 1916, Fondo: Justicia, Asunto: Falta de respeto a la autoridad. Archivo General del Estado de Nuevo León, Monterrey.

21. Sandos, *Rebellion,* 81–82.

22. A. S. Garza, Laredo, to Basilio Ramos, January 14, 1915, typed letter, Museum of South Texas Archive (MOST), Agustín S. Garza Collection (Plan de San Diego), File, 2009:006.001, G. de la Garza Correspondence, Basilio Ramos Jr.

23. Sandos, *Rebellion,* 84–85.

24. Ibid., 83–84. In an effort to receive military retirement, Agustín S. de la Garza needed to verify his participation in the Mexican Revolution. In a letter to President Lázaro Cárdenas, he provided the aliases and the real names of the signers of the second manifesto as proof of his military participation. The aliases and names were León Caballo (de la Garza); J. Z. Walcker (León Cárdenas Martínez, president); J. R. Becker (Francisco Múzquiz Guzmán, secretary); and J. N. Nagazaqui (Rafael Ochoa, treasurer). However, de la Garza fails to identify the real names for the following aliases who were signers: F. F. Lippi (vice president), P. Veeni, Jonás Bub, W. Córcega, and Inctlaca Ubaqui. See Agustín S. de la Garza to President Lázaro Cárdenas, December 31, 1938, MOST, Agustín S. Garza Collection File, 2009.006.010, G. de la Garza Correspondence, 1930s.

25. Agustín S. Garza, Saltillo, Coahuila, to General Victoriano Huerta, MOST, Agustín S. Garza Collection File, 2009.006.010, G. de la Garza Correspondence, 1930s.

26. Sandos, *Rebellion,* 84

27. Ibid., 94.

28. Ibid., 88.

29. Ramón Saldívar, *The Borderlands of Culture: Américo Paredes and the Transnational Imaginary* (Durham, N.C.: Duke University Press, 2006), 121–122.

30. Sandos, *Rebellion,* 100.

31. Ibid.

32. My translation: "*¿Cómo permanecer indiferentes y tranquilos ante semejantes atentados? ¿Cómo permitir semejantes ofensas inferidas a nuestra raza? ¿Acaso ya se acabó en nosotros el sentimiento de la humanidad y de patriotismo? ¡No! estará adormecido pero es fácil despertarlo.*" For a reproduction of the manifesto, see Sandos, *Rebellion,* 95.

33. Ibid., my translation: "*Basta ya de tolerancia, basta ya de sufrir insultos y desprecios, somos hombres conscientes de nuestros actos, que sabemos pensar lo mismo que ellos 'los gringos,' que podemos ser libres y lo seremos y que estamos suficientemente instruídos y fuertes para elegir nuestras autoridades y así lo haremos.*"

34. I would like to thank Victor Gómez, my colleague at South Texas College, for telling me about the use of this symbol on Mexican pesos in the early twentieth century.

35. See *Brownsville Herald*, "Gen. Nafarrate Denies Charge in Local Paper" (February 6, 1915); "Gen. Nafarrate Opened Way to Frustrate Plot: Commander of Constitutionalist Forces on Lower Border Says He Imparted Information Which Led to Important Discovery," and "Statement By Consul J. H. Johnson. Concerning Charge" (February 8, 1915).

36. Sandos clearly points out that Carranza was unable to fully control Nafarrate, *Rebellion,* 117–120.

37. John Mason Hart, *Revolutionary Mexico: The Coming and Process of the Mexican Revolution* (Berkeley: University of California Press, 1987), 280–281.

38. Sonia Hernández, "Military Activities in Matamoros During the Mexican Revolution, 1910–1915" (M.A. thesis, University of Texas–Pan American, 2001), 61.

39. Ibid., 65–68.

40. "Weekly Report of General Conditions along the Mexican Border," March 8, 1915, Roll 43, 812.00/14526, *Internal Affairs of Mexico* [hereafter, "Weekly Report"].

41. *Brownsville Herald*, "May Have Been Attempt to Rob a B&M Train: Bandits Burn Bridge Near Sebastian and Cut the Wire Communication: Sheriff's Department Again is Called to North End of Cameron County," July 26, 1915.

42. *Brownsville Herald*, "Masked Men Hold Up Officer, Take Prisoner, Lynch Him: San Benito Deputy Sheriff held up Near Town, His Prisoner is Wrested From Him and Lynched: Occurred at 10 O'Clock Last Night On Road Two Miles From San Benito" (July 29, 1915).

43. *Brownsville Herald*, "May Have Been Attempt to Rob a B&M Train.

44. "Weekly Report," August 7, 1915, 812.00/15730.

45. *Brownsville Herald*, "May Have Been Attempt to Rob a B&M Train."

46. *Brownsville Herald*, "Possibly a Filibuster Movement," August 5, 1915.

47. For an analysis of the staging of these photos as a method of imitation, see Richard Henry Ribb, "José Tomás Canales and the Texas Rangers: Myth, Identity, and Power in South Texas, 1900–1920" (Ph.D. diss., University of Texas, 2001), 315–324.

48. F. W. Berkshire report to Commission-General of Immigration, October 4, 1915, Reel 5, frames 0507–0511, Department of Labor, *Records of the Immigration and Naturalization Service Series A: Subject Correspondence Files Part 2: Mexican Immigration, 1906–1930* (Bethesda, Md: University Publications of America, 1993) microfilm [hereafter, *Records of the Immigration and Naturalization*].

49. *Brownsville Herald,* "Troop Trains Reinforce the Mexican Army: Considerable Increase in the Carranza Forces Reported from Reliable Source: Troop Trains Arrived in City of Matamoros Wednesday—Not Considered Bad Sign," September 30, 1915; and "Nafarrate Has Arrested Five Texas Raiders: Matamoros Commander Out With Statement Action Taken Nearly a Week Ago: Indicates No Immediate Action Will Follow Possible Shells Over Rio Grande" (October 1, 1915).

50. *Brownsville Herald,* "General López On Border May Take Command: Gen. Nafarrate May Leave In Eight Days For Vera Cruz To Take New Command: Nightly Checker Game Among Bends Of Rio Grande Passes Without Any Fighting" (October 4, 1915).

51. Space does not allow for an extended examination of the *revolución de Texas,* but there were over seventy engagements in total. See Rocha, "The Influence of the Mexican Revolution on the Mexico–Texas Border," 279.

52. "Memorandum" is divided into two sections: "Activities of Luis De la Rosa and Aniseta [sic] Pizano [sic]" and "Raids made in the U.S. territory by armed Mexicans, exclusive of those made by the bands of Aniseta [sic] Pizano [sic] and Luis De la Rosa . . . acts and quotations from weekly reports of commanding officers to the Department Commanders, Southern Department, March 20, 1915 to August 12, 1916." The first report on De la Rosa and Pizaña is dated October 25, 1915, and concludes on July 22, 1916. It is in these reports that De la Rosa and Pizaña's connection to de la Garza is mentioned. The last activities associated with the *Plan de San Diego* were during June 1916, when U.S. military commanders anticipated a raid into the Laredo area.

53. *Brownsville Herald,* "Guards Can Be Withdrawn, Say Some Ranchers: Tell Military Headquarters At Harlingen Everything Is Quiet Once Again: However, There Is Said To Be No Let Up By Army, And All Patrols Will Be Held"; see subheadline "Mexican Citizens Will Help Officials" (September 22, 1915).

54. Harris and Sadler, *The Texas Rangers and the Mexican Revolution,* 220, 295–297, 322.

55. *Brownsville Herald,* "No Fighting On American Side For Sergeant: Member Of López Army Tells An American Of Attempt Made At Recruiting: Innocently Tells Of How 8 Men Accepted Offer Of The 'Revolution' Agent" (October 19, 1915). Recruits were offered $10 gold and 75 cents a day plus a share of any spoils.

56. This is not surprising, though, considering that there are only two works devoted to the study of extralegal killings of Mexicans in general. See F. Arturo Rosales, *¡Pobre Raza!: Violence, Justice, and Mobilization Among México Lindo Immigrants, 1900–1936* (Austin: University of Texas Press, 1999); and William D. Carrigan and Clive Webb, "The Lynching of Persons of Mexican Origin or Descent in the United States, 1848 to 1928," *Journal of Social History* 37 (Winter 2003): 411–438.

57. Letter from American Consul to Secretary of State, January 26, 1915, 812.00/17186, Roll 51, *Internal Affairs of Mexico.*

58. "Weekly Report" October 30, 1915, 812.00/16752, Roll 49, *Ibid.*

59. Letter from E.P. Reynolds, Inspector in Charge, to Supervising Inspector, Immigration Services, El Paso, August 12, 1915, Reel 5, frames 0202–0204, *Records of the Immigration and Naturalization.*

60. Cosme Casares Muñoz, interview by Leticia Miroslava Gamboa, June 25, 1987, tape 00654, Lower Rio Grande Valley Oral History Collection, located at the Lower Rio Grande Valley Archives Collection, University of Texas-Pan American.

61. Testimony of R.B. Creager, *Investigation of the Texas Ranger Force,* 355.

62. Testimony of A. G. Crawford, R. B. Creager, and J. J. Busby, *Investigation of the Texas Ranger Force,* 46, 356, 646; and Johnson, *Revolution in Texas,* 115.

63. Testimony of Henry J. Kirk, *Investigation of the Texas Ranger Force,* 599; and Ribb, "José Tomás Canales," 98.

64. Testimony of W. T. Vann, *Investigation of the Texas Ranger Force,* 562; and Johnson, *Revolution in Texas,* 115. This reference was to the nine Mexicans mentioned at the beginning of this essay.

65. Martha Minow, *Between Vengeance and Forgiveness: Facing History after Genocide and Mass Violence* (Boston: Beacon Press, 1998), 1.

66. Ribb, "José Tomás Canales," 365–368.

67. *Border Bandits,* DVD, directed by Kirby Warnock (Dallas, Tex: Trans-Pecos Productions, 2003).

68. Texas State Representative Aaron Peña proposed that a marker or memorial be erected to remember those killed during these events, but the Texas Legislature failed to act, Elizabeth Pierson, "Legislation Inspired by Border Film," *The Monitor,* January 10, 2005, accessed January 19, 2006, from http://themonitor.com/PrintIt.cfm?Template=/GlobalTemplates/Details.cfm&StoryI. . . .

69. Ibid.

The El Paso Race Riot of 1916

MIGUEL A. LEVARIO

Their bodies lay stripped nearly naked and strewn about the train like fallen leaves. Pools of blood marked their final resting place. This sketched the scene near the Cusihuiriáchic (Cusi) Mines in Santa Ysabel, Chihuahua. Seventeen[1] American engineers, travelling on the Mexican Northwestern Railroad to their reopened mines under the protection of their passports and their *salvo conductos* furnished by de facto Chihuahua governor Ignacio

Consul General T. D. Edwards, Ciudad Juárez, México. Courtesy El Paso Public Library, Aultman Collection.

Enríquez, met this brutal demise.[2] A band of soldiers led by *Villista* officer Pablo López hijacked the train and demanded that all Anglos disembark. Their subsequent fate hung at the end of bayonets and rifle shots as the revolutionaries mercilessly executed Americans for simply being "*gringo*."[3] This event, the Santa Ysabel massacre, served as a catalyst for one of the largest race riots ever to occur in West Texas.[4]

Historiography of Mob Violence

Recent scholarship on mob violence in Texas at the turn of the twentieth century sheds light on the complexities of race and culture and their impact on conflict. Although race plays a critical role in such bloody episodes, other variables such as social tolerance and culture act as instigating forces as well. Scholars such as William D. Carrigan (*The Making of a Lynching Culture,* 2004) try to understand mob activity through the perspective of historical memory. Carrigan's study of the 1916 horrific lynching of seventeen-year old African American Jesse Washington in Waco, Texas, seeks to understand "how a culture of violence that nourished lynching formed and endured for so long among ordinary people."[5] Carrigan digs into Washington's lynching with at least two purposes: to demonstrate why members of the mob and residents of the community tolerated the lynching and to reveal a deeply disturbing part of American racist culture in the early twentieth century.[6] Carrigan's review of Texas' culture of violence since 1835 allows the reader to grasp how extralegal activity and brutal acts can be accepted by a progressive society in the early twentieth century.

Cynthia Nevels's (*Lynching to Belong,* 2007) study on whiteness and the lynching of five black men in Brazos County, Texas, argues that foreign-born European immigrants claimed whiteness by engaging in the South's most brutal act of racial domination through lynching. The participation of foreign-born immigrants in this act prompted Nevels to delve deeper to ascertain the incentive foreigners had to engage in such a characteristically southern act. Her study revealed that many of the immigrants had experienced racial discrimination in other parts of the South and realized the "power of white skin."[7] Many of the Italians, Irish, and Bohemian immigrants living in Brazos County experienced an ambiguous place in the South's black–white racial categorization. By participating in the lynching of five black men, they helped to resolve their enigmatic racial identity and became white.[8] Nevels's study offered a unique perspective into mob activity, revealing the racialized motivations of the immigrants propelled by their sense of whiteness and first-class citizenship.

In another study on mob action, Walter L. Buenger (*The Path to a Modern South,* 2001) identifies a dramatic shift in racial demography as contributing significantly to racial violence and the lynching of blacks in the town of Paris, Texas.[9] The escalation of the black population in the town contributed to lynching and other gruesome deeds used to intimidate the African American community, Buenger found. By 1890, the African American population had increased 187 percent and now constituted about one-third of the total number of people there.[10] Whites throughout northeast Texas, meanwhile, grew increasingly fearful of newly arriving blacks and "decried the breakdown in black behavior" and condemned those that "no longer knew their place."[11] Whites thus resorted to violent means to control the social and political ambitions of blacks at the turn of the twentieth century.

This essay contributes to the expanding literature on mob activity in Texas by noting that factors similar to the ones listed above apply to contexts involving ethnic Mexicans. However, it goes further by explaining how circumstances of a transnational nature reinforced long-standing characterizations of Mexican Americans as being "un-American" or an "enemy other" and by examining the projection of anger through violence upon an innocent group. First, a review of the 1916 events in West Texas will address the latent racial tension that persisted in the region, one that paralleled the friction that prevailed in central and northeast Texas between whites and blacks. It is through this brief analysis of the region's history of racially motivated violence and resistance that understanding of the events leading up to 1916 in El Paso will be reached. Second, an evaluation of these events will try to demonstrate that international militarization during the Mexican Revolution, specifically in 1916, contributed to the definition of Mexicans as an "enemy other." For most of the twentieth century in the southwest United States, "American" generally meant white, while "Mexican" referred to race and not citizenship.[12] Lastly, an assessment of the riot will establish in stark fashion that Mexicans, despite their citizenship or long residence in El Paso, came to be easily identified as proxies for the Mexican revolutionaries responsible for taking American lives.

The Legacy of Violence

The El Paso race riot of 1916 and its consequences can be best understood by examining the history of the development of conflict and militarization in the El Paso/Ciudad Juárez region. Although numerous confrontations occurred between law enforcement officials and El Paso residents in the late nineteenth century, none matched the San Elizario Salt War of 1877 in significance. The Salt War revealed the growing tension between Anglo entrepreneurs and Mexican residents and highlighted the use of local, federal, and state-based authority to impose law that clashed with the daily and accepted practice of the locals. Resistance by the residents in turn called for a greater degree of law enforcement and supervision.[13]

The Salt War involved a dispute over the free access to local salt licks located in El Paso County. Both American citizens and Mexican nationals had long used the lakes; however, local officials privatized the area and denied them access. Many residents continued to frequent the salt licks and eventually decided to challenge the exclusivity of the land. Louis Cardis, an Italian stagecoach manager and local political boss, and Judge Charles Howard, who had bought the salt beds in 1877 and declared them off limits to local residents, became embroiled in the early phase of the confrontation. The conflict worsened when the Texas Rangers and the U.S. Army arrived to suppress the popular insurgency. A semblance of order returned when law men and other volunteers enacted vigilante law upon the population of the valley.[14]

The Salt War underscored two developments that reappeared during the 1916 riot. First, residents were "swept up" by circumstances that quickly took on a life of their own. In the process, the participants took the law into their hands and violently expressed simmering racial feelings. Second, the opposing factions generally divided themselves along racial lines that transcended citizenship and class. As a consequence, the dispute left a bitter impression on many Mexicans, especially on merchants excluded from the opportunities of the new developing economy. The Salt War also left many Mexicans with the distinct impression that social relations had become more racialized than ever.

In the time period between the Salt War of 1877 and the outbreak of the Mexican Revolution in 1910, relations between Anglos and Mexicans in the region remained superficially peaceful. The railroad made its way to El Paso and Ciudad Juárez by the mid-1880s and helped provide the accoutrements of a modern city. However, underneath the façade of prosperity and goodwill, violent confrontations often pitted the predominately Mexican populace against law enforcement officials. These conflicts between the two ethnic communities often occurred throughout West Texas.

Several cases of violence occurred, including gunfights between the officers and local residents, producing popular discontent toward local law enforcement.[15] The growing civilian reaction toward police authorities became increasingly more aggressive and assertive as law enforcement officials sought to establish their authority in an isolated and semiautonomous region. Whites in West Texas assumed a greater role not only in protecting local custom but also in serving their own justice, a trend that would later contain a strong racial undercurrent.[16]

In 1908, for instance, Mexican residents from the Big Bend district confronted Texas Ranger Captain John R. Hughes near the Shafter Mines and San Antonio Canyon. Ranger Alex Ross, Ranger Sergeant J. D. Dunaway, Sam McKenzie, and a justice of the peace from the mines had gone to arrest S. A. Wright, an Anglo, for killing a Mexican. As they made their way back to Marfa, approximately thirty-five armed Mexicans demanded that Wright be handed over to them. But according to Hughes's report, "The Rangers refused to give [Wright] up and it looked for awhile like there was going to be war between the Rangers and the Mexicans."[17] The encounter finally passed when the Mexican lynch mob gave ground and Hughes assured them that justice and due process would be carried out. Although this incident did not escalate into a full-blown "war" as feared, the Rangers did "stir up more trouble than they put down."[18] Such confrontations, which occurred regularly, led to uneasy relationships between Anglos and Mexicans in the region.

In another case, citizens of Clint, a town located southeast of El Paso, petitioned the Texas Adjutant General in December 1917 for aid in keeping the peace, although they did not note the source of their concern. Adj. Gen. James A. Harley responded by sending several Rangers led by Jeff Vaughn. The Rangers did not quell the "troubles," but escalated them. Clint's justice of the peace Homer Wells stated:

> Some months since Clint and [the] surrounding country petitioned the state for some Rangers and in answer to that petition you sent four men, but the one whom was put in charge of the bunch (They call him Jeff Vaughn.) has acted in such a way as to cause more trouble in the past few months than has been here for months before. . . . I hope some action will be taken at once as the longer he remains here the more liable is there [to] be trouble.[19]

According to the complaint, Jeff Vaughn assaulted an innocent Mexican man for no apparent reason. Wells also added in his letter that if the Rangers stayed in the area, there was "liable to be serious trouble,"[20] for many residents of Clint and the surrounding area informed the judge that they would take matters into their own hands in reaction to Vaughn's behavior. Popular discontent and action thus existed as a viable option for Mexicans in these isolated pockets of West Texas when government responded too slowly to immediate threats. The Vaughn case, among many others, demonstrated how disturbing local affairs could produce popular action.

Changing Demographics in West Texas and Revolutionary Mexico

The "great migration" beginning in the early 1900s, with its roots in the economic destabilization of northern Mexico and broadened by the Mexican Revolution (1910–1920), caused both social and racial tensions to simmer among the Anglo-American population of El Paso. Many among the city's business elite supported an order by the president of the United States in 1916 to racially identify and classify Mexicans separate from whites in order to have a "better grasp of the population on social and economic problems."[21] Reports of the period in the national press described the refugees, exiles, and immigrants as "homeless, poverty stricken, chronically hungry, [and] alien in speech, manners, habits, and ideas."[22] They seemed no more than social stressors bound to complicate racial matters in the United States. At the turn of the twentieth century, larger issues of an international nature, including immigration and revolutionary turmoil in Mexico, often acted to bring local policy in line with state approaches then redefining relations between Mexico and the United States.[23]

The Mexican Revolution, apart from straining diplomatic relations between the United States and Mexico and begetting ill feelings between citizens of the two countries, expectedly caused distress in the United States over the welfare of American citizens in Mexico. The clashes of rival revolutionary factions forced many American workers and residents to abandon their homes in Mexico and head north to the United States. Anti-American feelings ran high in Mexico and along the border.[24] Anglo residents in El Paso feared that assaults and casualties inflicted on Americans in Mexico would translate to attacks upon whites in the city. In their apprehension, citizens and local officials requested protection by Texas Rangers and the U.S. Army.

The economic backlash of the Revolution equally concerned Americans as chaos plagued the Mexican landscape. American investments all over Mexico faced serious risks as Americans abandoned private property and industries in places where battles raged. Businessmen in El Paso, home for one of the largest smelting companies in the United States, worried as revolutionary forces closed or occupied mines in Chihuahua.[25] The economic ties between the United States and Mexico, magnified in El Paso, brought the Revolution to the doorstep of the United States.

American residents in Mexico as well as those along the international boundary did not escape the violence of the Revolution. Ranch raids caused great distress among Anglo property owners living along the border on the U.S. side. Some of these attacks were the work of individuals who, driven by need and the opportunity to retaliate for past wrongs, sought justice through banditry. Many local Mexican residents accepted some of them as heroes, champions, and defenders, but Anglo ranchers and authorities, specifically the Texas Rangers, viewed the marauders as nothing more than arrogant outlaws who threatened the lives and livelihood of residents in West Texas.[26]

In El Paso, furthermore, Anglos grew increasingly suspicious of all things Mexican, especially of Mexican refugees and their intentions. White El Pasoans entertained dreaded fears of attacks on their city either by revolutionary troops or soldiers from Mexico's army. In response, U.S. military officials moved to fortify El Paso and other strategic locations along the border.[27] Racialized tensions spread unchecked throughout the region.

The Santa Ysabel Massacre

Events in Chihuahua acted as a major source of uneasiness among Mexicans and Anglos in the city of El Paso. On December 30, 1915, El Paso honored *Carrancista* officer General Alvaro Obregón with a banquet and an audience with notable individuals.[28] Various political and military dignitaries, including El Paso mayor Tom Lea, Consul Andrés G. García, and Gen. John J. Pershing, attended.[29] The spectacle attempted to promote the beginning of a peaceful era in Mexico by emphasizing the removal of Pancho Villa (following his defeat at the Battle of Celaya in April 1915) as a threat to American mining interests in Chihuahua. Mexican American businessman and politician Félix Martínez furthered the rhetoric at the occasion by stating that Obregón had assured him that U.S. capital and American personnel would be safe and protected in Mexico. Days later the statement proved false when *Villista* troops led by Col. Pablo López hijacked a train carrying seventeen American engineers on their way to Cusihuiráchic, west of Ciudad Chihuahua.[30]

General Alvaro Obregón and the de facto government overlooked two critical facts with their proclamation. First, the supposed deposition of Pancho Villa as leader amounted to an overstatement, as his downfall did not minimize his influence over his loyal soldiers and officers. Second, the de facto government had grossly underestimated Villa's furor toward Woodrow Wilson when, on October 19, 1915, the U.S. president recognized Venustiano Carranza as the de facto president of Mexico and extended to him special military concessions. Villa saw these actions by the United States as betrayal, disrespect, and a clear violation of American neutrality. Public anti-American rhetoric from Villa forced both the Texas and federal governments to examine security concerns along the border. Villa's antipathy is well documented in various academic and popular works; however, it is relevant to note for this discussion that the reaction by Villa to the recognition of the Carranza government served as a catalyst for intense racialized conflict and for attacks on Anglos and Mexicans alike.[31]

In December 1915, just a few weeks prior to the massacre, Villa delivered a statement before the Cusihuiriáchic mining district in front of manager C. R. Watson and his men, warning them that they would no longer be protected and they should leave the country:

> Since your government has seen fit to recognize Venustiano Carranza, I no longer consider myself responsible for the safety of you or your countrymen in the territory dominated by my men. Your government has advised you to leave Mexico. Now leave. If you ever come back I'll kill you and kill you quick.[32]

Following Villa's speech, Watson quickly gathered his men, boarded a train, and safely arrived in El Paso. But several weeks later, *Carrancista* troops reoccupied Chihuahua City and secured the region. At the behest of Obregón and in defiance of the ominous threat by Villa on that fateful night in December, Watson and his men contacted Customs Collector Zach T. Cobb and Mexican consul general Andrés G. García for passports and *salvo conductos* for their trip back to the Cusi mines in Chihuahua.[33]

Watson and several men made their way back through Chihuahua to the properties of the Cusihuiriáchic Mining Company.[34] At approximately two o'clock in the afternoon on January 12, a band of one hundred soldiers under the command of Col. Pablo López attacked a "stalled" passenger train that contained the Cusi mining men. One eyewitness claimed that the band shouted, "Viva Villa!" and "Death to the Gringos!"[35]

According to another person at the scene, Juan Vásquez, the rebels lifted a rail to sidetrack the locomotive, which consisted of two passenger coaches, one carrying Americans and the other about twenty Mexican male passengers. Pablo López and his men quickly surrounded the train, entered the coach occupied by the Mexican men, searched all passengers, and stole their "bread and lunches."[36] Five Americans jumped from the train upon hearing shouts from the *Villista* band, but the rebels easily captured them and summarily executed the hapless miners.

The soldiers marched to the "American coach" and commanded that "all Gringos step out" of the car.[37] They then ordered the Americans to line up and strip themselves of their clothing. López then ordered two troopers with Mauser guns to prepare to kill the Americans; the soldiers walked down the line and shot them one by one. Americans attempting to flee fell prey to other rebels, who mortally shot them in their tracks.[38] According to reports, bodies lay strewn about in grotesque positions. The top of one American's head had been shot off, and his brains had spilled onto the ground.[39]

The targeting of Americans aboard the train took an interesting turn when Col. López identified a brown-skinned man, ostensibly Manuel Bonifacio Romero, a Mexican American native of Las Vegas, New Mexico. López inquired suspiciously of his association with the "*gringos.*" Romero replied, "I too am an American." "*Pues se quede allí entonces* (Well, then stay put)," López shrugged, and Romero died with the rest of the Americans.[40] In an ironic twist of fate, a Mexico–U.S. Claims Commission later refuted Mr. Romero's citizenship because the absence of a birth certificate could not authenticate his New Mexico residence. Romero's wife presented other forms of evidence, including their marriage certificate, to support his American citizenship claim, but to no avail. The Mexican representatives doubted his American status and therefore denied his widow compensation in the lawsuit.[41]

Killing of Americans during the Revolution did not commonly occur; however, the Santa Ysabel incident underscored the failure of the Chihuahua government to guarantee Americans safe passage. The activities of *Villista* forces further angered Americans who feared for the security of their fellow citizens. Villa's anti-American harangues and his public denunciation of President Wilson made Villa a *persona non grata,* especially among the Anglo residents of El Paso.[42]

Whereas Anglos viewed Villa as a callous murderer, Mexicans in El Paso held an opposing opinion of him. In the early years of the Revolution, Villa had often visited El Paso for diplomatic and personal reasons and, as evidenced by his loyal followers, enjoyed considerable and favorable support from many of the Mexican residents in El Paso's Mexican district, called Chihuahuita.[43] Even after Wilson's official recognition of Carranza, Villa still wielded extraordinary power and influence, a fact that made Mexicans grateful and respectful toward him and Anglos fearful and resentful of the revolutionary leader.[44]

The El Paso Race Riot of 1916

The death train carrying the bodies of the seventeen Americans murdered at Santa Ysabel, Chihuahua, arrived in Juárez on the morning of January 13. From there, it crossed the river to the Santa Fe railway freight depot in El Paso, where citizens unloaded the corpses and an armed escort accompanied the bodies and took them to various undertaking establishments.[45] The local police and military guard took precautions against any disturbances.[46] However, many Americans refused to stand idly by as they witnessed their comrades arriving in caskets.

In the early afternoon hours of January 13, shortly after the bodies of the dead Americans reached El Paso, U.S. Consul T. D. Edwards was jeered and verbally attacked by a mob of Americans. Many screamed, "Villa's consul, not ours!" and "Go back to Juárez with the Mexicans where you belong!" The protestors felt that Consul Edwards had not done enough to protect the men traversing Chihuahua despite the fact that he had personally received assurances by top Carranza officials of safety measures to be taken and the assignment of a military guard to protect them. Nevertheless, a petition circulated throughout hotel lobbies and the city asking President Wilson to remove Edwards because he allegedly gave Villa advice whenever the General visited Juárez.[47] The verbal and political ambush of Edwards soon gave way to a much more aggressive, retaliatory initiative by a mob.

Several groups of Americans took to El Paso streets and organized a variety of retributory responses to the atrocities committed in Santa Ysabel. Thirty or so men of various backgrounds, including prominent local businessmen, conducted a meeting in El Paso proposing to organize a volunteer "foreign legion" of one thousand men for service in Mexico under the protection of the Carranza government. The men felt confident that their unit could be financed and outfitted by a majority of those present at the meeting, but more fully by mining interests in Mexico.[48] There exists, however, no record of anyone heeding the call to ride into Mexico. Mining and cattle men elsewhere in El Paso organized a secret meeting to gather a second expedition to go into Mexico to capture those responsible for killing the American engineers.[49] Apparently, such a plan did not materialize either. But as fate would have it, people of all sorts responded to their instincts and on impulse amassed for action on the streets of El Paso.

Throughout the afternoon, tensions escalated close to downtown El Paso that fateful day in January. American soldiers stationed at Fort Bliss attacked two Mexican men near the Chihuahuita district. Scuffles between other U.S. soldiers and Mexicans occurred later that evening, and many police wagons returned to their respective stations with Mexicans who had been attacked and "civilians" who had participated in the sporadic disturbances.[50] Before long, soldiers and Anglo civilians in saloons began to take their drunken escapades to the streets and assault Mexicans they apprehended. Women, children, and the elderly did not escape the terror of the vigilante group. According to Hortencia Villegas, who recalled the rioting years later: "*Me acuerdo que a toda la gente dándoles golpes, a viejitos y a jóvenes y a todos*" (I remember everyone receiving blows, the elderly and young people, everyone).[51] Hundreds of Americans amassed in the principal downtown streets that outlined Chihuahuita, clearly intending to exact revenge on local Mexicans.[52] The confrontation then morphed into a full-fledged riot, turning into a shadow of a war that involved two primary sides: Anglos and U.S. soldiers on one side, Mexicans on the other. The crowd bent on retaliation swelled to nearly fifteen hundred men, and it would take another two to three hours after the first reports of the fighting began before the police successfully dispersed the deluge. Military reports claim that the disturbances surprised police officials who had concluded earlier that "there will be no trouble that evening."[53]

The Anglo rioters, however, met resistance. Once word of the turmoil spread throughout the *colonia,* groups from "El Segundo Barrio" began to show up with sticks, bats, pipes, and anything else they could muster to defend themselves.[54] According to Villegas, residents of Ciudad Juárez, including soldiers, joined their Mexican brethren from El Paso:

> *Yo le digo que se vino toda la mexicanada, y luego los de Juárez. Creo que eran todos los soldados de allá de Juárez, porque los tranvías empezaron a pasar con gente que se fue pa' Juárez y avisaron allá como andaba aquí el mitote.*

> [I tell you that all the Mexicans came and then from Juárez. I be-
> lieve they were the soldiers that were stationed there in Juárez because
> the trolleys began to take people to Juárez to tell everyone there of the
> ruckus that was going on.][55]

Toward the climax of the rioting, Gen. John J. Pershing, who commanded forces at Fort Bliss, ordered the Sixteenth Infantry to take charge of the downtown area because police officers seemed unable to control the mêlée. Lines of troops four abreast bulldozed through the streets and established sentries on street corners and in the middle of the plaza. American soldiers conducted a search for weapons and for additional Villa sympathizers in Chihuahuita until well after midnight. The troopers prohibited residents from walking the streets without a permit signed by the provost marshal.[56] Despite the military occupation, soldiers and Mexicans continued to brawl in the streets.

After the riot, General Pershing and the El Paso Police Department sent their respective units on a "cleanup" mission of the Mexican quarter in order to avert further violence. About fifty soldiers and as many police officers went "looking for Mexicans" and rounding up suspected Villa associates during their "cleanup" of the Chihuahuita streets.[57] As the "cleanup" campaign diminished and soldiers and police officers spread out over the bustling downtown area, General Pershing declared martial law. Despite this drastic military measure, Anglo rioters defiantly frequented saloons and other public establishments, searching for more trouble. A few intrepid Mexicans also congregated in open places, but police officers ordered them to leave because of "concern for their safety."[58]

An article in the otherwise progressive *Labor Advocate* revealed the outrage smoldering among Anglos who increasingly saw the conflict in nationalistic terms. The writer called on "Americans" to defend their country, suggesting that doing so would avenge the murder of American engineers and other foreigners in Mexico.[59] Such exaggerated nationalism that gave meaning to the attack on Chihuahuita only deepened a racial line of division as real as the international border that separated Mexico from the United States.

General Pershing reinforced racial divisions by instituting martial law—based on a policy of containment—on Mexican neighborhoods. One of his more creative enforcement practices included the enactment of "dead lines," physical demarcations that set aside the Mexican neighborhoods from the rest of the population. As Pershing concluded, Mexicans needed to be separated from Anglos in order to halt any further rioting. As he phrased it, "[T]he excitement on Friday was still intense, and but for the presence of the troops on the streets separating the Mexican from the American part of the city, there would certainly have been serious rioting."[60] The Pershing directive prohibited Mexicans from leaving the Chihuahuita district and Americans from entering it.[61] General Pershing next closed the international bridge, thereby extending the dead line to a separation of the United States from Mexico. This order denied American residents access to Ciudad Juárez and prohibited Mexicans from crossing into El Paso.[62]

Although the dead line was intended to quell the disturbance, it reinforced the racial division that incidentally indicted the larger Mexican community for the atrocities associated with the Santa Ysabel Massacre. Moreover, the order and its execution recalled the imaginary point beyond which prisoners during the U.S. Civil War could not cross lest they be shot. In the case of Chihuahuita, Mexicans who violated the dead line faced legal and physical repercussions. Many residents, including Hortencia Villegas, feared to cross the line: "*Yo pa' la Plaza no me voy, no me vayan a golpear*" (I don't go to the Plaza; they are not going to assault me).[63] In one case, a dark-skinned Mexican left a bar after the curfew established by the dead line and received a severe beating by soldiers. Not until he claimed to be a "nigger" did the soldiers release him.[64]

Pershing's containment measure also made it possible for the Army to continue searching Mexican homes for armed "Villa sympathizers." Subsequent declarations by officials that they had "cleaned up El Paso Street" further implicated Mexicans in the rioting and stigmatized them as a threat to the social order in El Paso.[65] The military strategy of separating the races, ostensibly for the protection of the Mexicans (who suffered an injustice during the upheaval), represented a repressive measure that strengthened Anglo anti-Mexican feelings and reaffirmed the position of Anglos as the final arbiters in cases involving racial conflict.

Conclusion

The 1916 El Paso riot stands as one of the most blatant expressions of ethnic amicus ever to be directed toward Mexicans during this time period. The Santa Ysabel massacre evoked past conflicts between Anglos and Mexicans in West Texas, and it unleashed entrenched anti-Mexican feelings. According to one newspaper report, fifty thousand cards that read "Remember the Alamo . . . Remember the Cusi" were ordered for distribution the day after the riot.[66] Subsequent to the mass rioting, plans for "revenge" were still being hatched up throughout El Paso, showing how historical memory (such as Carrigan found in central Texas) could spark mob violence, pitting Anglos against Mexicans.

Local newspapers, among them the *Labor Advocate,* played on the exaggerated nationalism of white El Pasoans, encouraging them to seek retribution against the "non-white and non-American" Mexicans in the city. The emphasis on race galvanized various segments of the white population, from private citizens to professional associations, into assuming their civic duty to intervene and make themselves available lest the large Mexican population rise up and retaliate. The remarkable appeal to active citizenship and nationalistic expression evidences Nevels's argument that whiteness often became a call to arms when people of color endangered white society.

The exponential population growth among Mexicans in El Paso had further heightened suspicions of Mexicans in the city and inflamed passions in the moment of crisis. Whites sensed their numerical disadvantage and moved to defend themselves at every cost, including violence. U.S. officials assisted them by pursuing strict punitive measures. Fort Bliss soldiers ransacked many Mexican homes in search of guns and other weapons, heeding rumors that Mexicans had heavily armed themselves and prepared to attack Anglos in the city.[67] As Buenger found in his study of Paris in northeast Texas, whites used violence in cases where racial groups needed to be "put back in their place."

Aside from illustrating that what occurred in El Paso conforms to patterns of racial violence toward other minority groups elsewhere in the state, the El Paso riot of 1916 offers other lessons. First, it indicates that when under stress, local authorities and Anglo citizens would use the opportunity to reinforce their position as the final mediators when racialized social conflict erupted. In fact, the episode legitimized the role of authorities (such as General Pershing and the U.S. Army) to segregate El Paso through militarized separation of the races. They had the consent of the dominant Anglo population to dictate a line of separation that could be militarily enforced and beyond which Mexicans could not travel. The separation of Mexicans from the rest of El Paso, the prohibition of passage across the border, and the establishment of martial law with the accompanying dead lines reinforced the verdict that Mexicans stood as a defeated minority. Mexican isolation and vilification, culminating from the massacre and the riot, succeeded in identifying them as an "enemy other."

Second, the riot exhibited a transnational character, as the Mexican Revolution figured prominently into relations between Mexico and United States and into local affairs. On the border, race relations had become increasingly problematic as Mexicans expressed mixed political allegiances and cultural attachments. Villa's assertion that Anglos were no longer safe in Mexico, and the subsequent proof of this statement through the racially motivated Santa Ysabel Massacre, ignited rage among the Anglo community, who then indiscriminately lashed out at all Mexican residents residing in the city. Anglos became anxious over the threat posed by the Revolution and acted out fears through violence in 1916.

Third, Anglo conduct during the riot validated the long-standing image whites held that Mexicans, regardless of citizenship status, were foreigners or, more specifically, the "enemy." The special census of January 1916 designed to identify and "segregate" Mexicans from Anglos had practically confirmed the Mexicans' position as such.[68] Immigration scholar Mae Ngai states that "foreignness" became a racialized concept extended to all Mexicans and Mexican Americans in the 1920s and carried the opprobrium of illegitimacy and inferiority.[69] American citizenship provided few benefits to Mexicans born in the United States or naturalized therein, states Ngai.[70] Public statements by Hispanos from New Mexico expressing their support for an American punitive operation against Villa went unheeded and received secondary coverage in local newspapers, suggesting that Mexican American loyalty was suspect and unwelcomed.[71]

Lastly, the El Paso Race Riot of 1916 demonstrates that resistance against violent aggression—as occurred during the disturbance—is very much a mark of Mexican American history. Many have been the times when Latino communities defended themselves against white aggression or aided and abetted one of their own who resisted Anglo injustice. Obvious cases where Mexican Americans retaliated against wrongdoings occurred in 1859, when a segment of the Tejano population around Brownsville joined forces behind Juan Cortina, or in 1888, when Tejanos in Rio Grande City threatened whites for an attempt on the life of Catarino Garza. Three years subsequent to that incident, Mexican Americans in South Texas shielded the same Catarino Garza from Texas Rangers who were hunting Garza down for violating the neutrality laws, and a decade later Tejanos gave succor to the fugitive Gregorio Cortez who was wrongly accused of horse stealing. In 1938, Tejanos extended moral support to Emma Tenayuca and the pecan shellers of San Antonio, then striking against the Anglo-dominated pecan-shelling industry; in 1949,

Mexican Americans coalesced behind Dr. Héctor P. García and the G.I. Forum, who protested the refusal of the Three Rivers mortician to hold services in his funeral home for the slain World War II soldier Félix Longoria; and more recently, communities have stood behind Mexican American activists challenging the malicious bashing of undocumented Mexicans. Such has been the stridency of a people unwilling to accept their condemnation as outsiders in the land of their birth or naturalization.[72]

The 1916 riot deepened racial divides between Mexicans and Anglos in El Paso, and for many years following altered relations between Americans and Mexicans in the border region. The riot exposed underlying anti-Mexican feelings and reinforced derogatory views of Mexicans. It provided local authorities and Anglos the opportunity to reinforce their positions to judge in cases involving racialized social conflict. Further, the episode sanctioned the role of authority to segregate El Paso through the militarized separation of the races with dead lines.

Notes

1. There is some confusion among scholars about the number killed, with numbers given ranging from sixteen to eighteen. There were eighteen dead, but one of those killed was Canadian, so, according to my research at National Archives, seventeen Americans were killed.

2. *Salvo conducto* was an official "safe pass" issued by representatives of the Carranza government to entice foreigners and capitalists back to northern Mexico in 1915. Cusi Mine's general manager Charles Watson met with de facto Chihuahua governor Ignacio Enríquez to negotiate terms for a return to the mines. On January 4, 1916, under the protection of Carranza General José Cavazos and one thousand troops, Watson and his men made their way to the Cusi mines. Christopher Lance Habermeyer, *Gringo's Curve: Pancho Villa's Massacre of American Miners in Mexico, 1916* (El Paso: Book Publishers of El Paso, 2004), 40–41; Eileen Welsome, *The General and the Jaguar: Pershing's Hunt for Pancho Villa, A True Story of Revolution & Revenge* (New York: Little, Brown, and Co., 2006), 64.

3. "Mining Men Stripped Naked and Ruthlessly Shot Down by Band of Villa Savages," *El Paso Morning Times* (January 12, 1916): 1.

4. Other similar episodes in West Texas in the nineteenth century included the Alpine race riot of 1886 and the San Elizario Salt War of 1877. The latter episode was not a riot per se; however, the conflict did exhibit strong racial undertones as participants lined up along racial lines. For more on the Salt War, see C. L. Sonnichsen, *The El Paso Salt War* (El Paso: Hertzog, 1961); W. H. Timmons, *El Paso: A Borderlands History*

(El Paso: Texas Western Press, 1990); Walter Prescott Webb, *The Texas Rangers: A Century of Frontier Defense* (Austin: University of Texas Press, 1935); and Paul Cool, *Salt Warriors: Insurgency on the Rio Grande* (College Station: Texas A&M University Press, 2008). On the Alpine riot, see Arnoldo De León, *They Called Them Greasers: Anglo Attitudes towards Mexicans in Texas, 1821–1900* (Austin: University of Texas Press, 1983), 92.

5. William D. Carrigan, *The Making of a Lynching Culture: Violence and Vigilantism in Central Texas, 1836–1916* (Urbana: University of Illinois, 2004), 2–3.

6. Ibid., 2–3.

7. Cynthia Skove Nevels, *Lynching to Belong: Claiming Whiteness through Racial Violence* (College Station: Texas A&M University Press, 2007), 6–7.

8. Ibid., 7.

9. Walter L. Buenger, *The Path to a Modern South: Northeast Texas between Reconstruction and the Great Depression* (Austin: University of Texas Press, 2001), 22–23.

10. Ibid., 22.

11. Ibid., 25.

12. David Montejano (ed.), *Chicano Politics and Society in the Late Twentieth Century* (Austin: University of Texas Press, 1999), xvi.

13. Sonnichsen, *The El Paso Salt War;* Webb, *The Texas Rangers;* Cool, *Salt Warriors.*

14. Cool, *Salt Warriors,* 2.

15. "When the Santa Fe Windows Were Shot Out, Rangers and Citizens Battle in the Street," *El Paso Times* (December 5, 1920), "Texas Rangers" Vertical File, Southwest Collection, Border Heritage Center, El Paso Public Library, El Paso, Texas.

16. In *Salt Warriors,* Paul Cool argues that the insurgency of 1877 was the "product of a deliberate, community-based decision squarely in the tradition of the *American* nation's original fight for self-government." However, the opposite may be the case. What we see emerge in the El Paso region is closer to what Américo Paredes identified as a "patriarchal system [that] not only made the Border community more cohesive, by emphasizing its clanlike characteristics, but it also minimized outside interference, because it allowed the community to govern itself to a great extent … the Border Mexican simply ignored strangers. . . ." Américo Paredes, *With His Pistol in His Hand: A Border Ballad and Its Hero* (Austin: University of Texas Press, 1958), 12–13.

17. Captain John R. Hughes, "Monthly Returns: Company 'D,' November 30, 1908," Adjutant General Records, Texas State Library and Archives Commission, Austin, Texas.

18. Paredes, *With His Pistol in His Hand,* 31; Julian Samora et al., *Gunpowder Justice: A Reassessment of the Texas Rangers* (Notre Dame: University of Notre Dame Press, 1979), 66; and Robert M. Utley, *Lone Star Lawmen: The Second Century of the Texas Rangers* (Oxford: Oxford University Press, 2007), 69.

19. "Ranger Force Correspondence, 1917," (1183–215) Texas Adjutant General Records, Texas State Library and Archives Commission, Austin, Texas.

20. Ibid.

21. Racial sentiment toward Mexicans in El Paso began to change when thousands of refugees began to flood the city. The influx led President Woodrow Wilson to order a special census on January 6, 1916, to quantify the number of refugees or persons temporarily residing in El Paso from Mexico. The 1916 census concluded that the city experienced a 57.6 percent population increase between 1910 and 1916, "Special Census of the Population of El Paso, Texas, Jan 15, 1916," Department of Commerce, Bureau of the Census (Washington, D.C.: GPO, 1916); "Americans and Mexicans to Be Segregated: New Federal Census Will List Each Race," *El Paso Herald* (January 14, 1916): 6. By 1920, some 42,305 of El Paso's population were foreign born. Of these, an overwhelming 91 percent came from Mexico. U.S. Bureau of the Census, *Population of Principal Cities [Texas] from Earliest Census to 1920,* Bureau of the Census, Washington, D.C., 1920; and Charles H. Harris III and Louis R. Sadler, "The 'Underside' of the Mexican Revolution, 1912," *The Americas* (July 1982): 69–83.

22. *The Survey* 36 (July 8, 1916), 380, Center for American History, University of Texas at Austin.

23. Miguel A. Levario, "Cuando vino la mexicanada: Authority, Race and Conflict in West Texas, 1895–1924" (Ph.D. diss., University of Texas at Austin, 2007), 136.

24. Clarence C. Clendenen, *The United States and Pancho Villa: A Study in Unconventional Diplomacy* (Ithaca: Cornell University, 1961), 135; Frederick C. Turner, "Anti-Americanism in Mexico, 1910–1913," *The Hispanic American Historical Review* 47 (November 1967): 502–518; and "Disorders Continue in Northern Mexico: Anti-American Outbreaks Will Probably Affect Our Reply to Carranza," *New York Times* (June 10, 1916): 5.

25. David D. Romo, *Ringside Seat to a Revolution: An Underground Cultural History of El Paso and Juárez, 1893–1923* (El Paso, Tex.: Cinco Puntos Press, 2005); T. Lindsay Baker, *Ghost Towns of Texas* (Norman: University of Oklahoma Press, 1986); and Mario García, *Desert Immigrants: The Mexicans of El Paso, 1880–1920* (New Haven, Conn.: Yale University Press, 1981), 19–20.

26. Levario, "Cuando vino la mexicanada," 22.

27. García, *Desert Immigrants,* 186–187.

28. Gen. Alvaro Obregón was one of de facto Mexican president Venustiano Carranza's top generals during the Revolution.

29. *El Paso Herald* (December 31, 1915): 6; and Jason T. Darrah, "Anglos, Mexicans, and the San Ysabel Massacre: A Study of Changing Ethnic Relations in El Paso, Texas, 1910–1916," (M.A. thesis, Texas Tech University, 2003), 70–72.

30. *El Paso Morning Times* (January 2, 1916): 2.

31. For more on Villa's anti-American rhetoric, see Haldeen Braddy, *Pancho Villa at Columbus: The Raid of 1916 Revisited* (El Paso: Texas Western College Press, 1965); John F. Chalkley, *Zach Lamar Cobb: El Paso Collector of Customs and Intelligence during the Mexican Revolution, 1913–1918* (El Paso: Texas Western Press, 1998); and Don M. Coerver and Linda B. Hall, *Texas and the Mexican Revolution: A Study in State and National Border Policy, 1910–1920* (San Antonio: Trinity University Press, 1984).

32. "Tragedy Declared Villa Reply to American Aid to Carranza Cause," *El Paso Morning Times* (January 12, 1916): 1.

33. Ibid.

34. The Cusihuiriáchic Mining Company was often referred to as "Cusi" by newspapers and workers.

35. Two eyewitnesses gave detailed accounts to the *El Paso Morning Times*. Juan Vásquez was identified as a "Mexican mining man." Tom B. Holmes, the lone survivor of the party of Americans who escaped to the border, did not witness the executions of the party, seeing only a few of them shot down. "Eye Witness Brings Tale of Butchery of American Mining Men in Chihuhua," *El Paso Morning Times* (January 13, 1916): 1; and "Eyewitness Tells of Killing of Eighteen Americans in Mexico," *El Paso Herald* (January 13, 1916): 2.

36. Ibid.

37. "Mining Men Stripped Naked and Ruthlessly Shot Down by Band of Villa Savages," *El Paso Morning Times* (January 12, 1916): 1.

38. *Villista* soldier and eyewitness, Adolfo Rivera, would recall several years after the incident that, "the Americans [miners] ran and ran." Habermeyer, *Gringos' Curve,* 59.

39. "Eye Witness Brings Tale of Butchery of American Mining Men in Chihuahua," *El Paso Morning Times* (January 13, 1916): 1.

40. Richard Estrada, "The Mexican Revolution in Ciudad Juárez-El Paso Area, 1910–1920," *Password* (Summer 1979): 69; and Romo, *Ringside Seat to a Revolution,* 220.

41. "Answer to Memorial before the Special Claims Commission Mexico and the United States," *The United States of America on behalf of Matilda Symansky Bodine, Administratrix of the Estate of Manuel Bonifacio Romero v. the United Mexican States,* The Santa Ysabel Cases (No. 7), Docket No. 449, Record Group 76, Records of Boundary and Claims Commission, 1923–1937, Records Relating to the Santa Ysabel Cases, 1924–1936, National Archives and Records Administration, College Park, Md.

42. Braddy, *Pancho Villa at Columbus: The Raid of 1916 Revisited,* 26.

43. "*Pasó por la Calle de El Paso cuando vino con el General Pershing . . . ¿Comó no lo voy a recorder, joven? Pero ni el golpe* (the young girl sustained a minor injury falling down some stairs) *sentí por llegar hasta ver a Pancho Villa.*" (He came through El Paso Street

with General Pershing … How could I forget, young man? Not even my injury was going to keep me from seeing Pancho Villa). (Unless otherwise noted, all translations are my own.) Hortencia Villegas, interview by Oscar J. Martínez, February 17, 1976, interview 235, transcript, Institute of Oral History, Special Collections, University of Texas at El Paso.

44. On October 26, 1915, Villa assembled the inhabitants of Colonia Morelos, Sonora, and delivered one of his most notable public speeches. His remarks were heavily laden with anti-American rhetoric. Villa promised that he would, "rescue the settlers from the tyranny of the North American Mormons, who exploit, vilify, and assassinate the Mexicans in the region." Charles H. Harris and Louis Sadler, "Pancho Villa and the Columbus Raid: The Missing Documents," *New Mexico Historical Review* L (October 1975): 335–346; Juan Gómez-Quiñones, "The Plan de San Diego Reviewed," *Aztlán: Chicano Journal of the Social Sciences and the Arts* 1 (Spring 1970): 125. In El Paso, Villa's anti-American rhetoric troubled many Anglo residents there and in parts of northern Mexico and it made them fear for their safety. Letter from U.S. Consul Edwards to Secretary of State Lansing, stating that "distress and fear is evident on every face [in Juárez and El Paso]," December 28, 1915, Records of the Department of State Relating to Internal Affairs of Mexico, 1910–1929, National Archives Microfilm, Microcopy No. 274, Records of the Department of State Relating to Internal Affairs of Mexico, 1910–29, Roll 50, 812.00/16776–17150, The National Archives and Records Service, Washington, D.C., 1959; and telegram from Zach Cobb to Secretary of State, stating that "[El Paso] as a whole is stirred deeply with quiet indignation because of the [Santa Ysabel] murders," January 11, 1916, Records of the Department of State Relating to Internal Affairs of Mexico, 1910–1929, National Archives Microfilm, Microcopy No. 274, Records of the Department of State Relating to Internal Affairs of Mexico, 1910–29, Roll 50, 812.00/16776–17150, The National Archives and Records Service, Washington, D.C., 1959.

45. "Mutilated Corpses of Murdered Americans Brought to El Paso," *El Paso Morning Times* (January 13, 1916): 1.

46. Report received by Commanding General, Eighth Brigade, Fort Bliss, Texas, "Weekly Report of General Conditions along the Mexican Border," January 15, 1916, no. 148, Headquarters Southern Department, Fort Sam Houston, Texas, Division of Mexican Affairs, National Archives Microfilm, Microcopy No. 274, Records of the Department of State Relating to Internal Affairs of Mexico, 1910–29, Roll 51, 812.00/17151–17575, The National Archives and Records Service, Washington, D.C., 1959 [hereafter, "Weekly report"].

47. "Consul Edwards of Juárez Jeered by American Crowds in El Paso," *El Paso Herald* (January 13, 1916): 3; "El Pasoans Petition President to Remove Consul T. D. Edwards," *El Paso Morning Times* (January 14, 1916): 5.

48. "Rodríguez Reported Prisoner," *El Paso Herald* (January 13, 1916): 1.

49. "Mexicans Chased Across Border," *San Antonio Express* (January 14, 1916): 2.

50. "Crowd Starts Riot on Broadway; Officers and Soldiers Stop It," *El Paso Herald* (January 14, 1916): 1.

51. Hortencia Villegas, interview by Oscar J. Martínez, February 17, 1976. Interview 235, transcript, Institute of Oral History, University of Texas at El Paso.

52. Crowds formed at Overland and Santa Fe Street, traveled along Santa Fe to Fifth, thence to El Paso, back along El Paso to Second, thence to Broadway, along Broadway to Overland, where they encountered still other crowds. "Villistas Vagged and Driven From El Paso, Near Riots and Sporadic Fighting in Downtown Streets Culmination of Day of Excitement Following Funerals of Masscre Victims," *El Paso Morning Times* (January 14, 1916): 1.

53. Report received by Commanding General, Eighth Brigade, Fort Bliss, Texas, "Weekly report"; and "Villistas Vagged and Driven From El Paso," *El Paso Morning Times* (January 14, 1916): 1.

54. El Paso's "Second Ward" was primarily inhabited by Mexicans and Mexican Americans. The area stretches east from the downtown area and along the Rio Grande.

55. Villegas, interview, February 17, 1976.

56. "Carranza Orders Assassins Captured Dead or Alive," *San Antonio Express* (January 14, 1916); "Mexicans Chased Across Border," *San Antonio Express* (January 14, 1916).

57. "Americans Fighting Mexicans in El Paso," *New York Times* (January 14, 1916); Pershing to Funston, Fort Bliss, Texas, January 17, 1916, National Archives Records of the Department of State, Relating to Internal Affairs of Mexico, 1910–1929, Roll 51, 812.00/17158.

58. "Carranza Orders Assassins Captured Dead or Alive," 1.

59. *Labor Advocate,* Front page (January 14, 1916) El Paso, Texas.

60. Pershing to Funston, January 17, 1916, National Archives Records of the Department of State, Relating to Internal Affairs of Mexico, 1910–1929; Roll 51, 812.00/17158.

61. "Troops Ready to Prevent Trouble," *San Antonio Express* (January 15, 1916).

62. "Slain Americans Buried in El Paso," *San Antonio Express* (January 15, 1916).

63. Villegas, interview, February 17, 1976.

64. El Paso resident Maurcio Cordero recounted an incident that took place in the aftermath of the Villa Columbus raid (March 1916), where his dark-skinned friend was beaten for violating curfew set forth by the dead lines established after the El Paso race riot in January 1916. Mauricio Cordero, Interview by Oscar J. Martínez, February 15, 1974, interview 250, transcript, Institute of Oral History, Special Collections, University of Texas at El Paso.

65. "Mexicans Chased Across Border," *San Antonio Express* (January 14, 1916).

66. According to the *New York Times,* the cards read, "Remember the Alamo, Did We Watch and Wait! Remember The Cusi. Shall We Watch and Wait!" "Americans Fighting Mexicans in El Paso," *New York Times* (January 14, 1916): 2.

67. Letter from Zach Cobb to Secretary of State Robert Lansing expressing fear that the "Carranza government is slipping backwards," and "if [Carranza is] not more aggressive against bandits, Villa and others may put them on the defensive in the garrisoned towns." February 1, 1916, NARA, Records of the Department of State, Relating to Internal Affairs of Mexico, 1910–1929, Roll 51, 812.00/17151–17575.

68. "Americans and Mexicans to Be Segregated, 6; and "Special Census of the Population of El Paso, Texas," January 15, 1916, Department of Commerce, Bureau of the Census (Washington, D.C.: Government Printing Office, 1916).

69. Mae Ngai, *Impossible Subjects: Illegal Aliens and the Making of Modern America* (Princeton: Princeton University Press, 2004), 131–132.

70. Ibid., 132.

71. "Indignation Meeting Is Called Off and Talk of Quick Revenge Subsides: Native Born New Mexicans Ready to Join Volunteers," *El Paso Morning Times,* January 15, 1916: 1.

72. Arnoldo De León, *Mexican Americans in Texas: A Brief History,* 3rd ed. (Wheeling, Ill.: Harlan Davidson Inc., 2009), 42–43, 56–57, 69–70, 104–105, 120–121, 172–173.

The Mexican Revolution and the Women of *El México de Afuera,* the Pan American Round Table, and the *Cruz Azul Mexicana*

JUANITA LUNA LAWHN

The role of *El México de Afuera* exiles in the history of San Antonio is critical to understanding the character of the city's diverse Latino population today. To the uninformed, political terminology can sometimes be misleading. Among those steeped in the experiences of México and Texas at the turn of the twentieth century, the reference *El México de Afuera* had a precise meaning, one expressing a reality more ideological than geographical.[1] Trans-

Camila Villasana Mata, president of La Cruz Azul, *1925–26. Courtesy Dominga Gómez Ybarra.*

lated superficially, word by word, *El México de Afuera* could be understood as "México on the Outside"—that is México outside of the lines or borders of its national territory. However, within the context of the cultural and political history of the México–Texas border, *El México de Afuera* is not correctly translated in a generic sense as *Mexicanos* or *Tejanos* who reside *al otro lado,* or north of the border—*El México de Afuera* is both and less than that.

As with so many other immigrant groups, when citizens of Mexico traveled to another country, they carried with them and within themselves all the individualizing traits of their history and social class, as well as their identifying political culture. As a whole, then, *Mexicanos* living in their "new land" exhibited and maintained all the political heritage of the land of origin. Most prominent in the official culture of textbooks (as well as in the popular culture of Mexico), and glaringly evident in almost every Mexican restaurant, are the images of *los revolucionarios*—Emiliano Zapata and Pancho Villa. For example, the image of Emiliano Zapata has been transformed into the mascot of many popular Mexican restaurants, such as *Mi Tierra,* in San Antonio, Texas. In the restaurant, a mural documents the history of the Tejano, Mexicano, Chicano, and/or Latino—Pancho Villa, Henry B. González, Emma Tenayuca, Dolores Huerta, and countless other figures from México and the United States. Of course, the image of Pancho Villa and Emiliano Zapata are most prominent and easily recognized. The mosaic wall mirrors the history of the Latino, symbolizing the Americanization of the Mexicano.

To look at the paintings and posters of the famous *Mi Tierra* restaurant, one acquires only the faintest suggestion of a reality that exists beyond the world of Zapata and Villa. Yet at the turn of the century came to San Antonio the conservatives who rejected revolution and embraced the politics and culture of the disgraced *Porfiriato* (the dictatorship of Porfirio Díaz which ended in 1911 with the start of the Revolution). These right-wing, conservative, and distinctly upper class immigrants were among those who first sought to maintain *El México de Afuera,* a Mexican universe of exiles. As the Mexican Revolution grew stronger and more dangerous, the face of the San Antonio *barrios* underwent a demographic change:[2] alongside the native Tejanos and *Porfiristas* settled *Maderistas* (supporters of Francisco Madero who fled north after Madero's murder in 1913 by opposing forces) as well as landless *campesinos* and even *revolucionarios*. After 1914 came *Huertistas* (out of favor in Mexico when revolutionaries ousted their leader president Victoriano Huerta). Collectively, these several exile elements constituted the community of *El México de Afuera*.

In San Antonio, the social and political allegiances of these various groups did not change course—conservatives did not suddenly embrace *revolucionarios;* nor did the *ricos* (the rich, or well-to-do class) mingle with the *pobres,* or the poorer masses. Actually, the elite Mexican immigrants established ties with their Euro-American affluent, elite, and distinctly upper-class counterparts.[3] Although the scholarship on the immigrants of the Revolution acknowledges these socially prominent members of the elites who came to stay in San Antonio (temporarily, they thought), less recognized are the accounts of the women of the Mexican community— the women of revolution, or women of *El México de Afuera.* The activities of these women émigrés and their involvement in local matters span the years of the turn of the century and reflect the cultural, social, and political character of their marriage and family background.

There is more to the chronicle of the Mexican women (as with the Mexican men) than first meets the eye. As historians, social scientists, and other scholars investigate the connection between the Mexican Revolution and the Tejano community, it becomes apparent that influences on Texas-Mexican society came as much from *El México de Afuera mujeres* such as Sara Madero, Angela Madero, Luz Corral de Villa, and Virginia Salinas Carranza as it did from luminaries like Francisco I. Madero, Pancho Villa, and Venustiano Carranza. Although it is difficult to identify the exact impact that these Mexican women had on the psyche of the Tejano, their effect becomes partially evident upon reading the narratives of these four political women—Sara Madero, Angela Madero, Luz Corral de Villa, and Virginia Salinas Carranza—who fled to the Southwest for sanctuary.

As the women of *El México de Afuera* became established in San Antonio, their inclination was to associate themselves with those of their own class. Elite women socialized among themselves; poorer women with others of their background. As to rico women, their activities are included in the standard publications of the time and illustrate the extent to which they became a part of San Antonio's transplanted circle of exiles, and also to the degree that the city's Anglo-American ruling class became a part of them. As members of the city's multi-ethnic community, these Mexican women participated within the Pan American Round Table and volunteered and carried out humanitarian work within the *Cruz Azul Mexicana* (the Mexican Blue Cross) of that city. In this way and others, the women of the Revolution worked to improve the social, intellectual, and material well-being of their own transplanted community, as well as that of the city's broader *colonial mexicana.*

The first chapter of this saga began with Madero in 1910. During the month of June, after being released from a Mexican prison on bail, Francisco I. Madero eluded "his guards and, donning the clothes of a working man, crossed the border at Laredo and came to San Antonio,"[4] where he began to plan the Mexican revolt.[5] Suspected revolutionary intrigue locally, the presence of a large Mexican American population there, and the proximity of San Antonio to México motivated newspapers in the city to stay abreast of events related to Mexico. The media thus chronicled the activities of *El México de Afuera* women in San Antonio.

The Mexican Revolution incited men and women on both sides of the border to military, social, and literary action. On February 13, 1913, Ignacio E. Lozano printed the first issue of the Spanish language newspaper, *La Prensa,* with its goal of keeping the community of *El México de Afuera* informed on the progress of the Mexican Revolution. During the early part of February, 1913, *The San Antonio Light* carried extensive coverage of the Revolution as well, reporting the murder of Francisco I. Madero and José María Pino Suárez, for instance. On February 24, 1913, *The San Antonio Light* printed a photograph of Mrs. Francisco I. Madero, offering the first characterization of *El México de Afuera* women in the person of Madero's widow, Sara Madero. Above the stern, determinate, and grieving woman were printed the words, "Widowed by Revolt."[6] Though a bold (albeit isolated) photograph of Señora Madero accompanied the *Light's* report, the print does not convey her personal story, even though the news items surrounding the image give extensive information on the particulars surrounding her husband's murder. Still, the story of Sara Madero does not end there.

On April 11, 1913, *The San Antonio Light* reprinted an interview with Mrs. Madero originally published in New York and titled: "Mrs. Madero Breaks Silence." In breaking her "silence," the widow revealed that "she approached Ambassador Henry Wilson to plead with him to use his influence to save her husband's life, only to encounter discouragement from the American ambassador."[7] Sara Madero reported that "Wilson declined to intercede on behalf of her husband. And when we pressed him to send a telegram to President Taft, he first said it was unnecessary, but later promised to send it."[8] Sara Madero's assertiveness and conviction to expose the hypocrisy of the U.S. ambassador is further revealed in the poignancy of her story: "From Havana, we wrote to President Taft asking him if he ever had received the message, but we got no answer to the letter. I am sure the message was never sent."[9] She continued firmly, "The ambassador told me he had conferred with Huerta regarding the fate of my husband and Vice President, José María Pino Suárez, and that he had advised Huerta to do what he thought best for the country."[10] As if what Sara had explained was not enough for the reader to infer Wilson's complicity in her husband's murder, she declared, "This was tantamount to advising Huerta that if he believed the death of my husband and *Señor* Suárez was for the good of the country to kill them. In any event, they were killed and I know that the ambassador had knowledge that such was to be done."[11] The distraught widow reported that Wilson responded to her anguish in the following manner: "Mrs. Madero, I will be frank with you; your husband's downfall is due to the fact that he never consulted with me—he never wanted to advise with me."[12] Wilson's reply implies that if President Madero had assumed a subordinate position, maybe, he would have protected him.

Sara Madero's accusations against Henry Lane Wilson reveal the unrelenting valor of a woman advocating for the lives of her husband and Vice-President, Pino Suárez. In retrospect, one can only wonder about what effect Sara Madero's interview had on *El México de Afuera* community in San Antonio. For those who supported the Díaz's regime, it might have been to retreat into denial; for the *Maderistas,* bitterness toward the enemies of democracy; for the working-class *campesinos,* it could have deepened their distrust in the U.S. government as well as in the government of Mexico because they could have seen Madero as their president—the president of the *campesino.* For the Tejano community, on the other hand, it could have been to believe that in México, in the realm of U.S.–México relations, no one was safe.

The well-to-do from Mexico had always envisioned Texas as a safe place for visits or residence. For example, various members of the Madero family resided in San Antonio before and during the Revolution. On October 24, 1916, *The San Antonio Light* reported on the marriage of Angela Madero, Francisco I. Madero's sister, to José Treviño García at the Ursuline Chapel, located in the center of San Antonio. The couple was accompanied by various members of the Madero family, including Madero's widow. According to *The San Antonio Light,* Angela Madero gained national prominence following the imprisonment of Madero and Pino Suárez when she allegedly faced Victoriano Huerta and denounced him. Like Madero's widow, Angela's status as a woman of privilege provided her with the life experiences of a good education, wealth, and politics. Angela had lived in San Antonio while her brother wrote the *Plan of San Luis Potosí.* After their marriage, Angela and José Treviño García returned to

Monterrey.[13] The movement between the United States and Mexico, exemplified by the newlyweds, served to arrest acculturation and assimilation in the Tejano community. Even today, the coming and going of individuals across the border continues to enrich the Mexican culture of Latinos over the entire United States.

On December 4, 1919, *The San Antonio Light* printed an interview titled "Mrs. Villa Laughs at Report of Warrior Husband's Capture: Late Advices Add Not One Whit to Many Worries of Woman, Resident of City Raising Family of Three."[14] In contrast to the Madero family, who lived among the upper-class Euro-Americans and other *Mexicanos* in the near North Side of San Antonio, Luz Villa resided at 815 Rivas[15]—the near West Side, the barrio where recent immigrants bonded with the existing working-class community. The connection between the San Antonio community and those directly involved in the fighting across the border is apparent in the *Light's* report that "Men friendly to Villa, Americans and others, who return from his haunts, bring back letters that they give or send to his wife."[16] The story continued that the last letter that came from Villa, "contained information that Villa had a 'garrison' in the Santa Rosalia district."[17] This news item reveals the immediacy of the Mexican Revolution to the barrios of San Antonio as it illustrates that the borders of the Mexican Revolution did not necessarily confine themselves to the Rio Grande—the fluidity of the border served also to provide a safe abode for the revolutionary, a retreat both for the woman and the man.

In the interview, Villa's children's tutor, Professor Matías C. García, related that Pancho Villa valued education for his own children as well as for the children of his country, and that Villa realized the "handicap that denial of education has put upon the lower classes of México and that he has always intended to remedy it."[18] Professor García continued, "Reynalda, the eldest, who is 16 [and] is studying shorthand . . . realizes that even the daughter of a man who means to be master of Mexico someday should be prepared to make her own way in the world."[19] In the kitchen, meanwhile, Luz had prepared breakfast, and the interview concluded with a repetition of her philosophy—"politics and nothing more,"[20] a reference to the latest report that her husband "is held prisoner by his own men and will be turned over to the Carranza government for a fifty-thousand-*peso* reward."[21] This story vividly captures the courage of Luz Corral de Villa; while Pancho Villa traveled over the northern states of Mexico fomenting revolution, she struggled independently on the West Side of San Antonio providing for her children and herself.

Finally, in the decade of the Revolution, on November 10, 1919, in a news brief titled "Mrs. Carranza Dies at Querétaro after Protracted Illness," the *San Antonio Light* announced the death of Virginia Salinas Carranza: "a descendent from the early settlers of San Antonio who lived in what is now known as Nogalitos beyond the Aransas Pass tracks on S. Flores Street . . . Salinas Street received its name from this old San Antonio family."[22] The report carried a brief biography of Virginia: "Her father moved the family to Coahuila during one of the revolutions of Texas."[23] The respect that Virginia attained among friends and acquaintances is evident in further details given: "a woman of many excellent qualities, highly educated, but of a retiring and modest disposition, and always greatly interested in her husband's future,"[24] who "while in this city, passed through many ordeals during her husband's struggles in the overthrow of Huerta."[25] In the story, Samuel Belden, a San Antonio lawyer closely aligned to the Tejano community, praised Virginia Salinas Carranza: "One of the greatest characters of recent Mexican history has succumbed. When women come into their own in México, as they are doing in other countries, full justice and credit will be extended this estimable woman who was untiring in her work for the betterment of México and its people."[26]

The news items that touched on the bearing and demeanor of notable exile women of the Revolution—Sara Madero, Luz Corral de Villa, and Virginia Salinas Carranza—function to illustrate that the women were not necessarily timid, silent, or irresolute, but leaders in their own right. Information concerning their activities is limited, however, and much research is needed to document women's roles in the Mexican Revolution, as well as their involvement in local community affairs while part of *El México de Afuera.*

The narratives of these four prominent women—Sara Madero, Angela Madero, Luz Corral de Villa, and Virginia Salinas Carranza—do divulge something about the lives of Mexican women exiles in San Antonio. They reveal that the political standing they held in Mexico persisted in San Antonio. The Madero family, judging from the social activities that *The San Antonio Light* printed in the 1910s, did not interact with the *Huertista* exiles—an expected course of behavior because the latter families supported the *Porfiriato.* Still, both groups lived among the well-do-to Euro-Americans in the near north side of the city. But as will be shown below, by the late 1910s and into the 1920s, the women of *El Mexico de Afuera,* notwithstanding their social standings, got involved in humanitarian activities for the common good of all Mexicanos in the city. Luz, on the other hand, lived in a modest home, on the *barrios* of West Side, where most of the recent Mexican *campesinos* as well as working-class Tejanos resided. The Carranza family lived in the south side of San Antonio.

More important, the same narratives confirm the forceful character of the women. Regardless of social class and political position, the four women—Sara Madero, Angela Madero, Luz Corral de Villa, and Virginia Salinas Carranza—challenged authority, whether the authorities were Mexican or American, or newspaper reporters. Furthermore, their personal accounts illustrate the women's loyalty to their husbands, their flair with language, their powerful spirits, their participation within the political systems of their country, and their uninhibited exercise of power when given the opportunity to tell their personal stories. The women who crossed the border into San Antonio displayed a pattern of resistance, one repeated by the Tejana, Mexicana, Chicana, and the Latina woman who in later years rebelled against social, political and economic disparity—in the Finck Cigar Company Strike (1933), the San Antonio Laundry Strike (1937), and the Pecan Shellers' Strike (1938)—strikes that occurred in San Antonio throughout the twentieth century.

While men of the exiled community in San Antonio forged their respective places within their professions and businesses, as well as in their literary endeavors in publishing houses and in various Spanish-language newspapers in San Antonio, such as *La Época, El Imparcial de Texas,* and *La Prensa,* the women joined local clubs devoted to preserving Mexican culture and ideals (both in Mexico and Texas), as well as other societies committed to humanitarian work in the city. Among the former was the Pan American Round Table (PART), an organization founded by Florence Terry Griswold, a humanitarian who responded emotionally to the disenfranchised citizens of the Mexican Revolution. Griswold reflected on her philosophy thus:

> We feel that as the women of the Western Hemisphere are the ones most keenly interested and have been the greatest sufferers by reason of political misunderstandings of the men, we consider that now is the time to begin educational propaganda of the sort that will mould the minds of coming generations into the sound principals of international amity, so that in the future, we may be one for all and all for one.[27]

On October 16, 1916, during a luncheon at the Menger Hotel, Florence Griswold organized PART.[28] The constitution of the Pan American

Round Table of San Antonio declared the organization to be nonpolitical, nonsectarian, and non-profit-sharing. Primarily, PART pursued two goals: (a) "To promote mutual knowledge, understanding and friendship among the people of the Western Hemisphere; (b) To foster all movements leading to a higher civilization, especially those affecting the women and children of the Pan American countries."[29]

As the Pan American Round Table favored learning the customs and culture of the Latin American countries, it attracted among others the women of *El México de Afuera,* who desired not to relinquish their Mexican citizenship and wished to maintain their language and heritage. They represented a resource that would facilitate the organization in reaching its goal: bringing together U.S. and Mexican women in the cause for Pan Americanism. Among the original charter members was Alicia Lozano, wife of Ignacio E. Lozano, the editor of *La Prensa* and a critic of the Revolution. Thus, while the fighting took place far away, the Mexican Revolution still touched Tejanos whenever *El México de Afuera* women, through local involvement, brought light to their city's *colonia mexicana* (constituted of both foreign and native-born Mexicans) and to it also, greater credibility.

As part of its campaign to foster Pan Americanism, PART on December 1–3, 1919, sponsored the first *Congreso Femenino* (Feminine Conference, or Woman's Conference) in San Antonio, a conference that would not have taken place if PART had not been first organized. Although the organization proclaimed to be nonpolitical, the conference *was* just that. Both U.S. and Mexican government officials attended and played an important role in the three-day meeting. The first session began without the delegation from the National University of México because two of its members, Dr. Hermila Galindo, a Mexican feminist, and Mrs. Eugenta [sic] Flores Meléndez, were denied passports by the U.S. consul in México City.[30] Florence Griswold greeted the audience. Among the participants in the first morning's sessions were San Antonio Mayor Sam Bell and other city officials, Father M. S. Garriga, *Señor* de la Mata (Mexican consul), and Guillermo Hall, head of the Mexican Trade Bureau of the Chamber of Commerce.[31]

Dr. W. E. Dunn, associate professor of Latin-American history at the University of Texas, presented on the first day of the conference. His address took the topic beyond mutual understanding and friendship to trade relations between Mexico and the United States. He issued an alert: "[A] bitter propaganda against this nation is being disseminated throughout

South and Central America by European powers, to prevent growth of trade relations and consequent diversion of that rich trade to this country."[32] For Dunn, to have European countries interfere with U.S.–México trade would be disruptive to the economic ties linking the two nations. On this practical attitude of cooperation between the United States and Mexico rested the essence of Pan Americanism.

The next presenter, Professor Slaughter, from Rice Institute, was equally pragmatic, but rather than focusing on commerce, addressed education. In his presentation, "Educational Opportunities for Latin Americans in the United States," he discussed the schooling problems facing Latin American countries, particularly illiteracy in México. He suggested that the United States might be able to aid the southern republics, and in particular México, by the establishment of training schools for teachers.[33] Esther Pérez Carvajal, Spanish teacher at the Main High School, translated Professor Slaughter's words for the benefit of the Spanish-speaking audience. One would assume that as a translator Carvajal was constantly involved in the conversation and personal dynamics of the various presenters. Her role must have been more than that of a mere translator: most likely, that of a negotiator.

James Slayden, an audience member, strongly declared "[I]t is not merely a matter of education that the matter of trade, of gain, is inextricably mixed up with the entire situation."[34] He concluded, "This nation must not only educate others, but can profitably turn its attention to educating its own citizens."[35]

Dr. Charles Cunningham of the University of Texas, on the second day of the conference, spoke on the "Fundamentals of Pan-Americanism." Dr. Cunningham defined Pan Americanism as embracing "All Americans"[36] and, according to the *San Antonio Light*, said that

> to reach this objective, it is necessary to know the background of each nation, first, as understanding is based on knowledge. He declared that commercial relations were great factors in determining the sympathetic understanding between the nations and that men doing business in the Latin-American countries were largely determining the opinion those nations held.[37]

Another speaker during the afternoon was the aforementioned Esther Pérez Carvajal, Chair of the Spanish department at Main Avenue High School, today known as Fox Tech. Carvajal offered methods for furthering the teaching of language in the schools.[38] The story of Carvajal, conference translator and speaker, merits its own study. Important known fragments of her life indicate that she was one of few Mexican-descent women educated in the United States (University of Chicago, 1919) and that she held a significant position in the San Antonio School District. Beyond that, there is some indication that she engaged in academic writing: she authored a brief article in the prestigious journal of the Modern Language Association (on nothing less than the American Flag) and collaborated in the writing of a book on the teaching of Spanish.[39]

During Wednesday's assembly, dubbed "México Day," the Mexican women (several of them from the *El México de Afuera* community) stepped forward. Among the day's organizers were Mrs. Juan Long, Mrs. Ernesto Madero, Mrs. Everisto Madero, and Mrs. C.B. Woods, predominantly *Maderistas*.[40] During the official proceedings, the Housewives Chamber of Commerce, through the president, Mrs. J. Bittles, presented a resolution directing U.S. congressmen and senators to investigate the reasons for permitting the importation of fruits and vegetables from México.[41]

> The resolution alleged that the fruit-growing industry in this country indirectly had framed narrow regulations regarding importation of cheap fruits and vegetables into those parts of the country safely removed by geographical distance from fruit-growing centers. This action was asked as a step in reducing the high cost of living.[42]

The conference was not only interested in commercial relations but also in sharing of ideas and language. Consequently, a second resolution encouraged the exchange of students between universities in Latin American countries and those of the United States, the promotion of a mutual understanding of ideals, and the teaching of English where groups of Spanish-speaking people lived.[43]

Dr. J. Z. Uriburu, president and chairman of the board of directors of the first Pan American University in this country, at Riverside near Los Angeles, California, introduced a resolution to build a second Pan American University in San Antonio.[44] Uriburu stated, "I am a firm believer in the Monroe doctrine modified so that it becomes the means of preserving the interest of the Western Hemisphere. . . . [It is] only through education that future generations of this hemisphere will unite their efforts in developing the commercial, economic and political levels of Pan-America."[45] Col. Francisco Chapa, a Tejano, read the clause that requested that a Pan American University be built in San Antonio.[46]

On the final day of the conference, Mrs. Muñoz Blanco, wife of Manuel Múzquiz Blanco, one of the editors of *La Prensa,* appealed in Spanish to the women to do all in their power to bring the two nations to closer friendly relations.[47] Mrs. Muñoz Blanco's appeal was within character for she was one of the *El México de Afuera* loyalists. Muñoz Blanco was Mexican in citizenship and heart. State Senator Harry Hertzberg predicted a brilliant future for the Pan American Round Table and offered his personal assistance and cooperation to the movement.[48]

The last day's program included talks by Mrs. Long, Francisco Oliveres [sic] Jr., Manuel Blanco of *La Prensa,* and Dr. Uriburu. One presenter read a message from Dr. Hermila Galindo, who had not been able to attend the conference.[49] Dr. Galindo had once joined a liberal club that opposed Porfirio Díaz, and in 1917 she "became the private secretary and propagandist to the liberal, reform-minded Carranza. Having won his trust, she proceeded to lobby for the rights of Mexican women. . . . In 1915 . . . she published her magazine, *La Mujer Moderna* [*The Modern Woman*]."[50] The fact that Dr. Galindo's essay was read in the same venue where *Maderista* and *Huertista mujeres* were well represented is an example of how Mexican women considered issues more important than political affiliations—an attitude that permeated the First Feminine Conference in San Antonio in 1916.

Hundreds of guests attended an evening banquet sponsored by Consul Mata and funded by local Mexican families who provided the music and dancing. The delegation from Mexico joined in "presiding, singing the national anthem of this country prior to singing their own, which followed as an international courtesy." The women from the *Huertista* and *Maderista* camps had heretofore retained their distance from each other in San Antonio because of political differences. However, as both groups were foreigners in the city, participation in the international feminine conference gave them an opportunity to bond with their mother country, Mexico. The two cohorts of women put aside their differences and united in solidarity in an effort to demonstrate their loyalty to their nation—"*afuera de México hay nomás una patria*" (beyond Mexico, there is only one nation). In getting involved in the cause of the Pan American Round Table (as well as in other local affairs) women of *El México de Afuera* sought not only to improve conditions in their beloved country but also to nourish the cultural and intellectual environment in San Antonio's Tejano community, of which they gradually became a part.

By the 1920s, the flow of people (who had arrived voluntarily and involuntarily) from Mexico to the United States witnessed a gradual reversal. The influx of Mexicans into the United States as a result of the Mexican Revolution had led to an overabundance of Mexican labor, and consequently mounting unemployment, vagrancy, hunger, illness, and unfair cases of incarcerations.[51] The United States thus approached Mexican consuls and requested that their government find a solution to the problems. On April 9, 1921, Mexican consuls convened in San Antonio, Texas, to deal with the difficulties. Among several resolutions approved during the conference was one to create the *Comisiones Honoríficas* (Honorary Commissions) and *La Cruz Azul Mexicana,* both under the auspices of the Mexican government. A man named Jesús Franco was entrusted with locating communities experiencing undue difficulty. He was to travel to those areas, identify Mexican or Tejana women who demonstrated leadership qualities, and found chapters of *La Cruz Azul Mexicana.* As members of *La Cruz Azul,* women—whether they were exiles of the Revolution, *rico* or *pobre,* or Tejanas—would be better able to provide assistance to their locales in a systematic manner.[52]

On April 14, 1921, Jesús Franco and a group of Mexican consuls traveled to San Marcos, Texas, where they installed the first *Comisiones Honoríficas* and a *La Cruz Azul* chapter as a response to the request from the Mexican community in that city. Jesusita Díaz was president of *La Cruz Azul* in San Marcos.[53]

As of March 5, 1922, María Luisa Garza (Loreley) headed the *brigadas de La Cruz Azul Mexicana* (Blue Cross brigades/chapters) in Texas, as president. Isabel Belden was the general treasurer, Concepción García Cuéllar was the "*abandera*" (flag carrier), and María Frobes [sic] was the Vice-President of *La Cruz Azul Mexicana.* When María Luisa Garza went to Austin to induct Governor of Texas Pat M. Neff as an honorary member of *La Cruz Azul,* she requested that the executive look into the case of Pedro Sánchez, a Mexican imprisoned in Marlin, Texas. The Governor eventually commuted Pedro Sánchez' death sentence to life imprisonment.[54]

As a voluntary organization led by women expelled by the Revolution or by Tejanas, *La Cruz Azul* encouraged Mexican-descent women to advocate for the disenfranchised members of the Tejano community. Loreley was one of several journalists who immigrated to the United

States in the Revolution's aftermath and continued their journalistic work in the Spanish-language newspapers. In San Antonio, she published regularly in *La Época, el periódico del obrero (The Epoch: The Workers' Newspaper);* becoming president of the *Cruz Azul Mexicana* was thus well within the framework of her commitment to the working-class community. It is interesting to note that she did not publish for *La Prensa* of San Antonio, even though it appears that she lived in San Antonio during the 1920s.

On May 5, 1922, the first state conference of the *Comisiones honoríficas* and of the *brigadas de la Cruz Azul* was held in Laredo, Texas. Isabel Belden, Tila Villegas, and Julia Flores attended as delegates of the San Antonio *Cruz Azul* chapter.[55] The work of the *Cruz Azul* included supporting charitable organizations such as the Red Cross, advocating for Mexicans, and creating libraries; the *brigadas* were encouraged to contact José Vasconcelos, Secretary of Public Education in México City, asking his office to provide available books, especially texts published for Mexicans living in foreign lands. Both the Mexican immigrant community and the Tejano community were to be important elements in meeting the goals of the *Cruz Azul,* according to one of the resolutions passed at the conference: it specifically encouraged *Cruz Azul* members to involve Mexicans (regardless of place of nativity) in fulfilling the organization's objectives. Additionally, the consul present at the conference exhorted those in attendance to seek wider support in efforts to increase the inventory of proposed libraries.[56] Obviously, the deliberations at the first conference of *Comisiones Honoríficas* and the *brigadas de La Cruz Azul* reflected the Mexican, Tejano, and Euro-American communities' concern for the welfare of all Mexicanos living in the United States.

Though the Mexican consuls held oversight over the *Cruz Azul Mexicana,* the women from the *barrios* did most of the field work. Labor in the trenches blurred the lines of national loyalties, as is evident in the fact that María Luisa Garza was a Mexican citizen,[57] whereas Isabel Belden was a Tejana. It is important to note that just as in other occasions, women despite the place of nativity came together in solidarity to work toward a greater issue: the erasure of borders.

Mexican immigrant and Tejano women carried on humanitarian work in cities such as San Antonio as well as in rural communities across the state such as Alice, Alpine, Austin, Asherton, Aransas Pass, Beaumont, Benavides, Corpus Christi, Charlotte, Carrizo Spring, Del Rio, Encinal, Pleasanton, Pharr, Rockdale, Uvalde, Sabinal, and many other towns in Texas and the United States.[58] On December 5, 1998, I interviewed Minga Villasana, the daughter of Camila Villasana, the president of the *Cruz Azul Mexicana* of Sabinal, Texas, my hometown. She shared a photograph of her mother that featured her in complete uniform. Minga also showed me her mother's gold organizational ring. My interview with Minga Villasana confirmed documentary sources that the women of *La Cruz Azul* were instrumental in providing humanitarian aid to individuals who were in need of food, medicine, and clothing.[59] As researchers continue to *platicar con la gente de los barrios* (to dialogue with people from Mexican communities), the history of these women will be made public.

In San Antonio, Texas, the activities of *La Cruz Azul* were reported in *La Época, La Prensa,* and in *El Imparcial de Texas.* According to reports, among the most important contributions made by the *Cruz Azul* to the colonia mexicana was the founding of *la clínica de la Cruz Azul Mexicana* (the Blue Cross Clinic), located on 933 South Laredo,[60] but later moved to Frio Road in the near West Side, a section of the city heavily populated by working-class and recently arrived Mexicanos.[61] The clinic opened for business on May 30, 1925; it included *a sala de ciruguía* (surgery ward) and a conference room that could hold as many as sixty individuals. Mr. Aaron Saenz, *Secretario de Relaciones Exteriores de México* (Ministry of Foreign Affairs), attended the inauguration. The clinic was housed in a building made available by R. W. Morrison, who rented it to *La Cruz Azul* for the nominal fee of a dollar a month. The philanthropic act of R. W. Morrison illustrates the collaboration of well-to-do Anglo citizens from the city working with the *El México de Afuera* community and with Tejanos to fulfill the goals of the *Cruz Azul*—a mandate of its constitution. The clinic extended its services to all persons, regardless of race, and at no cost, although individuals could extend whatever possible to pay for their medical services. Monies were set aside for the care of children who received immunization to guard against childhood diseases.[62] The success of the clinic depended on the willingness of the city's residents to donate money for its maintenance, and the newspaper *La Época* volunteered to solicit donations from its reading public. The clinic also relied on women for operating staff. In sustaining the clinic, the Mexican and Tejana women demonstrated their assertiveness, their business capabilities, and their ability to run a medical facility that served the Mexican community of San Antonio.

Just as the *Cruz Azul Mexicana* chapter in San Antonio worked to help Mexican American communities, so did other brigades across Texas and throughout the nation. For example, in Luling, Texas, *La Cruz Azul* assisted the following individuals: Juan Flores with $1.50; Sr. Domingo Martínez with 35 cents; Mrs. Concepción O. de Flores with 75 cents; and Mrs. Sara Barbosa with 75 cents.[63] These funds had been acquired by public donations; in keeping with a requirement of the bylaws, the *Cruz Azul* practiced a policy of transparency, making a public announcement of assistance given to individuals.

To collect funds for the organization, the *Cruz Azul* also organized and celebrated Mexican national holidays by holding fiestas, as in the case of one such observance in Eagle Lake, Texas. During the festival, organizers announced that a member of the Mexican community would be given money to join his family in Wharton, Texas.[64] In Waco, Texas, *Cruz Azul* members similarly struggled to strengthen their financial resources, and thus launched a benefit drive. A news item stated: "*Con objeto de cumplir con la misión que tiene encomendada, la brigada de la Cruz Azul de este lugar llevó a cabo una colecta de dinero, siendo comisionadas para recoger los donativos las Sras. Severa F. de García y Feliciana R. de García.*" [With the goal of fulfilling its mission, the Blue Cross of the city conducted a monetary collection, placing Mrs. Severa F. de García and Felicina R. de García in charge of gathering the donations].[65] Although the organization was formed as a response to what the United States saw as a problem of Mexican public dependency, the *Cruz Azul's* actions were those of a self-sufficient, self-reliant organization—a community taking care of its own.

Additionally, the *Cruz Azul* provided intellectual activities in an effort to culturally enrich the *colonia mexicana*. On October 30, 1925, *La Prensa* announced, "*Hoy Habrá Una Velada Literario Musical en el Teatro Nacional*" [Today there will be an evening soiree of music at the National theater],[66] not an uncommon community-wide program set in the center of the city. Such activities for the good of the community displayed the loyalty that women of *El México de Afuera* involved in the *Cruz Azul* had toward their nation and their language and culture. So did other kinds of presentations. On October 24, 1926, *La Prensa* printed a news release that stated that the *señorita* Elena Landazuri, who was visiting San Antonio, would give a lesson, free and opened to the public, on Spanish.[67] It also announced that for those *compatriotas,* who were already literate in Spanish but who wished to perfect their language and grammatical skills, a class would be held in the classroom of the *Cruz Azul* clinic. The clinic was a refuge for the disenfranchised but also offered its space for those who were not on the fringe of their community. It would not be surprising to find out that the doctors serving this clinic were the same ones from the community of *El*

México de Afuera, as for example, Dr. Urrutia who had a daily morning talk show in the Spanish-language radio station.

Although these are just a few of the examples that illustrate *La Cruz Azul's* work within the barrio, many news items in *El Imparcial de Texas, La Prensa,* and *La Época* make known how women of *El México de Afuera* were intricately involved in the social, political, and intellectual activities of their communities in Texas. As the women of the *Cruz Azul* worked for the welfare of the Mexican community of the barrios across the state, their activities blunted the process of assimilation because such ventures acted to reinforce Mexican identity in the face of a strong movement to Americanize the Mexicano.

In conclusion, the personal narratives of Sara Madero, Angela Madero, Luz Corral de Villa, and Virginia Salinas Carranza reflect the complexity of the Mexican woman. Despite the travail they faced, each woman was strong in her own right, intelligent, indomitable, and liberated. One would be remiss to ignore their commitment to what they believed, not unlike their husbands, was just and equitable. Once they crossed the border, they honored their *patria* in their heart and intellect as one might assume they had done within their own country. It is this tradition and history that is their legacy to the contemporary Chicana—a history extended by Emma Tenayuca and all the working-class women in San Antonio who organized to fight big business and city hall by joining strikes such as the Finck Cigar Company Strike, the San Antonio Laundry Strike, and the Pecan Shellers' Strike, among others.

The women of *El México de Afuera* did not stop their civic activities when conferences such as those sponsored by PART, among them the *Congreso Femenino,* ended. PART continued to organize other clubs in the United States and in Mexico; women who had access to political capital made use of it to advance their own political ideologies—they were the "Wise" Latinas of the our past. They were and are our mentors if we continue to uncover and disseminate their influence to the young hybrid generations of our present—this is their legacy as it is our heritage—to share so that we may learn from each other.

La Cruz Azul illustrates the paradox of the immigrant—the immigrant comes to a new land to partake of its fruits, but once in that new land, yearns for *la patria.* Thus, *La Cruz Azul* with its humanitarian activities neutralized the loss of cultural identity—it intellectually challenged the Americanization of the Mexicano. The women of *La Cruz Azul* took care of the medical needs of Tejano communities and ensured that Mexicans living in the United States maintained their Mexican identity, and that Mexicans and Mexican Americans enjoyed good health—jobs no one woman can accomplish alone. Thus, immigrants have gone through a life of the pendulum. This is our legacy today—we move back and forth between one land and another, between one culture and another—and in the process we become neither this or that, but something distinct in itself. What it is that we become is for each one of us to define for ourselves—a daily creation, a daily search.

Notes

1. Federico Allen Hinojosa, *El México de Afuera: y u reintegración a la patria* (San Antonio: Artes Gráficas, 1940). See also Mario T. García, *Mexican Americans: Leadership, Ideology, and Identity, 1930–1960* (New Haven, Conn.: Yale University Press, 1989), 15.

2. John Mason Hart, *Revolutionary Mexico: The Coming and Process of the Mexican Revolution* (Los Angeles: University of California Press, 1987).

3. Richard A. García, *The Rise of the Mexican American Middle Class: San Antonio, 1929–1941* (College Station: Texas A&M University Press, 1991).

4. "Madero Led Revolution Against Díaz," *The San Antonio Light* (February 10, 1913): 3.

5. *Plan de San Luis: Manifiesto a la nación. Redactado por Don Francisco I. Madero y sus colaboradores en San Antonio, Texas en Octubre–Noviembre de 1910:* Instituto de Estudios Históricos de La Revolución Mexicana *(Plan de San Luis se edita, en ocasión de la visita del C. Presidente de Los estados Unidos Mexicanos, Lic. Luis Echeverria Alvarez A la ciudad de San Antonio, Texas, E.U.A. El 19 de junio de 1972):* n.p.

6. "Widow by Revolt," *The San Antonio Light* (February 24, 1913): 3.

7. Ibid., April 11, 1913: 11.

8. Ibid.

9. Ibid.

10. Ibid.

11. Ibid.

12. Ibid.

13. "Miss Angela Madero to Be Married Here," *The San Antonio Light* (October 24, 1916).

14. "Mrs. Villa Laughs at Report of Warrior Husband's Capture," *San Antonio Evening News* (December 4, 1919): 1, 2.

15. Ibid.

16. Ibid.

17. Ibid.

18. Ibid.

19. Ibid.

20. Ibid.

21. Ibid.

22. "Mrs. Carranza Dies at Querétaro after Protracted Illness," *The San Antonio Light* (November 10, 1919): 14.

23. Ibid.

24. Ibid.

25. Ibid.

26. Ibid.

27. Collected History—Outline of Pan American Activities under Directions of PART of San Antonio, Texas, 1916–1936, Box 1, Folder 3, n.d. Original Document at the UTSA Archives, University of Texas at San Antonio.

28. *Handbook of Texas Online,* "Pan American Round Table," accessed February 1, 2010, from http://www.tshaonline.org/handbook/online/articles/PP/vwp1.html.

29. Constitution and By-Laws. Pan American Round Table Constitution, 1916. Original Document at the UTSA Archives.

30. "Women Pledge Friendship Link ith Mexico," *San Antonio Evening News* (December 1, 1919).

31. *"Celebró su primera sesión el Congreso Femenino,"* *La Prensa* [San Antonio, Texas] (2 diciembre 1919): 1.

32. *"El Congreso Feminino Trabaja Por El Acercamiento de EE Unidos a la America Latina,"* *La Prensa* (3 diciembre 1919): 1.

33. Ibid.

34. Ibid.

35. Ibid.

36. "Pan Americanism Sum Up Ideals in Conclusion," *San Antonio Light* (December 3, 1919): 4.

37. Ibid.

38. "Pan Americans Show Needs for New Friendship," *San Antonio Evening News* (December 2, 1919): 9.

39. Esther P. Carvajal, "A Spanish Lesson on the American Flag," *The Modern Language Journal* 17, No.1 (October 1932): 47–48.

40. *"Celebró su primera sesión,"* *La Prensa* (2 diciembre 1919).

41. "Pan Americans Sum Up Ideals in Conclusion," 4.

42. Ibid.

43. Ibid.

44. "Pan American Is Urged for San Antonio by Head of California University," *San Antonio Evening News* (December 4, 1919): 5.

45. "Dinner Closes Convention of Pan Americanism," *San Antonio Evening News* (December 4, 1919):12.

46. Ibid.

47. Ibid.

48. Ibid.

49. Ibid.

50. Emma Pérez, *The Decolonial Imaginary: Writing Chicanas into History* (Bloomington: Indiana University Press, 1999): 43–44.

51. Jesús Franco, *El Alma de La Raza* (El Paso, Texas: *Companía La Patria,* 1923): 38.

52. Ibid., 43.

53. Ibid., 51–52.

54. "*Dos Pasos del Patíbulos, Fue Salvado Un Acto de Justicia,*" *La Época* (San Antonio, Texas) (5 marzo 1922): 1.

55. Franco, *El Alma de La Raza,* 108.

56. Ibid., 127–128.

57. Irma Braña Rubio and Ramón Martínez Saenz, *Diccionario de Escritoras* (Monterrey, Nuevo León, México: Ediciones Castillo, S.A. De C.V., 1996):10–20.

58. Franco, *El Alma de La Raza.*

59. Minga Villasana interview with Juanita Luna Lawhn, December 5, 1998, Sabinal, Texas.

60. "*Inauguración de la Clínica de La Cruz Azul Mexicana,* " *La Prensa* (30 mayo 1925): 1.

61. "*La Moderna Clínica de La Cruz Azul*" *La Época* (18 enero 1929): 1, 6.

62. "*Inauguración de la Clínica de La Cruz Azul Mexicana,*" *La Prensa* (30 mayo 1925): 1.

63. "*Auxilios de La Cruz Azul Mexicana de Luling,*" *La Época* (10 julio 1927): 5.

64. "*En Eagle Lake Hizo La Cruz Azul Una Bonita Fiesta,*" *La Época* (year unknown): 5.

65. "*Una Buena Acción de La Cruz Azul de Waco, Texas,*" *La Época* (30 marzo 1924): 6.

66. "*Hoy Habrá Una Velada Literario Musical en el Teatro Nacional,*" *La Prensa* (30 octubre 1925): 6.

67. "*Da Clases De Español Gratuitamente Una Mexicana,*" *La Prensa* (24 Octubre 1926): 3.

Women's Labor and Activism in the Greater Mexican Borderlands, 1910–1930

SONIA HERNÁNDEZ

When noble and loyal friends of the revolution appeared at my door with the mutilated and bloody bodies of our soldiers, my heart jumped, and since that moment, my life was transformed. . . .

—Jovita Idar, Laredo, Texas

The ideology of *cooperativismo*,[1] access to arable land, worker rights, and dignity were some of the principles that guided much of the revolutionary agenda in the years leading up to the 1910 Mexican Revolution. In the greater northern borderlands extending from central Nuevo León to northern Tamaulipas, up to the hill country of central Texas, the ideology of the Revolution resonated and shaped social and cultural relations in profound ways. Perhaps the bloodiest revolution of the twentieth century, the Mexican Revolution offered hope to scores of Mexicans in southern Texas. These Mexicans resided and worked in one of the last regions to be colonized by the United States; their counterparts in northeastern Mexico also experienced economic colonization by American and other foreign interests. Of particular importance was the influence of the Revolution on labor organizations and their activism. Although historians have examined the role of the Revolution with regards to the labor of men, labor unions, and related themes, there has been less attention paid to that of women's labor on both sides of the border. Chicana historians and other scholars have analyzed women's labor relations and activism within the context of the Mexican Revolution as a transnational phenomenon. However, with few exceptions, there remains a wide gap in the historiography of women's labor in the greater borderlands as a whole. I argue that ethnic Mexican (i.e., persons of Mexican descent who may be either U.S. or Mexican citizens) working-class women used the rhetoric of the Revolution to address their marginal position in the crossroads of two nation-states that had denied them rights and excluded them from access to resources.[2] What follows is an examination of women's labor during the Revolution in the greater borderlands region, which included south Texas and northeastern Mexico. Based on binational archival research, I analyze the influence the Revolution had on women's labor experiences and activism.

Women's labor proved critical to the making of the Mexican borderlands in the late nineteenth and early twentieth centuries. To gain a better understanding of women's extensive contributions to labor as well as how they used the rhetoric of revolution to improve working conditions, their experiences must be placed in greater regional and historical context. Because of extensive ties between northeastern Mexico and south Texas, the experiences of women residents and transients at this crossroads are better understood within a transnational framework. Women migrated back and forth, maintained ties with family "back home," and shared a common labor experience.[3] More real on a map than in people's everyday life, the border did not stop the flow of ideas and certainly did not stop cultural exchange, particularly before 1930 and in later years as security intensified in the form of placing more boots on the ground and using more technology. In the decades before the massive federally funded deportation campaign targeting Mexicans, the porous nature of the border sustained a revolving door for laborers from both nation-states. Laborers, mutual-aid societies, and labor organizations—comprised of both male and female workers— maintained close ties with one another and, whenever possible, supported each other's agendas; to a great extent they were fighting for the same kinds of things: livable wages, the right to organize and strike, safe working environments, and their right to a dignified way of life. Women also fought for these guarantees, yet they advanced a specific female worker, or *obrera,* agenda for gender equity and general women's rights.[4]

One of the central debates in the historiography of Mexican women's history is whether the Mexican Revolution was in fact revolutionary for women. In particular, the questions of whether and how the Revolution altered labor and gender relations have been posed by scholars. Although historians of women's history tend to agree that the Revolution had a direct influence in creating opportunities for women to fight alongside their male counterparts and to express their views concerning women's rights in journals, magazines, and newspapers, the stands these historians take on whether the Revolution altered gender relations vary.[5] Given the Revolution's transnational influence, the same questions can be posed for Mexican American women, or Mexican immigrant women residing on the northern bank of the *Río Grande*. What exactly did the Revolution mean for working women in this extended borderlands region? What kinds of work did working-class women perform, and what was the legacy of the Revolution in the Texas borderlands for them? The Revolution provided a unique opportunity for women to voice their labor demands within a revolutionary framework. However, their success was limited given that gender relations were not altered significantly; gender inequities continued in the labor realm and beyond. Although women's activism was articulated in a broad context, this paper focuses only on women's experiences in labor and their activism in this particular arena.

Revolutionary Women

Recently, scholars' research has shed new light on women's active participation in the Mexican Revolution in the battlefield, as spies, providing key assistance to female and male soldiers, and promoting revolutionary ideas through their writings in newspapers and magazines.[6] Mexican women joined the fight, picking up arms and playing key roles in the civil war. In the Matamoros-Brownsville corridor, *The Brownsville Herald* reported in March 1913 that "five women under the orders of [General Lucio] Blanco … took an active part in combat on their horses and shooting their pistols …," citing key witnesses from nearby San Benito, Texas.[7] In the El Paso region, Señora Flores de Andrade made her mark crisscrossing the border, like many other women, supplying arms to revolutionaries and acting as a spy. When not acting as spies or handling weapons, women assisted as nurses, caring for the wounded and aiding other *compañeras*. Some joined *La Cruz Blanca,* a transnational organization founded by Leonor Villegas de Magnón to assist *Carrancista* soldiers.[8] Still other

Mexican women took advantage of the revolutionary atmosphere to advance their own agendas promoting social and gender equity. This revolutionary idealism was expressed in the actions and texts by female journalists, writers, and activists in political parties such as the *Partido Liberal Mexicano* (PLM).[9]

In the late nineteenth century and first years of the twentieth century, activists who opposed President Porfirio Díaz met to plan a revolutionary movement against him. Organizing the main PLM branch from San Luis Potosí in northeastern Mexico were Camilo Arriaga, an affluent *norteño,* and Ricardo and Enrique Flores Magón, the intellectual siblings who would come to represent the anarchist branch of the Revolution. What set this particular anarchist-based, socioeconomic, and political party apart was its stance with regards to women. The PLM bypassed national boundaries, garnering female support from both sides of the border. As historian Emma Pérez has argued, "The discourse of the Revolution knew no boundaries. Language, words, *corridos,* and concepts crossed back and forth along the Mexico–U.S. border...."[10] Women proved critical in carrying the Revolution's message and acting on it, and they fully participated in the PLM and other radical groups. Whereas much attention has been paid to the wave of immigration produced by the Revolution, and to women immigrants to a lesser extent, not until recently have scholars addressed the revolutionary work performed by women transnationals, who frequently criticized both nation-states. Sara Estela Ramírez and the Villarreal sisters, Andrea and Teresa, were women who represented the radical wing of the Revolution, playing a crucial role in spreading revolutionary ideology. Ramírez, born in Coahuila, immigrated to Texas and eventually settled in Laredo at the age of seventeen. She was a poet and activist who wrote on behalf of Mexican women. Her writings in the form of articles, poems, and other works were published in *La Crónica* and *El Démocrata Fronterizo.* Andrea and Teresa Villarreal addressed issues affecting the binational community while writing for newspapers, including *El Obrero* and *La Mujer Moderna.*[11] They wrote about "the need to educate the proletariat along the U.S.–Mexico border."[12]

Women writers who adhered to the PLM used a gendered rhetoric to promote women's rights. Isidra T. de Cárdenas, for example, founded *La Voz de la Mujer* in El Paso to advance a pro-women, pro-PLM agenda. Like *La Voz de la Mujer, El Obrero,* founded in 1909 in San Antonio by Teresa Villarreal, represented Mexican women's decision to act on "the need to disrupt the social formation."[13] *La Voz de la Mujer* employed the concept of the family, and as one editorial stated, "Women are an integral part of the great human family; therefore, it is their duty and right to demand and struggle for the dignification of their country."[14] One of the main concerns of the revolutionary movement, particularly of the PLM and Ricardo Flores Magón, was implementing a minimum wage for women. In Mexico's textile mills, women earned two-thirds to three-fourths of males' wages and even less as compared to men in heavier industries, particularly steel and oil. In 1906, the Flores Magón brothers noted the depressed wages of women, calling for a minimum national daily pay of 40 *centavos*.[15] The activism of the Mexican brothers and their supporters in the United States also incorporated the same rhetoric to address conditions for women on the Texas side.[16] Sara Estela Ramírez, a PLM supporter herself and a major player in the organization, used the leadership experience gained advancing the PLM and general socioeconomic issues founded on revolutionary principles in Mexico to then apply them to the Texas situation, particularly to improve the labor conditions of fellow working Mexicans.[17]

Indeed, the Revolution provided a unique opportunity to address labor conditions in Texas. Scores of peons and small *rancheros* in northern Mexico joined revolutionary factions addressing the harshness of the debt-peonage system as well as the increased competition with American companies over natural resources, gross wage discrepancies between foreign and native workers, and political repression. Others crossed the border but maintained communication with residents in Mexico; this, in turn, created a new space for them to address labor concerns, among others. PLM supporters active in Tamaulipas and workers who had heard about the PLM's agenda brought with them their ideas about socioeconomic justice when they crossed the river. The ideas that the PLM had espoused, particularly those of Ricardo Flores Magón, stressed Mexican nationalism, anti-American sentiment, and worker autonomy that challenged the burgeoning industrial capitalism in the Northeast and provided an alternative for workers. They also questioned the low wages in the expanding commercial agricultural enterprises led by Anglo and affluent Mexican growers in the nearby fertile Rio Grande Valley. In 1911, Flores Magón published a proclamation in the PLM's magazine *Regeneración,* addressing workers' concerns: "We need to take possession of the factories, the mines, the smelters . . . instead of abandoning our tools and crossing our arms . . . my brothers, let's continue to work, but not for the bosses but for ourselves and our families."[18] As Aurora Mónica Alcayaga Sasso has vividly described in her doctoral thesis, the workers heeded the call. In the Gulf Coast region of the Mexican northeast, they did not destroy the machines; they did however, slow down production, stop production altogether, and employ other strategies.[19]

That same ideology appealed to *Tejanos* and Mexican immigrants residing and working in Texas during the Revolution. As working and living conditions for Mexican-descent people in Texas worsened, the revolutionary cause made a lot of sense to them. From 1911 through 1917, scores of PLM-affiliated branches emerged. A total of fifty-two branches, and possibly more, were organized throughout Texas (see table). A handful of PLM-affiliated groups either had been organized by women or included women. In 1913, women founded *Grupo Regeneración "Prismas Anarquistas"* in Burkett, Texas. The group was founded by Alida Martínez, who delivered a speech to commemorate the inauguration of *Prismas Anarquistas.* She reminded her *compañeras* that "what brings us together, our goal, is to come together as a group so that our demands may be heard . . . although we are weak women, we also have rights to life, especially when it is us that sustain the human race." She closed by reminding the women that "we have the unavoidable obligation to defend this right and to die for it if possible."[20] Similar groups emerged in the state; in Morin, Texas, for example, *Grupo Femenino Aspiraciones Libres* was founded in 1912.[21]

Mexican women on both sides of the border worked, offering the public their services. One organization that comprised a great number of women dedicated to advancing the goals of the Mexican Revolution in the areas of labor, education, and medical assistance was the *Brigada Cruz Azul.*[22] The *Cruz Azul* member, Sra. Vallado de González spoke of "*abnegación, caridad y patriotismo,* virtues held close to the bosom of women."[23] In fact, "abnegation, charity, and patriotism" formed the main tenets of the *Cruz Azul.* A large female membership comprised the *Cruz Azul* and its numerous branches throughout the region. The *Cruz Azul* became one of the leading organizations to use the unique opportunity that the Mexican Revolution and its aftermath offered to women. It also blurred gender lines, if only temporarily, combining women and men's charitable work for a common good. As Ephraim Frisch, Rabbi of Temple Bethel in San Antonio put it, "[The *Cruz Azul*] is engaged in a noble labor of bringing relief to the stricken and of uniting men and women into the common bonds of humanitarian sentiment and service."[24] In 1920, female members of the *Cruz Azul* participated in a parade in the main street of San Juan, Texas, to commemorate Mexican independence.[25]

Speaking on behalf of all working Mexican women and moving beyond women's roles as mothers, Jovita Idar, the activist, educator, journalist, and supporter of the *Cruz Blanca,* vehemently advocated gender equity. She wrote, "[I]f men and women are to be made better spiritually, better morally, and if they are to enjoy a better social life and greater opportunities for education, self-expression, and self-development, then they must live under conditions that make for the enjoyment and realization of these things."[26] To be sure, Idar exemplified the ardent activism expressed by female labor and social leaders on both sides of the border. Idar is well-known for her leadership and participation in the *Primer Congreso Mexicanista,* the first cultural conference organized by ethnic Mexicans to address Mexican issues affecting the community. As scholar José Limón has pointed out, "Texas-Mexican women and their particular social problems received the attention of the congreso. . . ."[27] Member and educator Soledad Flores de Peña expressed her concern about Mexican women: "It is necessary to understand each and every one of our responsibilities. . . . I believe that in order to achieve this, the best means is to educate woman, instruct her, and at the same time respect and support her."[28] Women also contributed to a broader discussion that was not necessarily viewed in gendered terms. They protested against lynching, social, political, and economic discrimination. In fact, like her African American counterpart, Ida Wells Barnett, Idar vehemently opposed the lynching of Mexicans throughout the Southwest. She also took it upon herself to write in opposition to President Woodrow Wilson's decision to send troops to the border during the height of the Mexican Revolution. The troops were to quell the revolutionary activity that had spilled to the American side of the border. Idar also stood up to a group of Texas Rangers who sought to close down her family's newspaper in Laredo, Texas.[29]

One of the pioneering organizations dedicated to the advancement of Mexican women's rights was *La Liga Femenil Mexicanista,* founded in October 1911, whose first president was Jovita Idar. A pioneer Chicana organization, it bypassed national boundaries by operating in the Tamaulipas town of Nuevo Laredo. Besides assisting in promoting women's education and children's bilingual education, the organization extended aid to immigrant families. Regarding the latter, Idar focused on the working conditions of immigrants but zeroed in on working women. Her activist writings advocated "equality with respect to men's work in order for women to integrate themselves into society and demand political rights."[30] Her article, "*Debemos Trabajar*" (We Should Work), which appeared on November 23, 1911, in *La Crónica,* expressed Idar's ideal of the modern working woman. According to Idar, women should strive to exit the domestic sphere and work. She wrote, "The *obrera* recognizes her rights, proudly raises her head and joins the struggle, the time of her degradation is over, she is no longer a slave sold for some coins, she is no longer a servant, but the equal of a man...."[31] The Revolution had provided an opening for women to vocalize issues of gender equity that could have appeared as radical during peacetime. For Idar, the Revolution did not create or lead to her activism; the Revolution strengthened her female consciousness. Idar had witnessed women's second-class status as well as the deplorable conditions in which her fellow Mexicans and Mexican Americans found themselves. The revolutionary rhetoric of worker autonomy, labor rights, and women's rights further heightened Idar's activist outlook.

The kind of revolution that had taken shape in Mexico and whose ideas had been carried over across the border influenced women to claim labor rights while at the same time addressing women's issues. In short, Mexican immigrant women and *Tejanas,* through their writings and activism, exemplified what historian Emma Pérez called "a kind of renaissance [for women]."[32]

In one of her writings, Idar wrote, "I am not content with what my modest cooperative work has accomplished for the present revolution [referring to her service to the *Cruz Azul*].... when noble and loyal friends of the revolution appeared at my door with the mutilated and bloody bodies of our soldiers, my heart jumped, and since that moment, my life was transformed."[33] Idar's position as an educated writer, from a progressive and well-established family as were the Idars from Laredo, allowed her to claim a privileged space in a transnational community to speak out on behalf of working-class women and their families. Idar wrote extensively for the family newspaper *La Crónica* (Laredo), as well as in *El Eco de Corpus Christi* and *La Luz* (San Benito). She also founded *Evolución* in 1916, which ran until 1920, and coedited *El Heraldo Cristiano,* published by the Rio Grande Methodist Church conference.[34] An activist, educator, and journalist, Jovita Idar addressed issues concerning working-class women who labored as cotton pickers, *lavanderas* (or public washers), domestic workers, and in other occupations, spreading a transnational labor activist message. Indeed, her writings, often times under the pseudonym *Astrea,* bypassed national and gender boundaries, addressing gender equity and other issues affecting the Mexican community on both sides of the border.[35]

It should be noted that Idar's contributions were highly radical as compared to those of other women from the region. Not all women experienced the Revolution in the same way. For Matamorense Esther González Salinas, the revolutionary rhetoric prevalent at that time produced different results. Salinas had spent her life as an educator for all-girls' schools in Matamoros, Reynosa, and Villa Hidalgo in Tamaulipas. Because of the civil war, she headed to Texas, where she continued to work as an educator. Within a short period of time, Salinas, who had been living in San Diego, founded a Spanish-speaking school that she named "México." She later opened up a similar school in Kingsville. After the Revolution, she returned to Matamoros, her hometown, where she lived the rest of her life teaching.[36] The threat of violence and war caused by the Revolution led to the increase in immigration, and for many, like González Salinas, it provided an opportunity to continue their work as educators on the north side of the border.

Women's Labor during the Revolution

Some women left their mark on the Revolution by contributing to newspapers, journals, teaching, and taking up arms or assisting in the acquisition of weapons in their cross-border activities; others helped to build the borderlands, working in factories, agriculture, and in a variety of other occupations. As women fled across the border, away from the war in Mexico, they found themselves selling their labor, working in predominantly low-paying jobs much like their *Tejana* counterparts. Working-class Mexican women's labor in the region was concentrated in specific "light" industries or in the burgeoning commercial agriculture. Their tasks were frequently paid by the piece, low paid, and considered unskilled. As in the Tamaulipas and Nuevo León countryside, the Texas greater border region, including the rural towns of the Rio Grande Valley, Robstown, Alice, and the farms in the central part of the state, was the worksite of scores of working-class *Mexicanas*. A small segment of the female population worked in industries, including laundry, cigar-making, and factories, but the majority of women labored as agricultural workers. Like their male counterparts, they formed part of the "seasonal and migratory workforce for the commercial agriculture that developed in the state in the late nineteenth and early twentieth centuries."[37] Women, working alongside men, contributed to the development of entire cities. In 1904, in San Juan, located in deep South Texas, women worked in the seven-thousand-acre San Juan Plantation, picking cotton and working the sugar cane, alfalfa, and onions; the plantation, owned by John Closner, would later become part of the city of San Juan.[38] Further north, in San Antonio and El Paso, as in the expanding urban and industrialized center of Monterrey, employed Mexican women tended to hold higher paying jobs than those held by their *campesinas* or farmworker counterparts.

The Revolution forced many Mexicans out of the country, fleeing for safety. A wave of immigrants from all social classes crossed the border, finding refuge and work in Texas. The Palomo Acosta sisters, Sabina and Juanita, formed part of this generation. Sabina arrived at the tender age of four, and Juanita was born several years after the end of the civil war. Coming from a *campesino* family background, the sisters labored in the spinach and onion farms of south and central Texas. In 1910, families could earn up to $5 a day for cotton picking in the higher paying counties, such as Collin. Several years after the war, each working family member could earn $3 a day laboring in Texas farms.[39] Like the Palomo Acosta family, Estéban and Piedad Tijerina Cantú immigrated to Texas during the Revolution. In 1912, the Cantus left rural General Bravo, Nuevo León, and settled in San Juan, where Piedad and her family became seasonal migrant workers. They travelled to Refugio, Texas, to work the fields; eventually they were able to purchase land of their own in San Juan "where they raised crops such as carrots and cotton."[40]

In the years leading up to the Revolution, an estimated 15 percent of Mexican immigrant women earned wages in the border region of south Texas. Some 17 percent of Mexican women in the El Paso area earned wages by 1920.[41] However, it is quite possible that the numbers are higher, given the nature of labor statistics, low reporting, transient working women, and other related factors. Although women in the Rio Grande Valley earned lower wages, the occupations they held were not as racially diverse as those in the border region; that is, the majority of the workers were of Mexican descent. Towns such as Laredo and Brownsville offered women teaching, typographical, and clerical positions. By 1910, ethnic Mexican women began to move to larger and more urbanized cities, including San Antonio, Houston, and Dallas. As historian Emilio Zamora explains, "Improved job opportunities [in these urban centers] encouraged the movement of Mexicana workers into industrial occupations."[42] In the larger urban areas like San Antonio, women worked in pecan-shelling and cigar-making establishments as well as candy and hat-making shops. In El Paso, large numbers of women filled the public laundry positions and garment factories.[43] Others, like Ms. Marcelino Solis and Leonor López Alonzo and their families, left Mexico during the Revolution and set up small shops. The Solis family opened up a shoe shop, whereas the Alonsos opened a barbershop. Both businesses are still family owned and are operating today in San Juan. In both urban and rural centers, ethnic Mexican women also performed the important job of *partera,* or midwife. Anselma Garza Sloss of San Juan was one of several midwives that performed services for numerous *Tejano* families.[44]

Women employed in the hotel and restaurant, manufacturing, and laundry industries earned substandard wages. Mexican women in the El Paso area, for example, earned on average a weekly wage of a little less than $9 laboring in hotels and restaurants. Those in manufacturing jobs could earn close to $8. On average, women employed in laundries could earn between $4 and $6.56 a week.[45] Many of the *Mexicanas* who worked in public laundries were heads of households or contributed significantly to the family income. As one laundry worker put it, "I find it difficult to live on my wages, which I turn into the family budget."[46] As the *obreras'* contemporary Mexican labor activist Clemente N. Idar said, referring to the existing wages paid to laundresses, "[They do not permit women] to live decent and respectable lives as American citizens."[47]

As early as 1918, women workers joined the numerous American Federation of Labor (AFL)–affiliated unions of workers in the "*planchaduría y limpia-ropa*" sector. However, apprentices and women were placed in separate categories related to their union membership. Although all union members were required to pay one dollar as an initiation fee, male workers paid a monthly fee of eighty-five cents, whereas apprentices and women paid only fifty cents. A fee reduction of over a quarter for *obreras* translated into extra income for the nuclear or extended family. Nonetheless, although the Revolution certainly shaped the rhetoric of labor activism in that gender equity and *compañerismo,* or camaraderie, were hailed as priorities, the reality was that much of the rhetoric did not alter women's status. The gender discourse grounded in nineteenth-century conceptions of morality, abnegation, and the idea of gender-specific occupations (linked to ideas of domesticity and femininity) persisted after the Revolution and continued to shape labor relations that helped to maintain women's separate status as reflected in the lower wages they received. Women continued to be barred from numerous traditional male unions and to assume the double burden of work both in and outside the home.[48]

Female and male cotton pickers who had left the nearby states of

Tamaulipas, Nuevo León, and Coahuila to escape debt peonage in the late nineteenth and early twentieth centuries encountered similar labor practices in Texas, although they earned higher wages. Referring to the Mexican agricultural workers, Clemente N. Idar, wrote to pro-labor Judge B. F. Patterson from San Antonio, and explained that they "are treated brutally, abused, and robbed. . . ."[49] Female farm workers were not exempt from this treatment or unfavorable labor conditions. Women, alongside their children, siblings, their husbands, and their fathers, toiled for long hours under the hot Texas sun. Frequently, women cotton pickers as well as their male counterparts faced harsh labor practices. In Central Texas, near Gonzales and the farms of Luling, Fentress, and Martindale, organized farm laborers reported "hundreds of complaints are made at all times of the year against the cruel treatment they ordinarily get from the landowners with whom they raise cotton crops. . . ."[50] One farm worker became ill, and he and his family "were left in a public road and all the work *they* had performed in the farm was lost with the exception of the miserable groceries they had been receiving."[51] It should not surprise us then, that as early as 1911, a PLM branch, *Grupo Regeneración de Agricultores,* was organized in the Fentress area.[52]

Working conditions for female migrant workers were among the worst in the region. One farmworker, Miguel Pavia, candidly described the situation for Mexican male and female agricultural workers. He wrote "with respect to the . . . agricultural workers' wages, it varies and *está al antojo del terrateniente* (is at the landowner's whim) . . . the most they'll pay when they are in real need is $1.50 per day."[53] He continued, "To sum it up, the Mexican farm workers in this area [Central Texas] are like slaves, wage workers and [we are] in the same system as Mexico's *hacendario* [sic]."[54] What Mexican immigrants with predominantly *campesino* backgrounds encountered was a brutal labor system; although it paid higher wages, it resembled the everyday harsh labor practices rampant in *haciendas* and *ranchos* throughout northern Mexico. Ironically, working-class Mexicans had protested precisely these kinds of labor practices before and during the Revolution, which had much to do with controlling labor in northeastern Mexico due to its proximity to Texas (and the United States, more generally).[55] Indeed, the abolishment of debt peonage had ranked high on the list of grievances outlined by revolutionaries.

Performing labor activism went beyond simply writing about it. As Pavia put it, "It was not easy to organize." He confessed that "the majority of Mexicans were afraid to organize . . . however, I have been working hard to promote the worker cause ... I hold meetings every Sunday ... and I have several individuals who have joined the union...."[56] Organizing mutual-aid organizations and/or unions had its challenges, particularly for women who continued to struggle for recognition of their contributions to labor.

Living conditions for Mexican migrant families were substandard, to say the least. If Mexican families were not housed in "empty farm buildings during harvest," they could find themselves "sleep[ing] and cook[ing] on the open road, waiting for seasonal work."[57] Women and their families followed the crops. During August, some Mexicans worked on the cotton harvest in nearby Corpus Christi, Robstown, and other small towns, while another group headed toward the Houston area. Growers from Austin and its vicinity then received the cotton pickers. By September, the workers headed to other parts of the state.[58] The women who picked cotton in extended families were for the most part transients, often crossing into New Mexico to perform work up until February, when they headed back south to places like the Rio Grande Valley.[59] To make ends meet, Mexican women also tended home gardens and preserved foods, particularly those who remained in their farm homes for long periods of time as compared to transient women workers.[60]

Although data are limited, early studies on Mexican agricultural labor reveal that for the most part, when a woman lived with her family, her wages were distributed to the head of the household, usually a male. For example, in a study of more than two hundred Mexican women in central Texas, more than half labored in the fields alongside their families. A much smaller percentage "performed field work for hire ... only three women besides the widows, received the income from their labor; one of the three was married and the other two, single ... in the case of the other married women the husband received all income...."[61] For those who received the wages directly, these amounted to approximately a dollar a day for up to ten hours of work. As has been argued by historians of labor, agricultural work, categorized and defined as unskilled, probably ranked among the worst paid.[62]

Labor contracts drawn up between farmworkers and landowners, or *terratenientes* (as Mexican immigrants called them), frequently involved migrant males and the landowner. However, part of the agreement of payment, housing, and related issues involved women. In a 1925 public announcement about information crucial to Mexican laborers, the anonymous writer(s) reminded *aparceros* and *medieros* "*que residen en el estado de*

Texas" (sharecroppers who reside in Texas) that they "all should have a written contract," particularly by late in the year, because it was in November and December that most contracts were renewed. These workers had to ensure that the landowners specified whether the agreement included "*troncos de caballo* (harnesses), field tools, housing, water, and firewood."[63] The announcement specifically stated that "no married man should accept a contract lacking prepayment of at least $30.00 per month."[64] The fact that male married workers were encouraged to seek this prepayment testifies to the critical role women played in the family for survival of the workers and the sustained household. As historian Zaragoza Vargas has explained, women and children contributed to all facets of agriculture work.[65] Female farm workers worked twice as hard—in the field and in the common makeshift homes—cleaning, washing, mending clothes, and preparing meals for the entire family. Women continued to perform the double work after the Revolution and up to the present day. As the *corrido* "*Bellos Recuerdos*" (song "Fond Memories") reminds us, the women workers of families laboring in El Chapeño, Robstown, and the Corpus Christi region provided meals on site: "Right at noon, my mother called us, come my children let us eat; under the big truck, we all ate refried beans, potatoes, and coffee."[66] Although they prepared meals and worked in the fields themselves, the majority of women did not receive wages directly. Frequently, payment to the patriarch (grandfather, father, husband, or the eldest son) included women workers' wages. The announcement further explained how the $30.00 should be divided: "$20.00 for provisions and $10.00 for clothes, doctor, and medicines . . . if family has more than two children, the prepayment should be increased proportionately."[67] Finally, Mexicans were advised to ensure that "at least two people you trust accompany you to speak with the *terrateniente*."[68]

To be sure, whether or not women earned "direct" wages, they nonetheless performed the work just like their male counterparts: on average, women picked anywhere between 100 to 150 pounds of cotton a day, and some up to 200 pounds.[69] Besides picking, women hoed and chopped, baled hay, and plowed. As one contemporary investigator explained, "From these Mexican peon women comes cheap labor for the farm and factory. With them, we can raise cotton, cheap cotton; in fact, we can meet almost any price the market will pay and still produce cotton, even though to do it we have to bring across the Rio Grande fresh supplies of labor each year."[70] The worker influx from Mexico included large numbers of women.

The Legacy of the Revolution on Women's Labor and Activism

The post-revolutionary period, particularly the late 1920s and 1930s, ushered a new era of labor activism, much of it influencing Mexican immigrant women. The kinds of gendered labor issues raised by Jovita Idar and others resonated with the large numbers of Mexican women workers even after the military phase of the Revolution had ended. In October 1918, ethnic Mexican women employed in the laundry business in El Paso vehemently protested the dismissal of two fellow female workers because of their union activism. The workers, who had recently founded a branch of the International Laundry Workers Union, objected to the dismissal of one sorter and one marker from the Acme Laundry in El Paso.[71] As Acme stepped up efforts to control the labor force, close to five hundred *obreras* from six different laundries walked out of their jobs.[72] The act of abandoning difficult-to-secure jobs on the part of ethnic Mexican women took on special meaning in El Paso. As the late historian Irene Ledesma has argued, "Anglo El Pasoans regarded Mexicans as foreigners, regardless of their citizenship status."[73] To protest working conditions in an era of intense anti-foreign sentiment and in a highly patriarchal society involved certain risks. Moreover, as violence crossed the border, Texas Rangers, vigilante groups, and even some affluent Mexican Americans quickly took action by frequently labeling Mexicans as "bandits." Hence, any uprising against authority and its representatives was seen as a transgression, and swift action could be taken.[74] In fact, nativist movements would continue to create obstacles to Mexican-based labor organizing throughout the 1920s in El Paso.[75] Nonetheless, AFL-organized *obreras* struck once again within two months that same year. The decision came quickly after a *mítin* (meeting). Within a week of planning, the women struck; they "asked for money to survive, food and work."[76] The walkouts organized by women took place within the wider context of revolutionary upheaval that reflected the decline of Mexican social, political, and economic power on both sides of the river.

The Revolution, on the one hand, was in great part, a reaction to the foreign capital accumulation and gross wage discrepancies between foreigners and Mexican workers widespread in the Mexican northeast. In south Texas, it reflected the discontent regarding the shift from Mexican to Anglo control of land and political power, and a response to rampant lynching and educational segregation.[77] Meetings outlining collective action organized by *mutualistas* and labor leaders took place on both sides of the border. The activism showcased by the female laundry workers in El Paso formed part of this extensive labor network throughout the borderlands.

As Ledesma has pointed out, "Labor union activity in the United States increased enormously in the 1930s because of economic conditions and encouragement from the national government in the form of the Wagner Act." Across the *Rio Grande,* Mexican labor union activity intensified and was strengthened with the passage of the *Ley Federal del Trabajo* (1931). Indeed, both pieces of legislation signaled a turning point in the labor relations in the greater borderlands. Mexican women wage earners stepped up efforts to organize. Like their *cigarrera* and *costurera* counterparts in Linares, Montemorelos, and Monterrey, Mexican women cigar makers and pecan shellers from the El Paso and San Antonio region rallied to voice demands regarding their dire economic situation. Emerging from the San Antonio region, the fiery young community labor organizer Emma Tenayuca combined the rhetoric of communism, feminism, and revolutionary ideology to organize cigar rollers and pecan shellers. Earning an average of $2.25 a week, pecan-sheller *obreras* worked in unsanitary conditions: the work rooms lacked proper ventilation, workers sat on backless benches, and their tool to crush pecans was no other than their hands.[78] Tenayuca, referencing revolutionary leaders like the Flores Magón brothers, later reminisced about the conditions of Mexican workers. She explained, "I started going to the plaza and political rallies when I was 6 or 7 years old . . . you had the influence of [the] Flores Magón brothers . . . you had *enganchadores,* contractors who came in and took people out to the Valley. I was exposed to all of that." She continued, "I had a basic underlying faith in the American idea of freedom and fairness. I felt there was something that had to be done . . . and I went out on the picket line. That was the first time I was arrested."[79] Tenayuca's exposure to radical ideas emanating from Mexico due to the revolutionary struggle and her understanding of "American" rights combined to produce a unique perspective on issues of labor and women's rights in the region.[80]

Ties between Mexicans and their counterparts in Texas remained and grew stronger precisely because a pro-labor agenda was incorporated on both sides of the border. This cooperation aided in setting up conferences advancing binational labor. Just one year before the El Paso women workers struck, a binational labor conference was organized in Laredo, and Mexican, Mexican American, and American labor representatives attended.[81] Although the more radical branches of Mexican labor decided not to support the endeavor given AFL leader Samuel Gompers's pro-war stance and the organization's failure to address the PLM jailed supporters, it is interesting to note the agenda promoted in 1918 in Laredo. The conference, *Confederación Obrera Pan Americana* (COPA), called for the "the improvement of Mexican immigrants' labor situation in the United States . . . we should fight to make the wages of immigrants the same as that of U.S. workers."[82] It also stressed the "fraternal and solidarity ties among workers on both sides of the border. . . ." The binational organizers advocated a transnational worker autonomy that would not be "under the tutelage of both governments."[83]

That a labor conference took place at this crossroads points to how the revolutionary rhetoric about labor rights influenced working class ideologies on both ends. Labor organizers in Texas, like Clement N. Idar, had considerable knowledge of post-revolutionary labor laws in Mexico and functioned as labor brokers or middlemen. Idar made it a point to disclose any new information about Mexican organizing activity to organizations in the United States. As he explained to the Bakery and Confectionary Workers' International Union in Chicago (AFL affiliated), "I have . . . gained considerable knowledge of the labor laws of Mexico as contained in the Federal Constitution and State Constitutions." In the spring of 1922, Clemente found himself in Torreón in the Mexican north. He was instrumental in organizing the local branches of the United Brotherhood of Carpenters and Joiners of America, as well as tailors and common laborers.[84] He added that his "experiences [have] broadened out considerably organizing Spanish-speaking workers" in Mexico. He would later return and continue aiding ethnic Mexicans throughout the United States. Idar had been instrumental in promoting labor unity across the borderlands since the days of the Revolution.[85]

Not being associated or affiliated with a union did not mean lack of activism. Particularly for working women who were not in a union, alternative cultural practices helped them to cope with labor issues. One popular practice was that of petitioning authorities for aid.[86] To cope with job loss, aid with children, or family-related issues, women petitioned for aid. Petitions were sent to both local and national authorities or to labor or *mutualistas,* even if women were not members. In El Paso, Guadalupe Garza wrote to the president of the *Sociedad "Melchor Ocampo."* She wrote about her *"necesidades"* and asked for any help possible "to cure her *hijita"* (young daughter). She explained that *"porque soy una mujer sola, no tengo a quien aclamar"* (because I am a single woman, I have no one to rely on). She closed by stating that she "awaited a favorable response."[87] The organization received similar petitions, including those by women from across the border in Piedras Negras, Coahuila.[88] Organizations continued to receive petitions and also maintained their transnational appeal.

Women's participation in promoting the Revolution's agenda during the PLM years and in organizations like the *Cruz Azul* helped to insert women's labor concerns in the greater conversation about labor. As the debate on women's labor and their place in society gained attention, organizations welcomed female workers or addressed women's issues. For example, the *Sociedad Mutualista "Melchor Ocampo"* in 1930 organized a "cultural conference" in its social hall, where "noted speaker" *licenciado* Paulino Rubio from the sister border town of Piedras Negras delivered a lecture entitled "*Mutualismo, La Mujer y el Hogar*."[89] Other organizations began to include more coverage on women's labor issues in their publications.

Although the Revolution had widened the space for women to advance their socioeconomic and political agendas, and despite the inclusion of a specific women's agenda, the Revolution did not totally erase gender inequity. However, the rhetoric to reconstruct the nation after the Revolution assumed a gendered tone whereby women were defined as "*compañeras*" and not "slaves," and men were encouraged to stand strong to support their new revolutionary and modern families.[90] As a gendered discourse to promote nationalism gained strength in the post-revolutionary period in Mexico, a similar discourse influenced the labor of women in Texas. Women workers, wives of fellow *obreros,* and even their children were spoken of in gendered terms. Women workers were also part of the larger working Mexican family. Local tailor unions and the *Hermandad Unida de Carpinteros y Ensambladeros* formulated gender-specific messages to aid the "*gran familia*" of tailors.[91] There would be a union creed for women, one for men, and one for the children; the entire "family was tied to the male union members." Integrating women and children became a top priority for the union,

> We have not given women and children much priority. If we have them on our side, helping them understand what we understand with regards to the aspirations, doctrines and principles that form the basis of our labor movement . . . our work will be more efficient and fruitful.[92]

The *Brigada Cruz Azul,* which included scores of women who assisted in a variety of ways during the Revolution, articulated a gendered discourse to promote ideas of nationalism and advocate for Mexican immigrant women and men in the post-revolutionary period. A. P. Carrillo, president of the organization, poignantly argued in his speech that "those of us who had to leave our nation to come to work honorably and with dignity ... need to respect this nation's flag ... but we should never forget to honor our own flag." He included women in his talk, expressing that "for you Mexican mothers, that is your task, to instruct your children ... to honor that tricolor flag, which is the symbol of our beloved Mother nation, which is the mother of our parents, the mother of our grandparents, the mother of our heroes, the mother of all of us, that is the Mother country!"[93] Female members were also encouraged to continue working, helping the poor, widows, and orphans. Women were spoken of in terms of their "power" and position as mothers first, then as workers. One activist from Laredo argued that "it was absolutely indispensable to educate women from our *raza* (people) so that she can further have an influence on her children's intelligence."[94] Another activist, Hortencia Moncayo, who spoke ardently against lynching, was compared to Mexican independence heroine Josefa Ortiz de Domínguez, or "*La Correjidora,*" and Leona Vicario.[95]

By the 1930s, the depression hit Texas. As historian Julia Kirk Blackwelder has shown, ethnicity would play a crucial role in the kinds of occupations women would have access to during the Depression. Of particular significance was Mexican American women's low labor participation. "Largely unskilled, geographically segregated, and greeted with prejudice, prospective Hispanic workers had few job choices."[96] Indeed, work was limited, and soon hundreds of thousands of Mexican American women and their families would face deportation. Many of the Mexican immigrant and Mexican American women workers who had contributed to the Texas economy in the early twentieth century and during the Revolution now planned their forced return to Mexico.[97] For those women who remained in their jobs, just like in factories and tobacco establishments throughout northeastern Mexico, technological innovations and sophisticated machinery replaced them.

During the Revolution, women participated by creating, sustaining, and promoting ideas about worker autonomy, fair wages, and gender equity. They took advantage of the environment produced by the war to formulate radical ideas about women's rights, which led to the creation of a "renaissance" for women, to quote Emma Pérez. Others continued to sell their labor, contributing to the expansion and modernization of

Selected PLM-Affiliated Organizations in Texas, 1911–1917

Name	Location	Date Founded
Grupo Regeneración	San Antonio, no. 25	1911
Grupo Regeneración "Tierra y Libertad"	San Antonio, no.25	1911
Grupo Regeneración "Tierra y Libertad"	San Antonio, no.131	1913
El Grupo Liberal Mexicano Práxedis G. Guerrero	Strawn, no. 25	1911
Grupo Regeneración	González, no. 35	1911
Grupo Regeneración Práxedis G. Guerrero	Amarillo, no. 35	1911
Grupo Regeneración "Pan Tierra y Libertad"	Brady, no. 40	1911
Grupo Regeneración Guillermo Stanley, Blo.	Grove, no. 40	1911
Grupo Regeneración de Agricultores	Fentress, no. 81	1912
Grupo Regeneración "Tierra y Libertad"	Beaumont, no. 81	1912
Grupo Femenino "Aspiraciones Libres"	Morin, no.81	1912
Grupo Regeneración "Ignacio Zaragoza"	Raton, no. 81	1912
Grupo Regeneración "Práxedis Guerrero"	Condado de Cameron, no. 83	1912
Grupo Regeneración "Blas Salinas"	Knippa, no. 87	1912
Grupo Regeneración "Tierra y Libertad"	Austin, no. 89, no.107	1912
Grupo Regeneración "Tierra y Libertad"	Austin, no. 149	1913
Grupo Regeneración Del Valle	Rio Grande Valley, no. 89	1912
Grupo Regeneración de Hutto	Hutto, no. 89	1912
Grupo Regeneración de Kyle	Kyle, no. 89	1912
Grupo Regeneración "Práxedis Guerrero"	San Marcos, no. 89	1912
Grupo Regeneración "Práxedis Guerrero"	San Marcos, no. 162	1913
Grupo Regeneración "Tierra y Libertad"	Uhland, no. 89	1912
Grupo Regeneración "Práxedis Guerrero"	Garfield, no. 89	1912
Grupo Regeneración "Tierra y Libertad"	Bluff Springs, no. 96	1912
Grupo Regeneración "Rebeldes sin Hogar"	Alba, no.96	1912
Grupo Regeneración "Rebeldes sin Hogar"	Alba, no. 131	1913
Grupo Regeneración "Benjamín Canales Garza	Malakoff, no. 98	1912
Grupo Regeneración "Vencer o Morir"	Como, no. 99 & 110	1912
Grupo Regeneración "Vencer o Morir"	Como, no. 131	1913
Grupo Regeneración "Higinio Tanguma"	Riesel, no. 103	1912
Grupo Regeneración "Tierra y Libertad"	Weir, no. 103	1912
Grupo Regeneración "Tierra y Libertad"	Weir, no. 149	1913
Grupo Regeneración "Tierra y Libertad"	Waxahachie, no. 107	1912
Grupo Regeneración "Bandera Roja"	González, no. 130	1913
Grupo Regeneración "Prismas Anarquistas"	Burkett, no. 148	1913
Grupo Regeneración "Solidaridad Perpetua"	Brownsville, no. 149	1913
Grupo Regeneración "Amor y Justicia"	Coleman, no. 149	1913
Grupo Regeneración "Práxedis Guerrero"	Hondo, no. 187	1914
Grupo Regeneración "Libertad o Muerte"	Rio Grande Valley, no. 257	1917
Grupo Regeneración "Juárez y Lerdo"	Reagan, no. 257	1917

Adapted from Aurora Mónica Alcayaga Sasso, "Librado Rivera y los Hermanos Rojos en el Movimiento Social y Cultural Anarquista en Villa Cecilia y Tampico, Tamaulipas, 1915–1931," Tesis Doctoral en Historia, Universidad Iberoamericana, México, 2006.

the borderlands. Building on the ideas espoused during the Revolution, women's activism helped to shape the larger conversation about labor and labor rights. However, the Revolution did not fix the widespread gender inequities present along the borderlands. Although the activism of women during the Revolution helped to bring women's labor issues to the forefront, and despite the advances made by women like Tenayuca in the postrevolutionary period, women's work was still gender specific and, even in the agricultural fields, considered family work; only a handful of women earned wages directly. It would take another "renaissance" for women—a massive movement concerned with issues that went beyond labor—some five decades after the Revolution to address the gendered, racial, political, and economic inequalities that continued to shape and affect their lives at work and at home.

Notes

I would like to thank the WAC (Writing Across the Curriculum) group at the University of Texas–Pan American for reading an earlier draft of this essay. Also, thanks to Guadalupe San Miguel Jr. for his helpful comments. I also extend my gratitude to the staff at the Nettie Lee Benson Library for their assistance.

1. The idea and practice of cooperativism formed part of the broader socioeconomic agenda of the Mexican Revolution. Much of it had been promoted by the early mutual-aid societies on both sides of the *Río Grande*. The practice of cooperativism can be traced back to preindustrial Mexico (i.e., *cajas de ahorro* [communal savings banks]). See Rosendo Rojas Coria, *Tratado del Cooperativismo En México* (México D.F: Fondo de Cultura Económica, 1982) Segunda Edición. See also John M. Hart, "The Evolution of the Mexican and Mexican American Working Classes," in *Border Crossings: Mexican and Mexican American Workers,* ed. John M. Hart (Wilmington, Del.: Scholarly Resources, 1998); and John M. Hart, *Revolutionary Mexico: The Coming and Process of the Mexican Revolution* (Berkeley: University of California Press, 1987).

2. I use the term "ethnic Mexican" to refer to Mexican-descent individuals residing in the United States. I borrow from Gloria Anzaldúa's concept of a borderlands as a place of constant negotiation, and borrow from Samuel Truett and Elliott Young's concept of the borderlands as a "crossroads." I also distinguish between border and borderlands. "Border" is used to refer to the geopolitical boundary between the United States and Mexico and "borderlands" refers to the region adjacent to the immediate borderline. Gloria Anzaldúa, *Borderlands/La Frontera: The New Mestiza* (San Francisco: Aunt Lute Books, 2007); and Samuel Truett and Elliott Young, eds., *Continental Crossroads: Remapping U.S.–Mexican Borderlands History* (Durham, N.C.: Duke

University Press, 2004). On the various definitions of border, frontier, and borderland/s from the perspective of different disciplines, see Hastings Donnan and Thomas Wilson, *Borders: Frontiers of Identity, Nation, and State* (Oxford: Berg Publishers, 1999).

3. Emilio Zamora points out that immigration in the pre-revolutionary period consisted of more of a cycle, in which Mexicans frequently returned to Mexico for periods of time and then headed back to the United States. He argues that "return migrations reinforced a pattern of cultural and political interactions between communities on both sides of the border." *The World of the Mexican Worker in Texas* (College Station: Texas A&M University Press, 1993), 15.

4. For women in the American Southwest, see Vicki Ruiz, *Cannery Women, Cannery Lives: Mexican Women, Unionization, and the California Food Processing Industry, 1930–1950* (Albuquerque: University of New Mexico Press, 1987). See also her *From Out of the Shadows: Mexican Women in Twentieth Century America* (New York: Oxford University Press, 2008). For the Mexican north, see Michael Snodgrass, *Deference and Defiance in Monterrey: Workers, Paternalism, and Revolution in Mexico, 1890–1950* (Cambridge: Cambridge University Press, 2003); and Jocelyn Olcott, *Revolutionary Women in Revolutionary Mexico* (Durham, N.C.: Duke University Press, 2005). For Mexico City, see Susie Porter, *Working Women in Mexico City: Public Discourses and Material Conditions, 1879–1931* (Tucson: University of Arizona Press, 2003).

5. See the various essays that address this question in Jocelyn Olcott, Mary Kay Vaughan, and Gabriela Cano, eds., *Sex in Revolution: Gender, Politics, and Power in Modern Mexico* (Durham, N.C.: Duke University Press, 2006).

6. Classic works on women and the Mexican Revolution include Elizabeth Salas, "The *Soldadera* in the Mexican Revolution: War and Men's Illusions," in *Women of the Mexican Countryside, 1850–1990,* eds. Heather Fowler-Salamini and Mary Kay Vaughan (Tucson: University of Arizona Press, 1994): 93–105 (and other essays in that same collection); *Las Mujeres en la Revolución Mexicana: Biografía de Mujeres Revolucionarias* (México: INEHRM, 1992); Anna Macías, *Against All Odds: The Feminist Movement in Mexico to 1940* (Westport, Conn.: Greenwood Press, 1982); Angeles Mendieta Alatorre, *La Mujer en la Revolución Mexicana* (México: Biblioteca del Instituto Nacional de Estudios Históricos de la Revolución Mexicana, 1961); Carmen Ramos and Ana Lau, *Mujeres y Revolución, 1900–1917* (México: Instituto Nacional de Estudios Históricos de la Revolución Mexicana, 1993); Andrés Reséndez Fuentes, "Battleground Women: *Soldaderas* and Female Soldiers in the Mexican Revolution," *The Americas* 51 (April 1995): 525–553; and Shirlene Soto, *Emergence of the Modern Mexican Woman: Her Participation in Revolution and Struggle for Equality, 1910–1940* (Denver, Col.: Arden Press, 1990).

7. See the various articles on the Revolution in *The Brownsville Herald* during the month of March 1913.

8. Teresa Palomo Acosta and Ruthe Winegarten, *Las Tejanas: 300 Years of History* (Austin: University of Texas Press, 2003), 76–7.

9. For a discussion of the intersections of "text," or "narrative," and "action," or politics, see Elliott Young, *Catarino Garza's Revolution on the Texas–Mexico Border* (Durham, N.C.: Duke University Press, 2004), particularly chapter 1.

10. Emma Pérez, *The Decolonial Imaginary: Writing Chicanas into History* (Bloomington: Indiana University Press, 1999), 56.

11. Pérez, *The Decolonial Imaginary,* 56–58; Teresa Palomo Acosta, "Sara Estela Ramírez," *Handbook of Texas Online,* accessed September 18, 2009; and Cynthia E. Orozco, "Mexican American Women," *Handbook of Texas Online.* See also Pilar Melero, "Sara Estela Ramírez and Andrea Villarreal González: Revolutionary Voices?" in *Recovering the U.S. Hispanic Literary Heritage,* vol. 6, eds. Antonia I. Castañeda and A. Gabriel Meléndez (Houston: Arte Público Press, 2006), 182–198. Immigration figures for the period of 1850–1920 are as follows: Adapted from table 6, in Zamora, *The World of the Mexican Worker.*

Year	Mexico-born	U.S.-Born	Total
1850	12,443	6,850	19,293
1900	71,062	92,555	163,617
1910	124,238	153,093	277,331
1920	249,652	255,705	505,357

See also Zamora, "Sara Estela Ramírez: Una Rosa Roja en el Movimiento," in *Mexican Women in the United States: Struggles Past and Present,* eds. Magdalena Mora and Adelaida R. del Castillo (Los Angeles: Chicano Studies Research Center Publications, 1980).

12. Clara Lomas, "The Articulation of Gender in the Mexican Borderlands, 1900–1915," in *Recovering the U.S. Hispanic Literary Heritage,* eds. Ramón Gutiérrez and Genaro Padilla (Houston: Arte Público Press, 1993), 294.

13. Ibid., 293–297.

14. Ibid., 300.

15. Although the historian Juan Mora-Torres does not focus on *obreras,* he acknowledges the lower wages they received in the textile industry, *The Making of the Mexican Border: The State, Capitalism, and Society in Nuevo León, 1848–1910* (Austin: University of Texas Press, 2001). The Magón brothers also called for a minimum national pay of 30 *centavos* for children and 75 *centavos* for men (in the textile industry).

16. In states such as Utah and California, for example, women made gains with regards to improvement of wages and general work conditions. The Utah State Federation of Labor Convention voted in favor of a minimum wage law for women. In California, unionized theater workers pressed for equal pay when they discovered that

theatrical managers planned to substitute women for male operators in their motion picture theaters. Given men's activism in unions, the theatrical managers saw women as cheaper alternatives and as passive and nonthreatening workers. However, the female operatives' actions contradicted this idea; in a cross-gender solidarity movement, their issues were made public, leaving theater managers with no other alternative than to address these issues. "Unions Favor Women's Minimum Wage" and "Organized Labor Protects Women," *Pan American Labor Press—El Obrero Pan-Americano, órgano de la confederación obrera Pan-American* (San Antonio), October 9, 1918, Box OS1, Clemente N. Idar Papers [hereafter, CNI], Nettie Lee Benson Library Latin American Collection [hereafter, NLBLAC].

17. Zamora, "Sara Estela Ramírez."

18. Aurora Mónica Alcayaga Sasso, "Librado Rivera y los Hermanos Rojos en el Movimiento Social y Cultural Anarquista en Villa Cecilia y Tampico, Tamaulipas, 1915–1931" (Tesis Doctoral en Historia, Universidad Iberoamericana, México, 2006), as quoted on page 107.

19. Ibid. Alcayaga Sasso's focus is on the Tampico region. However, workers from throughout Mexico employed similar strategies. The PLM had branches throughout the country and in the United States.

20. "'Discurso' Grupo Regeneración 'Prismas Anarquistas' de Burkett, Texas," *Regeneración,* no. 147 (June 28, 1913) [online] Archivo Electrónico de Ricardo Flóres Magón, accessed November 30, 2009, from www.archivomagon.net/Periodico/Re generacion/CuartaEpoca/PDF/e4n147.pdf

21. Alcayaga Sasso, "Librado Rivera y los Hermanos Rojos, 138.

22. Acosta and Winegarten, *Las Tejanas,* 211–212.

23. *Album Conmemorativo de las Comisiones Honoríficas y Brigada Cruz Azul,* microfilm 1, 1925, Eustacio Cepeda Papers [hereafter, ECP, NLBLAC].

24. Ibid., 61.

25. Roseann Bacha-Garza (and the San Juan EDC), *Images of America: San Juan* (Arcadia, 2010), 102.

26. Transcription of speech by Clemente N. Idar, n.d., Box 9, Folder 14, CNI, NLBLAC.

27. José E. Limón, "El Primer Congreso Mexicanista de 1991: A Precursor to Contemporary Chicanismo," *Aztlán* 5 (Spring/Fall 1974): 95.

28. Ibid., 95–98. Women also continued to participate in mutual-aid societies in the 1930s. Dolores Charó represented the Club Social Recreativo "Latino Americano," a mixed-sex organization in Robstown, Texas. Women also formed part of the various activities in the *Sociedad Mutualista "Hijos de Hidalgo"* also in the same town. See "Notas de Robstown" in *El Paladín* (Corpus Christi) *órgano de LULAC,* February 7, 1930, Box OS1, CNI, NLBLAC.

29. Acosta and Winegarten, *Las Tejanas,* 85. On race and Mexicans in Texas, see the various studies by Arnoldo De León, particularly, *They Called Them Greasers: Anglo Attitudes towards Mexicans in Texas, 1821–1900* (Austin: University of Texas Press, 1983).

30. Edna Ochoa, "El Periodismo, la mujer y la frontera en Laredo: propuesta de cambio en la obra de Jovita Idar," ponencia en *Primer Simposio de la Historia del Noreste y Sur de Texas, Archivo Histórico de Reynosa, Reynosa, Tamaulipas, México* (octubre 2, 2006): 6; "150 Years of Work for Women's Rights," *San Antonio Express News* (July 19, 1998): 6A.

31. Ochoa, "El Periodismo, la mujer y la frontera en Laredo . . . ," 7.

32. Pérez, *The Decolonial Imaginary,* 56.

33. Undated three-page letter by Jovita Idar, Box 1 Folder 2, CNI, NLBLAC.

34. Ochoa, "El Periodismo, la mujer y la frontera en Laredo . . . ," 7–8.

35. Ibid., 3.

36. "Esther González Salinas," unpublished biography written by Rosaura Alicia Dávila, Archivo Histórico de Matamoros. I thank Ms. Dávila for providing me with a copy of this essay.

37. Palomo and Winegarten, *Las Tejanas,* 97.

38. Bacha-Garza, *Images of America,* 12–13.

39. Ibid., 100.

40. Ibid., 34.

41. Orozco, "Mexican American Women," *Handbook of Texas Online,* accessed September 18, 2009.

42. Zamora, *The World of the Mexican Worker,* 26; Emilio Zamora, "Mexican Labor Activity in South Texas, 1900–1920" (Ph.D. diss., University of Texas at Austin, 1983), 42–44.

43. Zamora, "Mexican Labor Activity in South Texas," 42–44.

44. Bacha-Garza, *Images of America,* 22, 44, 52.

45. Zamora "The World of the Mexican Worker," 214, table 6; Irene Ledesma, "Texas Newspapers and Chicana Workers' Activism, 1919–1974," *The Western Historical Quarterly* 26 (Autumn 1995): 312.

46. As quoted in Ledesma, "Texas Newspapers and Chicana Workers' Activism," 312.

47. Ibid., 314.

48. To Margarito Romo, Laredo, from Clemente N. Idar, Laredo, October 10, 1918, Box 2 Folder 3, CNI, NLBLAC, October 10, 1918.

49. To Judge B. F. Patterson, San Antonio, from Clemente Idar, AFL organizer, Laredo, June 24, 1921, Box 2, Folder 3, CNI, NLBLAC.

50. To Judge B. F. Patterson, San Antonio, from Clemente Idar, AFL organizer, Laredo, June 24, 1921, Box 2, Folder 3, CNI, NLBLAC.

51. Ibid., *"They,"* my emphasis.

52. See table.

53. To Clemente N. Idar from Miguel Pavio, Fentress, No month, 27, 1920, Box 2, Folder 3, CNI, NLBLAC.

54. Ibid.

55. See Miguel Angel González Quiroga, in "Guerra y Comercio en Torno al Rió Bravo (1855–1867), Línea Fronteriza, Espacio Económico Común," Mario Cerutti, *Historia Mexicana* 40 (Octubre–Diciembre 1990): 217–297. For a discussion of peasant petitions to authorities to address labor control mechanisms, see Sonia Hernández, "Mexicanas and Mexicanos in a Transitional Borderland, 1880–1940" (Ph.D. diss., University of Houston, 2006), particularly chapters 2 and 3.

56. To Clemente N. Idar from Miguel Pavio, Fentress, No month, 27, 1920, Box 2, Folder 3, CNI, NLBLAC.

57. José Guillermo Pastrano, "The Bureaucratic Origins of Migrant Poverty: The Texas Cotton Industry, 1910–1930," *The Journal of Peasant Studies* 35 (October 2008): 688.

58. Ibid., 711–712.

59. Ruth Allen, "The Labor of Women in the Production of Cotton," Bureau of Research in the Social Sciences Study, no. 3 (Austin: University of Texas at Austin, The University of Texas Bulletin No. 3134, 1931), 103; Emilio Zamora, *Claiming Rights and Writing Wrongs in Texas: Mexican Workers and Job Politics during World War II* (College Station: Texas A&M University Press, 2009), 106; see also Neil Foley, *The White Scourge: Mexicans, Blacks, and Poor Whites in Texas Cotton Culture* (Berkeley: University of California Press, 1999).

60. Allen, "The Labor of Women in the Production of Cotton," 220.

61. Ibid., 231; Acosta and Winegarten, *Las Tejanas,* 104. Acosta and Winegarten also discuss women's fieldwork during the 1930s in the same chapter (5).

62. Allen, "The Labor of Women in the Production of Cotton," 233.

63. "Algunos datos de interés general para los Mexicanos que residen en el estado de Texas" in *Album Conmemorativo de las Comisiones Honoríficos y Brigada Cruz Azul,* 18, microfilm 1, 1925, ECP, NLBLAC.

64. Ibid., 18.

65. Zaragosa Vargas, "Mexican Migrant Workers in the Midwest," in *Major Problems in Mexican American History,* ed. Zaragosa Vargas (Boston, New York: Houghton Mifflin, 1999).

66. "Bellos Recuerdos" by Los Fantasmas del Valle, in "Tacuachito Nights: Conjunto Music from South Texas," Smithsonian Recording (CD 1999); See also Acosta and Winegarten, *Las Tejanas,* 106.

67. "Algunos datos de interés," 18.

68. Ibid., 18.

69. Allen, "The Labor of Women in the Production of Cotton," 233. The numbers are based on a sample group of 106 Mexican women.

70. Ibid., 239.

71. Ledesma, "Texas Newspapers and Chicana Workers' Activism," 310–311.

72. Ibid., 311–312.

73. Ibid., 314.

74. See Benjamin H. Johnson, *Revolution in Texas: How a Forgotten Rebellion and Its Bloody Suppression Turned Mexicans into Americans* (New Haven, Conn.: Yale University Press, 2003); Rodolfo Rocha, "The Influence of the Mexican Revolution on the Texas–Mexico Border, 1910–1916" (Ph.D. diss., Texas Tech University, 1981); and James Sandos, *Rebellion in the Borderlands: Anarchism and the Plan de San Diego, 1904–1923* (Norman: Oklahoma University Press, 1992).

75. Ledesma, "Texas Newspapers and Chicana Workers' Activism," 317.

76. "Las Trabajadoras Mexicanas de Lavanderías de El Paso, Fueron Indignamente Engañadas y Perjudicadas Bajo el Pretexto de Una Unión," *La República* (El Paso), 23 de diciembre, 1919, Box OS1, CNI, NLBLAC. For a discussion on newpaper perceptions of Mexican women workers, see Ledesma, "Texas Newspapers and Chicana Workers' Activism."

77. For the Mexican North, see Mora-Torres, *Making of the Mexican Border;* for South Texas, see Young, *Catarino Garza's Revolution.*

78. Ledesma, "Texas Newspapers and Chicana Workers' Activism," 317; see also Gabriela González, "Carolina Munguía and Emma Tenayuca: The Politics of Benevolence and Radical Reform," *Frontiers: A Journal of Women Studies* 24, no. 2/3, Gender on the Borderlands (2003): 200–229; and Carmen Tafolla's "La Pasionaria" in the same volume, as well as other works on Tenayuca by Tafolla.

79. Sonia Hernández and Charles Waite, ed., *The Mexican American Experience in Texas: A Primary Source Reader* (Dubuque: Kendall Hunt Publishers, 2009), 109–110.

80. Although women's labor activism in the 1930s and 1940s is not the focus of this study, it is important to note that women, individually and collectively, took it upon themselves to address unfair labor practices and push for labor rights using various approaches. See González, "Carolina Munguía and Emma Tenayuca," 200–229; Ruiz, *Cannery Women, Cannery Lives;* see also Ruiz, "Una Mujer Sin Fronteras: Luisa Moreno and Latina Labor Activism" *The Pacific Historical Review* 73 (February 2004): 1–20.

81. "Lo que serán las conferencias obreras en Laredo el próximo 13 de Noviembre: Los obreros de los dos paises tratarán importantes asuntos, un abrazo fraternal, se darán en el Puente, las fiestas se preparan," *Evolución* (Laredo), 26 de octubre, 1918, Box OS1, CNI, NLBLAC.

82. Alcayago Sasso, "Librado Rivera y Los Hermanos Rojos," 144.

83. Ibid., 144.

84. To the Bakery and Confectionary Workers' International Union, Chicago, from Clemente N. Idar, Torreón, April 20, 1922, Box 4, Folder 5, CNI, NLBLAC.

85. Limón, "El Primer Congreso Mexicanista," 97.

86. Rooted in the colonial tradition of mutual reciprocity, *vecinos* in the frontier region frequently used the written petition to voice concerns and negotiate socioeconomic conditions. Indeed, the use of the written petition survived the modernization of the borderlands. Extensive social networks of support were well in place since the turn of the twentieth century, and possibly prior to that Mexicanos from Monterrey who adhered to the *Círculo de Obreros* received communication from their *compañeros* across the border. When Texas authorities detained and imprisoned Mexican Gregorio Cortéz for the murder of a sheriff in self-defense, Laredo-based *Sociedad Obreros Igualdad y Progreso,* with the assistance of Monterrey *obreros,* sought to intervene, *Sociedad Obreros Igualdad y Progreso,* Laredo, to Governor, Nuevo León, July 30, 1901, Fondo: Trabajo, Asunto: Asociaciones, Organizaciones, y Sindicatos, Archivo General del Estado de Nuevo León [hereafter, AGENL]. See also letter dated September 17, 1901.

87. Al Presidente y Socios de la Sociedad Melchor Ocampo de Guadalupe V. de Garza, 8 junio 1936, Box 1, Folder 2, SMMO [hereafter, SMMO, NLBLAC]. Unfortunately, we do not know whether Guadalupe received aid. We do know, based on other documents, that other women who petitioned the organization did acquire help. See, for example, al Sociedad M. Melchor Ocampo de Juana V. de Flores, 10 de noviembre, 1936, Box 1, Folder 2, SMMO, NLBLAC.

88. Sociedad M. Melchor Ocampo de Victoria Ureste, n.d., Box 1, Folder 2, SMMO, NLBLAC. Similar to the *campesinas* and *campesinos* of northeastern Mexico, Mexican immigrants whose agricultural skills were once again put to use in Texas negotiated labor conditions through the assistance of a public officials. The naming of honorary members was a Mexican common cultural practice in existence years prior to the outbreak of the Revolution. If anything, the Revolution enhanced and encouraged this practice, particularly because it extended rights to those at the very bottom of the power structure. By doing so, workers adopted the politics of servitude and loyalty. The organized farm workers from central Texas, for instance, sought to make the progressive Judge B. F. Patterson their honorary member, to help them negotiate working conditions with their respective landowners. See Judge B. F. Patterson, San Antonio, from Clemente Idar, AFL organizer, Laredo, June 24, 1921, Box 2, Folder 3, CNI, NLBLAC; see also *Sociedad Mutualista "Hijos de Hidalgo,"* San Diego (Texas), to Governor, Nuevo León, and *Sociedad Unión Fraternal Obreros de Brownsville,* to Governor, Nuevo León, March 30, 1892, in Fondo: Trabajo Asunto: Asociaciones, Organizaciones, y Sindicatos, AGENL.

89. "Atenta Invitación" de parte de Sociedad Mutualista "Melchor Ocampo, April 14, 1930, Box 1 Folder 2, SMMO, NLBLAC.

90. Olcott, Vaughan, and Cano, eds. *Sex in Revolution.*

91. To J. M. Plata from Clement N. Idar, March 19, 1920, Box 2, Folder 3, CNI, NLBLAC.

92. Ibid.

93. "Acta de la sesión inaugural del tercer congreso de delegados de las comisiones honoríficas y brigadas de la Cruz Azul Mexicana, de la Primera Divisón efectuado en la ciudad de San Antonio, Texas, durante los días 12, 12, 14, y 15 de octubre de 1925," in *Albúm Conmemorativo de las Comisiones Honoríficas y Brigadas de la Cruz Azul Mexicana* (1925), on microfilm reel, ECP, NLBLAC.

94. As quoted in Limón, "El Primer Congreso Mexicanista," 95.

95. Ibid., 95.

96. Julia Kirk Blackwelder, *Women of the Depression: Caste and Culture in San Antonio, 1929–1939* (College Station: Texas A&M University Press, 1984), 60–62; see also Zaragoza Vargas, "Tejana Radical: Emma Tenayuca and the San Antonio Labor Movement during the Great Depression," *Pacific Historical Review* 66 (November 1997): 553–580.

97. There were also Mexicans and Mexican Americans who left the country voluntarily.

Salt of the Earth The Immigrant Experience of Gerónimo Treviño

ROBERTO R. TREVIÑO

"They tried to warn them, 'Look out—Indians!' But it was too late. I guess one of them was deaf and the other one couldn't see," the old man half-joked, wide-eyed and gesturing to make his point to the gaggle of kids gathered at his feet. "Anyway, the Indians killed those two *mexicanos* who were working way out at the other end of the fence line, and they escaped into a *sacatal* there, a thicket as tall as this house! And *that's* why they

Mexican immigrants Gerónimo and Francisca Treviño and their Texas-born children, Gerónimo Jr. (oldest), Beatriz, and infant Zulema, ca. 1925.

named the place *El Rancho de los Difuntos* (the Ranch of the Dead)."[1] Silence engulfed my brothers and cousins as we looked at each other, replaying the vivid images conjured by our grandfather's storytelling. Growing up in Mathis, Texas, in the 1950s, I heard many such tales about his life in northern Mexico and South Texas. Enveloped in balmy darkness, we spent many a summer evening on his front porch, transfixed as the master narrator regaled us with stories that were exciting, scary, and funny but, at times, also tinged with sadness and anger. They were accounts about the everyday dreams and struggles of ordinary Mexican Revolution immigrants, like the storyteller himself, Gerónimo Treviño from Parás, Nuevo León.

Don Gerónimo, as he was known to friends and acquaintances, knew the stories of his people and his times intimately; he had lived them. His life was not glamorous because he was not famous, and it was not always tranquil because the hard realities of the times often made mere survival a challenge in itself. He was simply a hard-working, honest man of a poor, rural upbringing, a man of few material resources but great determination—the salt of the earth. In many ways *Don* Gerónimo's life paralleled the experiences of the multitude of immigrants who escaped the chaos of the Mexican Revolution, hoping to find a better life in Texas in the 1910s and 1920s.[2] Like countless other common folks who came to Texas from Mexico in those years, Gerónimo Treviño's life was marked by severe hardships, frustrations, and disappointments. Yet, it was also a life lived with zest and a sense of adventure, buoyed by unflinching courage, perseverance, and hope. It is an important story that should be told.

For, indeed, ordinary *mexicanos* like Gerónimo Treviño were makers of history in their own right. Born into poverty, Gerónimo relied on his innate capacity for hard work and dogged determination to forge a productive life as an immigrant in the Coastal Bend region. Even though he was a poorly paid common laborer and cotton sharecropper, his labor had large implications. Gerónimo's work not only provided for a large family but also helped to give rise to an agricultural boom in Texas and a flourishing Mexican American community in the 1910s and 1920s.

The state of Nuevo León, like its neighbor states that make up the Mexican North, has a unique geography and history that set it apart and explain its central role in the forging of modern Mexico. For one thing, Nuevo León's rugged terrain and climate have always challenged its inhabitants with extremely hot and cold temperatures, dust storms, and severe droughts, giving rise to the common saying, "Our land is not bad, but heaven does not help us." Moreover, the region's history has been characterized by ongoing cycles of violence—Indian wars, banditry, civil wars, and foreign interventions—resulting from the efforts of Spain, Mexico, and the United States to exert control over the land and its people in the name of nation building. Indeed, life in Nuevo León had been a continual challenge since 1596, when Spain's colonization began with the arrival of its first *vecinos,* the peasant farmer-soldiers who received land grants, water rights, and tax exemptions in return for pledging their allegiance to the local governor and agreeing to pacify the region and defend its borders at their own expense.[3]

In that harsh and unforgiving land, a young woman named Toribia Rubio gave birth to Gerónimo Treviño on September 30, 1885, in Parás, a small village lying some forty miles from the Río Grande and about midway between Laredo and Brownsville, Texas. Almost from the start, hardship marked Gerónimo's life. The first of several tragedies that befell his family in his formative years came as a child. Gerónimo's father Lauro Treviño never married his mother, and left her with three children when he moved away to marry someone else in the nearby town of Agualeguas. The deserted mother took her children—Gilberto the oldest, Gerónimo, and their younger sister Lauriana—to live with her at her father's ranch on the outskirts of Parás, the Ranch of the Dead.[4] The ranch's morbid name speaks volumes about the hard life and personal tragedies that shaped the young Gerónimo, and it also reflects the conflicted history of the frontier region of Nuevo León and its people, the Nuevoleoneses.

The story the elderly Gerónimo recounted to his grandchildren about Indians killing some *mexicanos* at the ranch where he grew up was no fairytale; it was a common experience on the Nuevo León frontier. A state of continual warfare, *guerra viva,* existed in the region from Spanish colonial times through most of the nineteenth century. As waves of settlers tried to wrest the land away from the different indigenous groups, Indians exacted a terrible toll, killing hundreds of intruders, burning their ranches and towns, carrying off their women and children, and stealing their horses and other livestock. Widespread and incessant, the attacks affected practically all of Nuevo León and reached eastward all the way to the border towns of Laredo, Mier, Camargo, and Reynosa, some of the places where, as a young man, Gerónimo would later cross into Texas in search of work. The bloodletting finally began to let up in the 1870s, but sporadic violence continued into the next decade. In fact, the last Indian attack in Nuevo León occurred at Bustamante in 1885, the year Gerónimo was born.[5] This prolonged history of conflict was still fresh in the minds of the people who surrounded him in his childhood. Hearing chilling stories about his people locked in a deadly struggle for survival undoubtedly helped shape the young Gerónimo's outlook and character.

The constant Indian wars forged the character of the many famous generals Nuevo León produced. "The Indian's audacity gave them boldness; his cunning, cautiousness. The eternal enemy's tirelessness produced in them tenaciousness; his ferocity, bravery on a heroic scale." One of those larger-than-life figures bore the same name as my grandfather. The famous Jerónimo Treviño rose to prominence fighting against the French invasion of Mexico in the 1860s and went on to become one of northern Mexico's most powerful *caudillos* (regional strongmen) of the nineteenth century. He was still a wealthy and prominent politico in the early 1900s, when my grandfather was a young adult.[6] My grandfather clearly admired the legendary general, seeing him as a "man of great merit." He delighted in telling a story about a U.S. border guard who, after hearing Gerónimo's name, jokingly pretended he was dealing with the famous general. And he spoke almost reverently about the time he had actually seen "el General"—"but only from a distance"—when the living legend visited Parás.[7]

But famous people like General Jerónimo Treviño were not the only ones tested and tempered by the challenges of frontier life in Nuevo León; the "ordinary" *vecinos* (settlers) of the region confronted those harsh realities too, albeit without wealth, influence, and small armies at their disposal. Poor farming families such as my grandfather's faced daily adversity as they scratched a living from the unpredictable land. Not surprisingly, the old man's storytelling was never more animated than when he talked about Mexicans and their land. The identity of Nuevoleoneses was deeply tied to their experiences on the land, bound up in the blood, sweat, and tears of generations of *vecinos* bent on subduing it and reaping its bounty. This was a large part of what set him and "his people" apart from others, especially *los indios.*

And "what kind of Indians" were those who killed those *mexicanos* and gave the ranch its name, his oldest grandson once asked *Don* Gerónimo, meaning what were they called? The old man stiffened with disbelief and stared at his young namesake as he pondered the question—what *kind* of Indians? "Well, they were *bad* Indians, what else?" *Don* Gerónimo's brusque response is noteworthy not simply for its disregard for political correctness; rather, his reaction reveals his nineteenth-century mindset and his understanding of who he was. "Do you know what they wanted?" he asked by way of explanation. "They wanted to do away with all of us so that they could get all the land."[8] Ignoring centuries of genocidal policies toward Mexico's indigenous peoples, his reference to the land meant, of course, *our* land—land claimed by *mexicanos* like himself and his *vecino* forebears; land they had cleared and cultivated; land they had fought to the death for; the land that had sustained them and made them who they were.

Life on that land had always been hard, but for rural poor folks it grew increasingly difficult—and eventually unsustainable—during the *Porfiriato,* the dictatorship of Porfirio Díaz that began in 1876 and ended with the cataclysmic Revolution of 1910. During the last three decades of the nineteenth century, a number of factors, including Mexico's economic policies, population pressures on the land, and expanding capitalism in Texas and the Southwest, combined to steadily impoverish and uproot small farmers in Nuevo León. For families like Gerónimo's, only periodic migration to the United States allowed them to continue traditional subsistence farming and ranching given their ever-shrinking parcels of land and dirt-cheap local wages.[9] Like others who began leaving the region as early as the 1870s, Gerónimo's older brother Gilberto had worked in Texas to help sustain the family on their small *rancho* outside of Parás, setting a precedent that Gerónimo would follow. But in 1901, just as the Nuevo León countryside entered "a profound crisis of subsistence," death claimed Gilberto at age eighteen. Things went from bad to worse for the family in the ensuing years. To begin with, Gerónimo's stepfather also died, making Gerónimo the "man of the house" in his early twenties. The responsibility of caring for his widowed mother and six younger siblings grew harder as the local economy deteriorated even further and the nation spiraled into civil war.[10]

The outbreak of the Revolution of 1910 wreaked havoc around Gerónimo's home region. When the fighting among revolutionary factions intensified in the mid-1910s, he was forced to move his family from Parás to Texas. The Revolution "was what drove us over here," he recalled. "In those years, salaries for poor people over there were worthless." Employers would pay workers a pittance—literally a few cents—to harvest corn and then would tell them, "Go ahead and take some corn home so you can make yourselves some tortillas." Late in life, the elderly *Don* Gerónimo still vividly remembered the fighting: "The *Carrancistas* (Venustiano Carranza's forces) got there first. And then came a *Villista* army (followers of Francisco "Pancho" Villa), laying a damned siege, . . . buildings collapsing all around! . . . Oh, things got really bad, yes. When they were fighting in Guerrero, they fought from La Quinta. From La Quinta over here to town, it's only about a mile. And from over there, the *cabrones* were bombing the Federales over here. Well, La Quinta was a place where they used to grow vegetables to sell, but when the Revolution started, well, you couldn't work anymore. . . . And so business came to a standstill; there was nothing." With the sense of humor that saw him through many tough times, he explained that "if you had a good horse or a good mule to work with, the soldiers would take it from you. They would replace it with another animal but—damn it—it was so skinny you could blow on it and it would fall over! But what could you do? You took it."[11]

With violence mounting in the area, farming and ranching interrupted, and soldiers beginning to steal their goats and cows—their main livelihood—Gerónimo knew he had to act to protect his family. "I'm going to bring my people with me, my mother and my little sisters," he decided while he was away on one of his stints for work in Texas around 1915. On his return, he told his mother, "We'd better sell the rest of the livestock because they're going to finish them off—we'd better move to Texas, Mamá." An uncle's protests that they were better off there in Parás, among family, failed to convince Gerónimo.[12] His uneasiness about the safety of his family, especially his mother and sisters, was shared by many who were caught up in the violence of the Revolution in northern Mexico. For example, Salvador Guerrero recounted how an uncle had warned his father about an advancing army whose "main objective was to kill, steal, and rape. So for the protection of his family and, more specifically, of his teenage daughters, my father gathered up everyone and joined other refugees heading for northern Coahuila in 1915."[13] At about the same time the Guerreros fled Coahuila, Gerónimo added his family to the exodus of *mexicanos* seeking safety and a living wage in the United States. What had eluded them in revolutionary Mexico in the 1910s, Gerónimo and thousands of other refugees would find in the Coastal Bend region of Texas.

Eventually, Gerónimo would settle permanently in Texas in 1919, but by then he was no stranger to the Coastal Bend. Since about 1914, he had gone to Texas many times to work for two or three months at a stretch around Corpus Christi to help the family make ends meet back in Parás. "I crossed over very early and was here in Texas five years while my family all was back in Mexico," he recounted later in life about his early adventures. "There I was, sending them money so they could make ends meet, . . . working on a ranch four or five miles outside of *el Sinto* (Sinton) . . . *ginando algodón* (working in a cotton gin)."[14] During the Mexican Revolution, the waves of *mexicanos* arriving in South Texas easily found work in the vast ranch lands that were being converted from raising cattle to growing cotton and vegetables during the 1910s and 1920s. Labor contractors like C. M. Posey constantly issued calls for Mexicans willing to clear land and pick cotton. Posey, whose advertisements in San Antonio's *El Imparcial* included a picture of himself smartly dressed in suit and tie and Stetson hat, wooed *mexicanos* with the line, "Ask for *El Panzón* (Fatso), who never denies a favor to an honorable and hard-working Mexican." Thousands of acres of dense mesquite and underbrush first had to be cleared before the rich Blackland Prairie could yield its fruits. "Grubbing," as Anglo employers called clearing the land, paid abysmal wages as it was considered "Mexican work." But it was plentiful, and early in his Texas travels Gerónimo did plenty of it, as did thousands of his compatriots expelled by the Mexican Revolution. Frank Treviño, the youngest of Gerónimo's children, recalled hearing his father and other family members talk about grubbing mesquite at "a dollar an acre" on the outskirts of Corpus Christi. "They said there were six hundred men clearing land over there around Bay Side" and Calallen, my uncle Frank recounted.[15]

Uprooting mesquite was brutal work done mainly "*a puro talache*" (using nothing but pickaxes) by small armies of Mexican immigrants working alongside native-born Tejanos. In the 1930s, the town of Taft published a pamphlet that celebrated its history and linked it to the fortunes of the Coleman-Fulton Pasture Company, a leading agribusiness giant in Texas in the 1910s and 1920s, commonly called the Taft Ranch. The largest and most successful cotton-farming corporation in Texas at the time, the two-hundred-thousand-plus acreage of the Taft Ranch covered a large swath of San Patricio County, and its cotton and other enterprises gave rise to Sinton, Taft, Mathis, and other towns in the Coastal Bend region. Gerónimo and other refugees from the Mexican Revolution flocked to these and other towns, where they found work, settled, and raised families and, in the process, enlarged and energized the established enclaves of native-born Tejanos and enriched local economies. The booklet stated that in 1909 the company started bringing in "hundreds of Mexicans," employing as many as "300 workers at a time on several occasions" for grubbing work.[16]

The pamphlet's account about Mexican "grubbers" confirms Frank Treviño's recollections, even though the two versions vary in scale. That the number of workers he recalled (600) was exactly double what the historical document reported may reflect my uncle's legendary tendency to exaggerate. On the other hand, there might well have been a larger grubbing operation in the area at some point. In any case, what is important is the invigorating effect that the Mexican Revolution's wave of immigration produced in Texas. *Mexicano* immigrants injected a demographic vigor that reshaped the Mexican American population and set it on a trajectory of viable growth and permanence. They also provided the back-breaking labor that was a crucial to the Texas agricultural boom of the early twentieth century. How Tejano history would have developed without the large influx of immigrants is impossible to say, but certainly the composition of the Tejano community would have remained much smaller, and most likely, its future cultural and political imprint less profound. What is clear, however, is that the cotton and vegetable farms that enriched Texas would not have blossomed. As a reporter wrote in 1915, "Palpably there would be no great farming enterprise in that [Gulf Coast] region of Texas today had it not been for the availability of cheap Mexican labor."[17]

Significantly, a variety of employers and Texas boosters in the 1910s and 1920s recognized the importance of Mexican labor. "We have confined our remarks so far to the advent and events of Anglo-Americans," the pamphlet lauding the Taft Ranch stated at one point, "but it is fitting and only proper that we mention the part played by Mexican immigrants in this section's early history." The booklet went on to praise the "many men from south of the Rio Grande" employed by the Taft Ranch, because "[t]hey made fine cowhands and later excellent farmers and farm employees." My grandfather may or may not have worked for the Taft Ranch at some point during the mid- and later 1910s. On the one hand, his name does not appear in the likeliest places, in the payroll ledgers listing seasonal cotton pickers by name and in the house rental records. On the other hand, in another place where Gerónimo's name might be expected to appear, in the entries for the company's grubbing operations, individual "grubbers" are not listed by name. However, it is possible that during his early years in Texas, Gerónimo worked for the giant Taft Ranch clearing land or in some other capacity. There seem to be hints of this in some of his recollections. For example, he once recalled that a friend on his way back to Mexico from Louisiana looked him up in Sinton, a town that lay within the boundaries of the Taft Ranch. "He found out we were in *el Sinto* . . . and he went over there," the elderly Gerónimo recollected. His account of the incident sounds similar to descriptions provided by sources in the 1910s about the rustic conditions endured by Mexican grubbers, cooking outside and living in tents: "My friends and I were cooking supper there outside when he arrived. It was getting dark and we had no light there, just the light from the fire."[18]

Still, it is unlikely that the free-spirited Gerónimo would have put up with the constraints the Taft Ranch imposed on its workers. Applying the techniques of scientific management to gain greater efficiency and larger profits, Taft Ranch managers not only closely regulated every step of cotton production, but they also required employees to live in company housing, shop in the company's stores, attend their company-owned and controlled schools and churches, and otherwise submit to strict economic and social controls. Perhaps Mexican laborers like Gerónimo were less affected by this regimentation than the company's salaried and other year-round workers. Regardless, the proud and strong-willed Gerónimo would have avoided work situations he found insulting or repressive, as did other common folk who lived by their wits and resisted exploitation as best they could. Historians and other scholars have amply documented the "brutal and volatile character of Mexican–Anglo relations in the farm areas" during the early twentieth century. Employers and state authorities devised a system of "labor repression" aimed at maintaining an abundant supply of cheap Mexican labor by establishing local vagrancy laws and pass systems for workers, manipulating labor agency laws and worker contracts, and using other coercive tactics. But many workers constantly resisted this "web of labor controls," most of the time simply by using their social networks to learn where better opportunities existed and moving around from employer to employer. "In their search for work in Texas," historian David Montejano wrote, "Mexicans were sensitive to rumors about bad treatment and poor working conditions at particular farms; for them, it was a matter of protection." Similarly, Gerónimo's years as a cotton farmer, which stretched from the 1910s into the 1940s, were spent moving between various *ranchos* in four Coastal Bend counties: Nueces, San Patricio, Refugio, and Bee. Working on a contract basis, he struck deals with different employers in a constant effort to find the best opportunities to earn a living in the Corpus Christi area.[19]

But getting from Mexico to the cotton country around Corpus Christi was not simple or easy. For one thing, the perils of migration were not to be taken lightly; crossing the rugged Borderlands terrain required plenty of fortitude and stamina as well as survival skills and knowledge of the territory. "You had to carry water because there were some parts of the journey that were very dry, and you went on foot," *Don* Gerónimo explained in his later years. "You didn't have the means you have now—you didn't have cars; a person who had a horse was rich. Lots of snakes crossed your path!" Even a trip that would be a short commute by car—say, between Alice and Kingsville—would be a serious walk through the South Texas chaparral of the early twentieth century. "That stretch between Alice and Kingsville, well, it's not very far," *Don* Gerónimo recounted. "Once a friend and I were going and we had a bottle of water. Well, that infernal sun beating down on us, the *monte* (dense woods) all around us like that, and nothing but that endless road stretching out for miles ahead of us. Well, we drank all our water and we still had a ways to go to get to the town." Luckily, they spotted a *papalote* in the distance and gleefully headed off toward the windmill, knowing a water well awaited them.[20]

Throughout his dangerous travels in the 1910s, Gerónimo always proved equal to the task. A hard rural life had given him a strong body. He was an excellent swimmer, who, in his seventies, would strip down, swim out toward the middle of the Nueces River, and coax his grandsons to join him. Despite my childhood recollections of him as a giant of a man, in his prime he was probably only slightly larger than the average *mexicano* of his time. Consular pictures and documents show a handsome mustachioed man with a piercing gaze, who stood 5 feet 9 inches tall, was of medium build, and weighed about 165 pounds. But besides being physically sturdy—*macizo,* as he put it—Gerónimo was prepared in other ways to cope with the harsh South Texas environment. He rarely traveled unarmed and often spoke proudly of his trusty .38 *pistolita* and his prized .30–.30 rifle. He became expert in their use, and they served him well in providing food and protection for his family. From his travels, Gerónimo gleaned valuable knowledge about the Texas terrain. He became a fine hunter and spent many days and nights alone in the woods stalking game.[21]

Gerónimo armed himself not only to hunt and protect himself from wild animals; other predators roamed the borderlands he traveled. Throughout much of its history, lawlessness and violence plagued the Texas–Mexico border region. On the Mexican side, in addition to the Indian wars, authorities had fought for generations against the violence associated with cross-border smuggling and banditry. Outlawry flourished on the Texas side as well, with the added scourge of vigilante violence and other periodic depredations perpetrated against *mexicanos* and native-born Tejanos. This violence flowed back and forth across the South Texas border during the late nineteenth and early twentieth centuries, making travel in the area risky. But it came to a head with devastating consequences for Mexicans and Tejanos at just about the time Gerónimo began his treks to work in Texas, during an uprising called the *Plan de San Diego* of 1915–1916. As the Mexican Revolution raged, some native-born Tejanos mounted an insurrection to try to liberate Texas and the Southwest. In response, vigilantes and Texas Rangers unleashed a reign of terror that suppressed the revolt, but in the process, killed hundreds, perhaps thousands, of innocent Mexicans and Mexican Americans in the border region.[22]

Thus, traveling through the Texas–Mexican borderlands during those troubled times, law-abiding migrants like Gerónimo risked their lives as they crossed the Río Grande back and forth in search of work. In Mexico, they could be caught in the crossfire of dueling revolutionary armies or assaulted by marauders who prowled the countryside. On the Texas side, they constantly ran the risk of being accused as a "border bandit" and summarily executed. Even in the more peaceful outer reaches of the Río Grande Valley, in the Corpus Christi area where he worked, suspicion hung over both immigrants like him and the native-born Tejanos among whom he lived, as rumors about impending bandit raids circulated. In Robstown, for instance, a long-time resident recalled that many newcomers to the area "made preparations two or three times . . . seeking refuge from an attack that never materialized."[23]

Little wonder, then, that Gerónimo often carried documents that might give him a bit of added security on his journeys, letters or passes from government officials that attested to the legitimacy of his travels and to his good character. On one occasion before leaving Parás, he sought "a letter of safe passage because I was young and needed the backing of someone influential. So it occurred to me to ask . . . for a letter that would help me where I was going to go work." In Gerónimo's world, the most "influential" man he could approach was the mayor of his tiny village, who gladly provided a letter. The document stated that "Gerónimo Treviño, a peaceful and honorable resident of this village, leaves today in search of work" and it asked that "civil and military authorities give him aid and all manner of guarantees."[24] Whether such documents ever actually helped Gerónimo in his perilous travels is not as important as what his seeking them reveals about him. Even though he was a poor, semiliterate farmer, Gerónimo understood U.S.–Mexico borderlands society and his place in that world well enough to navigate its turbulent times relatively successfully. He understood that poor people like himself needed any advantage they could muster and that his frequent trips through a region inflamed with violence and racial strife posed serious threats for him on both sides of the border. So he did not act recklessly. Rather, his awareness of the social and political climate allowed him to plan and prepare intelligently to minimize the dangers of migration.

Yet, all these attributes only partly explain the man from Parás. Equally important were his human qualities and values. A profound sense of responsibility toward his family motivated Gerónimo. Having become the so-called man of the house after his older brother and his stepfather died, Gerónimo took to heart the traditional role of family patriarch. Representative of his time, he lived by a code steeped in concepts of male privilege and dominance, embodying, in other words, Mexican *machismo*. Demanding unquestioning obedience from his family, Gerónimo could be insensitive and sharp-tongued. Yet, at the same time he expressed a caring for others that was deep and genuine and made him fiercely loyal and protective of his family and his *raza* (the larger *mexicano*-Tejano community). A strong work ethic, another deeply engrained cultural value, also defined Gerónimo. Simply put, he valued hard work and people who worked hard. But his attitude toward manual labor was not simply born of necessity. The way he *enjoyed* working, especially reaping the fruits of the land as a farmer, reflected his belief that being *muy trabajador* (a good worker) was an essential trait of manliness, and his view of the land as sacrosanct. Gerónimo was also very much an optimist. I grew up constantly hearing him use a sing-song phrase, "¡*Todavía hay chanza, todavía hay chanza!*" (There's still a chance!) Frequently, when he talked about a difficulty of some kind or playfully challenged us in a game, he would repeatedly utter that ditty as a way to keep us from giving up. It was his way of saying that hope and persistence would see a person through hard times. Lastly, he summed up matter-of-factly another element of his character that sustained him: "I have never been afraid." Such a statement, of course, actually reflected an internalized cultural belief that Mexican men should not *show* fear but *overcome* it. Throughout his life, Gerónimo strove to do both convincingly.

Although his abilities and confidence allowed Gerónimo to cross the Río Grande and traverse South Texas at will when he traveled alone, moving his widowed mother, his beloved little sisters and half-brothers from Mexico to Texas proved to be a more complicated process, done in fits and starts. "I would cross over anywhere, swimming the river and crossing at any place," he recounted later about the ease with which he came and went as a single young man in the 1910s. "My friends from town would ask me how I could go and come so frequently. I would work two or three months and return to Parás, and I wouldn't cross on the bridge."

But replanting a family was not as simple as traveling alone. Apparently, Gerónimo would "cross over anywhere" when he was on his own, but when family members accompanied him in the late 1910s and early 1920s, he crossed "on the bridge" at official—and safer—ports of entry. For example, the photo on the passport issued in 1920 by the Mexican Consulate in Laredo shows him, his wife Francisca, and her youngest sister, a toddler named Rita. "I brought the whole family," *Don* Gerónimo often reminded us in his later years. "I brought my sister Josefa along with her husband and everybody—*I* did, with my own money," he liked to emphasize. With the exception of his sister Agripina, who married and settled in the state of Tamaulipas near the Texas border, by the early 1920s Gerónimo had relocated his mother and the rest of his siblings in Texas, where they settled permanently and started families—sister Lauriana outside of Bruni, in Webb County; sister Josefa near Woodsboro in Refugio County; half-brother Román Gonzales in Nueces County around Corpus Christi; and half-brother Jesús Gonzales, the youngest of the family, in Corpus Christi.[25]

World War I had interrupted the family's planned move to Texas. *Don* Gerónimo had seemingly relocated his family to Texas just prior to 1917, when the United States declared war on the Central Powers. Upon the U.S. entry into World War I, rumors circulated that *mexicanos* would be drafted into the Army even as a significant number of them volunteered for military service. Not surprisingly, Gerónimo felt no such compulsion. He knew his history well, and for him and countless other fiercely proud *mexicanos* the loss of Texas and the Mexican War still resonated deeply. Those feelings were kept alive by the bitter wine of racial hatred *mexicanos* and Tejanos often still imbibed in the Lone Star state. "In those days," the elderly *Don* Gerónimo recounted, "they would call those who didn't defend themselves 'Mexican . . . greaser.' When they'd get mad with a worker they would say, 'Get away, Mexican greaser.'" *Don* Gerónimo's choice of words implied that he was not among "those who didn't defend themselves," and the bitterness with which he spoke left no doubt there was no love lost between him and the *"ojitos azules"* (Anglos) whom he preferred to keep at arms' length. Besides, it did not make sense to leave his own war-torn country to join a foreign army. Caught between a rock and a hard place, Gerónimo left Texas with his mother and siblings sometime in 1917 and returned to Parás. There, among extended family and friends, they waited out the end of World War I, even as the Mexican Revolution wore on.[26]

Back in his native village, Gerónimo renewed his acquaintance with Francisca Ruiz, and romance entered the life of the man who until then had put his family's needs ahead of his own. But marriage would have to wait. Once World War I ended in 1918, Gerónimo, with his immediate family in tow, returned to Texas and found work in the farm lands around Robstown, in Nueces County. However, the early part of the next year found him on the way back to Parás yet again. This time Gerónimo returned to marry his sweetheart, Francisca Ruiz, who had grown up in the same town and was ten years younger than the well-traveled thirty-three-year-old bachelor. Gerónimo and Francisca celebrated their wedding on March 9, 1919. Five days later, the newly-weds headed for Texas. Like so many others who left Mexico during the Revolution, my grandfather and grandmother held on to the hope of someday returning to their *"México lindo"* (beloved Mexico). As they left Parás in mid-March 1919, they could not have known that would never be, that instead they and other *mexicanos* fleeing the Revolution were already engaged in building and becoming a permanent part of a new Mexican American community in Texas.[27]

The couple crossed the Río Grande at a point called Barranco Blanco, slightly southeast of Ciudad Mier, Tamaulipas, not far from Parás. According to family lore, Gerónimo swam and pulled his bride across in a tub. On the Texas side, an elderly couple Gerónimo knew put them up for the night and the next day arranged for someone to take them to Hebbronville, some seventy-five miles north. Hebbronville was one of the stops along the Texas–Mexican Railroad that ran between Laredo and Corpus Christi, connecting northern Mexico and the Coastal Bend. Most likely, Gerónimo and Francisca boarded a train at Hebbronville and a bit farther up the line connected with the St. Louis, Brownsville & Mexico Railway to reach their destination, Sinton, the seat of San Patricio County. Francisca later recalled, "We arrived in Sinton as newlyweds. We slept in a hotel there because Gerónimo had a job around there in the *tierras prietas* (the Blackland Prairie), so we slept there and waited for the foreman to come take us to the *rancho.*"[28]

Arriving in Sinton in March 1919 marked both an end and a beginning. Unbeknownst to Gerónimo at the time, his migrations between Mexico and Texas had ended and he was now in the region where he would spend the rest of his life. There would be other moves, but they would be less frequent and occur within the adjoining San Patricio, Refugio, and Bee Counties. As his life began to take on somewhat more predictable rhythms, the new challenge became to provide for a growing family as a sharecropper in cotton country.

In February 1920, a census taker canvassing a cotton farm near the Odem and Taft Road in San Patricio County found two families living in "dwelling #94." The enumerator reported as one head of household Gerónimo Treviño, age thirty-three. Listed as part of Gerónimo's household were his wife, Francisca, age twenty-three; his widowed mother, Toribia Rubio, age fifty; and his seventeen-year-old brother, Jesús Gonzales. Twenty-six-year-old Román Gonzales and his twenty-five-year-old wife Augustina made up the other family in the dwelling. The occupants of dwelling #94 shared the characteristics of being Mexican-born of Mexican parents, noncitizens ("aliens") who had immigrated in 1919, and unable to speak English (with the exception of Román). Everyone could read and write, except Gerónimo and his mother. None of the women were employed, whereas all the men were listed as "laborer on cotton farms."[29]

The census enumerator's report provides a snapshot of Gerónimo's life after he settled in the Coastal Bend. The details mesh with what historians have written about the world of Mexican and Tejano sharecroppers whose labor fueled the cotton boom of the 1920s, a world controlled by notions of white racial superiority that severely limited opportunities for people like Gerónimo. For example, the Coastal Bend's phenomenal cotton production relied heavily on two classes of workers who grew cotton on someone else's land: tenant farmers and sharecroppers. Tenant farmers had the most favorable arrangements with landowners. They farmed on "thirds and fourths," keeping two-thirds of the grain and three-fourths of the cotton they grew; were allowed to rent more land; and enjoyed a higher social standing, as reflected in the title "farmer." This arrangement was reserved for whites. In contrast, sharecroppers farmed on "halves," meaning they turned over half of the profits to the landowner, were allowed to farm far less acreage, and bore the stigma of being considered not farmers but common laborers. This arrangement was reserved for Mexicans and Mexican Americans (and occasionally African Americans).[30]

The 1920 census information about Gerónimo and his family affirms what scholars have written about cotton tenant farming in Texas. Gerónimo's neighbors, the people who lived around him in dwellings sequentially numbered from 88 to 95, were all Anglos or Mexicans and Mexican Americans involved in growing cotton. All the white men were described as "farmer," whereas all the Mexican and Mexican American men were designated as "laborer." The designation of both *mexicano* immigrants *and* native-born Tejanos as "laborers" rather than "farmers" is instructive. On the one hand, it reflected the custom of the time to limit the social status and economic opportunities of Mexican-origin people by racially lumping them together into a category of outsiders who could be exploited as cheap labor and denied human rights. On the other hand, however, the census information shows that *mexicanos* and Mexican Americans were living and working in close proximity. And this, along with their shared experience of discrimination, served to bind immigrant and U.S.-born together, providing the social glue for community building as they created a new Texas Mexican community.[31]

Based on the census data, Gerónimo apparently worked as a typical Mexican sharecropper in rural San Patricio County, at least in 1920. But scholars have also noted that relations and agreements between Anglo landowners and their tenant farmers and sharecroppers varied a lot. Thus, depending on local conditions at different times, sharecroppers moved around seeking better opportunities.[32] Gerónimo likewise exercised his options and tried to make the most of the meager opportunities that existed. Sometimes he was able to do what *mexicano* sharecroppers were not supposed to do. For example, as a rule, working on fourths was supposed to be reserved for whites but, as Frank Treviño recalled, "Sometimes we worked on fourths and sometimes on halves." Moreover, sharecroppers were closely supervised and not allowed to sell the crops themselves, but at least at one farm, "We did everything ourselves and harvested everything and Father sold it," Gerónimo's son recounted.[33]

In 1922, after two years in the Sinton area Gerónimo, Francisca, and their first-born child, named Gerónimo, moved to a farm near Woodsboro in adjacent Refugio County, where they stayed several years. The later twenties found the family back in the Sinton area, but they again returned to a *rancho* outside of Woodsboro about 1930. There were difficulties involved in moving a household and a family that by 1930 included six children. Still, Gerónimo's moves were actually infrequent compared to many cotton sharecroppers, thousands of whom were used to hitting the road at the end of every cotton harvest.[34] When it came to moving, Gerónimo had to consider many factors—and undoubtedly my grandmother Doña Panchita made sure he did. By 1922, her widowed mother and some of her siblings had left Parás and moved to the Coastal Bend. There, Francisca's two younger sisters Carmen and Rita later married the Texas-born brothers Epifanio and Ilifonso Gonzales, who also farmed cotton in the area. Emblematic of the marriages between *mexicano* immigrants and native-born Tejanos that would solidify the emerging Mexican American community in Texas, Gerónimo's family and the two Gonzales families became linked for life. Throughout many years, as they often lived and worked together or nearby, they were able to help each other bring into the world and provide for their children. The years Gerónimo and Francisco lived in the Woodsboro area, for example, coincided with the birth of several of their children and the time the Gonzales families lived there. The families later lived and worked near each other in Bee County.[35] Thus, Gerónimo's moves around the cotton counties were not just about getting a little more money for his cotton; they were more about family. Marriages between Mexican immigrants and Tejanos and their shared values about the family reflected yet another way the Mexican Revolution structured Mexican American life in the early decades of twentieth-century Texas.

No doubt Gerónimo calculated his moves to earn as much as possible farming cotton but also to keep his family in as stable and supportive an environment as possible. Living near relatives ensured that, as did working for landowners who allowed him to stay for years at a time and raise other crops and maybe a few animals to feed his family. Frank Treviño remembered that on the Steinmeyer Ranch in Bee County, "We raised corn, sugar cane, sorghum, onions, watermelons [and] cantaloupes. But we didn't give those other crops to the *patrona,* only [her part] of the corn, sorghum, and cotton." The strategy worked pretty well—well enough that sometimes Gerónimo had to hire other people to help with the sorghum and corn harvests. Eventually, he was able to buy a truck, which he used to transport his family and other workers to West Texas and the Panhandle, where he had contracts to harvest cotton, beans, and other crops. "There were some years that we did real well," recalled Frank Treviño.[36]

Indeed, as Mexican Revolution immigrants Gerónimo and Francisca incorporated themselves into the Tejano community, they did well on several counts: for themselves and their family and for others. In different ways their efforts helped to build the Texas Mexican American community of the early twentieth century. As Gerónimo and Francisca raised their seven children, they baptized them in the Catholic Church and enrolled them in local schools.[37] In doing so, they helped spur the growth of Catholicism in Texas. In addition, their children's presence in the schools not only revealed the couple's recognition of the importance of education but also added to the Tejano community's steadily building demand for better education. Over time, the Treviño family became more deeply imbedded in the expanding Tejano community, as other *mexicanos* continued to arrive in large numbers. Along with established Mexican Americans, many of the immigrants would set up businesses the Treviños would patronize. Among this growing mix of immigrants and native born, the family would forge supportive life-long ties as neighbors, coworkers, and *compadres* (god-parents), all of which helped to lay the basis for a viable Texas Mexican American community that was taking shape in the 1910s and 1920s. The Mexican Revolution of 1910 drove the couple from Parás, Nuevo León, to a new land; there they helped pioneer the rise of a new Mexican American society.

Sometimes the experiences of so-called ordinary folks get short shrift in the pages of history, not so much because they are altogether left out but because of the way they are sometimes presented—reduced to faceless, voiceless statistics neatly quantified in the charts and graphs of scholarly books, but lacking a human dimension. To be sure, some skillful historians have made brilliant use of aggregate data about common folks, synthesizing enormous amounts of facts about them to illustrate patterns in their experiences that reveal how they shaped and were shaped by history.[38] Still, it is important that whenever possible historians put flesh and bone on abstractions such as "historical agency" and catch-all terms like "ordinary people"; we should give them a face as well as a voice that includes the narratives of the common people as they themselves constructed them. Doing so can bring history to life by revealing that which makes historical agents human—their personalities, motivations, and ways of interacting with historical events and forces. Such an approach can not only uncover previously unknown history makers but, more importantly, it can also deepen our understanding of how history is shaped and who shapes it.

Gerónimo Treviño and ordinary *mexicano* immigrants like him helped mold an important chapter in Texas history. Despite the limitations imposed on him by historical forces more powerful than he—poverty, war, racism—the man from Parás used his strong back and determination to become a productive member of his adopted country. Even as his labor enriched those who exploited him, it contributed significantly to the flourishing Texas economy and to the building of a vibrant Tejano community during the early twentieth century. An editorial in the Spanish-language press poignantly summed up the important role of salt-of-the-earth folks like Gerónimo:

> The State of Texas knows the Mexican people very well. In its country-
> side, towns, and cities live thousands upon thousands of Mexicans who
> are honest people, respectful of the laws, inexhaustible workers, men of
> good hearts and genuine religiosity. They have watered this land with
> the sweat of their brow and have made it blossom; because of them—
> humble but heroic collaborators—Texas holds a prominent place in
> agriculture and industry. In short, thousands of Americans have built
> their fortunes on the Mexicans' labor.[39]

Stories about the lives of people like Gerónimo, then, illustrate that the cli-
chéd saying about ordinary people doing extraordinary things in American
history applies as much to Mexican Americans as it does to other Americans. Even more importantly, however, stories like *Don* Gerónimo's deserve to be told because they help us make better sense of a larger drama.
On the one hand, the experiences of ordinary folks like my grandparents
are an integral part of Mexican American history. On the other hand, they
must also be recognized as an important part of the building of Texas and
the nation.

Notes

1. Gerónimo Treviño, interview by Jerry R. Treviño, Mathis, Texas, 1975, tape recording and transcript in author's possession [hereafter, GT/JRT interview].

2. The literature on the Mexican Revolution is voluminous. For the Revolution in
general see Alan Knight, *The Mexican Revolution,* 2 vols. (Cambridge: Cambridge University Press, 1986). On pre-revolutionary northern Mexico, see Juan Mora-Torres, *The
Making of the Mexico Border: The State, Capitalism, and Society in Nuevo León, 1848–1910*
(Austin: University of Texas Press, 2001). Two excellent historical studies about Mexican
immigrants in Texas are Mario T. García, *Desert Immigrants: The Mexican of El Paso, 1880–
1920* (New Haven, Conn.: Yale University Press, 1981), and Emilio Zamora, *The World
of the Mexican Worker in Texas* (College Station: Texas A&M University, 1993). Con-
temporary accounts include the classic anthropological studies, Paul Schuster Taylor,
An American-Mexican Frontier, Nueces County, Texas (Chapel Hill: University of North
Carolina Press, 1934), and Manuel Gamio, *Mexican Immigration to the United States: A
Study of Human Migration and Adjustment* (Chicago: University of Chicago Press, 1930).

3. Enciclopedia de los Municipios de México online, s.v. "Parás," accessed December 9, 2009, from http://www.e-local.gob.mx/work/templates/enciclo/nuevoleon/
municipios/19040a.htm; and Mora-Torres, *The Making of the Mexican Border,* 15–16,
quote 109.

4. Gerónimo Trevino, interview by author, Mathis, Texas, ca. 1975, tape recording and transcript in author's possession [hereafter, GT/RRT interview]; letter by Civil Magistrate Valentín V. Hinojosa attesting to the birth of Gerónimo Treviño, July 6, 1918, personal papers of Jerry R. Treviño, Paige, Texas [hereafter, JRT Papers], copy in author's possession.

5. *Enciclopedia de México,* 2nd ed., s.v. "Estado de Nuevo León"; Mora-Torres, *Making of the Mexican Border,* 17–18, 36–41.

6. "Estado de Nuevo León"; Mora-Torres, *Making of the Mexican Border,* 52–84. Quote in "Estado de Nuevo León"; translation by author.

7. GT/JRT interview; GT/RRT interview.

8. GT/JRT interview.

9. Mora-Torres, *Making of the Mexican Border,* 19–20, 109–11, 153–55.

10. GT/JRT interview; Mora-Torres, *Making of the Mexican Border,* 166–91.

11. GT/RRT interview; GT/JRT interview.

12. GT/RRT interview.

13. Salvador Guerrero, *Memorias: A West Texas Life,* ed. Arnoldo De León (Lubbock, Tex: Texas Tech University Press, 1991), 3–4. Historian Vicki Ruiz also alludes to sexual violence against Mexican women during the Revolution; see *From Out of the Shadows: Mexican Women in Twentieth-Century America* (New York: Oxford University Press, 1998), 8.

14. GT/RRT interview; Francisca Treviño, interview by author, Mathis, Texas, ca. 1978, tape recording and transcript in author's possession.

15. *El Imparcial* (San Antonio), January 1, 1920, November 25, 1920, July 22, 1920; Zamora, *World of the Mexican Worker,* 14–15, 31–33; Neil Foley, *The White Scourge: Mexicans, Blacks, and Poor Whites in Texas Cotton Culture* (Berkeley and Los Angeles: University of California Press, 1997), 123, 130; and Frank Treviño, interview by author, Mathis, Texas, July 23, 2009, tape recording and transcript in author's possession. The Blackland Prairie of the Coastal Bend (called *"las tierras prietas"* by Mexicans) got its name from the rich humus content that gives the soil its dark appearance and great fertility, as locals often boasted. See May Mathis Green Watson, *Taft ranch: a history of the fifty years of development sponsored by Coleman-Fulton Pasture Company, with sketches of Gregory and Taft, the two towns it created* (n.p., ca. 1930), unnumbered, and any number of local newspapers such as the *Robstown Record* in the 1920s.

16. Frank Treviño interview; Watson, *Taft ranch;* "San Pat historical site to be honored," clipping, April 11, 1989, Ranches and Ranching Folders, *Corpus Christi Caller* Vertical Files, Corpus Christi Public Library, Corpus Christi, Texas [hereafter, CCCV Files/CCPL]; "Taft," clipping, February 19, 1934, Taft, Texas Folder, CCCV Files/CCPL.

17. Barton W. Currie, "100,000 Acres of Business Farming: Farm and Packing-

House Departments of the Taft Ranch," *The Country Gentleman,* June 19, 1915,:1043, copy in Taft Ranch Folder, CCCV Files/CCCPL. On the boom in Texas agriculture, see David Montejano, *Anglos and Mexicans in the Making of Texas, 1836–1986* (Austin: University of Texas Press, 1987), 106–219.

18. Watson, *Taft Ranch,* unnumbered; GT/RRT interview. The Gerónimo Treviño who worked for the Coleman-Fulton Pasture Company from 1919–1921 is most likely not the man from Parás, as he was a salaried employee of the Company's store and its telephone department. The Company's records are held at the Center for American History at the University of Texas at Austin.

19. Montejano, *Anglos and Mexicans,* 197–219, quotes on 197 and 217–18; see also Foley, *White Scourge,* 118–40; GT/RRT interview; Frank Treviño interview; and Francisca Treviño interview.

20. GT/RRT interview.

21. Gerónimo Treviño passports, 1920, 1923, JRT Papers, copies in author's possession; GT/JRT interview.

22. Benjamin Heber Johnson, *Revolution in Texas: How a Forgotten Rebellion and Its Bloody Suppression Turned Mexicans into Americans* (New Haven, Conn.: Yale University Press, 2003); Rodolfo Rocha, "The Tejano Revolt of 1915," in *Mexican Americans in Texas History: Selected Essays,* ed. Emilio Zamora, Cynthia Orozco, and Rodolfo Rocha (Austin: Texas State Historical Association, 2000), 103–19.

23. Marion Keach, "Mrs. H. J. 'Miss Nettie' Bryden," clipping, Oct. 31, 1957, Cities and Towns, Robstown Folder, CCCV Files/CCPL.

24. Letter of introduction for Gerónimo Treviño by Ygnacio Pérez, February 7, 1918, JRT Papers; Mexican Consulate of Zapata, Texas passport for Gerónimo Treviño, February 8, 1919, JRT Papers, copies in author's possession.

25. GT/JRT interview; GT/RRT interview; Francisca Treviño interview; Mexican Consulate of Laredo, Texas passport for Gerónimo Treviño, Oct. 26, 1920, JRT Papers; and family history notes, JRT Papers, copies in author's possession.

26. José A. Ramírez, *To the Line of Fire: Mexican Texans and World War I* (College Station: Texas A&M University Press, 2009); Francisca Treviño interview; and GT/JRT interview. On anti-Mexican racism, see Taylor, *An American-Mexican Frontier* and Gamio, *Mexican Immigration.*

27. Francisca Treviño interview; letter by Civil Magistrate Valentín V. Hinojosa attesting to marriage of Gerónimo Treviño and Francisca Ruiz, March 9, 1919, JRT Papers, copy in author's possession. On the immigrants' longing for "*México lindo,*" see F. Arturo Rosales, "Shifting Self Perceptions and Ethnic Consciousness Among Mexicans in Houston, 1908–1946," *Aztlán* 16: 1&2 (1987): 71–94; and Roberto R. Treviño, "*Prensa y patria:* The Spanish-Language Press and the Biculturation of the Tejano Middle Class, 1920–1940," *Western Historical Quarterly* 22: 4 (Nov. 1991): 451–72.

I recall the story about how greatly disappointed *Don* Gerónimo was when his eldest son (my father) rejected the idea that the whole Treviño clan should move to Mexico after World War II.

28. GT/JRT interview; map, "THE TEXAS MEXICAN RY. CO. and connections," File Railroads, Tex-Mex, 1882–1998, Vertical Files, CCPL; map, "COLEMAN-FULTON PASTURE COMPANY LAND SALES 1928, A. Ray Stephens, *The Taft Ranch: A Texas Principality* (Austin: University of Texas Press, 1964), 233; broadside, "THE TEXAS MEXICAN RAILWAY COMPANY TIME TABLE," File Railroads, Tex-Mex, 1882–1998, Vertical Files, CCPL; and Francisca Treviño interview.

29. 1920 U.S. census, population schedule, San Patricio County, Texas, Enumeration District 190, sheet 26, dwelling 94, family 97, Gerónimo Treviño household; National Archives microfilm publication T625, Roll 1843; and digital image, Heritage Quest.com, accessed July 2, 2009, from http://www.heritagequestonline.com.

30. Montejano, *Anglos and Mexicans,* 169–78; and Foley, *White Scourge,* 10, 64–91, especially 69–71, 85–86.

31. 1920 U.S. census, Gerónimo Treviño household.

32. Foley, *White Scourge,* 220, note 30, 70–71; and Montejano, *Anglos and Mexicans,* 171, 217–18.

33. Frank Treviño interview.

34. Francisca Treviño interview; family history notes, JRT Papers, copies in author's possession; and Foley, *White Scourge,* 71.

35. Frank Treviño interview; Francisca Treviño interview; and family history notes, JRT Papers, copies in author's possession.

36. Francisca Treviño interview; and Frank Treviño interview.

37. Baptism certificate for Gerónimo R. Treviño, JRT Papers, copy in author's possession; and Frank Treviño interview.

38. For Texas, see Montejano, *Anglos and Mexicans,* and Foley, *White Scourge;* for California, see Albert Camarillo, *Chicanos in a Changing Society: From Mexican Pueblos to American Barrios in Santa Barbara and Southern California, 1848–1930* (Cambridge Mass.: Harvard University Press, 1979).

39. "Replica a Mr. Ferguson," *El Imparcial* (San Antonio), December 23, 1920, translation by author.

Sleuthing Immigrant Origins Felix Tijerina and His Mexican Revolution Roots

THOMAS H. KRENECK

When Felix Tijerina died on September 4, 1965, at age sixty, he was widely viewed as the most esteemed and influential Mexican American resident of Houston, Texas, and a much heralded citizen of the state. Businessman, civic leader, and nationally recognized advocate of Mexican American education, Tijerina rose to special prominence in the post–World War II era. Like no one before him, he bridged the traditional ethnic gap through his leading roles in mainstream organizations as well as in Mexican American groups. His life story was common knowledge to most Houstonians: his humble birth in 1905 (reportedly in Sugar Land, Texas), his early days in Houston as an uneducated laborer, his Horatio Alger–style rise to wealth and status as owner of a chain of Mexican food restaurants, his leadership position among Mexican Americans, and his many philanthropic endeavors. He reportedly became the first Mexican American millionaire in Houston. Tijerina was particularly well recognized for his tenure as national president of the League of United Latin American Citizens (LULAC) during the late 1950s. Many awards and accolades came his way. As just one example, this prominence led him to be the first Mexican American resident in Houston to have a school named in his honor.[1]

My own interest in Tijerina resulted from my tenure at the

Houston Metropolitan Research Center (HMRC) as an acquisitions archivist/historian. Felix's name seemed ever present in the historical records from the 1930s to the 1960s that I accumulated for our Mexican American archival component. HMRC's materials on his life and work increased significantly when his widow, the late Mrs. Felix Tijerina Sr., donated his papers to our institution. My interest in him grew, and over a twenty-year period I produced a book-length biography of him (published in 2001) that examined Tijerina both as a Mexican American leader and as a reflection of the Mexican American experience during the first seven decades of the twentieth century.[2]

Early on, my research indicated that Tijerina was one of the more significant figures in the Mexican American community of his time and that his story seemed critical for understanding Mexican American history in Texas and the United States. Through his efforts as LULAC national president from 1956 to 1960, LULAC gained the status of a national organization for the first time. Tijerina expanded the League from five states in the Southwest into eight more in the upper Midwest and Northeast, paralleling what Dr. Héctor P. García did with the American G.I. Forum during the same decade. Felix's development of the Little School of the 400 is a milestone in the history of Mexican American education. The Little School brought national attention to LULAC, support to the educational needs of Mexican American youngsters, and influenced state and federal policy during the 1960s and beyond. Moreover, for many Mexicans and Anglos alike, Tijerina served as a state and national role model regarding the proper behavior of Mexican Americans.[3]

The other aspect of his life, that is as representative of Mexican American development, especially among the middle-class entrepreneurial element of the Depression and World War II eras, proved equally important. Felix's participation in 1920s Mexican American urbanization, his involvement in 1930s Mexican organizations, his remarkable adaptation, his growing activities within Anglo organizations as a bicultural person, his activities as an entrepreneur, the self-determination he managed to negotiate, his relations with other peoples of color, and many other elements common to Mexican American existence in the twentieth century all reflected larger experiences.[4]

I was prepared to deal with the above-mentioned aspects of Felix's life. But I encountered the hidden theme that he had Mexican Revolution immigrant roots. Contrary to his public image that he was Texas born, I discovered and verified that Felix Tijerina was in fact a Mexican immigrant who, as a youngster, had fled the deprivations and violence of the Mexican Revolution of 1910. His foreign-born origins thus wove throughout the book and became the most engaging, profound, difficult, and moving aspect of the research. It also turned out to be one of the more significant elements of the volume.

According to the extant literature, the Mexican Revolution expelled immigrants of many types into Texas, transforming established Tejano settlements significantly. These multitudes comprised elements from every social stratum; *ricos* (wealthy), middle classes, and *pobres* (poor) fled north to escape the violence and dislocation afflicting their homeland. Most of these exiles and refugees—especially the common working people—melted into the mass of laborers and saw little improvement in their material condition once in Texas. Some from the prosperous classes found a niche in the new society and embarked on fresh beginnings (the families of Henry B. González, Albert Peña, Héctor P. García, and others are examples). A fortunate few from the modest folk, like Felix Tijerina, went on to achieve Horatio Alger greatness. Thus, the Mexican Revolution affected Texas Mexican communities in varied manners.[5]

The secret of Felix Tijerina's Mexican Revolution background plagued him throughout his life. This essay accordingly seeks to explain two important points revolving around his nativity: first, how and why he maintained this fiction; and second, what circumstances actually surrounded his birth and immigration. Just as importantly, I also explain the difficult personal journey I undertook in search of his roots—the physical, intellectual, and cultural odyssey that I had to make in sleuthing his immigrant origins. This essay likewise enumerates the many implications Tijerina's seemingly harmless alteration of his origins has on writings about Mexican American history and on biography.

Maintaining the Fiction of His Birth

Why did Felix Tijerina alter the story of his nativity? According to the literature generated during his later life and even after, especially the many newspaper articles about him, Felix was born in Sugar Land, just southwest of Houston, and he came to the Bayou City as a Texas-born urban immigrant. The many stories written about him pictured Tijerina as a homegrown rags-to-riches individual. Houston, Texas, prized such a Horatio Alger image. U.S. Immigration and Naturalization Service (INS) agents during the 1950s, however, maintained that Tijerina had actually been born in Mexico, and this accusation became a public controversy. Tijerina cleared up this situation legally in court, and once and for all a federal court declared that he had been born in the Lone Star state.[6]

As a biographer, I took Felix's version at face value at the beginning of my research in 1979. He was, after all, a person of great veracity, and if he claimed Sugar Land as his hometown, then it must have been so. But my research quickly began to show otherwise, and the deeper I delved, the more interesting the story became, and his nativity became even more important on many levels.

The first publicly documented evidence in the controversy over his birthplace came in 1925, when, as a young man working as a waiter in a Houston restaurant, Felix journeyed to the small *villa* of General Escobedo, Nuevo León, in Northern Mexico, to visit relatives. On the way back, INS officials detained him at Laredo because he could not offer sufficient proof of U.S. citizenship. Felix later maintained that in order to get back to work in Houston without delay, he signed an application for an immigration visa to enter the United States. On it, he swore that he was born in General Escobedo. He then proceeded to Houston. This incident would haunt Felix Tijerina's future.[7]

The next time that anyone questioned his citizenship status occurred in 1940. Of course, 1940 came toward the end of the repatriation efforts of the 1930s, when Mexican nationals and their children either went or were sent to Mexico during the Great Depression. Again, on his return from a trip to Mexico in March 1940, immigration officers detained Felix temporarily in Laredo because his declaration of being an American citizen did not fully satisfy them.[8]

A week later, two immigration officers in Houston told Tijerina that he should "get the matter [of his citizenship] straight." Alarmingly, they possessed the visa document he had signed in 1925.[9]

By 1940, Felix was already a rising star on the Houston scene, and he had ample reason to claim U.S. nativity. In response to this 1940 trouble, Felix went to elaborate lengths to obtain a so-called delayed birth certificate stating that he was born in Sugar Land (Fort Bend County), Texas, on April 29, 1905, the son of Rafael Tijerina and Dionicia Villarreal Tijerina. He made a trip to the Sugar Land area, where remarkably he obtained the assistance of one Buck Flanagan, who had been a captain of guards at that notorious local penitentiary. Imaginably a "walking boss" similar to a character from the feature movie *Cool Hand Luke,* such an individual did not seem to be the sort of person who customarily assisted Mexican immigrants. Together, Captain Flanagan and Tijerina located one Easter Fueler, an elderly African American midwife who, after some conversation, signed an affidavit that she had delivered Felix. One can readily assume that money changed hands from Felix to Mrs. Fueler and/or that Fueler might have done Captain Flanagan a favor. Doubtless, she was not the first black person Flanagan had convinced to do what he asked. One also wonders how Felix knew Flanagan well enough to obtain such services. This episode did, however, serve as an example of how well Felix Tijerina worked with people. Back in Houston, the INS officials still expressed skepticism regarding Tijerina's place of birth; for his part, Felix thought the matter closed.[10]

Felix would have chosen to claim U.S. nativity for obvious reasons. In 1937, during the height of the Depression he had opened what instantly became a successful restaurant. With family to support, he could ill afford deportation amid the repatriation taking place in Houston. Attempts at naturalization could be tricky. By the late 1930s, he had also achieved an impressive level of recognition in Anglo Houston for his civic activities. He may even have innocently claimed U.S. birth years before, especially to mainstream Houston; he had not taken the opportunity to seek naturalization and did not want to appear as if he had told a falsehood. Between 1940 and the early 1950s, Felix became even more prominent. He served in the army during World War II and prospered in the restaurant business beyond his wildest dreams. He also participated in a host of Mexican American and Anglo-American civic organizations. Most conspicuously, in early 1953, Felix became the first Mexican American appointed to the board of the Houston Housing Authority (HHA). He came in as part of a slate of reform-minded appointees to clean up administrative problems in the city's public housing, which they did. This new board discharged several employees, while others resigned.[11]

A couple of the disgruntled people who left the HHA struck back at Felix by attacking his citizenship status. According to Federal Bureau of Investigation (FBI) records, two of these unidentified individuals presented themselves at the Houston FBI office in May 1953 and questioned the veracity of Tijerina's 1940 certificate of birth on file in Fort Bend County. Although this accusation ultimately came to nothing, the report made its way to the attention of J. Edgar Hoover, the bureau's legendary Director.[12]

Trouble over Felix's nativity soon erupted more publicly. Felix and his wife of many years had adopted a child in Monterrey in 1948. Their right to petition for the child's American citizenship came in 1953. In September of that year, the Tijerinas filed the naturalization petition with the U.S. District Court in Houston, which then referred the case to the INS.

Apparently, at the filing of this petition the INS questioned Felix's citizenship status by presenting him with two crucial documents. First of all, the INS produced the 1925 visa application. And second, the INS had a certified copy of a document that purported to be the record of the birth of a son named Feliberto Tijerina to Rafael Tijerina and Dionicia Villarreal Tijerina (the same names as Felix's parents). This birth record further stated that the child had been born in the village of General Escobedo, Nuevo León, on April 29, 1905, the same time that Felix used as his birth date. The INS offered him the chance to straighten things out by seeking naturalization for himself.

Someone, perhaps the two unidentified individuals associated with the earlier FBI inquiries, had probably provided or helped to provide the INS with this new record. What happened after the agents presented Felix with this document is a complex story that comprises chapter 7 of the biography. Suffice it to say, this time Felix struck back at his tormentors.[13]

He soon contracted the services of an extremely competent, prestigious Houston civil attorney named William J. Knight, who in March 1954 filed suit in federal court to have the court declare Felix a citizen of the United States and acknowledge that he was native born in Fort Bend County, Texas. Clearly, Felix wanted to settle the matter once and for all, and he probably did not want to admit that he had altered the story of his origins all along.

The suit lasted from 1954 until mid-1956. The Houston media gave it much attention and made it a highly public affair. Tijerina and Knight placed a great deal on the line, including Felix's good name and legality in the court case *Felix Tijerina v. Herbert Brownell Jr.,* Attorney General of the United States and the INS. It culminated in a one-day formal hearing before Federal Judge Joe M. Ingraham. The sides presented all the evidence, including the undisputable birth record from Mexico and the fact that Felix's older sister affirmed that she had been born in General Escobedo. Felix had many things going for him, including a close relationship between Ingraham and Knight, a sympathetic young district attorney named Sidney Farr who did not vigorously press the state's case, and favorable public sentiment. Judge Ingraham especially favored Tijerina; he dined regularly at Felix's restaurant, thought highly of Felix's civic activities, and served as a fellow member of the Democrats for Eisenhower campaign.

And Felix won his suit. Judge Ingraham, a very decent man and moderate Eisenhower appointee, in May 1956, granted Felix Tijerina the declaratory judgment stating that he was a native-born citizen of the United States. He rested his decision on his belief that "a preponderance of the evidence" showed that Felix Tijerina "was born at Sugarland in Fort Bend County, Texas." I conclude in the biography that Judge Ingraham's ruling served justice rather than the truth.[14]

Needless to say, much jubilation took place. That same month, May 1956, Felix threw his hat in the ring for LULAC National President, won the office unanimously that summer, and went on to serve an unprecedented four terms in which he and his cohorts accomplished some important things, including the implementation of the Little School of the 400 and expansion of LULAC into a national organization, much of both bankrolled personally by the affluent Tijerina.[15]

Tijerina's Actual Birth and Immigration

Of course, what the court stated and the truth (as near as can be determined) conflicted. The search for historical fact forced me to write a much different version of Felix's origins than that assumed in the judge's ruling or in the literature on Tijerina. To the biographer, then, Felix's birthplace meant a great deal as scholars are duty bound to be factually truthful. The quest to determine the place of his birth sent me on a difficult research journey, one which entailed extensive digging in court records, company employee ledgers, genealogical microfilm, church records, FBI files, oral interviews with Felix's acquaintances and relatives, and finally two very memorable research trips to the little town of General Escobedo, Nuevo León.

The end product of my search (chapter 1) comprised what I felt to be the most fundamental part of the biography. It treats Felix's Mexican birth and immigration to Houston, Texas. My research uncovered that he was born on April 29, 1905, as Feliberto Tijerina Villarreal, in the *villa* of General Escobedo, some 12 kilometers north of downtown Monterrey. His father, Rafael Tijerina Alvarez, was a farmer of modest means and his mother, Dionicia Villarreal Ayala, a housewife. After his father died of cancer in 1915, to escape the deprivations of the Mexican Revolution that had the area of General Escobedo in turmoil, the Tijerinas immigrated to the United States in 1915 or 1916 as part of what scholars label the Immigrant Generation. As near as can be ascertained, Felix had no formal education and could not read or write. He and his mother and sisters (along with other members of his extended family) worked their way up the Texas Coastal Bend in the cotton fields, amid great hardships. His mother's father accompanied them, but he died of natural causes in Victoria, Texas. In Sugar Land, where they settled for a couple of years, Feliberto lost his youngest sister to the effects of diarrhea. Both grandfather and sister were buried in now unmarked graves. Tijerina worked in Sugar Land as a water boy for Sugarland Industries, a large agricultural enterprise.[16]

Feliberto and the rest of the family finally reached Houston in 1922, through much travail. He became principal breadwinner of the family by the time he entered his teens. When he arrived in Houston, he abbreviated his name from Feliberto to Felix and labored at menial jobs on Houston's produce row and in a Houston restaurant as a busboy and then waiter. He was unattended by any advantages. His early years and his journey of immigration amounted to a crucible in Felix's (née Feliberto's) life and show him as a truly heroic figure for what he endured, overcame, and then achieved. He went from an inauspicious product of the Mexican Revolution to become a millionaire, a respected member of the community, and an associate of such luminaries as Senator Lyndon B. Johnson and Governor Price Daniels.[17]

My Journey In Search of Tijerina's Roots

My sleuthing the facts of his Mexican immigrant origins proved to be a laborious yet rewarding odyssey, one during which I had to surmount many obstacles not normally associated with biographical writing. The first step in this journey started during a conversation in 1980 or 1981 with one of Tijerina's most trusted former LULAC lieutenants, an attorney who shall remain unnamed here because he made his comment off the record. But this individual was in a position to know about the case. He and I sat in his office, discussing various topics with a third party to whom I remarked that Felix was born in Sugar Land, Texas but had as a youth unwisely declared to INS officials that he was Mexican born. This misstep, I opined, Felix made because he was "green" and wanted to return to work in the most expeditious manner. Felix's associate quickly remarked that such constituted the "official story." That comment piqued my curiosity and sent me in search of Felix's authentic roots.[18]

Two other contemporary associates of Tijerina who had reason to know the true account soon supported this initial revelation by the attorney. Neither of them wanted to go on the record, as much because they were hesitant to embarrass a deceased man whom they respected, though they often disagreed with him publicly. In delving into the oral history memoirs of other elderly people who remembered Felix from the 1920s, one of his former neighbors (who as a child had met the family when they first moved to Houston) later told me the Tijerinas spoke rapid Spanish, as did most people "from Monterrey."[19] These comments gave me insight into the common knowledge of the members of the Mexican American community who knew Felix best, though other people said they felt he was born in the United States.

A huge side of me did not welcome the news that Tijerina may have fabricated the story of his origins. When I had first interviewed Mrs. Felix Tijerina about her late husband's nativity, she staunchly maintained that Felix was a native-born Texan. She stated that the birth certificate in Mexico was of another relative who had actually cheated Felix's father out of property and that this miscreant later met an untimely death in a bar under suspicious circumstances. She said that authorities had confused Felix with this Mexico-born relative, which led to a case of mistaken identity. She defended the truthfulness of Easter Fueler, the African American midwife. Mrs. Felix (as she was widely known) greatly assisted in the writing of her husband's biography, and I counted her as a friend. She was a serious person, worthy of respect, and I had no desire to embarrass Tijerina's memory. As trite as it might sound, however, the truth of history propelled me forward.

Of course, I conducted my paper research in the United States first. I searched exhaustively and in vain for any birth record of Felix Tijerina in Texas. It would have proved to be much easier and quicker for me if I could have located records of his Sugar Land birth. But he simply was not born in Sugar Land, no matter how much I wished that he had been.

Primary materials available in the United States did reveal much. Ironically, the public court records generated by his 1950s lawsuit led me to solid proof of his nativity. In trying to clear this situation up legally, Felix left a public document trail for this later biographer to follow. A federal records repository provided me with these materials upon request. These court proceedings and their ancillary documents revealed a number of leads, including the revelation of the *villa* of General Escobedo as his family's hometown, the INS official's 1940 doubts about Felix being born in Texas, and so forth.

To find evidence of Felix's General Escobedo birth, I visited a Church of Jesus Christ of Latter-Day Saints genealogical library in Houston. The Mormons thankfully had microfilmed and cataloged the vital statistics in Mexico, such as civil and church records. I requested the civil marriage and birth records of General Escobedo, Nuevo León, and quickly found the marriage entry for Felix's mother and father and, most importantly, the birth records of Feliberto Tijerina and his five sisters, one of whom had died shortly after birth. In those reels, I also located the death record of Rafael Tijerina Alvarez. To reconfirm my research on these births, I later called upon the services of the ultimate authority, Monterrey historian and genealogist extraordinaire Israel Cavazos Garza, who provided me with the same information.[20]

Luckily, Sidney Farr and Judge Ingraham still lived in Houston, and I then interviewed them both. Farr recalled that they knew the true facts of Felix's birth, but he said it mattered little to him. He viewed Tijerina as a good man and solid, contributing citizen. Héctor de la Peña (a LULAC stalwart in Corpus Christi) had befriended Farr when the latter began his legal career after World War II, so Farr forever felt gratitude to Mexican Americans like de la Peña and Tijerina. Nor did Farr relish the INS agents whom he felt harassed Felix in the 1950s and had a "police mentality." It seemed easy for Farr to acquiesce to Felix's case when he felt it was the right thing to do. Farr likewise wanted no trouble with Ingraham and Knight, men of substance in the Houston legal establishment who clearly sided with Tijerina. Besides, just as Ingraham and Knight, Farr ate at Felix Mexican Restaurant and saw the genial restaurateur regularly. (I ate at the same Felix Mexican Restaurant on Westheimer years later, where my personal choice was always the Felix "All Time Special.") One can easily appreciate why so many people could throw in together to cover Felix's nativity without exchanging a word about the matter.[21]

On the day following my meeting with Farr, I interviewed Judge Joe Ingraham. He was in semiretirement and heard cases only as a visiting jurist. His suite of offices in the Houston Federal Building and his position were imposing, but he treated me well. I wondered going into the appointment whether he had known something I did not. I had to get his perspective. His interview clearly indicated that Ingraham ignored most of the "facts" and simply wanted to put things right, regardless of the "truth" of the matter. Originally from Oklahoma, Ingraham called himself a "Red River Wetback" who had simply been born away from home. One could readily imagine that he reasoned the same for Felix Tijerina. No money or favors changed hands with his decision. The cabal among powerful people to protect Felix, like most conspiracies among white men, remained subtle and silent. Felix had gone along and gotten along, and Ingraham, the rest of the individuals in the court, and Houston media liked and respected him.

In an oral history interview, a question often presents itself that the interviewer would rather not ask, but must. I had to press Judge Ingraham about the birth certificate from General Escobedo that appeared in the court documents as evidence against Felix. My question slightly irritated him, and he politely, but firmly, curtailed that line of inquiry by saying, "I don't know how many Mexicans may be named Felix Tijerina." He went on to note solemnly that "Felix is dead and gone now; but he died a citizen of the United States." Ingraham seemed gratified that his decision had quieted the controversy of Tijerina's citizenship.[22] I responded to Judge Ingraham's final comments by dropping the subject. I added a few pleasantries and clichés to mollify what little tension had resulted from my question. I thanked him for his time, indicated what a great man I thought Felix Tijerina had been, and made my way to the door. His young attorney assistant gave me a wink and nod as I scurried out with the information I needed. Judge Joe Ingraham had done the right thing in Felix's case, and I held a kind thought for him when several years later I saw a picture of his younger, benevolent face in a newspaper article that announced he had died. The obituary stated that Ingraham was by nature a fair judge. I could attest to that by his dealings with Felix Tijerina.

Perhaps consciously or subconsciously, Mrs. Felix helped lead me to the truth by giving me the names of early family members on her husband's mother's side that would prove crucial. Felix's elderly first cousin, to whom she referred me, I found still living in San Antonio. He told me that he thought the Tijerina siblings were all born in Mexico. He referred me to his elder sister, who could speak with more firsthand authority. She lived out of state and I communicated with her by telephone through her son. She remembered when the Tijerinas came from Mexico in 1915, including young Felix. She noted that they had fled economic hardship following the death of Felix's father. She recalled that when Felix came to Texas, he was a rugged youngster from having associated with unruly *Carrancista* revolutionaries in Mexico. When I asked about a child named Feliberto, she replied, "That was Felix."[23]

Mrs. Felix was an extremely intelligent person, so perhaps she wanted the truth told as much as anyone, even though she personally guarded Felix's public image. Perhaps she had come to trust that I would couch the story in a sympathetic manner to him and his memory. At the conclusion of one of our last conversations, held at the main Felix Mexican Restaurant in the early 1990s, she and I walked to the front door and the topic of Felix's nativity came up, and she said, "Maybe you could write it both ways." In a sense, I tried to do that by explaining the complexity of the entire story. Perhaps she knew it truly made no difference to his memory. Felix had legendary status; she knew his positive legacy could handle whatever truth would be revealed because it showed him as an honorable man. But my thoughts on Mrs. Felix's motives consist of mere speculation. I am a historian, not a psychologist.

Regardless of the essentials about his birth that I possessed, I needed to place "Feliberto" in Texas, either before or after he came to Houston. The evidence indicated that he was born Feliberto in 1905, and by the time he first appeared in the Houston city directory in 1923, he was Felix. But when—and if so, why—did he make the name change? My "ah-ha moment" came with what I discovered in the personnel records of Sugarland Industries. HMRC already possessed those records, but although an archivist there, I had not thought to check them. I found the slim employee ledger from the 1920s, which had miraculously survived. I recall vividly the day I sat on the floor in an aisle in the dim stacks and thumbed through the pages of this ledger to the pages containing entries from 1921. On page 18 it appeared in bold hand—"Filiberto Tyerina." He made wages somewhat less than the normal field hands, likely the pay of a water boy. Doreteo Pena and Félix Joso (Jasso), acquaintances he mentioned in his conversations with the INS in 1940, appeared in close proximity to "Filiberto" in the ledger.[24] This link created the connection between the Feliberto of General Escobedo and the Felix of Houston. He still called himself Feliberto in Sugarland, but when he moved to Houston he had to make a mental leap and altered his name to Felix. Feliberto did not translate well into English. Felix was a big city name for a new life. One can only speculate how he came by this name. Maybe someone gave it to him for ease of pronunciation. One's environment changes one as one changes to fit one's environment, especially as the individual moves from the rural to the urban setting. (I had experienced my own similar transition when I moved in 1966 from a cotton farm in Karnes County, Texas, to Houston.) Perhaps Tijerina adopted Felix Jasso's first name. The first four letters of Feliberto and Felix are the same. Felix translates well into English or Spanish. One can be Felix or Félix, depending upon which ethnic community one is interacting with. I could identify with him, and I felt deep compassion the moment I read his name in the Sugarland Industries ledger. I envisioned him as a seventeen-year old fellow, barely 5 feet 3 inches tall, who could not read or write, with few possessions, and who had to make his way and be the principal breadwinner for his mother and three sisters. Perhaps anti-immigrant xenophobes can condemn honest, hard-working "undocumented" Mexicans among us, but I cannot. I respect them, and at that point my admiration for Felix Tijerina soared.

Doubtless, I could have written an adequate story of Tijerina's Mexican origins with what I had by the mid-1980s, but for several tangible and intangible reasons I needed to journey to the place of his birth truly to understand his roots and subsequent life. Candidly, as much time and concern as such a trip entailed, I welcomed it. The history, literature, and mystique of the Mexican Revolution of 1910 had long captivated me. The classes on Mexico's history I took at the University of Houston in 1960s and early 1970s from Professor Jack Allen Haddick helped to launch my serious interest in the topic. I had learned that one needed to understand the Mexican Revolution, the first of the great twentieth-century revolutions. Names like Porfirio Díaz, Francisco Madero, Pancho Villa, Felipe Angeles, Emiliano Zapata, Venustiano Carranza, Alvaro Obregón, and many others entered the vocabulary and thoughts of our own society in Texas. They helped to ingrain many symbols of *mexicanidad* into the consciousness of Mexico, Texas, and ultimately the United States. Many *corridos* (folk ballads) emanated from the almost two decades of turmoil, immortalizing songs such as "*La Adelita*" and "*Siete Leguas*" and enhancing our culture. The Chicano Movement of the late 1960s and 1970s, which influenced me, had adopted images from the Revolution. Works by such authors as Mariano Azuela (*The Underdogs, The Bosses,* and *The Flies*) and John Reid (*Insurgent Mexico*) ranked among my favorite literature. I always identified with Reid, the romantic revolutionary, whose grave I had visited some years earlier at the foot of the Kremlin Wall in Red Square, when the Soviet Union still existed. Of course, the Mexican Revolution was fundamental to understanding Mexican American history as it sent hundreds of thousands of people north across the Mexico–U.S. border to augment our population. Today, millions of American citizens can trace their forebears' immigrant crossings to that era. Altogether, the Mexican Revolution represents an important and interesting topic.

Armed with the above information and spirit, I made two research trips to Mexico to round out my understanding, and they proved to be transformational to my study. The people I met, the information I gained, and the feelings evoked during those two field trips positively affected the biography and me.

The first trip took place in August 1993 and amounted to a reconnaissance, a time for gathering general information and to stake out future research. A colleague accompanying me acted as a sounding board for ideas and as someone to offer additional insight into what I observed. We flew to Monterrey, where we stayed and rented an automobile. While in Monterrey, we visited the Gran Ancira Hotel, built in 1912, which had served as temporary headquarters for revolutionary forces and where reportedly General Villa had ridden his horse up its grand staircase. I had seen a photo of Felix Tijerina there with fellow LULACs many years later, when he had achieved prominence as a businessman. We also visited the *Palacio del Obispado* (Bishop's Palace), site of some of the fiercest fighting in the 1846–1848 Mexican War, the topic upon which I had written my Master's thesis. From that prominence, we could survey the distant mountainous terrain to the north of the city where General Escobedo lay. At the *Obispado,* I happened upon a displayed map of the area from the turn of the twentieth century that located General Escobedo when it was a far-off *villa,* unconnected to the city. Relevant documents sometimes serendipitously turn up where you least expect, and historic maps prove helpful.

We set out for General Escobedo in our rental car and found it after wandering circuitously from downtown Monterrey with map in hand. By 1993, General Escobedo had long since become a suburb of Monterrey, swallowed by the urban sprawl of that giant city. General Escobedo is both a *villa* and a *municipio* (a municipal district much like a county).

When we finally located the heart of the old *villa,* we immediately recognized it as such. Most tellingly, the historic, central plaza still served as its focal point, circled by the oldest *sillar* and stucco buildings in the area. At the risk of sounding mystical, I sensed at first sight that here Felix Tijerina (née Feliberto) spent the first decade of his life. Perhaps revealing my own streak of romanticism, I felt that I looked at the plaza with the sense of discovery and expectation of a latter-day John Reid, much as Reid peered across the border at Ojinaga from Presidio, Texas, in anticipation of his adventure that resulted in *Insurgent Mexico.*

Although I said nothing to the locals I met there regarding the exact nature of my visit (I never mentioned Felix's name on that 1993 trip), I gathered some key information. Clearly, the 12 kilometers represented no small distance from Monterrey in 1905–1915. We located the remodeled civil administration building (*Palacio de Gobierno*) where Felix's relatives reported his parents' marriage, his birth, his father's death, and other family matters. We easily found the church *San Nicolás De Bari* (built in 1826) on the plaza's east side, where I suspected that events of Felix's youth took place, the family having had a religious background. We discovered the *villa's* cemetery, where his father must have been buried, but found no trace of his grave, though there were many Villarreal and Ayala tombstones. The earliest surviving, marked interments dated from the 1920s; former ones have either gone unmarked or have been reused by subsequent graves. We savored the general ambience of not only the *villa,* but its surrounding semi-arid terrain, how it was set among the mountains, especially the distinctive Cerro del Topo Chico, which I described as shaped like a whale lying on its belly. Topo Chico dominated the horizon to the southwest. The *villa* sat perched on a rise above the muddy Río Pesquería. The terrain and its climate starkly contrasted with Houston's flat, humid, green area, where Felix would make his mark and become so identified. He made no small adjustment between where he originated and where he finally settled and prospered.

The local folks proved very friendly and helpful. In our inquiries about the history and nature of the *villa,* someone set up a meeting for us with a man in his early eighties, Jesús Ayala López, clearly a man of standing in the community, who told me he had relatives who had immigrated to Corpus Christi, where I worked by 1993. He noted that many people in the early decades of the century had gone to Texas. He also related many things that, embarrassingly, I could not understand because of my lack of fluency in Spanish. I knew that I wanted to return at some future date armed with a translator to interview this individual as he knew much about the history of the town and region. I simply could not accomplish everything I wanted to do in one several-day visit. This initial trip had been to reconnoiter and savor the town and region. Candidly, the surreptitious nature of this 1993 research trip sprang from the fact that Mrs. Tijerina might learn that I had gone. As it turned out, she heard that I had, though she made little mention of it.

Perhaps my most important broader insight from this trip came from my associate, who noted that the Tijerinas probably "got by" until tragedy struck with Felix's father's death, and then they could no longer make it. This profound observation came from seeing the *villa's* modest features, even by northern Mexican standards. To the sensitive eye, the folks of General Escobedo in the 1910s surely lived a hardscrabble existence. Once

Felix left, not much remained there for him to return to except for visits with extended family members.

Equally important, my 1993 trip convinced me that I had to return for a more thorough inquiry. Other people whom I needed to question and research resources that I needed to explore surely existed there. I truly wanted to speak with *don* Jesús again. Whatever my Spanish language deficiencies, I would compensate for by marshalling the resources and perseverance I needed.

In September 1997, after Mrs. Tijerina's death, I returned to General Escobedo in full force and hit research pay dirt. In the company of a scholarly translator and another academic associate—the former Hispanic and latter non-Hispanic—we represented a range of perspectives, expertise, and sensitivity to the subject and people. We telephoned ahead, alerted local officials that we would come, and communicated the exact nature of our interest. When we arrived by automobile from Reynosa, the *villa* and its residents gave us a grand welcome.[25]

The 1997 research visit provided a bonanza of in-depth discoveries on Felix. We had a meeting, arranged in advance, with the *municipio's* secretary of the *ayuntamiento* (city council), Oscar Garza Guajardo, who warmly greeted us and gave us over to his able assistant Gerardo García Guajardo. Gerardo immediately took us to the house that reportedly belonged to Rafael Tijerina, father of Felix Tijerina. This edifice faced the town plaza and proved to be one of those picturesque *sillar* buildings I had admired in 1993. Poetically, it now served as the *villa's* library, so in keeping with Felix's love of education. I later took a picture of it with massive Topo Chico in the background; the image would appear in my biography of Tijerina. Gerardo also showed us some of the local historic spots. He proved to be an educated, intelligent young man, who confided to us that he and his wife might move to Chicago to better themselves. I hope they made it. The United States would gain much from their presence here.[26]

The next day we met Juan Ramón Garza Guajardo, General Escobedo's *cronista* (official historian) and an author in his own right of several books on the town's past. We learned a great deal from him regarding the *villa's* development from colonial times to the present. During the Revolution, he noted, the folks of General Escobedo generally sided with Pancho Villa (it was a "*Villista* town") and as a consequence took hard knocks from the *Carrancistas*. Mainly, he noted, the local populace at that time were *pacíficos*, people who only wanted to live in peace, and as a consequence men fled to avoid conscription. The Tijerinas were probably such

The one-storied sillar *and stucco structure directly across from the* plaza *in General Escobedo, Nuevo León, identified by local oral tradition as the house of Rafael (and Feliberto) Tijerina. The slope of the immense* Cerro Del Topo Chico *in the left background, 1990s.*

pacíficos. Juan Ramón even located another probable location of a house where the Tijerinas resided. We could only have obtained these facts and others he shared with us from the local *cronista* of this small place. Learned, kind, and generous with his time, he proved to be a fountain of information.

With the assistance of Gerardo and Juan Ramón, we located three key persons in the *villa* who provided us with more crucial information. The first of these individuals whom we interviewed was the owner of the Tijerina home on the plaza, who turned out to be none other than *don* Jesús Ayala López, the man we had met in 1993. What a happy eventuality. Clearly a man of substance, he had formerly served as the *alcalde* of General Escobedo. This time I could understand everything he knew about the town's history through my interpreter. We met with him on his patio off the plaza, the same spot from four years before, but this time, armed with an intelligent, insightful scholar/translator and tape recorder, we conducted a full, systematic interview. Born in 1911, he was now in his mid-eighties, but he still possessed a keen memory. He told us a great deal about the town's history, including the rampages of revolutionary soldiers during the teens. Among other things, he confirmed that Felix Tijerina had left General Escobedo when he was very young and had been known there as Feliberto, but he denied having personally met him.

After interviewing *señor* Ayala López, we met and spoke extensively with Francisco Peña Ayala and his son Francisco Peña Garza in Monterrey proper. Born in 1912 in a house on the plaza in General Escobedo, Peña Ayala informed us he moved to Monterrey in 1924 for better opportunity. He came to know Felix after he grew up and in fact became Felix's *compadre.* He and his family actually moved to Houston for a time, where his son worked for Tijerina to learn business skills. The elderly gentleman told us that many people left General Escobedo for the United States because of the Revolution. Most tellingly, he remembered from his earliest childhood being at the local railroad station when the Tijerinas left the villa "with just their clothes, to fight for their lives" to survive.[27]

Both of these men clearly still understood the sensitivity of Felix's birth controversy and tried in their own way to avoid directly betraying Tijerina, although what they said validated my research about his nativity. *Don* Jesús may have claimed that he never met Felix, but he clearly must have known him well. He recalled where Felix's father tilled a plot of land east of the *villa,* he knew he owned the house where Tijerina had lived, and he confirmed that Felix (Feliberto) was born in the town. *Don* Jesús had ranked as a substantial citizen of the region at the time when Tijerina returned for visits over the years. He and Felix were probably both part of the local Ayala clan. Cleverly, he stated that he was not certain whether Felix had been born in the house on the plaza, but he said that the structure belonged to Rafael Tijerina; and because his birth certificate ("*los documentos*") maintained that Feliberto had been born in the house of his father, then it was logical that Felix had been born in the building facing the plaza. To me that amounted to a judiciously worded, circuitous way to tell us exactly where Felix was born without directly betraying him. Most subtly, at the end of our interview, he tapped with his index finger on a portrait of Felix I had brought with me, and said quietly, almost imperceptibly: "Feliberto, Feliberto." To the sensitive eye, he made this gesture in recognition, respect, and affection. He also asked if he could keep the portrait.

While *señor* Peña Ayala remembered Felix and his family leaving, he stoutly (almost humorously to the listeners) declared that he knew not where they had gone. He thus stopped short of saying Felix went to the

United States. Most interesting, when we asked the elderly gentleman these direct questions, his son, Francisco Peña Garza, quickly moved around the table, seated himself next to his father as if to ensure that his father would be circumspect. In my years as an oral historian, I have seen younger family members employ such a gentle tactic many times to govern what their elders would say.

My colleagues and I drew from our meetings with these two informative elders that far from being censorious of Felix for his fabrication and subsequent legal troubles, they appreciated their friend's plight. They recognized that Felix Tijerina was a generous man who never forgot his family or his native country, but simply did what any practical man had to do to survive and prosper in a perilous world. In a sense, they still guarded his secret.

The third older person we interviewed was María Villarreal Sepúlveda, a cousin of Felix and the sister of his most loyal Houston employee, Domingo Villarreal. Born in 1912, *señora* Sepúlveda noted that she did not actually know Tijerina as a child, but in our conversation she consistently referred to Felix as Feliberto and confirmed that the people of General Escobedo always called him Feliberto, though, she opined, he may have been known as Felix in the United States. She saw him when he returned for visits and distributed gifts to family members. She flatly stated that he never said where in General Escobedo he was born.

Señora Sepúlveda was most graphic in her stories about the Revolution and the depredations of the *Carrancista* soldiers and their practice of looting and pillaging the town, stories she had heard from her parents. Most important for my vocabulary, we learned that the locals made a verb "*acarranciar*" (a play on the word "Carranza"), meaning "to take" or "to steal." Her many stories mentally transported me back in time to the days of the Revolution. I enjoyed those tales immensely, though living through them must have been terrifying and something that helped to make such refugees as Felix and his family members grateful to the United States and the safety they found there. (These stories of *Carrancista* depredations corroborated the comment made to me by Felix's elderly cousin years before that Tijerina had associated as a child with these hard-bitten revolutionary soldiers.)

My contacts in General Escobedo made our 1997 research trip of inestimable value for it gave me more than enough material to round out the sections on Felix's first ten years. Walking those dusty streets and speaking with the local folks had born fruitful results, allowing me to appreciate his story as a child of the Mexican Revolution—a heroic person whose story embodied the brutality, drama, peril, bravery, and complexity that was revolutionary Mexico, and how it sent people north to make an indelible imprint on Texas and the United States. No one could fail to be captivated by such an understanding. I know that I will never have such an experience again but am thankful for having it at least once.

As an addendum, through Juan Ramón I would discover more written records once I returned to the United States. He had revealed that the church at General Escobedo was part of the parish of San Nicolás Tolentino. I later located those files on microfilm and found the entries for Feliberto's baptism and confirmation as well as mention of various members of the Tijerina family (including Feliberto) taking part in other confirmation sacramental ceremonies. This discovery proved correct the hunch I had in 1993 that the church had been the site of many religious events for the youngster and his family before they left the area.

Implications

Obviously, Felix's Mexican nativity and immigration during the Mexican Revolution holds many implications for Mexican American history and biography in particular, perhaps too many to list here. The more salient ones follow.

First, his true birthplace influences the understanding historians develop regarding the relationship between the group of immigrants who came during the Revolution and the succeeding Mexican American generation. Felix's roots in the former and his status as a role model for the latter blurs the division between the two cohorts.

Second, his origins compel scholars to consider Mexican American–Mexican relations. Felix had extensive interactions with Mexico and his roots there made him more sensitive to that nation. As one public example of this relationship, he served as the ex-officio ambassador from Houston to Mexico on many occasions. Another example relates to the position he took on the deportation drive of the 1950s. In 1954, LULAC supported Operation Wetback (a campaign to expel undocumented Mexican workers), but Felix, as the organization's state director of Texas, did not join the chorus calling for expulsion. While he served as national president of LULAC (the organization required American citizenship for membership), he had much positive interaction with Mexico.[28]

Third, his birthplace and the chagrin it cost him compel students of

Mexican American history to consider the complexities of race relations in Texas. Although immigration laws and officials in the INS made his life difficult, his many friends within the Anglo establishment went to great lengths to quiet his citizenship status in his favor. They rallied to him and gave legal validity to his story.

Though still a worthy role model, Felix, as an example of proper Mexican American behavior, contains an intrinsic contradiction. This problem arises because he presented himself as a native-born American while actually a product of the Mexican Revolution. Native-born citizens could afford to be more assertive as a general rule in their quest for full equality in American society, but immigrants from Mexico during the teens and twenties tended to keep a low profile. Felix Tijerina epitomized the circumspect, moderate immigrant style to gaining equal status. Whether Felix's approach came from his immigrant roots, his standing as a minority businessman who catered to Anglo clientele, or his natural disposition is impossible to determine, but as an immigrant (and one who hid this fact) such would doubtless have made him less prone to be adversarial regarding the troubles that his ethnic population faced. Instead, he chose to deal with problems facing Mexican Americans by fostering education, in his case, the Little School of the 400. He advocated this more discreet prescription for all Mexican Americans, and many in Texas and across the nation followed his example. Certainly, powerful forces acting upon him influenced Felix's public comments and actions.[29]

Conversely and fifth, his Mexican Revolution origins doubtless helped make Tijerina the deeply appreciative, accomplished, loyal citizen of the United States whose presence had no little positive impact on Mexican American, Texas, and U.S. history. He experienced the travail that his native country underwent in the 1910s, and he showed a genuine gratitude to his adopted country for the benefits it bestowed upon him. He turned LULAC into a national organization and continually demonstrated his thankfulness for the United States, just as Dr. Héctor P. García (who immigrated to Texas in 1917 but did not naturalize until *after* World War II) became a deeply loyal benefactor to this country. Far from being a burden on society, both Tijerina and García contributed more than most native-born citizens did.[30]

Sixth, as a result of Felix's example I advise potential biographers and other scholars to view delayed U.S. birth certificates with skepticism when dealing with Mexican Americans born during the era of the Revolution. During my research, I encountered other persons who, doubtless for their own reasons, claimed to be native-born Texans (as Felix did) but I suspect had Mexican origins. In other words, Tijerina's case could represent a broader phenomenon and have larger implications for understanding an entire important period of Mexican American history.

Lastly, Felix's Mexican immigrant story and how he tried to hide his origins make his biography a much better book—a more interesting, dramatic, informative, and relevant history. His early background made Felix an even more human, sympathetic, and heroic figure. The question clearly made me a better researcher. Candidly, I remain disappointed that none of the book's reviewers fully recognized or seemed to appreciate the research odyssey involved in unearthing the total story of his immigrant roots. They seemed apparently to find it something of little difficulty (or even consequence), even though previous Tijerina biographers had missed it. For me, however, the unexpected, lengthy sleuthing of his nativity and the Revolution in Northern Mexico amounted to an experience that helped to refine me as a scholar and as a human being.

After the biography appeared, I journeyed to Monterrey and General Escobedo one final time, where I presented a complimentary copy to those persons who had helped clarify the mystery of Felix's birth for me. The three octogenarians were still alive, thankfully, and seemed genuinely pleased to receive their book. I also placed a copy, inscribed as "Libro Número Uno," in the little library of General Escobedo that today occupies the house where Felix Tijerina was said to have been born. I hope that it serves some future, positive purpose.

Notes

1. The author delivered the initial draft of this essay as a presentation at the Texas State Historical Association in March 2001, under the title "What Did It Matter Where He Was Born: Writing the Biography of Felix Tijerina." The author wishes to acknowledge the pioneering work on Houston Mexican American history by Arnoldo De León, Tatcho Mindiola Jr., and F. Arturo Rosales, as well as thank them for their support of my research on Felix Tijerina. *Houston Chronicle* (September 4, 1965), 1; *Houston Post* (September 5, 1965): 1, 4; *Houston Press* (August 26, 1948): 9; Daniel Sandoval, telephone interview by author, June 12, 1997; and Approval of Name for School in the Franklin-Burnett Area, June 27, 1977, Records of the Houston Independent School District Board of Education.

2. Thomas H. Kreneck, *Mexican American Odyssey: Felix Tijerina, Entrepreneur and Civic Leader, 1905–1965* (College Station: Texas A&M University Press, 2001).

3. Ibid., 192–193, 226–227, 266–272.

4. Ibid., 4–11.

5. As indications of the Mexican immigrant experience in survey literature, see Mark Reisler, *By the Sweat of Their Brow: Mexican Immigrant Labor in the United States, 1900–1940* (Westport and London: Greenwood Press, 1975), 3–17; Manuel G. Gonzales, *Mexicanos: A History of Mexicans in the United States* (Bloomington and Indianapolis: Indiana University Press, 1999), 11–138; and Arnoldo De León, *Mexican Americans in Texas: A Brief History,* 3rd ed. (Wheeling Ill.: Harlan Davidson, Inc., 2009), 71–84.

6. For representative biographical treatments on Tijerina during his life, see Silas Ragsdale, "Biography: Felix Tijerina," *The Log: Weekly Bulletin of the Rotary Club of Houston* 36 (August 19, 1948): 4; Marie Moore, "The Cap Still Fits: When Felix Tijerina Feels Like a Big Shot, He Thinks of a Beer Truck," *Houston* Post (August 8, 1955): 1, 11; and Louis Alexander, "Texas Helps Her Little Latins," *Saturday Evening Post* (August 5, 1961); 30–31, 54–55.

7. Kreneck, *Mexican American Odyssey,* 43–44.

8. Ibid., 80.

9. Ibid., 81; "Restaurateur Continues Fight on Citizenship," *Houston Chronicle* (February 15, 1956): sec. B, 9.

10. Kreneck, *Mexican American Odyssey,* 81–82.

11. Ibid., 88–115, 127–128.

12. Ibid., 128–129.

13. Ibid., 172–174.

14. Ibid., 171–189; and "Opinion of the Court" (May 25, 1956): 10–12, Civil Action No. 8113, *Tijerina v. Brownell.*

15. Kreneck, *Mexican American Odyssey,* 175–190.

16. Ibid., 16–30. Although I concluded that the Tijerinas first came to Texas in 1915, the Census of 1930, which became available after the publication of the biography, notes that the family entered in 1916.

17. Ibid., 35–36.

18. Off-the-record conversations during my research at times proved problematic, but they generally were beneficial.

19. Dianicia Contreras, telephone interview by author, January 19, 1985.

20. Kreneck, *Mexican American Odyssey,* 321. The author wishes to thank the late Dr. Clotilde P. García for introducing me to Israel Cavazos Garza, and Mira Smithwick for facilitating my research with him.

21. Kreneck, *Mexican American Odyssey,* 185–187; and Sidney Farr, interview by author, Houston, Tex., Apr. 23, 1981.

22. Kreneck, *Mexican American Odyssey,* p. 189; and Joe Ingraham, interview by author, Houston, Tex., Apr. 24, 1981.

23. Anselmo Villarreal, telephone interview by author, February 5, 1985; and María Villarreal Bosmans and Tony Bosmans, telephone interview with author, February 10, 1985.

24. Kreneck, *Mexican American Odyssey,* 29, 33, 35, 326; statement of Felix Tijerina made at Houston, Tex., before Acting Naturalization Examiner William P. Autrey on March 26, 1940, in the English language, 1–2, Exhibits, Civil Action No. 8113, *Tijerina v. Brownell,* February 15, 1956.

25. I wish to thank Marie Theresa Hernández and C. Elaine Cummins (who served as scholar/translator and academic associate, respectively) for their indispensible roles on this research trip.

26. For my initial acknowledgments of the individuals I encountered in General Escobedo, see Kreneck, *Mexican American Odyssey,* xii.

27. Francisco Ayala Peña, interview by author with assistance of Marie Theresa Hernández, Monterrey, Nuevo León, September 27, 1997.

28. Kreneck, *Mexican American Odyssey,* 155–158, 239, 295.

29. Ibid., 134, 170, 270.

30. Certificate of Naturalization, Hector Pérez García, November 7, 1946, Dr. Hector P. García Papers, Special Collections & Archives, Mary and Jeff Bell Library, Texas A&M University–Corpus Christi.

"The Population Is Overwhelmingly Mexican; Most of It Is in Sympathy with the Revolution. . . ."
Mexico's Revolution of 1910 and the Tejano Community in the Big Bend

JOHN EUSEBIO KLINGEMANN

The waters of the Rio Grande ran swiftly during the month of December 1913. The small ranching community of Ojinaga lay dormant that winter and the mountains in the background overpowered the landscape. Occasionally, a passerby, a merchant perhaps, crossed the river into Mexico, momentarily interrupting the everyday life of the townspeople. The Revolution had erupted a few years earlier, but those times had come and gone.

Refugees cross into Presidio, Texas, in late 1913, fleeing in advance of the Villista atack on Ojinaga. Courtesy West Texas Collection, Angelo State University.

Only recently, the Constitutionalist forces under Francisco Villa had taken up arms in Chihuahua against the dictatorship of Victoriano Huerta, sending the surrounding countryside into warfare. The *villista* campaign had provoked many people to flee Chihuahua into the United States through Ojinaga. The exodus to escape the horrors of warfare included many of the state's elite as well as soldiers from the federal army.

Santos Serrapio had been among the federal troops crossing into Texas. His command under General Salvador Mercado had disembarked at San Sóstenes, the last station north of Chihuahua City on the railway line. It had then wound its way through the cold desert mountains before arriving at Ojinaga in December. But the next month, they fled across the Rio Grande into Presidio, Texas, following a long battle against forces led by Francisco Villa. Soldiers in Mercado's first line of defense, it seems, had abandoned the trenches in the heat of battle—ostensibly, their movement prompted many in the second line to imagine that a full-scale retreat had been ordered. Before long, the majority of federal combatants and other loyal units had spilled across the river in search of safety, leaving behind the Mexican border town in the hands of the *villistas*.

U.S. Army personnel in Presidio grouped Santos and his fellow soldiers and marched them toward Marfa, Texas, where a train awaited the entire army, prepared to transport them to El Paso for internment until the American government decided on their future. On the group march through the West Texas mountains, the procession stopped at the small mining town of Shafter, where the marchers bivouacked for the night next to the town's cemetery. In the darkness, Santos and some of his friends stole away and wandered into the tunnels of a local silver mine, hoping to avoid apprehension. There they waited until the convoy departed; they then filtered into the community in search of employment.[1]

Santos Serrapio's experience hints at the Revolution's effects upon Tejano communities along the Big Bend area of Texas. But because few scholars have examined the consequences of the revolution on the region, several questions remain unanswered.[2] How did Tejanos participate in the Revolution? Did they join revolutionary forces? Did the Revolution disrupt Tejano life? How did the violence in Mexico contribute to a flow of immigrants into the Big Bend? Did raids along the Big Bend reach Tejanos and their homes in the Big Bend country? These are but a few of the questions this paper will pursue.

For the purposes of this essay, focus will center on the combative phase of the Revolution from 1910 to 1920. More precisely, the work examines the early revolutionary movements and their influences upon Tejano society in the Big Bend. During this period, Chihuahua and Coahuila witnessed significant revolutionary activity, due, in 1910, to the Madero Revolution, and three years later, to the Constitutionalist movement against Victoriano Huerta. During this latter time, Chihuahua became the center for *villismo,* with major clashes also occurring in Coahuila and Durango to the South.

The areas herein defined as constituting the southern portions of the Big Bend are the counties of Brewster and Presidio. I have excluded other counties because little revolutionary activity occurred there. Undoubtedly, sections beyond Presidio and Brewster counties received Mexican immigrants, and Tejano communities there experienced the revolution, but these two particular counties lay adjacent to the border and experienced the consequences of the revolution hardest. The border cities of El Paso and Ciudad Juárez have received extensive analysis from numerous scholars.[3]

I have also included as a part of the Big Bend expanse those areas parallel to Texas, primarily the state of Chihuahua at its northwesternmost section and the northeastern regions of Coahuila. Not only did these locations witness some of the first movements of the Revolution of 1910, they also served, especially in the case of Chihuahua, as the birthplace of *villismo* and the *División del Norte* in 1913. Brigades belonging to Francisco "Pancho" Villa's *División del Norte,* for the most part, originated as rebel cells in Chihuahua, some in the northeastern region of the state abutting the Big Bend.[4] Parts of both states consequently witnessed some of the most historic revolutionary turmoil in northern Mexico.[5] Such activity contributed to the immigration of many Mexicans into the Big Bend.

The Revolution and the Big Bend

As rebel forces and federal armies waged a war against each other in Chihuahua and Coahuila, they created a combat corridor that contributed to the making of a hostile environment. In much the same manner, the deployment of U.S. troops to the Big Bend in reaction to revolutionary events created a type of militarized zone and an atmosphere of heightened tension in the region. But for people in Mexico seeking to escape the horrors of combat, the Big Bend seemed a safer haven. Their arrival increased the size of the Tejano community.

Perhaps the two greatest examples of revolutionary conflict and its repercussions in the Tejano community in areas throughout the Big Bend were two major attacks in 1911 and 1913 on the city of Ojinaga, a small port of entry across from Presidio, Texas.[6] In 1911 and 1913, respectively, rebels forces attacked the federal army and waged a war for the right to command the city's garrison. These confrontations generated much change in the region. Moreover, both incidents prompted a general flight from Mexico by Mexican refugees seeking a better life in the United States. In turn, the circumstances surrounding both events intensified the demand for commerce, legally and illegally, drawing Tejanos into the hostilities.

Many throughout Mexico, including members of Chihuahuan society, met Francisco Madero's *Plan de San Luis Potosí,* a pronouncement that called for a general uprising on the 20th of November 1910, with action. In northwestern Chihuahua, the region opposite to the Big Bend, Toribio Ortega, a local politician and member of the Antireelectionist Club in Cuchillo Parado, and José de la Cruz Sánchez, a local leader from the Ojinaga area, responded to Madero's call for recruiting local men to form a rebel unit.[7] For several months, the two organizers and their followers waged a revolutionary conflict—against the forces of the federal government—that produced a wide-ranging transformation in northwestern Chihuahua.

Two years later in 1913, many former *maderistas* in Chihuahua, Durango, and Coahuila melded into a movement against Victoriano Huerta. In areas adjacent to the Big Bend of Texas, small rebels cells led by one-time *maderistas* including Toribio Ortega and others from his command, grew and coalesced into a much larger brigade, to carry on the fight against federal troops in northern Mexico. The conflict, which lasted several months, recreated conditions in the area that resembled those of 1910 and 1911.

The Madero Revolution

As mentioned above, Francisco Madero's call to arms according to the *Plan de San Luis Potosí* generated considerable revolutionary excitement in Chihuahua in 1910. Skirmishes between revolutionary bands and federal troops ultimately resulted in a long-fought battle for the port of entry at Ojinaga. Although revolutionary attacks upon federal garrisons throughout the north were slow to develop, the Ojinaga surroundings became a focal point as *Maderistas* could acquire weapons and supplies for their cause should they capture the city. Government attacks upon revolutionary bands in other parts of Chihuahua, including the El Paso-Juárez area, had forced *Maderistas* to search for an alternate base of operations.[8]

Prior to the direct confrontation for Ojinaga between federal forces and *maderistas* in 1911, several skirmishes erupted in lands below the southern edges of the Big Bend. As revolutionary cells of *maderistas* sprang up across northern Chihuahua, they launched sporadic attacks on federal troops that pushed the latter into a defensive position at Ojinaga. Soon the rebels merged under one leader in the region. But at the same time, federal troops continued to reinforce the garrison at Ojinaga. Inevitably, skirmishes took place; the first one occurred one December 15 at Venegas Ranch some fourteen miles west of Ojinaga, where a force of fifty *maderistas* engaged two hundred federal soldiers. Each side suffered a casualty, and the fighting ended when the revolutionists expended their ammunition and retreated to the nearby town of El Mulato.[9]

Although numerous skirmishes followed, the major push by revolutionists to defeat the federal army did not take place until a few months later, presumably as a result of revolutionary forces needing supplies and time to coalesce. The final confrontation at last took place during the months of March through May of 1911.

The revolutionists began their attempt to defeat their enemy by laying a siege to the city. Through the leadership of the aforementioned José de la Cruz Sánchez, the attackers surrounded the small town (a difficult task due to the terrain), a tactic de la Cruz Sánchez felt was the best method to utilize his forces instead of launching a direct assault. Federal General Gonzalo Luque had under his command a total of about one hundred men, with the nearest reinforcements located at some distance south of Ojinaga in the small town of Cuchillo Parado, where two hundred soldiers were stationed. Rebel forces, however, controlled the roads between both places, making the reinforcement of Ojinaga a formidable operation.[10]

On March 22, 1911, rebel forces numbering some six hundred men commenced their siege upon the small town located at the confluence of the Conchos and Rio Grande rivers. Over the course of a short time period, the revolutionists built several trench lines two to three hundred yards distance from federal positions. Federal efforts to prevent trench construction by clearing land of brush and trees proved ineffective as by April 14 the attackers had already established two long trenches on both sides of the town.[11]

The stranglehold lasted nearly two months, and in the end, rebel forces withdrew to nearby El Mulato. Although both sides worked to outmaneuver the other, neither ever gained a substantial advantage to inflict a defeat. Although *maderista* trenches surrounded the town, the federal army averted the effects of the quarantine by successfully procuring supplies through contacts in the United States.[12] On the other hand, revolutionary forces lacked the proper training to mount a solid attack on the defensive perimeter of the federal garrison. Ultimately, federal forces evacuated Ojinaga and returned to Chihuahua after Diaz's resignation, and the revolutionary forces were able to take the town.[13]

Villismo and the Movement against Victoriano Huerta

Porfirio Diaz's resignation did not, however, bring an end to revolutionary activity in Chihuahua. Less than two years later, the assassinations of President Francisco Madero, Vice-President José María Pino Suárez, and Chihuahuan Governor Abraham González solidified Chihuahua, Durango, and Coahuila into a campaign against Victoriano Huerta; this movement eventually fell under the leadership of Pancho Villa and his army, known as the *División del Norte.* Once again the border region between the Big Bend and northern Mexico experienced conflict that wrought havoc on the Tejano community.

Much like 1911, revolutionary activity in Chihuahua and Coahuila in 1913 produced prolonged warfare along the U.S.–Mexico border. For a second time, Ojinaga became the focal point for a battle between rebel forces in that sector, now under the command of Toribio Ortega, and President Victoriano Huerta's federal army. Many ex-*maderistas* in the region returned to fill the ranks of rebel units in northwestern Chihuahua, and an epic showdown reminiscent of 1911 reappeared. There again occurred several skirmishes in small towns surrounding Ojinaga and eventually a substantial battle in December for the garrison in the city. These ex-*maderistas* formed the core of Pancho Villa's *División del Norte.*[14]

The *villistas* had met with success during the months of April through December, having defeated federal troops in the state under General Salvador Mercado.[15] Victories at Ciudad Juárez and Tierra Blanca as well as the occupation of Ciudad Chihuahua had left the state in hands of the *villistas;* the exception was Ojinaga, where Mercado's men controlled the garrison. Mercado had evacuated Ciudad Chihuahua, avoiding a direct conflict with rebels; from there the general headed north toward the border, where he remained with a force of about five thousand men, including irregulars. In Ojinaga, then, a sizeable force awaited an attack by Villa's army.[16]

To overthrow Mercado's army commanded by a cluster of generals there at Ojinaga, Villa ordered Generals Pánfilo Natera and Toribio Ortega to attack the border town and oust the defenders. Natera and Ortega's first actions against Ojinaga involved assaults on forward positions situated in the small settlements of El Mulato, Candelaria, and San Juan, all of these on the outskirts of Ojinaga. It seems that Natera and Ortega's forces, numbering some three thousand, planned to encircle the city and attack from various positions instead of mounting a frontal assault from one direction. At El Mulato, the *villistas* warded off a small force of federal soldiers, who then retreated across the international border into Texas. Shortly afterward, however, a U.S. Army scouting party captured the fleeing soldiers trying to reenter Mexico at a location upstream.[17]

Once the outlying settlements had fallen, Natera and Ortega deployed their forces and launched a multi-thronged attack on Ojinaga on December 31. Major M. McNamee, the officer in charge of the U.S. military detachment at Presidio, watched as the battle unfolded. According to McNamee, the *villistas* bombarded the city with artillery and small arms fire throughout the night, yet could not penetrate the town's defenses. During the course of the fight, several shells landed on U.S. soil, and McNamee quickly dispatched a note to Ortega warning him of consequences should American lives be lost. According to McNamee, Ortega reassessed his strategies and no shells fell on the U.S. side again.[18]

Intermittent gunfire continued for the next few days before the *villistas* made another serious attempt to breach Ojinaga's protective barriers. At 2:00 P.M. in the afternoon of January 4, 1914, Natera and Ortega rallied their troops and once again attacked. For several hours both sides exchanged artillery bombardments and small weapons fire. When darkness set into the valley, Mercado deployed a detachment of cavalry along the exposed southern flank of the rebel forces then executing an attack on Ojinaga from the west and northwest. In a brilliant maneuver, the federal cavalry detachment crashed the exposed flank of the *villista* forces, inflicting on them heavy losses. Forced to flee, the rebels retreated to the nearby settlement of San Juan.[19]

Upon reaching San Juan, Natera and Ortega and their battered soldiers made camp at a local ranch and sent word to Villa that the battle had been lost and that Ojinaga remained in the hands of Mercado. Aside from smarting from the loss, the *villistas* grew to hate Mercado and his men for they had committed many atrocities against the rebels, including shooting the wounded and dragging them by horseback. Several rebels had been executed, and their bodies burned and buried in a common grave. For the next six days, the *villistas* regrouped, recuperated, and waited for further instructions from Villa.[20]

In Chihuahua, Villa gladly terminated his month-long stint as governor (Villa formally resigned his position) and directed his attention to the quagmire in Ojinaga. He gathered together the commands of Generals Rosalio Hernández and Maclovio Herrera (about fifteen hundred men) and began a march to the dusty border town. He arrived at San Juan on January 9, when the weather had turned bitterly cold, and called a meeting with Natera and Ortega. He heavily criticized both men for their earlier blunder but discussed with them a subsequent maneuver. The following day, Villa's artillery and cavalry deployed to different strategic positions at Ojinaga and readied for the attack scheduled for that night.[21]

Despite their initial victory, the federal army's situation had deteriorated measurably, and they expected Villa, whom they knew had arrived, to attack imminently. As General Mercado reported later, ammunition and morale were low, and a number of federal officers were considering plans to escape to the United States. Many of the horses in the federal camp had died, and officers who needed funds were selling many of their mounts in Presidio. Nevertheless, during the lull in the battle the federal army regrouped and the wait began.[22]

The final attack at Ojinaga commenced on January 10. At dusk, the more than thirty-five hundred *villistas* descended on the small town from all sides, with deadly artillery and small weapons fire. During the confusion, the first line of Mercado's defenses pulled back to replenish their supply of ammunition, in the act creating the specter of a called retreat. Within a matter of thirty minutes, the entire federal army poured across the Río Bravo in a mad frenzy. American patrols scuttled about the area trying to corral the federal soldiers and maneuver them toward a makeshift camp. In less than two hours, the victorious *villistas* had successfully routed a larger but demoralized federal force.[23]

Villa's takeover of Ojinaga marked one of the most impressive victories for the *villistas* during their campaign of 1913–1914. They had now completely eliminated the federal army from Chihuahua and taken control of the state government. In addition, they had gained access to supplies from a secure location adjacent to the U.S.–Mexico border.[24] Villa and the *División del Norte* had removed any doubts as to their success against the government of Huerta.

The Big Bend as a Militarized Zone

The *Maderista* revolution in northern Chihuahua during 1910 and 1911 altered the lives of border residents, including Tejanos who constituted the majority of the inhabitants along the Big Bend. The numerous skirmishes that took place in early 1911 and the subsequent siege upon Ojinaga in 1913 begot a hostile environment along the border that split families in both communities and forced many in Mexico to flee into the United States. As prospects of revolutionary conflict surfaced in late 1910, the United States reacted by deploying troops along the U.S.–Mexico border including the Big Bend region. In essence, areas such as the Big Bend began to resemble militarized zones—a condition that lasted several years—where local citizens, including Tejanos, were subjected to military authority.

The American presence along the border including the Big Bend acted as a base for cavalry, mounted infantry, coast artillery, and signal corps. The Department of Texas Command had a total of about twenty-eight hundred troops stationed from El Paso to Brownsville, with some stationed at several locations in the Big Bend. Two detachments received temporary duty along the border at Presidio and at Boquillas, a small mining community in the southeast across from Boquillas, Coahuila. The remaining two detachments were stationed in Presidio County at Marfa and in Brewster County at Marathon.[25]

These units were to guard certain areas in order to enforce neutrality laws and prevent the flow of arms and munitions destined for rebel units in Mexico. The troops stationed in Marfa had the responsibility of patrolling from Marfa to Presidio, while those in Marathon scouted the area from their home base to Boquillas. Under this structure, the southern areas of Brewster and Presidio Counties resembled militarized zones where local citizens were subject to searches at the hands of service personnel.[26]

In other ways, the *maderista* revolution brought disruption to border residents, as in the consequences created by the closure of international traffic through the Ojinaga–Presidio port of entry. In a letter to the Secretary of State, Representative William R. Smith noted that one of his constituents, a local merchant named John Kleinman in Presidio, Texas, had reported the action by Ojinaga authorities. In his opinion, the unnecessary suspension had been done to exact revenge upon Mr. Kleinman for deny-ing the sale of weapons to the municipal government in that city. In the merchant's opinion, the steps taken by Ojinaga's officials had caused much damage to the people of both communities.[27]

Other incidents that affected the local community stemmed from stray bullets that fell upon U.S. soil during clashes between federal and rebel forces. In one particular occasion, however, a federal patrol in Mexico at El Mulato fired in error upon U.S. soldiers, sending the latter scurrying in search of safety. It seems the federal patrol had mistaken the U.S. Army patrol for a group of insurgents. Tragically, the perpetrators wounded a young boy pulling his packhorse. The incident received much attention from both governments in the aftermath, but nothing could be ascertained as to the condition of the injured boy.[28]

The Revolution and Tejanos

Participation in the Mexican Revolution by Tejanos from the Big Bend region came in many forms. The call to arms by Francisco Madero in 1911 or *villistas* in 1913 brought, in northern Chihuahua, an eager response from many throughout the region. Some Tejanos traveled south to enlist, while others opted to help the revolution by supplying rebel forces with equipment, munitions, and weapons.

Reports concerning the provisioning of revolutionary forces by mer-chants in the United States (including Texas and the Big Bend region) came from American consular officials in cities along the U.S.–Mexico border. In one telegram dated October 15, 1910, Consul Luther Ellsworth noted the trade already established before the outbreak of the revolution. He described merchants in Texas supplying potential rebels across the bor-der with .30–.30 Winchester rifles and ammunition of the same caliber. Ellsworth's memorandum noted that U.S. border federal officers had ob-served that revolutionary sympathizers often purchased these munitions and then smuggled them across the Rio Grande after darkness.[29]

In the Big Bend, several isolated locations along the U.S.–Mexico bor-der, far removed from the watchful eye of American agents, offered mer-chants and gunrunners (both Tejanos and Mexican nationals) opportune ports of entry, where large loads of munitions and rifles could be crossed. The rugged terrain of the region that included mountain ranges, valleys, numerous dried creeks, and caves with limited access via a roadway offered smugglers plentiful places to avoid detection. The adjacency of the Big Bend to the border also offered smugglers an exit in case of discovery.

Supplies could also be crossed at legally designated avenues such as Presidio, but the presence of Mexican federal army and U.S. Army patrols increased the risk of failure. In certain instances, the possibility of smuggling at these points proved problematic as the warring factions closed bridges to traffic, as in the previously mentioned Ojinaga controversy. As a consequence, merchants and intermediaries sought other exits to avoid detection and to successfully smuggle their merchandise.

Several sites along the Rio Grande could be safely forded at night on horseback. These points included Ruidosa and Candelaria, small farming communities upriver from Presidio and El Mulato, another small farming community down river. At the far end of the Big Bend, Boquillas, a small mining town, served as yet another route for introducing weapons into Mexico.[30]

In order to arm their troops in 1911, José de la Cruz Sánchez and other rebel officers depended upon, among others, entrepeneurs located in the town of Presidio, Texas, directly across from Ojinaga. In Presidio, one particular merchant turned arms agent (who only accepted cash for weapons and would not sell on credit) employed local Tejanos as middlemen in the business of dispersing purchased munitions and collecting cash money. Once U.S. troops arrived, however, his activities came under the scrutiny of authorities, who forced the supplier to seek other surreptitious methods of providing weapons to the *maderistas*.[31]

Tejanos living along the border were not the only ones active in gunrunning during the earliest phase of the revolution; the commerce in weapons also engaged Tejanos removed some distance from the border. The railway line from San Antonio to El Paso passed through several points in the Big Bend or at its margins, so Tejanos and Mexican agents in the interior sent large shipments of munitions to the region destined for border crossings. Tejanos close to these railway stops received shipments and then transported the goods to the Rio Grande.

In Alpine, a small ranching community in northern Brewster County, a Tejano ranch owner served in one such capacity. Shipments arriving at the Toyah whistle stop were taken by wagon to his ranch until ready for transfer to rebels in Mexico.[32] Similarly, in Valentine, a railway stop, a local Tejano engaged in gunrunning until becoming the target of an anti-smuggling sting by U.S. authorities. Agents tracked his shipments through

Marfa and to the store, and then to Candelaria. It seems the U.S. cavalry successfully followed the munitions to Candelaria and seized them before they were whisked across the border.[33]

In 1913, increased commerce in contraband developed along the Big Bend area as a result of the constitutionalist movement in Chihuahua. Local former *maderistas* taking up the struggle against Victoriano Huerta organized into various rebellious cells in the northwest region of Chihuahua that eventually coalesced into the Brigada González Ortega of Villa's *División del Norte.* In order to wage an effective campaign against the federal army in the state, cell leaders turned to residents in the Big Bend to help procure munitions. Once these cells had defeated local federal troops, the acquisition of more weapons for constitutionalist forces increased.

Several of these brigade officers, most notably Toribio Ortega and Albino Aranda, called upon their former contacts on the Texas side to bring them a steady supply of weapons and ammunition. Toribio Ortega's position as the sole military force in the region allowed him to act expeditiously to accumulate weapons through purchases in the Big Bend. Well situated in Ojinaga by mid-April 1913, he worked diligently for the next two months to acquire supplies in the United States. Meanwhile, he mounted a campaign of recruitment locally around Ojinaga. His unit soon swelled to five hundred well-armed men with another three hundred volunteers (though these possessed no weapons). During the next two months, an additional three hundred men joined Ortega from the small settlements and towns surrounding Ojinaga, such as El Mulato, San Antonio, Barrancas and San Carlos.[34]

To arm all his troops, Ortega once again communicated with local merchants in Presidio, who, as they had done earlier, utilized local Tejanos as intermediaries to buy weapons and turn them over to Ortega. In one particular instance, a man named Pedro (last name unknown) purchased five cases of ammunition through the town merchant Kleinman for the revolutionists, but authorities seized the shipment in Marfa before it could be sent overland to Presidio. When questioned, Kleinman denied any involvement in the trafficking.[35]

Ortega's efforts to acquire weapons and supplies in the United States suddenly halted when the Mexican Consulate in Marfa, Texas, persuaded U.S. authorities to investigate the rebel officer's activities. As a result, the United States issued an arrest warrant for Ortega, charging him with violation of neutrality laws. Seemingly, his purchase of weapons and merchandise in the United States violated the arms embargo established by the U.S. government. Arrested in Presidio, Ortega was taken to Marfa and placed in the local jail.

Papers found on Ortega's person identified the many individuals who sold the revolutionists weapons and supplies. Included in the bundle were receipts signed by Tejanos, implicating them in abetting the constitutionalist cause. Ortega's incarceration, however, proved to be brief as he was released on bond. The old soldier returned to Ojinaga and resumed his revolutionary activities.[36]

Tejanos also participated in the war as soldiers in the ranks of the revolutionary forces. Several motives explain their desire to join. Some were removed by only one or two generations from Mexico, and they sympathized with the old homeland. Many were friends of revolutionaries. From Eagle Pass to El Paso, Texas, reports from officials stationed at the border noted that parties with Texas–Mexicans in their ranks had crossed the Rio Grande into Mexico, some armed and carrying supplies for revolutionaries. They had either been recruited by revolutionists or had volunteered to fight.[37]

From the Big Bend proper, U.S. federal agents reported that people on horseback, carrying loads of provisions, at times crossed the Rio Grande, destined to help the *maderistas.* In one particular case, eighty rebels with pack mules crossed from the United States into Mexico at Ruidosa, upriver from Presidio, intent on uniting with the nearly six hundred rebels at Ojinaga. Because the communiqués do not differentiate between Mexican citizens and Tejanos, the exact numbers of the latter heading south remains unclear.[38]

In 1913, Tejanos responded to the call of the *constitutionalists.* Malías C. García, a member of the constitutionalist revolutionary junta in El Paso, was arrested on July 5, 1913, along with five other men in the United States, for alleged recruitment efforts along the border. Authorities charged García with violations of U.S. neutrality laws.[39] They seized a letter from García that introduced him to Toribio Ortega as a brave soldier, but it also implicated him in recruitment efforts in the Big Bend area of Texas. The evidence suggests that at least one of them was recruiting for the Brigada González Ortega.

Many Tejanos who did not join the *maderistas* in 1911 or the constitutionalists after 1913 participated in the revolution through monetary donations. They contributed funds that could be utilized to purchase supplies, weapons, and ammunition. For Tejanos living in the Big Bend region, their proximity to the border allowed them to be in direct contact with members of Madero's forces and later those of the Constitutionalist forces.[40]

Immigration and the Revolution

One of the greatest effects the revolution had on the Tejano community of the Big Bend came as a result of massive immigration. During both the Madero and Constitutionalist movements, Mexicans fled their native country to escape the horrors of warfare; in doing so, they contributed to the growth of population and strengthened Tejano life and culture there. Although some left the Big Bend region and moved into the interior of the United States, many stayed behind in the area to begin a new life. In lower Brewster County, refugees in early 1911 settled in the worker housing of mining complexes located at or near Terlingua; there, Tejanos provided them with food and shelter. Within nearly two months, the community had grown by three hundred. Local authorities, alarmed by the numbers of refugees, feared that food supplies would eventually be exhausted. The concern prompted the local sheriff to declare that many ex-patriots would eventually turn to theft to supplement their needs.[41]

A similar movement of refugees into upriver Presidio occurred in May of that same year. General Gonzalo Luque's evacuation in the aftermath of the Ojinaga siege and the subsequent occupation of Ojinaga by Madero's forces prompted many to seek safety across the river, where they constructed a shantytown. Nearly a thousand refugees came to live in Presidio, inhabiting crude dwellings close to the river. The *maderistas,* however, soon appointed local authorities to Ojinaga and restored order there. As the revolution subsided and local authorities in Ojinaga began safeguarding the rights of citizens, many of the exiles returned to their place of origin.[42]

In 1913, Ojinaga once more became the entry path for refugees fleeing the revolution into Texas. As mentioned earlier, the federal army under the command of General Salvador Mercado, after several months of fighting the *villlistas* in Chihuahua, found itself almost trapped in Ciudad Chihuahua with few alternatives. General Mercado faced a major decision in December. The constitutionalists controlled Torreón to the southeast and Hidalgo del Parral to the south; guerrillas infested the mountains to the west; and worst of all, Villa was heading toward Ciudad Chihuahua from the north. After some disagreement among Pascual Orozco, José Inés Salazar, and himself, Mercado opted not to fight his way south, but instead to abandon the capital and transport his troops to the northeast and occupy the garrison in the city of Ojinaga. Perhaps Mercado understood the importance of situating his force next to the international border. If need be, he and his forces could seek sanctuary in the United States.

Mercado's decision to abandon Ciudad Chihuahua had far-reaching consequences. Villa's approach and the rumored departure of the federal army for the north set off a wave of panic locally because of widespread fears and rumors that Villa's troops would destroy everything. Many of the wealthy families in Chihuahua City began to gather as much of their fortunes as possible and made plans to follow the army to Ojinaga. Although the city was well defended, a battle in the streets meant the possible death of many civilians.[43]

The first column to leave Chihuahua City and reach Ojinaga was led by H. B. Freeman, the superintendent of the Alvarado Mining Company of Hidalgo del Parral. The entourage consisted of sixteen wagons carrying an estimated $750,000 worth of silver bars from the Alvarado and Inde mines. The caravan proceeded toward Ojinaga, carefully guarded by a detachment of *colorados* (irregulars loyal to Huerta) led by Pascual Orozco and accompanied by Generals José Inés Salazar and Caraveo (first name unknown). Once the column had reached Presidio, the silver shipment changed hands and was directly transported to Marfa by a U.S. cavalry escort. From there, the mining companies shipped the silver bars by rail to New York City.[44]

The second group to evacuate Ciudad Chihuahua and head north toward Ojinaga consisted of the city's civilian population. Here went a substantial portion of the wealthiest families in Chihuahua, including General Luis Terrazas Sr., as well as members of the Creel, Escobar, Quilty, and other well-to-do families. The families utilized the trains from the Kansas City, Mexico and Orient Railway line to make the trip from Ciudad Chihuahua to Falomir. From there, they proceeded on horseback and used whatever means of transportation available.[45]

The final group to leave the capital city was Mercado and the main body of his army, which included four hundred officers with their families; twenty-five hundred soldiers, their wives, and camp followers (*soldaderas*); and an uncounted number of children. In addition to the troops, nearly two hundred miscellaneous refugees trailed the long column. This last contingent also rode the train to Falomir, then continued on horseback or by foot until they reached Ojinaga on December 13 after an exceedingly difficult trip.[46] Food and water were scarce and the weather had begun to turn cold. Many animals and some people died along the difficult desert trek. In his memoirs, Mercado referred to the trip as "*la caravana de la muerte*" (the caravan of death).[47]

In a span of nearly two weeks, the small northern Chihuahuan village received a population of nearly eight thousand refugees. Many did not remain in Ojinaga, but rather crossed the Rio Bravo into the United States, where immigration authorities and officers of the U.S. Army registered them for entry into the country. Officials briefly interrogated the refugees, asked them to provide proof of identity, and released them on the Texas side, after stating that they had no desire to return immediately to Mexico. In addition to the fleeing masses, many townspeople from Ojinaga crossed the border into safety. Mercado and his forces, meantime, held their position at Ojinaga to defend the town garrison against the impending attack by *villistas*.[48]

Presidio was not the only point at which refugees from Ojinaga crossed the river, seeking temporary safety. On December 18, 1913, Supervising Inspector J.W. Berkshire of the U.S. Immigration Service informed Washington that some two hundred refugees, mostly farmers and their families from nearby villages across from Lajitas, prepared to cross into Texas. Inspector Robb (first name unknown), temporarily assigned to the port at Lajitas, reported to Berkshire that "the aliens are of a superior class and have plenty of funds, and have no desire to proceed beyond La Jitas [sic], but only intend to remain on the Mexican side until such time as they become satisfied they can return to their homes in safety." Robb additionally reported that many were living without shelter but were acting as if "on a protracted picnic," having ample food and drink and engaging in music and dance each night. Robb also located about two hundred and fifty to three hundred refugees near the mouth of Santa Elena Canyon, with sufficient food and a herd of fifteen hundred goats. Some were sleeping in tents, huts, wagons, or in the open. One entrepreneur from San Carlos thought it safe enough to sell men's wear and bolts of cloth to the refugees. Robb also reported finding a sewing machine, a typewriter, and a phonograph in one of the camps.[49]

Immigration during the ten-year revolution increased the number of Tejanos in the Big Bend. Tejano society in Brewster, Presidio, and Jeff Davis Counties expanded by 56 percent between 1910 and 1920. From a total of 7,582 people of Mexican descent in the Big Bend prior to the revolution, the population grew to 11,863 at the decade's end. By 1920, Tejanos comprised 73 percent of the population in the Big Bend.[50]

Although many Mexicans succeeded in fleeing the revolution, their fate in the Big Bend region of Texas varied. Some were successful in finding jobs in numerous markets that flourished in the Big Bend, including the mining and railroad industries, the ranching trade, and the candelilla wax business, among other enterprises. Others faced marginalization in the form of racial discrimination, rejection when seeking residence in certain neighborhoods, or obstacles to integrating themselves into mainstream society. Their assimilation into Big Bend society proved difficult.[51]

Conclusion

In his memorandum of April 1913 to the Adjutant General of the Army, the Commanding General for the Southern Department headquartered at Fort Sam Houston, Texas, reported on conditions along the U.S.–Mexico border. According to the Commanding General, Mexicans comprised the principal part of the population along the border from Texas to California, and in his opinion the majority sympathized with the constitutionalist movement of 1913 and many remained ardent supporters of the revolution of 1910. He further stated that many Mexicans supported the Revolution with substantial quantities of money due to the fact that "Mexicans are employed at good wages on our side of the line. . . ."[52]

Mexico's revolution of 1910 had a considerable effect on Tejano society in the Big Bend throughout the course of the Madero revolt of 1910 and the Constitutionalist movement of 1913. The mobilization of revolutionary forces during both periods and the subsequent attacks upon federal garrisons in northeastern Chihuahua and northwestern Coahuila contributed to the creation of a hostile environment along the border that, on some occasions, resulted in injury or death to Tejanos. The deployment of U.S. troops to patrol the border and the expansion of federal troops on the Mexican side intensified the contentious atmosphere there and transformed the region into a militarized zone for a period of nearly five years, escalating tensions between citizens on either side of the Rio Grande and authorities.

Tejanos along the Big Bend adjusted to the war conditions that plagued both sides. Many participated in the event as intermediaries between revolutionary forces and merchants in the United States eager to make a profit. Tejanos purchased supplies and munitions for their friends in Mexico and crossed them clandestinely at low fords along the Big Bend's section of the Rio Grande. Although profit motivated some, others patriotically supported the revolution and utilized their earnings from employment in the

United States to purchase war material. In some instances, Tejanos paid the ultimate price, facing incarceration for their actions, as they had violated neutrality laws.

Still others contributed to the revolution as soldiers in the ranks of Madero's army (as did members of Toribio Ortega's forces in the Ojinaga) or as *villistas* in the *División del Norte,* Fancisco Villa's group of army brigades within the Constitutionalist forces that fought against Victoriano Huerta. Agents of the Madero and Constitutionalist forces had recruited some, while others crossed into Mexico as part of large groups volunteering to join *la bola* (the fight). Tejanos in the Big Bend took up arms on both occasions to confront federal troops.

The revolution further contributed to community building in the Big Bend. Refugees fleeing the revolution found a niche in the Big Bend, as did those who went to work in the mines in lower Brewster County in 1911. Federal army soldiers who left the ranks of their brigades in 1913 settled in different towns, where they began life anew, relying on local occupations. Other refugees utilized Big Bend locales as a springboard for their introduction into the United States, as evidenced by the many who remained temporarily in the region, then left in search of employment in the interior.

Notes

1. Serrapio and his companions found employment in one of the local mines. A mine owner offered them jobs after discovering them hiding in the various tunnels. In time, Serrapio married a local woman and eventually moved to the nearby town of Marfa, where he remained until his death. Frances Faver Cline, interview by Jim Cullen, June 16, 1983, Archives of the Big Bend, Sul Ross State University, OHC64/ca1983, 45–51; and Salvador R. Mercado, *Revelaciones Históricas* (Las Cruces: Private Publication, 1916): 41–45.

2. Notable exceptions include Rodolfo Rocha and Paul Wright. See Rodolfo Rocha, "The Influence of the Mexican Revolution on the Mexico–Texas Border, 1910–1916" (Ph.D. diss., Texas Tech University, 1981); and Paul Wright, "Starting Over: Impacts of Mexican Revolution Refugees on Big Bend Society," *The Journal of Big Bend Studies* 13 (2001): 195–213.

3. See Oscar Martínez, *Fragments of the Mexican Revolution: Personal Accounts from the Border* (Albuquerque: The University of New Mexico Press, 1983); David Romo, *Ringside to a Revolution: An Underground Cultural History of El Paso and Juárez, 1893–1923* (El Paso: Cinco Puntos Press, 2005); and Miguel A. Levario, "Cuando vino la mexicanada:

Authority, Race and Conflict in West Texas, 1895–1924" (Ph.D. diss., University of Texas at Austin, 2007), among others.

4. In 1913, the majority of the brigades in the *División del Norte* formed in the state of Chihuahua, while others were organized in the states of Coahuila and Durango. See Friedrich Katz, *The Life and Times of Pancho Villa* (Stanford: Stanford University Press, 1998); Juan Bautista Vargas Arreola, *A Sangre y Fuego con Pancho Villa* (México: Fondo de Cultura Económica, S.A. de C.V., 1988); Arturo Ramírez Langle, *El ejercito villista* (México: Instituto Nacional de Antropología e Historia, 1961); Alberto Calzadíaz Barrera, *Hechos reales de la Revolución,* primer tomo (México: Editorial Patria, S.A., 1961), 99; Pedro Salmerón, *La División del Norte: La tierra, los hombres y la historia de un ejercito del pueblo* (México: Editorial Planeta Mexicana, S.A. de C.V., 2006); and E. Brondo Whitt, *La División del Norte, 1914 por un testigo presencial* (México: Editorial Lumen, 1940).

5. The northwestern and southernmost regions of Chihuahua have been excluded. These regions have received extensive analysis by scholars of the Revolution. See John Mason Hart, *Revolutionary Mexico: The Coming and Process of the Mexican Revolution* (Berkley: University of California Press, 1987); Alan Knight, *The Mexican Revolution, 2* vols. (Lincoln: University of Nebraska Press, 1986); and William H. Beezley, *Insurgent Governor: Abraham González and the Mexican Revolution in Chihuahua* (Lincoln: University of Nebraska Press, 1973).

6. It should be noted that Pascual Orozco Junior attacked the city of Ojinaga during his revolt of 1912 and defeated the federal garrison on September 11. The city served as a capital for his movement until January of the following year. Michael C. Meyer, *Mexican Rebel: Pascual Orozco and the Mexican Revolution 1910–1915* (Lincoln: University of Nebraska Press, 1967): 87.

7. Francisco P. Ontiveros, Ortega's biographer, describes Cuchillo Parado as a town dedicated to liberal ideology and freedom. Francisco de P. Ontiveros, *Toribio Ortega y la Brigada González Ortega* (Chihuahua: Talleres Gráficos del Estado, 1924), 5.

8. According to William H. Beezley, Provisional Governor Abraham González, "intended to occupy a port of entry on the international frontier to serve as a Mexican headquarters for the rebel junta, provide an entrance for war material from the United States, and possibly supply income from customs receipts." Plans for such as base in Ciudad Juárez had faltered, and focus had shifted to Ojinaga. See Beezley, *Insurgent Governor,* 41.

9. According to Earl H. Elam, El Mulato, a farming community east of Ojinaga, served as a regional supply base for the *maderistas*. Earl H. Elam, "The Madero Revolution and the Bloody Bend," *The Journal of Big Bend Studies* 13 (2001): 176–177.

10. Ellsworth notes in his report the testimony of a correspondent concerning de la Cruz Sánchez's siege tactic. According to the correspondent, the rebel leader claimed that the town would eventually be taken. Luther T. Ellsworth to Secretary of

State, January 31, 1911, *Records of the Department of State Relating to the Internal Affairs of Mexico, 1910–1929,* Film 812.00: 720, Roll 11.

11. According to the submitted report, the rebels utilized local resources (including some of the material cut down by federal forces but not used for their own trenches) to construct the trench lines. Secretary of War to Secretary of State, May 6, 1911, *Records of the Department of State Relating to the Internal Affairs of Mexico, 1910–1929,* Film 812.00: 1692, Roll 13.

12. General Gonzalo Luque's efforts to acquire U.S. help involved the procurement of supplies from the nearby town of Marfa, Texas, where a Mexican consular officer operated.

13. Captain A. E. Williams to Adjutant General, Department of Texas, May 9, 1911, *Records of the Department of State Relating to the Internal Affairs of Mexico, 1910–1929,* Film 812.00: 1898, Roll 13.

14. See John Klingemann, "Triumph of the Vanquished: Pancho Villa's Chihuahuan Army in Revolutionary Mexico" (Ph.D. diss, University of Arizona, 2008).

15. It should be noted that the first military action taken by anti-*huertistas* occurred in April 1913 as collective assault by rebel units under the command of Toribio Ortega. Ortega's attack resulted in a successful rout of the small federal military garrison in Ojinaga. As previously mentioned, the small town lay on a plateau and could not easily be defended by an inferior force. The small federal detachment of two hundred men in the town, under the command of Artillery Captain Alberto Ortiz, was no match for Colonel Ortega's units. Upon hearing the news of an imminent attack, Captain Ortiz fled to Presidio, Texas, and then to Marfa, where the Huerta government had consulate offices. Francisco de P. Ontiveros, *Toribio Ortega y la Brigada González Ortega* (Chihuahua: Talleres Gráficos del Estado, 1924), 62–65.

16. Marion Letcher to Secretary of State, November 30, 1913, *Records of the Department of State Relating to the Internal Affairs of Mexico, 1910–1929,* Film 812.00: 10054, Roll 32; and Secretary of War Lindley M. Garrison to Secretary of State, December 4, 1913, *Records of the Department of State Relating to the Internal Affairs of Mexico, 1910–1929,* Film 812.00: 10047, Roll 32.

17. Sergeant Ludwig Feldman reported that exactly forty-one rifles, fifteen sabers, and several thousand rounds of ammunition were confiscated from the federal soldiers apprehended in the United States. None was taken prisoner and all were allowed to reenter Mexico without their weapons. Major M. McNamee to Company Officer, South Department, January 3, 1914, National Archives, Washington D.C., RG 393, E4440, Box 1; J. W. Berkshire to Commissioner-General of Immigration, January 5, 1914, National Archives, Washington D.C., RG 85, 53108/711.

18. Major M. McNamee to Company Officer, South Department, January 3, 1914, National Archives, Washington D.C., RG 393, E4440, Box 1.

19. Reports from American officers at Presidio, Texas, note that the federal soldiers committed several acts of atrocity against the rebel forces at Ojinaga, including the multiple shooting of wounded rebels willing to surrender. Lindley M. Garrison to Secretary of State, concerning the situation at Ojinaga, January 5, 1914, National Archives, RG 85, 53108/711.

20. Ontiveros' and McNamee's descriptions of the events that transpired at Ojinaga contain the same information. McNamee's reports provide better descriptions of the battles as they unfolded, whereas Ontiveros provides the personal perspectives of the men in combat. Major M. McNamee to Company Officer, Southern Department, January 10, 1914, National Archives, Washington D.C., RG 393, E4440, Box 1; and Ontiveros, *Toribio Ortega y la Brigada González Ortega,* 108.

21. American military units constantly patrolled the border in search of refugees and fleeing soldiers. In addition to immigration inspectors and military personnel, the U.S. government sent the American Red Cross to the border in anticipation of having to treat the wounded at Ojinaga. Authorities were alarmed at the possibility that thousand of refugees, wounded and sick, would enter at Presidio, Texas. In some instances, people suspected of being smallpox cases had been quarantined by the U.S. Army. At least two thousand refugees and five thousand federal soldiers were expected to enter the United States. J. W. Berkshire to Commissioner General of Immigration, January 5, 1914, National Archives, Washington D.C., RG 85, 53108/71J; and Secretary of War, Lindley M. Garrison, to Secretary of State, January 9, 1914, National Archives, Washington D.C., RG 85, 53108/711.

22. Mercado, *Revelaciones Históricas,* 67–68.

23. George Harris to Supervising Inspector, February 24, 1914, National Archives, Washington D.C., RG 85, 53108/71J; and Major M. McNamee to Commanding General, Southern Department, January 17, 1914, National Archives, Washington D.C., RG 393, E4440, Box 1.

24. The refugees arriving at Presidio were eventually marched overland to the town of Marfa, where they were sent to Fort Bliss in El Paso to be interned for an unspecified amount of time. The group sent to Fort Bliss included 509 officers, 3,212 men, 1,081 women and 533 children. Nearly 100 federal soldiers were treated for rifle wounds at Presidio. Among the animals allowed to enter the United States were 983 horses, 383 mules and 414 burros. Captain Lear noted that few of the soldiers possessed money as they had not been paid since the 10th of December. He also noted that General Mercado did not have funds to pay his men. Captain Ben Lear Jr. to Major M. McNamee, January 15, 1914, National Archives, Washington D.C., RG 393, E4439, Box 4, Doc. 3172.

25. Secretary of War, J. M. Dickinson to Secretary of State, February 6, 1911, *Records of the Department of State Relating to the Internal Affairs of Mexico, 1910–1929,* Film 812.00: 754, RG 11.

26. Ibid.

27. According to Kleinman, the port closure injured "hundreds of people, dividing families and causing needless suffering." It should be noted that animosity by Ojinaga's authorities toward Kleinman also stemmed from the fact he had sold weapons and munitions to rebel forces. William R. Smith to Secretary of State, February 3, 1911, *Records of the Department of State Relating to the Internal Affairs of Mexico, 1910–1929,* Film 812.00: 717, RG 11.

28. In a report to his superiors, General Luque, commander at Ojinaga, claimed that his men had received strict orders to avoid confrontation with U.S. troops. The episode at El Mulato, according to Luque, resulted from fire directed at his soldiers from rebels in the vicinity of the Rio Grande. Attorney General George W. Wickersham to Secretary of State, March 23, 1911, *Records of the Department of State Relating to the Internal Affairs of Mexico, 1910–1929,* Film 812.00: 1057, RG 11; Embajada de México en los Estados Unidos de América to U.S. Secretary of State Philander Knox, May 3, 1911, *Records of the Department of State Relating to the Internal Affairs of Mexico, 1910–1929,* Film 812.00: 1629, RG 13; and Acting Secretary of War to Secretary of State Philander Knox, May 20, 1911, *Records of the Department of State Relating to the Internal Affairs of Mexico, 1910–1929,* Film 812.00: 1898, RG 13.

29. Luther T. Ellsworth to Secretary of State, October 15, 1910, *Records of the Department of State Relating to the Internal Affairs of Mexico, 1910–1929,* Film 812.00: 409, RG 10.

30. Ellsworth's report includes a passage from other agents. One particular reference describes rifles purchased at Marathon, Texas, that were subsequently smuggled to revolutionary forces at Boquillas. Ibid.; Vice Consul Charles M. Leonard to Secretary of State, January 13, 1911, *Records of the Department of State Relating to the Internal Affairs of Mexico, 1910–1929,* Film 812.00: 656, RG 10; and Captain Frank A. Barton to Adjutant General, Department of Texas, May 7, 1911, *Records of the Department of State Relating to the Internal Affairs of Mexico, 1910–1929,* Film 812.00: 1908, RG 13.

31. Information concerning those in Presidio is in author's private archive. Other Tejanos not only operated as gunrunners but also fought alongside revolutionaries. Receipt signed by Máximo Castillo, July 10, 1911, Ramo Gobernación, Sección: Sin Sección, Caja 865, Expediente 4, Galería 5, Archivo General de la Nación, Mexico D.F., Mexico.

32. According to William H. Beezley, Abraham González, a supporter of Francisco Madero constructed a system of provisioning rebel forces that entailed the recruitment of ranch foremen, freight dockworkers in rail yards, and others. His supporters also crossed the border and purchased weapons throughout West Texas, including the Big Bend region. Beezley, *Insurgent Governor,* 45–46.

33. The shipment included three boxes of .30–.30 Winchester rifles and ten boxes of ammunition that totaled ten thousand rounds. Captain Frank A. Barton to Adjutant General, Department of Texas, May 7, 1911, *Records of the Department of State Relating to the Internal Affairs of Mexico, 1910–1929,* Film 812.00: 1908, RG 13.

34. U.S. Department of State. Reports of special agents to Bureau of Investigation concerning activities in the Big Bend district. *Records of the Department of State Relating to the Internal Affairs of Mexico, 1910–1929,* Film 812.00: 7713, RG 26.

35. Deputy Collector J. R. Weisiger to Dr. A. H. Evans, Collector of Customs, May 27, 1913, *Records of the Department of State Relating to the Internal Affairs of Mexico, 1910–1929,* Film 812.00: 7794, RG 26.

36. As a matter of fact, the report indicated that many Mexicans living in the Marfa area visited Ortega during his incarceration, among them the local judge, who indicated a willingness to help the rebel secure his freedom from jail. U.S. Department of State. Reports of special agents to Bureau of Investigation concerning activities in the Big Bend district. *Records of the Department of State Relating to the Internal Affairs of Mexico, 1910–1929,* Film 812.00: 7867, RG 26.

37. These reports indicate the presence of armed groups in the United States that crossed into Mexico at one point or another during the early phase of the Madero revolution. Luther T. Ellsworth to Philander Knox, Secretary of State, November 24, 1910, *Records of the Department of State Relating to the Internal Affairs of Mexico, 1910–1929,* Film 812.00: 504, RG 10; Unknown to Secretary of State, December 24, 1910, *Records of the Department of State Relating to the Internal Affairs of Mexico, 1910–1929,* Film 812.00: 618, RG 10; and Assistant Secretary of War Robert Shaw Oliver to Philander Knox, Secretary of State, January 6, 1911, *Records of the Department of State Relating to the Internal Affairs of Mexico, 1910–1929,* Film 812.00: 619, RG 10.

38. Luther T. Ellsworth to Secretary of State, January 31, 1911, *Records of the Department of State Relating to the Internal Affairs of Mexico, 1910–1929,* Film 812.00: 720, RG 11.

39. U.S. Department of State, Internal Affairs of Mexico, 1910–1929, by unknown special agent of the Bureau of Investigation. Report on *U.S. v. Malías C. García et al.,* July 8, 1913, *Records of the Department of State Relating to the Internal Affairs of Mexico, 1910–1929,* Film 812.00: 8060, RG 27.

40. Brigadier General Tasker H. Bliss to the Adjutant General of the U.S. Army, April 19, 1913, *Records of the Department of State Relating to the Internal Affairs of Mexico, 1910–1929,* Film 812.00: 7229, RG 25.

41. "Return from Chisos Mines," *Alpine Avalanche* (January 19, 1911).

42. "Federals Abandon Town of Ojinaga," *El Paso Morning Times* (May 20, 1911): 1.

43. Oscar Lesser Norwald contends that Villa paid Mercado to abandon the city.

Moreover, Norwald stated that he and another man, in the company of two hundred soldiers that Mercado had abandoned, formally handed the city over to Villa. Oscar Lesser Norwald, interview by Rubén Osorio, tape recording, 1975, collection not catalogued, Archives of the Big Bend, Sul Ross State University, Alpine, TX.

44. Earl Elam, "Revolution on the Border: The U.S. Army in the Big Bend and the Battle of Ojinaga, 1913–1914," *West Texas Historical Association Yearbook* 46 (1990): 5–25; and Gerald G. Raun, "Refugees or Prisoners of War: The Internment of a Mexican Federal Army after the Battle of Ojinaga, December 1913–January 1914," *The Journal of Big Bend Studies* 12 (2000): 133–165.

45. Lona Teresa O'Neal Whittington, "The Road of Sorrow: Mexican Refugees Who Fled Pancho Villa through Presidio, Texas, 1913–1914" (M.A. Thesis, Sul Ross State University, Alpine, Texas, 1976): 12.

46. R. A. Brown to Commanding General, Southern Department, Fort Sam Houston, Texas, National Archives, Washington D.C., RG 393, E4439, Box 4, 3172; and Report from Supervising Inspector at El Paso, Texas, to Commissioner General of Immigration, National Archives, December 12, 1913, Washington D.C., RG 85, 53018/71I.

47. Mercado, *Revelaciones Históricas,* 58–59.

48. It seems the immigration agents stationed at Presidio wanted to prevent the purchase of weapons in the United States and therefore asked whether the refugees planned to return to Mexico. The agent noted in his report that a board of inquiry had not been formed to further interrogate any of the refugees as they entered the United States. Evidently, they were not considered a threat. It must be noted that the agents described the refugees as the better classes of Chihuahuans. John F. Carraway to Supervising Inspector, El Paso Texas, December 14, 1913, National Archives, Washington D.C., RG 85, 53108/71I.

49. Inspector Robb's report to the Supervising Inspector at El Paso, Texas, illustrates the desperate measures taken by many refugees to escape the horrors of the Revolution. Their makeshift cities in the United States provided temporary relief. Immigration agents at Presidio persuaded refugees to return to Ojinaga, assuring them they [refugees] could return to Presidio once Ojinaga was attacked. U.S. authorities were temporarily successful, but many of the refugees returned once the *villistas* began an offensive on Ojinaga. J. W. Berkshire to Commissioner-General of Immigration, December 26, 1913, National Archives, Washington, D.C., RG85, 53108/71I; and J. W. Berkshire to Commissioner-General of Immigration, January 29, 1914, National Archives, Washington D.C., RG 85, 53108/71J.

50. Wright, "Starting Over," 195–213.

51. The *Alpine Avalanche* contains numerous articles concerning the expansion of industry in the Big Bend. The construction of the railroad further facilitated such

growth as it made available the transportation of products from the Big Bend to other locations. See *Alpine Avalanche* from 1910 to 1914.

52. General Tasker proposed that the U.S. Army patrol the Mexican side of the border in order to curb the introduction of weapons into the country via the international boundary. U.S. Army Brigadier-General Tasker H. Bliss to Adjutant General of the U.S. Army, April 13, 1913, *Records of the Department of State Relating to the Internal Affairs of Mexico, 1910–1929*, Film 812.00: 7229, RG 25.

Smugglers in Dangerous Times Revolution and Communities in the Tejano Borderlands

GEORGE T. DÍAZ

Late in December 1910, Deputy U.S. Customs Collector Luke Dowe wrote his superiors of a troubling problem he faced in his efforts to prevent illegal arms smuggling on the border. Dowe complained that "ninety-nine percent of the Mexican population residing along the Texas border are in sympathy with the revolutionists as well as a great many of the American ranch-

Postcard photograph of downtown Laredo, Texas, early 1900s. Courtesy Laredo Public Library.

man [sic]."[1] Dowe continued that sympathetic borderlanders were "willing and ready to render them [revolutionists] assistance."[2] Collector Dowe's concerns about borderlanders' complicity in affairs in Mexico were well founded as the Revolution did impact communities on the Texas side.

Between the years of the onset of the Mexican Revolution and the First World War, many Tejanos, as well as some Anglos, broke U.S. law in order to aid the Revolution in Mexico or profit from it. Whereas the United States saw arms smuggling as a violation to its neutrality, those in sympathy with the various movements had few qualms about taking arms illegally across the Rio Grande. Local hardware merchants cashed in by selling arms to all buyers against the desires of the federal government. Support for the Revolution and a desire for personal gain led most Tejanos to accept arms smuggling across the border. Moreover, World War I–related trade restrictions on foodstuffs such as sugar and lard, coupled with food shortages in war, ravaged Mexico and created a market for contraband consumables that sympathetic and entrepreneurial borderlanders readily filled. Border residents' personal and economic motives trumped U.S. prohibitions on arms and food exports and frustrated federal efforts to regulate this trade on the border.

Although a prevalent occurrence, smuggling as an enduring borderlands phenomenon remains underexamined. Scholars such as Peter Andreas have provided insight into contemporary smuggling on the U.S.–Mexico divide, but only a handful of historians have examined the topic of smuggling along the same region. Articles by James Sandos and Gabriela Recio have contributed to the scholarly understanding of drug smuggling across the borderlands in the early twentieth century, and Luz María Hernández Sáenz does an excellent job of showing how a U.S. embargo failed to prevent arms smuggling across the Arizona–Sonora border during the Mexican Revolution. Charles H. Harris and Louis R. Sadler's combined efforts have made significant strides in informing readers of the depths of arms smuggling during the Mexican Revolution and the practice of smuggling rationed foodstuffs, but the topic is far from exhausted. This essay contributes to Mexican American and borderlands scholarship by examining how the Mexican Revolution prompted borderlanders to disregard federal laws by smuggling arms and rationed foodstuffs into Mexico out of sympathy for the revolutionaries and a desire for monetary gain. Moreover, it examines how U.S. federal laws coming out of the Mexican Revolution made ordinary borderlanders into smugglers.[3]

Unraveling the hidden history of smuggling along the lower Rio

Grande borderlands offers a host of challenges. Smugglers themselves sought to avoid detection and became known mostly for the occasions in which they were apprehended. The best smugglers, however, were never caught. Despite these challenges, Mexican and U.S. government attempts to police their borderlands did leave a window into smugglers' "secret trades."[4]

Revolutionary Smuggling

The Mexican Revolution did not stay in Mexico; it spilled north of the border. Supporters of various factions worked to aid their compatriots from bases in the United States. Francisco Madero's call appealed to many of his countrymen in the United States, who chose to support the Revolution by smuggling arms. Late in December of 1910, Luther Ellsworth, U.S. Consul in Ciudad Porfirio Díaz (Piedras Negras), reported that Madero's "rebellion is very popular in the border on the American side where there are thousands of Mexicans, a great number possessing rifles and ammunition."[5] Ellsworth further warned that "Mexicans are crossing [arms], not only at El Paso, Texas, but at many other points up and down the line."[6] U.S. Customs agents did work to prevent arms smuggling, but stopping determined arms smugglers proved difficult.[7] U.S. Customs agents reported a typical case of clandestine activity early in 1911. In January of that year, Deputy Collector Dowe and several other Mounted Inspectors investigated a report of a wagon carrying contraband arms being smuggled into Mexico thirty miles west of Del Rio. Dowe and the other agents searched for several days before coming to a partially burnt heap of empty UMC cartridge boxes at the Rio Grande's edge. Inspectors' subsequent search of a nearby ranch uncovered one horse, two rifles, and 144 cartridges that they believed the smugglers had left behind. Customs agents seized the property and filed a report.[8]

The United States and Mexico stationed federal forces on their shared borderlands specifically to protect their territory and police arms trafficking. Additional U.S. Calvary units patrolled the border as early as January 1911. On March 3, 1911, a small biplane took off from Ft. McIntosh just outside Laredo on a surveillance mission along the border to Eagle Pass. The Army pilots may not have seen signs of traffickers or enemy movements that day, but their flight became the first service mission in U.S. military aviation.[9] The largest force of Texas Rangers assembled until that time arrived in Laredo in the fall of 1911, after hearing that Bernardo Reyes, a former general under President Porfirio Díaz, planned to use the town as a base against Mexico's new president Francisco Madero. Anti-Reyes forces tipped off U.S. authorities of a cache of arms secreted near the Texas-Mexican railroad depot. The information proved accurate. U.S. Customs officers and Rangers uncovered sixteen Mauser rifles along with several boxes of ammunition on November 20, 1911. Nor were those arms all authorities uncovered that day. Texas Rangers captured a Mexican Army Captain along with sixty dynamite bombs nearby. Texas Rangers and other American forces would go on to seize at least 152 horses, twenty-one thousand cartridges, and over one hundred rifles during their heightened occupation of Laredo that fall.[10]

Tejanos sometimes used American forces to aid their favorite revolutionary faction. Although anti-Madero forces controlled Nuevo Laredo in 1911, Madero's promise of a democratic Mexico had gained him supporters in *los dos Laredos. Maderistas* could and did inform American authorities of their enemies' activities when possible. The information that resulted in the seizure on November 20, 1911, of a bounty of sixteen Mauser rifles and a large quantity of ammunition that Reyistas had hidden in a field outside of town, for instance, came from a young ethnic Mexican boy who informed a U.S. Customs inspector.[11] In the uncertain atmosphere of the Mexican Revolution, even the hated *rinche* (a term Tejanos applied generally to U.S. peace officers) could prove an ally.[12]

Government investigations into arms trafficking through Laredo revealed the complexity of arms smuggling and its place within local perceptions of criminality. Rather than discovering mounted bandits, authorities found local Tejano elites involved in weapons smuggling. Suspect Amador Sánchez descended from one of Laredo's founding families. Sánchez served as Laredo's mayor from 1901–1910, and at the time of his arrest served as the sheriff for Webb County. Sánchez's sympathies resided with Mexican expatriate Bernardo Reyes's plot against Madero's government. Investigators found that Sánchez had used the county jail as storeroom for weapons destined to be smuggled to Mexico, and on November 16, 1911, a local grand jury indicted him for conspiracy to violate the neutrality laws of the United States.[13] Although Sánchez pled guilty, the former political boss never saw the inside of a jail cell. The court fined Sánchez $1,200 for his role in the plot, which he promptly paid and returned to work as the county sheriff. Although several of Sheriff Sánchez's coconspirators could not afford to pay their fines and were ordered to incarceration, Sánchez used his power to grant his friends special privileges such as allowing them to go home at night.[14] Political rivalries among other members of the local elite eventually dethroned Sánchez in 1914, but it is significant that a convicted felon could remain county sheriff and president of the Webb County school board. Sánchez's political ties were substantial enough to secure him a presidential pardon in May 1912, five months after his conviction. Sánchez's recovery from his conviction for violating U.S. neutrality laws is more than an example of local corruption; it illustrates locals' tolerance of arms smuggling.[15]

Neutrality Violations

Arms trafficking may have captured headlines, but it is important to remember that less conspicuous U.S. neutrality laws also shaped the lives of ordinary borderlanders. National and international crises affected federal border polices in ways that border peoples deemed problematic. Francisco Madero may have succeeded in ousting Porfirio Díaz in May 1911, but Madero's new government itself faced a series of revolts. Early in 1912, Pascual Orozco, a military commander who had once supported Madero, rebelled against the embattled president and further plunged the border into crisis. In response to such ongoing turmoil, the U.S. Congress passed a resolution prohibiting the export of arms or ammunition to any country in the hemisphere where conditions of domestic unrest prevailed. Late in February 1913, Tejano Pedro Villarreal knowingly or unknowingly violated the resolution when he attempted to take a .22-caliber rifle and three hundred rounds of ammunition across the border into Mexico. Although it is highly unlikely that Villarreal took his .22-caliber Savage rifle to wage war in Mexico, American neutrality laws were not only strict, but strictly enforced. The court ordered Villarreal to jail after he defaulted on his $500 bail.[16]

Historians can only imagine Villarreal's thoughts over his ordeal. Did he understand that by carrying a rifle and ammunition across the river he violated an American presidential proclamation and U.S. federal law? Records do not indicate how federal agents discovered Villarreal. Did he try to cross the border at the bridge, or did federal authorities arrest him as he tried to ford the river? Did Villarreal hide the rifle and the ammunition, or did he carry them openly, unaware that crossing arms, even those for personal use, ran contrary to American policy? That Villarreal had approval from Nuevo Laredo's Colonel Jefe de Armas (Chief of Arms) to transfer the rifle to his own residence in Nuevo Laredo did nothing to excuse his actions in the eyes of American law. Villarreal may have felt his sentence an injustice, but he was pragmatic. A declaration of innocence which ended in a guilty verdict would likely lead to a stiffer sentence than a plea of guilty. Lacking the money for a good attorney, he pled culpable to violating U.S. neutrality laws.[17]

Personal sympathies factored into some arms sales, but the desire to make a profit motivated numerous transactions. Actually, even before Madero's call to arms in November 1910, Díaz opponents engaged in the trafficking of military merchandise. U.S. gun merchants cashed in by running ads in border papers. On September 20, 1910, U.S. Consul Ellsworth complained of an American arms company's troubling ad in a prominent Spanish-language paper. Translated, the ad read, "Do you want a good rifle? Remember that an unarmed man is of no value. Write today . . . It is our desire that each Mexican has [sic] a rifle."[18]

Illicit arms deliveries to revolutionaries once conflict erupted came from complicit American merchants. Legal loopholes hamstrung U.S. law enforcement efforts to prevent arms smuggling. Neutrality laws forbade the vending of arms to foreign nations in states of domestic unrest, for instance, but Laredo's historic ties to Mexico made it difficult for Tejanos to consider their neighboring country as a "foreign nation." Though U.S. neutrality laws made it illegal to attempt crossing arms and munitions into Mexico, buyers could still purchase arms legally. Thus, unless officers uncovered plans of a conspiracy or encountered suspects in the very act of smuggling, they had no case. As to be expected, arms smugglers exploited this weakness. On October 15, 1910, Ellsworth noted in his dispatches that Texas merchants were already "doing quite a business in 30–30 Winchester Rifles and Cartridges . . . and it is of the opinion of several of our . . . Officers that they are purchased by friends of the Revolutionists in Mexico."[19] Ellsworth stated that anti-Díaz conspirators took these arms to "out of the way places" and "after nightfall smuggled [them] across the border."[20] Customs Collector Robert Dowe complained that merchants, both Anglo and those of Mexican descent, made it a "practice to supply all comers with arms and cartridges even when aware they were used for revolutionary purposes."[21] U.S. government agents noted that arms sales on the border were to such an extent that local hardware stores had trouble keeping up with demand.[22] Manuel Guerra, the proprietor of Guerra & Son of Roma, Texas, engaged in arms dealings so extensive that the Mexican government took note. Late in September 1912, Alberto Leal, the Mexican Consul in Rio Grande City wrote his superiors that U.S. Customs had recently seized three thousand rounds of .30–.30 shells consigned to "Manuel Guerra, a mexicotexano who is always involved in our civil difficulties to profit from the sale of arms and horses."[23] Aside from the seizure, Leal warned that he was informed that Guerra awaited another order of two thousand rounds of .30–.30 shells and over ten thousand rounds of other assorted ammo.[24]

Although American arms shipments to Mexico may have been forbidden, arms orders in Laredo increased as local merchants became international arms dealers: hardware stores became small armories as legitimate businessmen became outfitters for anyone with money to buy. Joseph Netzer decorated his show window in downtown Laredo with life-sized models of Remington arms' trademark bear cubs, "armed to the teeth" with rifles they held in their paws.[25] In late September 1913, a Bureau of Investigation agent operating in Laredo looked deeper into Netzer's disturbingly large arms orders. Investigations revealed that Netzer sold nine thousand rounds of seven-millimeter ammunition to a Mexican citizen and that Netzer had placed an additional request for one hundred and sixty .30–.30 rifles and seven thousand shells. The .30–.30s could be used for sport, although they were more likely used for war. Seven-millimeter rounds, indeed, were strictly military-grade ammunition commonly used in machine guns. Nor was this the limit of Netzer's enterprises. An examination of Netzer's account books disclosed that he sold 20,000 seven-millimeter cartridges for $784,000 on a single day in October of that year. Netzer claimed he could not remember the name of the man who made the procurement, only that he had paid in cash. The Bureau of Investigation, delving into railroad shipping records, revealed that in addition to Netzer's shipments of guns and ammo, he also received blasting caps and explosives for which he could not account. Investigators further discovered that Netzer sold his arms to a local grocer who worked as a middleman for Mexican arms buyers.[26]

The U.S. government's efforts to impose its will on the borderlands foundered because its policy conflicted with local sympathies and the aims of border peoples. Jurors heard this seemingly compelling evidence against Netzer, yet refused to indict him. Although Netzer had clearly broken federal law, his illegal arms sales had not offended community values. Locals did not seem to have seen Netzer as a smuggler at all. Netzer did not transport contraband across the border; he sold merchandise out of his establishment. He was a prominent businessman who had migrated from Germany as a young man and had served in the army before starting a life in Laredo; breaking national laws simply made his business more profitable.[27] No matter what the law said, locals did not see selling prohibited arms destined to be smuggled as a punishable crime. Even Mayor Robert M. McComb was rumored to have sold arms to persons of dubious nationality.[28] Indicted neutrality violators and suspected illicit arms dealers like Netzer and others like him did not serve prison sentences and continued to be active in their communities. Netzer reprised his role as the President of the Washington Birthday Celebration Association (WBCA), the community's largest and most lucrative festival, in 1914.[29] Subsequent probes by the Bureau of Investigation into Netzer's questionable sale of pistol ammunition in 1919 did not prevent him from continuing to serve as president of the WBCA until 1923.[30] Charlie Deutz, whose gun ads routinely competed with those of Netzer, would go on to serve as the President of the WBCA in 1930.[31] That Netzer and others overcame their charges indicates that illicit trade could be part of licit business in the borderlands and that smuggling, even in some cases gun smuggling, could be acceptable in locals' eyes if done to support a popular cause.[32]

World War I Export Violations

Federal power not only sought to prevent the export of arms but also to keep certain staples in the country. During the First World War, the U.S. government restricted from export a litany of produce and consumer goods necessary to America's war effort. As to be expected, this prohibition did not slake borderlanders' need for these items. In actuality, it likely increased demand. Years of war devastated Mexico's national infrastructure and left the country in chronic need of basic foodstuffs and material goods. Bureau of Investigation agents monitoring the border observed that conditions along the lower Rio Grande were desperate. Late in December 1917, Bureau of Investigation Agent M. E. Parker reported that along the Mexican side of the border the prices for "groceries of every kind were high," forty-pound sacks of flour sold for $7.00 gold, two pounds of lard sold for $3.50, while sugar and corn were "very scarce."[33] On January 13, 1918, the *Laredo Weekly Times* commented there was "much need in Mexico. Almost every item of food is scarce and some articles cannot be had at all without importing them from this country."[34]

The U.S. prohibition on the exportation on certain foodstuffs and their scarcity in Mexico created a particular market for contraband sugar. On February 12, 1918, U.S. Customs agents John Chamberlain and Robert

Rumsey apprehended Mauricio Carreno smuggling six 100-pound sacks of sugar out of the United States without a license from the War Trade Bureau. For this transgression, the court sentenced Carreno to serve ten days in the Webb County jail.[35] Carreno's operations were small compared to those of Juan Lozano and Jacinto Esquamia, who attempted to sneak one thousand pounds of sugar and four hundred pounds of lard out of the United States. The court's sentence of twenty days in county jail seemed a small deterrent to determined traffickers.[36] Sugar smuggling was so lucrative *contrabandistas* devised elaborate ruses to get their goods across. Early in February 1918, U.S. Customs agents working in Laredo became suspicious of a Mexican man making frequent wagon trips across the border. Upon stopping him, agents discovered a false compartment at the bottom of a can of gasoline containing twenty-five pounds of contraband sugar. That the suspect claimed to have done the work on behalf of another suggests that U.S. trade prohibitions and Mexican needs had transformed the sugar trade on the border into a profitable organized activity.[37]

U.S. war restrictions also adversely affected unsuspecting members of the pastoral economy. Pedro Benavides, Refugio Domínguez, and Eulalio Palacios were not traffickers but area ranchers. On February 1, 1918, the trio became smugglers in the eyes of Customs agents when they unlawfully transported four bulls into Mexico. Bulls had been on the War Trade Bureau's conservation list since October 1917, and could not be taken out of the country without a license. Whether out of ignorance, laziness, or spite, the three did not obtain the necessary documentation. U.S. Customs agents arrested them, an examining trial held each of them on a $500 bond, which they failed to meet, and the three went to jail.[38]

Given the scarcity in Mexico, it is reasonable to assume that many Tejanas/os smuggled foodstuffs out of necessity or pity for those in need, but given suspects' scale of operations it seems more likely that many smuggled out of greed. Take, for example, the case of Macedonio García, who seems to have trafficked restricted staples as part of his wholesale grocery business in Matamoros, Tamaulipas, across from Brownsville. Unlike other foodstuff smuggling cases that depended on arresting officers' testimony, the government's case against García rested on the word of local witnesses. Six Brownsville merchants testified that over the course of eleven days late in the fall of 1917, García unlawfully exported some $8,282 worth of rationed sugar and lard into Mexico using a variety of third-party buyers so as not to arouse the inquiry of U.S. Customs forces. Further Treasury Department investigations revealed that the "malevolent practice" of subtly crossing sizeable amounts of contraband foodstuffs as part of larger trafficking missions could be "encountered anywhere there is a settlement between Eagle Pass and Point Isabel."[39]

U.S. trade restrictions created a demand for many other types of prohibited American consumer goods in Mexico. Antonio Rojano and Anslemo Chapa saw the niche in the market and on February 2, 1918, tried to smuggle a vast assortment of restricted commodities, including seventeen woolen suits, eighty-eight leather shoes, and 109 pieces of roofing tin weighing 214 pounds.[40] On January 18, 1918, U.S. Customs agents apprehended José Guerra, unlawfully exporting six leather purses, seven boxes of chewing gum, twenty-four yards of cotton mull, and three dozen silk ties out of the United States into Mexico.[41] Although what Rojano, Chapa, and Guerra attempted to export were victimless consumer products, federal forces arrested and indicted them because the U.S. government saw Rojano and his companions' trafficking as undermining the war effort on the home front. In truth, however, their offense was not so much taking banned items out of the United States, but boldly engaging in large-scale ventures. Rojano, Chapa, and Guerra were traffickers, perhaps merchant dealers, but they got greedy. It is important to note that in the considerable boxes of case files examined in this research, no casual smugglers of prohibited export items appear. Customs officials and the court do not seem to have prosecuted persons who confined themselves to exporting prohibited items for personal use. Taking restricted goods out of the country does not seem to have been the crime. What constituted a punishable criminal act was exporting prohibited items commercially. Locals, however, did not seem to see Rojano and his companions' operations as criminal. Only the Customs agents involved in the cased testified against them, and a local jury acquitted the defendants.[42]

Illegal commerce to Mexico was so extensive by the end of the decade that associations of smugglers carved out mercantile slots for themselves along the lower Rio Grande. On February 24, 1920, J. Rábago, Mexico's Vice Consul in Hidalgo, warned of an "Association of Contrabandistas" dominating the town of Reynosa, Tamaulipas.[43] Although Rábago conceded that it is "certain that there is smuggling across all borders, in Reynosa, it is virtually the only profession."[44] In Reynosa, the Consul continued, there is a "band of smugglers, an Association" made up of sixty-eight individuals led by four brothers. Rábago stated that the Association was well organized and held regular meetings to discuss company matters. In truth, the Association operated just like a business, although an illicit one. Principally the Association made money trafficking livestock, wax, cinnamon, whiskey, and other consumer goods around federal tariffs and trade prohibitions. Rábago estimated that the Association's activities defrauded the Mexican government of $200,000 worth of revenue annually. Moreover, Rábago warned that in Reynosa "no one voted except those 68 in the band of contrabandistas; and in this way they control the municipality."[45] Simón González, one of the four brothers heading the Association, even served as the town's *presidente*. With smugglers wielding such influence and trafficking popularly desired items, Rábago wrote that along the border "it is not a discredit to be a smuggler, even though he is an evildoer."[46]

Conclusion

The Mexican Revolution thrust upon border people difficult choices between obeying or violating U.S. and Mexican law. Whether out of genuine sympathy or a desire for personal gain, many border people—Tejano, Mexicano, and Anglo—chose to disregard federal laws to support revolutionary forces in Mexico. Anglo arms merchants desiring to profit from war in Mexico and sympathetic Tejanos both violated U.S. national law by conducting illicit trade in support of revolutionary groups in Mexico. Aside from arms trafficking, ethnic Mexicans from both sides of the Rio Grande smuggled rationed food stuffs into blighted Mexico. Despite its illegality, Tejanos largely tolerated this illegal trade because it supported popular factions in Mexico and aided people in need. U.S. vigilance against neutrality violations and war trade prohibitions not only failed to deter the trafficking of guns and rationed goods, it spurred a highly profitable illegal arms and rationed foodstuff trade and contributed significantly to the rise of organized bands of smugglers on the border.

Notes

1. Deputy Collector Luke Dowe to The Collector of Customs, Eagle Pass, Texas. December 27, 1910, Letters Sent to the Collector of Customs at Eagle Pass, DL 1 A-32–8–6, NARA., Fort Worth.

2. Ibid.

3. Peter Andreas, *Border Games: Policing the U.S.–Mexico Divide* (Ithaca: Cornell University Press, 2000); Luz María Hernández Sáenz, "Smuggling for the Revolution: Illegal Trafficking of Arms on the Arizona–Sonora Border, 1912–1914," *Arizona and*

the West 28 (Winter 1986): 357–377; James A. Sandos, "Northern Separatism during the Mexican Revolution: An Inquiry into the Role of Drug Trafficking, 1919–1920," *The Americas* 41 (1984): 191–214; Gabriela Recio, "Drugs and Alcohol: U.S. Prohibition and the Origins of the Drug Trade in Mexico, 1910–1930," *Journal of Latin American Studies* 34, (2002): 21–42; and Charles H. Harris II and Louis R. Sadler, *The Secret War in El Paso: Mexican Revolutionary Intrigue, 1906–1920* (Albuquerque: University of New Mexico Press, 2009).

4. Given the fragmented nature of sources on illicit trade, statistical analysis of smuggling would be conjectural, therefore this essay rests on an interpretive analysis of accused smuggling cases. For more on the subject of illicit trade, see Alan L. Karras, *Smuggling: Contraband and Corruption in World History* (New York: Rowman & Littlefield, 2009); Moisés Naím, *Illicit: How Smugglers, Traffickers, and Copycats Are Hijacking the Global Economy* (New York: Anchor Books, 2005); Eric Tagliacozzo, *Secret Trades, Porous Borders: Smuggling and States along a Southeast Asian Frontier, 1865–1915* (New Haven, Conn.: Yale University Press, 2005); and William van Schendel and Itty Abraham, eds., *Illicit Flows and Criminal Things: States, Borders, and the Other Side of Globalization* (Indianapolis: Indiana University Press, 2005).

5. Luther Ellsworth to The Honorable Secretary of State, Ciudad Porfirio Díaz. December 25, 1910, Records of the Department of State Relating to the Internal Affairs of Mexico, 1910–1929, Reel 10.

6. Luther Ellsworth to The Honorable Secretary of State, Ciudad Porfirio Díaz, December 24, 1910, Records of the Department of State Relating to the Internal Affairs of Mexico, 1910–1929, Reel 10.

7. U.S. law over arms exports was a web of confusion. American neutrality law forbade the outfitting of an army or expedition against a friendly power, but not the sale of arms. Technically, anyone could legally purchase as many arms as desired and export them. However, U.S. officials on the border, such as Consul Luther Ellsworth, did direct Customs agents to intercept arms exports to Mexico. Various Presidential embargoes such as those instated by William H. Taft and Woodrow Wilson did make it illegal to export arms into Mexico later in the decade. Despite early confusion over the letter of the law, U.S. Customs agents on the border knew the sentiment of their government and worked to prevent arms exports of all kinds. Michael Dennis Carman, *United States Customs and the Madero Revolution* (El Paso: Texas Western Press, 1976), 33; and Hernández Sáenz, "Smuggling for the Revolution," 358.

8. Deputy Collector Luke Dowe to The Collector of Customs at Eagle Pass, Texas, Jan. 16, 1911, Records of the Department of State Relating to the Internal Affairs of Mexico, 1910–1929, Reel 10. Scattered newspaper reports, U.S. State Department, Bureau of Investigation, and the Secretaría de Relaciones Exteriores records indicate prevalent arms smuggling across the border into Mexico, but in most cases arms smug-

glers seem to have evaded U.S. authorities. With the notable exception of a group of arms smugglers capturing two county law enforcement agents near Carrizo Springs, torturing and killing one of them, arms smuggling was a discrete affair with few violent encounters. "Fought Smugglers on Soil of Texas," *Laredo Weekly Times,* Laredo, Texas, (September 14, 1913); and Harris and Sadler, *The Secret War in El Paso,* 87–89.

9. James Garza, "On the Edge of a Storm: Laredo and the Mexican Revolution, 1910–1917" (M.A. thesis., Texas A&M International University, 1996), 29.

10. Garza, "On the Edge of a Storm," 35–36; Charles Harris III and Louis Sadler, "The 1911 Reyes Conspiracy: The Texas Side," *Southwestern Historical Quarterly* 83 (April 1980): 325–48; and "Startling Developments Follow Indictments By the Grand Jury," *Laredo Weekly Times* (November 26, 1911).

11. "Startling Developments Follow Indictments By the Grand Jury," *Laredo Weekly Times* (November 26, 1911). Perhaps because he married a local ethnic Mexican woman and started a family in Laredo, Customs Inspector Rumsey was particularly adept at securing informants against alleged neutrality violators. Late in December 1917, an informant provided Rumsey with information on thirty individuals organizing a band to invade Mexico from the United States. J. J. Lawrence, "Prudencio Miranda, General Cuéllar, and Col. Braniff Alleged Vio. Neutrality Laws" (December 25, 1917), Investigative Records Relating to Mexican Neutrality Violations ("Mexican Files"), Investigative Case Files of the Bureau of Investigation, 1908–1922, 1909–1921, National Archives and Records Administration [hereafter, "Mexican Files"]. In this essay, the term "ethnic Mexican" refers to persons of Mexican descent who could be either U.S. or Mexican citizens.

12. *Rinche* is an extremely negative term for a U.S. law enforcement agent. Although most often used to refer to Texas Rangers, noted Tejano scholar Américo Paredes informs, and the author's own investigations confirm, that ethnic Mexicans often labeled other groups of U.S. law enforcement personnel *rinches.* Américo Paredes, *With His Pistol in His Hand: A Border Ballad and Its Hero* (Austin: University of Texas Press, 1958), 24.

13. Garza, "On the Edge of a Storm," 35; and Harris and Sadler, "The 1911 Reyes Conspiracy," 331.

14. Harris and Sadler, "The 1911 Reyes Conspiracy," 338.

15. Harris and Sadler, "The 1911 Reyes Conspiracy, " 341; and Movimentos Revolucionarios en Tejas y Otros Puntos Contra el Gobierno de la Republica, LE 719, Leg 3, Secretaría de Relaciones Exteriores, Mexico City.

16. *The United States v. Pedro Villarreal,* Western District Court of Texas Criminal Case Files for Laredo. A-20–51–2 NARA, Fort Worth; Hernández Sáenz, "Smuggling for the Revolution," 358; and Michael C. Meyer et al., *The Course of Mexican History* (New York: Oxford University Press, 1999), 496–97.

17. *The United States v. Pedro Villarreal,* Western District Court of Texas Criminal Case Files for Laredo, A-20–51–2 NARA, Fort Worth. For more on guilty pleas, see, F. Arturo Rosales, *Pobre Raza! Violence, Justice, and Mobilization among México LIndo Immigrants, 1900–1936* (Austin: University of Texas Press, 1999), 124; and Charles L. Zelden, *Justice Lies in the District: The U.S. District Court, Southern District of Texas, 1902–1960* (College Station: Texas A&M University Press, 1993), 65.

18. Luther Ellsworth to The Honorable Secretary of State, Ciudad Porfirio Díaz. September 20, 1910. Records of the Department of State Relating to the Internal Affairs of Mexico, 1910–1929, Reel 10.

19. Luther Ellsworth to The Honorable Secretary of State, Ciudad Porfirio Díaz, October 15, 1910, Records of the Department of State Relating to the Internal Affairs of Mexico, 1910–1929, Reel 10.

20. Collector R. W. Dowe to Honorable Luther T. Ellsworth, Ciudad Porfirio Díaz, October 15, 1910; and Luther Ellsworth to The Honorable Secretary of State, Ciudad Porfirio Díaz, October 15, 1910. In Records of the Department of State Relating to the Internal Affairs of Mexico, 1910–1929.

21. Luther Ellsworth to The Honorable Secretary of State, Ciudad Porfirio Díaz, December 5, 1910, Records of the Department of State Relating to the Internal Affairs of Mexico, 1910–1929, Reel 10.

22. Dorothy Pierson Kerig, *Luther T. Ellsworth: U.S. Consul on the Border during the Mexican Revolution* (El Paso: Texas Western Press, 1975), 36. For an excellent examination of U.S. security forces efforts to investigate neutrality violations, see José A. Ramírez, *To the Line of Fire: Mexican Texans and World War I* (College Station: Texas A&M University Press, 2009).

23. Mendoza y Vizcano, Servicio Consular Mexicano, September 25, 1912, in Movimento Revolucionario, LE 830, Leg 30, Secretaría de Relaciones Exteriores, Mexico City.

24. Ibid.

25. "An Attractive Display," *Laredo Weekly Times* (November 23, 1913).

26. Garza, "On the Edge of a Storm," 48–49.

27. For more information on Joseph Netzer and other businessmen and women on the border, see Alicia M. Dewey, "Risk and Opportunity on the U.S./Mexico Border: Credit, Bankruptcy, and the Emergence of the Anglo and Mexican-American Middle Classes in South Texas, 1898–1941" (Ph.D. diss., Southern Methodist University, 2007), 171; and Elliott Young, "Red Men, Princess Pocahontas, and George Washington: Harmonizing Race Relations in Laredo at the Turn of the Century," *Western Historical Quarterly* 29 (Spring 1998): 57.

28. Garza, "On the Edge of a Storm," 48–49; and J. B. Wilkinson, *Laredo and the Rio Grande Frontier* (Austin: Jenkins Publishing Co. 1975), 395.

29. Stan Green, ed., *A History of the Washington Birthday's Celebration* (Laredo: Border Studies Publishing, 1999), 152. For more on the George Washington's Birthday celebration, see Young, "Red Men, Princess Pocahontas, and George Washington."

30. J. J. Lawrence, Jan. 18, 1919, *Smuggled Ammunition,* "Mexican Files"; and Green, *A History of the Washington's Birthday Celebration,* 152.

31. Green, *A History of the Washington's Birthday Celebration,* 152. For Mexican investigations into Deutz's arms sales, see Revolución Mexicana, LE 718, Leg 1, Secretaría de Relaciones Exteriores, Mexico City.

32. Local elites' involvement in illicit arms dealing occurred along the U.S.–Mexico border. Adolph Krakauer knowingly sold untold quantities of arms to revolutionaries yet served as the President of the El Paso Chamber of Commerce. Harris and Sadler, *The Secret War in El Paso,* 87. Complaints of locals' complicity in arms sales extended to the Mexican government. In the summer of 1913, A. M. Lozano, a Mexican consul inspector monitoring arms sales on the border complained that authorities in Laredo did not cooperate in investigations because they "sympathize notoriously with the Carranza movement," Revolución Mexicana, LE 718, Leg 1, Secretaría de Relaciones Exteriores, Mexico City.

33. In re Conditions in Monterrey, Mexico, M. E. Parker, Brownsville, Texas, December 20, 1917, Investigative Records Relating to Mexican Neutrality Violations, "Mexican Files."

34. "Evading Export Laws," *Laredo Weekly Times* (Jan. 13, 1918).

35. *The United States v. Mauricio Carreno,* Western District Court of Texas Criminal Case Files for Laredo, A-20–51–2 NARA, Fort Worth.

36. *The United States v. Juan Lozano and Jacinto Esquamia,* Western District Court of Texas Criminal Case Files for Laredo, A-20–51–2 NARA, Fort Worth.

37. "Clever Smuggling Stunt Unearthed by Inspector," *Laredo Weekly Times* (February 3, 1918).

38. *The United States v. Pedro Benavides et al.,* Western District Court of Texas Criminal Case Files for Laredo. A-20–51–2 NARA., Fort Worth; and "Trio Mexicans Arrested Charged With Smuggling," *Laredo Weekly Times* (February 10, 1918).

39. "García Case Law Evasion is one of the Most Typical," *Laredo Weekly Times* (Jan. 13, 1918). For more on low-level "ant" or "armpit" smugglers, see Paul Nugent, *Smugglers, Secessionists & Loyal Citizens on the Ghana–Togo Frontier: The Lie of the Borderlands since 1914* (Athens: Ohio University Press, 2002); Silvia Rivera Cusicanqui, "'Here, Even the Legislators Chew Them': Coca Leaves and Identity Politics in Northern Argentina," in *Illicit Flows and Criminal Things,* eds. Willem van Schendel and Itty Abraham (Bloomington: Indiana University Press, 2005); and Mélissa Gauthier, "Fayuca Hormiga: The Cross-Border Trade of Used Clothing between the United States and

Mexico," in *Borderlands: Comparing Border Security in North America and Europe,* ed. Emmanuel Brunet-Jailly (Ottawa: University of Ottawa Press, 2007), 95.

40. *The United States v. Antonio Rojano and Anslemo Chapa,* Western District Court of Texas Criminal Case Files for Laredo, A-20–51–2 NARA, Fort Worth.

41. *The United States v. José Guerra,* Western District Court of Texas Criminal Case Files for Laredo, A-20–51–2 NARA, Fort Worth.

42. *The United States v. Antonio Rojano and Anslemo Chapa,* Western District Court of Texas Criminal Case Files for Laredo, A-20–51–2 NARA, Fort Worth. Of the numerous cases examined during the war years, no suspects were charged in unlawfully exporting rationed items in small amounts. Western District Court of Texas Criminal Case Files for Laredo, A-20–51–2 NARA, Fort Worth.

43. Asociación de Contrabandistas, En Reynosa, Tamp, Topografica 17–20–272, Secretaría de Relaciones Exteriores, Mexico City.

44. Ibid.

45. Ibid.

46. Ibid.

Eureka! The Mexican Revolution in African American Context, 1910–1920

GERALD HORNE AND MARGARET STEVENS

"Good Lord!" exclaimed President Woodrow Wilson when his secretary of state, Robert Lansing, told him about the "authentic" evidence of a German-Mexican plot that was uncovered by British authorities concerning the "Zimmerman Telegram" of 1917. In the midst of World War I, this telegram revealed an alleged German-Mexican plan to retake territory seized by the United States from Mexico in the war of 1846. The

Soldiers of the U.S. Tenth Cavalry Regiment, June 21, 1916. Courtesy New Mexico State University Library, Archives and Special Collections.

German diplomat, Zimmerman, "frankly acknowledged that the message, as printed, was genuine and attempted to justify his sending it," thereby strengthening U.S. resolve to enter World War I against Germany, in part to thwart any potential trouble on the Mexican border that might be fomented by German aggressors.[1]

President Wilson's fears brought on by the Zimmerman Telegram were also the result of lingering apprehensions about Mexican and Mexican American plans to revolt against specific regions in Texas and across the southwestern portion of the United States as part of the 1915 *Plan de San Diego.* Notably, this plan was predicated in part on the promise of securing an independent state—or states for that matter—to dissident African Americans who would agree to support the radical Mexicans' effort in overthrowing U.S. territorial acquisitions that had been won from the Mexican government in the decades before. The plan "called for Mexicans and Mexican Americans to rise up against American authorities on the Texas side of the border, to declare their independence from the United States and then to invade the rest of Texas, New Mexico, Arizona, California, and Wyoming." In addition, the plan sought to subsequently annex six states currently in the United States that would, in turn, be rendered over to African Americans as a basis for their own independent republic— a goal that anticipated by several decades the Communist Party's call for an independent "Black Belt" in the U.S. South that would be led by black workers in the process of realizing their right to self-determination, according to the Leninist doctrine of the time. Another group of oppressed national minorities, the Apaches, were supposedly "to be given back their lost lands, and all white American males over age of sixteen were to be killed."[2]

Needless to say the *Plan De San Diego* never came to fruition. However, the historical role of African Americans who supported Mexicans in revolt against the empire hovering to the north, and reciprocally, the role of Mexicans in inspiring and at times directly supporting African American revolt against a white supremacist government to which they were subjects, is often obscured in narratives about U.S.–Mexican relations during the revolutionary era. This essay addresses two fundamental issues with regard to the Mexican Revolution: how Mexico played an important role in shaping the experiences of African Americans prior to, during, and after the Revolution, and how the revolutionary government helped radicalize African American communities across the border in Texas. Indeed, the relationship between the Mexican Revolution and African Americans living in the region north of Mexico—particularly those inhabiting Texas—forms an integral component of this narrative about Tejanos and the Mexican Revolution.

Mexico was historically a place for African American refuge from and protest against Jim Crow, the racially based system of white ruling class hegemony predicated upon the economic, political, and social oppression of black people in the United States. In the antebellum United States, thousands of enslaved Africans fled south to Mexico rather than north to Canada. Even Africans who were not enslaved sought refuge in Mexico. For example, in 1857 Luis N. Fouche, a free African American from Florida, had established a colony named Eureka near Tampico. That same year, forty other—presumably free—African Americans from Florida settled near Vera Cruz.[3]

During the postbellum period, African American migration to Mexico persisted and at times surpassed the movement to Mexico during slavery, primarily in the aftermath of the defeat of Radical Reconstruction and its efforts toward granting socioeconomic gains to former slaves. The family background of famed poet and leftist Langston Hughes reveals this history of African American migration to Mexico in the postbellum period. More particularly, Langston Hughes's father is a testament to the exodus to Mexico of African Americans in the aftermath of the defeat of Reconstruction. According to Hughes, his father wanted to go "where a colored man could get ahead and make money quicker, and my mother did not want to go. My father went to Cuba, and then to Mexico, where there wasn't any color line, or any Jim Crow." Also there was a colony of black people from Alabama in Mexico in the 1890s; in fact, there were "ten large colonies." A Mexican official told them that Mexico would be "their Canaan, the land of hope and promise, where they would find relief from the persecution of southern whites." Although this characterization of Mexico as a "Canaan" for African Americans was only partially accurate, it was indeed the case that Mexico often afforded them opportunities toward economic and social advancement that were not made as readily available in the "colossus to the North."[4]

This is not to romanticize the place of Mexico as simply a haven for black racial solidarity in the struggle against white supremacy, because black military involvement in struggles against Mexico during the revolutionary era directly undermined this radical process. As early as 1877,

"Mexicans and Tejanos . . . began to riot, looting homes and villages with cries of 'kill all Americans' and 'death to the gringos'" in El Paso, Texas, only to be suppressed brutally by black soldiers in this period that were referred to as the "Buffalo Soldiers." But pervasive anti-American sentiment along the border toward "all Americans," including African American soldiers, sporadically morphed into racially-based anti-Anglo hostility that amalgamated the causes of black, brown and red, in this case the latter signifying Native Americans.[5]

In the period following the abolition of slavery in the United States, a surge of antiracist mobilization sparked by Radical Reconstruction in the south and abolitionist progressives in the north was counteracted by a white supremacist ruling class that sought to maintain a racial hierarchy in the United States with zero tolerance for people of color ascendency, especially in Texas. It is now widely acknowledged that fears of a "multiracial coalition of blacks, Indians and Mexicans had accompanied the first Anglo settlers to Texas and remained a continuing source of anxiety through the post–Civil War years." These fears were apparently somewhat well founded, for as "the conquest of the Rio Grande reached its final stage, policymakers noticed a change of demeanor in black servicemen, who refused to capitulate to racial discrimination; the same weapons that had opened the frontier to settlement could just as easily be turned on racist whites." Toward the latter part of the nineteenth century, in 1883 to be exact, African Americans in Harrison County, Texas, organized their own militia for self-defense against mob attacks from white racists. In turn, "local whites, with the help of state forces, crushed the movement, but rumors about armed, uniformed blacks provoked paranoiac fears that lasted for months." Well aware of the potential for non-Anglos along the border to join forces in the common cause against white supremacy, U.S. authorities struggling to maintain economic and military predominance within their own borders, much less over their brown neighbors to the south, were met with the recurring question of whether African Americans could "be trusted to fight other people of color."[6]

In point of fact, there were only about fifty-five black people in Duval County in 1880; therefore, any fears on the part of the U.S. elite of black and Mexican racial collusion in opposition to white supremacy would not have been based on the demographic problem of a heavily populated "Black Belt" on the Mexican border. Still, the fact remained that blacks in Texas post-Reconstruction were part of the borderlands population and culture, no matter how small in number, and this presence was a persistent thorn in the side of U.S. business and military enterprises in the period leading up to the Mexican Revolution.

William Ellis from Victoria, Texas, described as a "mulatto," was an "entrepreneur who often claimed Cuban and Mexican origins." By 1896, he was the "first Negro broker" on Wall Street and then considered the "Duke of Harrar, an Ethiopian province" resulting in "two million acres of land" that were "bestowed upon him." He was a broker in NYC with a branch in Mexico City where he "died on a business trip." To Ellis, Mexico was "not only closer but more civilized than Africa. . . . as the Negro is suppressed as he is in the United States . . . the better class of them will seek new fields, and Mexico, standing at the very doors of the United States, offering inducements to all, will prove a welcome home to the Negro."[7]

Ellis reported in 1889 from Mexico City that he had "just received my concessions from the Mexican government for the introduction of (20,000) twenty thousand Afro-American colonists from the southern United States of America into the states of Vera Cruz, Tamaulipas and San Luis Potosoi," and his goal was to utilize "over three million acres of rich lands" thus receiving from the Mexican government "($50) fifty dollars in government bonds bearing (6%) six percent interest" for every "colonist" over twelve years of age. Ellis claimed at this time to have "2000 (two thousand) families ready to start within the next (60) days," and adventure capitalist that he was, he was willing to "furnish all the colonists for the first two years with all necessary farming tools, implements, wagons, also clothing and provisions of every kind" in order to reap his reward from the Mexican government. Although Ellis's ventures never fully materialized, it was precisely this type of space for economic entrepreneurship that the Mexican government carved out for capitalist-minded African Americans who would not live idly under Jim Crow, thus adding to U.S. rulers' unease about Mexican-African American collusion in the postbellum period.[8]

Pre-revolutionary racial intermingling between black Texans and Mexico—though not of a particularly political variety—was especially visible in El Paso, Texas. In 1893 in El Paso, black men were rallying at City Hall, protesting against the enforcement of antimiscegenation law that jeopardized their marriages to their Mexican wives. Many were former soldiers who had come west and had employed Mexican women to "do their washing, which facilitated their becoming intimate with one another. . . . A judge in El Paso threw out the pending cases against these 'mixed' families."[9]

The history of racially mixed Mexican and African American families along the border was indeed a significant factor in shaping black and brown political collusion in the period leading up to the Mexican Revolution. The ancestry of Alva Stevenson, a contemporary in Los Angeles, reveals a maternal grandmother who was Mexican and a native of San José de Gracia, Sinaloa. She had been a cook in the army of General Plutarco Elías Calles during the Revolution. She "met and married Stevenson's grandfather, an African American from Kerr County, Texas . . . he migrated from Texas to Guadalajara at the turn of the century and got a job as a foreman on the railroad. The couple returned to the United States and settled in Nogales, Arizona."[10]

Given the substantial number of African American troops in the region surrounding El Paso, many African American civilians in this vicinity worked mainly for the railway and the military. There were fourteen hundred black people in El Paso in 1910 during the beginning of the Mexican Revolution, out of a population of thirty-seven thousand. Black soldiers in uniform created a funny admixture of racial tension and relative decrease in white supremacy in relationship to the rest of the south. In this way, black business in the El Paso region was more prosperous than normal for African American communities at the time, and this was due in no small part to Mexican patronage of such businesses. In "most places you live in a ghetto, but not in El Paso," said Mrs. Nixon; her husband was a doctor and "his practice was almost entirely Mexican. . . . We used to say it was the United Nations in his office. He had quite a few Philipinos [sic]. . . . The most he ever charged was $2 for an office call and $4 for a house call." This cultivation of black business enterprise in the wake of the Mexican Revolution—though hardly radical in itself—became a key component of left-wing and black radical movements that incorporated such notable figures as radical heavyweight pugilist Jack Johnson, discussed subsequently.[11]

As a point of clarification, the Texas–Mexico border was not the only locale for this black and Mexican cultural mixing, because states like New Mexico, California, and Arizona also gave rise to populations in which black and brown intermingling was an aspect of borderland demographic and cultural development. In one case, George McJunkin was "born a slave in Texas," came to New Mexico after the Civil War, and resided in Folsom, New Mexico, acting "as a kind of bridge between the Mexicans." "Mexican cowboys . . . taught him the things he wanted to know—how to swing a rope and drop a loop over a horse's head or how to snap a loop up under its heels." He "liked some of the young Mexican women and they liked him. . . . [He] felt very close to the Mexicans. They and he both were nonwhite and because of that they had many experiences in common."[12]

There were evidently "many experiences in common" that far exceeded the realm of familial bonds, for as the Mexican Revolution took shape there was evidence of African Americans volunteering to fight on the side of the Mexicans. In the early stages of the revolutionary process, Clarence Harris of San Diego recalled seeing African Americans fighting a fierce battle in "Tijuana"—Baja California. This now sprawling metropolis was then "just a little town . . . some people, maybe they were citizens or a few soldiers of Tijuana, I don't know, put up a fight and it lasted quite a while. It started early in the morning and it was over about three o'clock in the afternoon." Harris recalled how he and his *compadres* "sat on a hill just about where the gate going into Tijuana is now. . . . The bullets were whizzing by."[13]

Problems intensified for U.S. authorities once it became clear that even elements within the established circles of the state apparatus in the border town of Laredo had sympathies for the Mexican cause. The Mexican Consul in Laredo, Texas, told the U.S. marshal there in 1911 that "it is a matter of common notoriety that the constabulatory of Webb County and a large party of the city police are in sympathy with those preparing an uprising in Mexico." In particular, he noted that "[s]ome of the principal peace officers of the county and city are actively espousing and assisting those who are attempting to subvert the peace of my country." That same year the Mexican consul in Calexico, California, (as anarchists and African Americans were embroiled in warfare just across the border) concluded that there were "three hundred" in revolt, "the majority" being "*Americanos.*" Later, after the Revolution had moved in a more radical direction, the U.S. revolutionary left—which included the African Blood Brotherhood, a radical organization of West Indians and African Americans dedicated to racial emancipation that eventually amalgamated forces with the Third International—was hailed by the Mexican consul in New York for its "energetic campaign in favor" of his nation.[14]

After repeated complaints about the murder of U.S. citizens and sacking of their investments at the hands of Mexican dissidents both within the country and also in Mexico, the U.S. government in 1914 sent troops to invade Mexico. This occurred after U.S. sailors were arrested in Tampico, near the rich oilfields. With a touch of pride, the NAACP noted that "twenty colored men, none more than twenty years of age, landed with the battalion of Blue Jackets from the U.S. warships and fought unceasingly at the recent taking of Vera Cruz, with "one . . . slightly injured." Still, the question persisted for U.S. authorities as to whether African Americans could be trusted to take up arms in defense of the racially prejudiced United States against the more socially progressive political regime engendered by the Mexican government to the south. History shows that they were in fact entrusted with this task, and many—though not all—honored their duties.[15]

Undoubtedly, there was a long and undeniable history of African American collusion in the implementation of American imperial policy and military occupation in Mexico. Henry O. Flipper, one of the first African Americans to attend West Point, is the personification of this trend. With his fervent loyalty to the U.S. government and impressive linguistic training in Spanish, Flipper singlehandedly helped produce research that was useful in orchestrating American reappropriation of lands that had been seized by the Mexican government during the Revolution. In the pre-revolutionary period as early as 1882 to 1891, Flipper "surveyed public lands in Mexico for American companies under concessions from the Mexican government." From 1901 to 1905, he was "resident engineer" for the "Balvanera Mining Company, a New York corporation," and from 1907 to 1919 he was "resident engineer and legal advisor to the Sierra Mining Company, a Duluth, Minnesota corporation" with vast holdings in Mexico.[16] Flipper served as an agent of the U.S. government, officially appointed as a "Special Agent for the Department of Justice," where his "duties," in his own words, were outlined as follows:

> [T]o go to Mexico and examine the grants on the ground, make such surveys as I thought necessary, hunt up witnesses, be myself the principal witness at the trial of the cases, hunt up and translate the Spanish and Mexican land laws [on the basis of] which the grants had been made and, in short, prepare the cases for the United States Attorney. In the course of this work, I collected, translated and arranged, and the Department of Justice published, a collection of Spanish and Mexican land laws running from the 16th century to 1853, which collection the Land Court and the United States Supreme Court used extensively in reaching their decisions.[17]

Above and beyond the individual actions of such avowed loyalists to U.S. empire as Flipper, the collective role of the Buffalo Soldiers in securing U.S. military domination over less powerful adversaries—Native American and Mexican alike—was critical both prior to and during the Mexican Revolution. Reflecting on the historic role of the Buffalo Soldiers, New Mexican writer, Tim Giago, stated in 1997 that "I believe African Americans everywhere should look upon this time in their history with extreme caution. Many American Indian men, women and children were mercilessly slaughtered by these Buffalo Soldiers who were led by white officers." Although conceding that "to the credit of some, they deserted and joined some of the American Indian tribes they had been hindered to annihilate," his larger conclusion was that "[t]his is not one of the prouder moments for African Americans." Many African American soldiers of the day, evincing an ideological loyalty to the U.S. government similar to that of Henry Flipper, reflected proudly on the fact that they had "battled and defeated the Apaches, Kiowas, Comanches, Cheyennes, Mexicans and Mescaleros."[18]

During the era of the Mexican Revolution, it was the Buffalo Soldiers who forced the Mexican revolutionary Pancho Villa back into northern Mexico after he attacked Columbus, New Mexico, in 1916, wounding thirteen and killing sixteen Americans. In response to Villa's attack, the U.S. military under the leadership of the African American soldier Colonel Charles Young, led fifteen thousand troops in a "charge at Agua Caliente" into Mexico, making it the "first time that American troops had attacked with the support of overhead machine gun fire." But this "punitive expedition," as it was later known, quickly turned sour for the United States once the Buffalo Soldiers were called upon to make even further attacks on Mexican soldiers on Mexican soil. The "charge at Carrizal" left ninety African American soldiers overwhelmed by over four hundred Mexican troops, eventually forcing the former into retreat and many into eventual death. Lem H. Spilsbury, a "scout and interpreter," recalled that they were "taken to the town of Carrizal. They took our clothes away from us and shoes and hats, also all jewelry and money . . . Most of the boys were barefooted and bare-headed and in their underclothes. The first detachment of six prisoners were robbed of everything in the way of outer clothing." Understandably, the embarrassed and defeated U.S. government opted that reports of the Carrizal defeat "should not be given press."[19]

The preeminent African American activist, sociologist, historian, and cofounder of the National Association for the Advancement of Colored

People, William Edward Burghardt Du Bois, however, was determined to broadcast this defeat of the Negro troops before the readership of *The Crisis,* literary organ of the NAACP. Above all, Du Bois was interested in responding to the highly publicized story of the troopers laughing and singing in the face of certain death at Carrizal. "Schoolboys of coming generations," said *The Crisis,* "will read how the troopers faced certain death with smiles on their lips; that they joked with one another, and burst into song as they fought their last fight against overwhelming odds." In other words, Du Bois was most struck by the fact that, in spite of their failure to advance the cause of American empire against the Mexican nation, the spirit of these African American troops was not one of fear or sorrow in the face of death, but rather one of cynical celebration and buoyancy. W. Ashbie Hawkins of Baltimore summed up the mounting crisis of U.S. hegemony over African Americans by declaring that "when respectable colored men in this city have difficulty in purchasing or renting homes for themselves and families simply because they are colored, they cannot be easily persuaded to fight to maintain such a condition." "[No] man, white or black," he continued, "can love a city, a state or a nation that restrains and hampers his activities on every hand and that endorses and perpetuates race friction by class legislation."[20]

As the Mexican Revolution overlapped with U.S. participation in World War I, and as African American soldiers drafted into the First World War to supposedly "make the world safe for democracy" began to return to the segregated, repressive dicta of Jim Crow, Texas became the focal point of a powerful admixture of militarism and racial pride that resulted in heightened racial tensions between African Americans and Anglos. And the Mexican border to the south was by no means irrelevant to this deepening crisis of white supremacy on the part of black Texans.

Well before black soldiers began to return to Texas from World War I, there was intelligence indicating that black veterans of the Mexican Revolution were conspiring to form race-based militias presumably against Anglos in the United States. U.S. intelligence "picked up new information that [an] organization and journal for black officers was about to be set up in the United States along the lines of a Masonic lodge. The man behind the scheme was "a Methodist or Baptist minister of Galveston, Texas, radical and probably militant in his views." Lieutenant Osceola A. McKaine was helping in "the formation in Harlem of the League for Democracy . . . the most radical and successful of the black veterans' associations." A native of South Carolina, he "joined the army in 1914, serving in the Philippines and afterward with the 24th Infantry at Columbus, New Mexico, and under Pershing during the latter's pursuit of Pancho Villa."[21]

In part, the spark that ignited this explosion of black militarist organization along the Mexican border was derived from the increase in white supremacist attacks on African Americans in that same zone during the Mexican Revolution and World War I and climaxing in the aftermath of the latter. In 1916, fifteen thousand Anglo-Americans in Waco, Texas, celebrated the torture and burning of seventeen-year-old Jesse Washington. As the NAACP put it, they "unsexed him; cut off his fingers, nose and ears; burned him alive . . . The teeth brought five dollars each." In a twist of irony, the NAACP noted that this lynching was concurrent with the "punitive expedition" of the Buffalo Soldiers to Carrizal. In 1918, sixty African Americans were lynched and seventy-six in 1919. Thus it was in this context of increasing racial tension that the NAACP of Texas grew rapidly, marking a new era of black militancy and helping to promote the radical upheaval that heavyweight boxer and "race man" Jack Johnson led along the Texas–Mexico border in the ensuing period.[22]

The NAACP was organized just as the Mexican Revolution was getting off the ground. Before 1918, the NAACP "had been completely unorganized" in Texas, but that year "twelve branches" were founded and a "further twenty-one in 1919. Within the space of one year the original membership of 2,774 swelled up to 7,960. In most of the new Texas NAACP branches, women made up at least a quarter of the charter members." In the fall of 1918, the NAACP leadership was informed that the strongest branch was in San Antonio, with almost one thousand members. In 1916, the entire national organization had nine thousand members, but by the end of 1918 there were 165 branches and forty-four thousand members.[23]

Across Texas, black militarism was mounting—and quickly. Texas Ranger Frank Matthews was told by "Mr. Davis, salesman at George Petchernick's Gun Store on East Houston St." in San Antonio that "they had sold a great many Negroes pistols and rifles and cartridges . . . in the last two months. . . . Several pawn shops had sold a great deal of arms and ammunition to Negroes." In Marshall, Texas, black radical papers were banned from sale and even circulation in the streets. U.S. intelligence agent reports revealed concern about a "Negro uprising in East Texas in opposition to the draft into WWI." Moreover, an agent in Texarkana heard a "Negro preacher [say] . . . 'Negroes should arm themselves with Winchester rifles . . . then we will have another war right here at home for

Democracy.'" In this same context, *The Crisis* defended the black residents of Houston, Texas, who retaliated against racial violence only to compound this valorization of black militancy by printing a letter from African American veterans in Columbus, New Mexico, who had formed a relief committee for victims of racist violence in East St. Louis: "*The Crisis* is held in very high esteem by the men of the 24th Infantry and we are always glad when it comes.... We want to become members of the NAACP." Such an amalgamation of forces between the generally pacifist NAACP and militant black veterans on the Mexican border during the Mexican Revolution—and now contemporaneous with the spread of socialist internationalism sparked by the Bolshevik Revolution of 1917—made the "Red Summer" of 1919 an especially hot period for Texas.[24]

In October of 1919, a Bureau of Investigation official reported nervously that "many Negroes are going into Mexico. Twenty were counted at the theatre in Mexico City one night. They are publicly in favor of riots in the United States and are conferring with many *Carrancista* generals ... with a view, supposedly, of assisting the *Carrancistas* in case of trouble with the United States." It certainly did not help matters any that these African Americans were headed to Mexico to meet with the acclaimed boxer, socialist sympathizer, and "race man" Jack Johnson.[25]

When Johnson had a boxing match in Nuevo Laredo, on the Mexican side of the border, "and something like 20 Negroes from the United States" reportedly "conferred" with him about matters above and beyond the fight, it was feared "by well posted Americans that this meeting was had in Nuevo Laredo for the purpose of giving Johnson a chance to have an understanding with his visitors and to further Carranza propaganda in the United States." Several African American informants, namely "three Negro musicians and a small well educated yellow Negro in Nuevo Laredo and several Americans" were said to have informed U.S. agents that they had seen Johnson "in close consultation with the *Carrancistas* there. It is rumored that Johnson has a commission under the Carranza government." The report also advised for scrutiny of black musicians near the border like Louis Markham and Jerry Smith of San Antonio and James Kelley of New Iberia, Louisiana, because there two films had "been exhibited in San Antonio recently showing Johnson in dress suit and stating he is a member of the best clubs in Mexico City."[26]

U.S. authorities became increasingly uncomfortable as ties between black militarism along the border and the Mexican government led by

President Venustiano Carranza became increasingly evident. In the aftermath of the Houston race riot of 1917, a mutiny of one hundred and fifty black soldiers from the 24th Infantry based out of Camp Logan, Texas, it was reported that "[o]ver the entire south, particularly Texas, Louisiana and Arkansas there are spread secret societies of Negroes for the purpose of aggressive action against the whites," "perhaps 1500" in Houston alone. Inspired by heavyweight boxer Jack Johnson, whose radical agenda was increasingly being supported both financially and politically by President Carranza, as well as the claims to self-determination and independence that were touted during World War I, many African American soldiers and veterans were reportedly procuring "arms in great numbers." In one race riot in Longview, Texas, apparently "everyone was greatly surprised to see Negroes coming out of the cane brakes with 30–30 caliber rifles and as much as 200 rounds of ammunition." Across the county in which Longview is situated, "approximately 8000 firearms" were confiscated by local authorities. Such militant direct action against white supremacy on the part of "Negro society" in Texas only exacerbated fears that "[e]fforts are thought to be under way by the *Carrancista* government to get Negroes into Mexico in order that they may assist the army, many of them having already been trained in our own service."[27]

It was in this context of race-based militancy that Jack Johnson settled down in—or more likely escaped to—Mexico in 1919. When James J. Jeffries lost to Jack Johnson leading to "several racial disturbances in Texas as a result of this fight," "Governor T. M. Campbell asked the legislature to bar any films of the fight, and it did so. Other legislators tried unsuccessfully to get a law passed which would bar for all time films in which Negroes were participants." As early as 1912, U.S. Attorney General George Wickersham was informed that "special interest [had been] manifested by the President in the investigation of charges against John A. Johnson, heavyweight pugilist." Johnson had long established himself as a formidable boxer who enjoyed pouncing on European-Americans from across the hemisphere—thus winning the hearts and minds of people of African descent from Texas all the way to Cuba.[28]

Captain Cushman A. Rice of Havana, Cuba, newly installed as President of the Sporting Club of Cuba, declared that if he had a choice, Johnson would not fight there. "Let me say for myself, as well as every man of means on the island that a bout between [Johnson and the challenger Jess Willard] will not be tolerated for a single moment . . . the race question is too delicate a subject to ever allow a white man to battle a Negro. Our interests are too valuable to allow the flames of race feeling to be fanned into a riot. . . . Never will we tolerate mixed bouts. . . . We don't want any civil war and that's what it would mean if a black started to muss up with a white man." Still haunting the memory of Cushman and most certainly the vast majority of non-black Cuban elites was the recent race rebellion of 1912 in Cuba. Cushman loosely referred to this rebellion when he concluded that "they [Negro Cubans] went off into the woods to run a government of their own about three years ago and we had to go out and shoot them. We don't want that. We don't intend to do anything that would put the idea in their heads again."[29] Clearly, radical African Americans and radical Afro-Cubans were seen as a double threat for U.S. and Cuban authorities alike, a threat that would endure well into the twentieth century, first under the leadership of the Communist Third International in the 1930s and later under President Fidel Castro, beginning in the 1960s.

But Johnson was not deterred by Cuba's racial backwardness. Rather, he just looked past Cuba to Mexico. According to Johnson, Mexico was "willing not only to give us the privileges of Mexican citizenship, but will champion our cause. . . . If you want us, Mexico . . . we are ready to become your citizens and willing to do all that we can to make you a great power among the nations." More broadly, he proclaimed, "If you want us, Latin America, we are ready to dwell among you and make you rich as we have made the southern white man rich . . . in other words, the Negro is on the auction block, and the nation or community that bids the highest will receive him." Someone who knew Johnson personally reported that "I have become a friend of Jack Johnson, and can positively assert that he has sent money and written articles to aid the Negroes in their struggle in the United States. He makes collections among the Negroes and their sympathizers. . . . He tried to go to the Antilles, especially Cuba, to foment a rebellion among the Negroes . . . calls himself a DEFENDER OF HIS RACE" (emphasis in original).[30]

When Walter Sanborn, an American drugstore and restaurant owner in Mexico, was forced to serve Johnson, William F. Buckley Sr., an (in)famous conservative oilman, noted the words of a U.S. Senate aide who said that "Sanborn was very badly treated by General Merrigo and General de la Torre and forced him to wait on Jack Johnson. . . . Johnson stands very high with the Carranza government and [there] are more Negroes now in Mexico City than ever before. Americans from there are of the opinion that the Carranza government is carrying out through Johnson quite a propaganda in the United States. Some time ago Johnson gave an exhibition in Nuevo Laredo and had about twenty Negroes from different portions of the United States to meet him there."[31]

Not only had Johnson proved to be a "race man" of significant stature for his time, but he had also established himself as a considerable ally of the fast-growing Bolshevik movement for socialist internationalism. Mike Gold, an early Red, or Communist, who also escaped to Mexico, came across Johnson when "[a]t one point collecting money in the streets of Mexico City for a Spanish translation of the Soviet Constitution, he encountered the African American boxer Jack Johnson, with whom he was acquainted." Johnson reportedly gave him ten dollars.[32]

In addition to monetary contributions to left causes, Johnson was also known as somewhat of a socialist ideologue. A spy who had infiltrated the Socialist Party in Mexico noted that "Johnson wished to spread race propaganda and he was interested in socialist ideology." According to U.S. intelligence, Johnson was not only "publicly in favor of race riots in [the] U.S." but was also a key promoter "of the Carranza propaganda in the U.S.," which included "efforts under way to get Negroes into the Mexican army." But just as the *Plan de San Diego* had never come to fruition several years before, neither had it occurred that considerable African Americans joined the Mexican military in an effort to overthrow Jim Crow domination over brown and black alike in the United States.

The Mexican Revolution undeniably shaped the experiences of African Americans in Texas and even more importantly helped radicalize African American communities in the state and even across the country. In the era prior to the Revolution, Mexico supported African American revolts against the white supremacist government of the United States. More generally, Mexico had always been a tolerant place in which African Americans could live. Further, Mexicans and Tejanos accepted African Americans into their communities and families, and had patronized African American businesses.

In the era of the Mexican Revolution, African Americans, and particularly those involved in the "New Negro" in the post–World War I period like the African Blood Brotherhood, supported the radical phase of the Mexican Revolution; in return, the Mexican consul expressed his gratitude. Reciprocally, in 1915 the Tejanos in the *Plan de San Diego* took into account the subordinate status of African Americans in the United States as they endeavored to strike a blow against U.S. domination in the south-west.

Most revealing about this historical black and brown nexus is the way in which African American veterans who returned from service in the Mexican Revolution seem to have exhibited exceptional racial pride. Upon their return, they refused to accept a Jim Crow Texas where lynching occurred. In several towns across Texas, they allegedly formed militias to combat prejudice and violence. In turn, the Carranza government, which tolerated notions of racial equality, supported African American radical ideas. In short, the transnational inroads constructed by black militants from Jack Johnson to the vigilance committees in Columbus, New Mexico, during the era of the Mexican Revolution are a testament to the long history of brown and black collusion against white supremacy that recurred time and again on the long road from slavery to freedom.[33]

Notes

1. "Memorandum on the Message of Zimmerman to the German Minister to Mexico," March 4, 1917, Box 7, Folder 2, *Robert Lansing Papers, Princeton University;* "Zimmerman Note," *Current History* 6 (April 1917): 3.

2. John S. D. Eisenhower, *Intervention! The United States and the Mexican Revolution, 1913–1917* (New York: Norton, 1993), 212.

3. Karl Jacoby, "Between North and South: The Alternative Borderlands of William H. Ellis and the African-American Colony, 1895," 2001, unpublished paper in possession of Gerald Horne, coauthor.

4. Langston Hughes, *The Big Sea* (New York: Knopf, 1942), 15; Edward J. Mullen, ed., *Langston Hughes in the Hspanic World and Haiti* (Hamden: Archon Press, 1977), 21; and Alfred W. Reynolds, "The Alabama Negro Colony in Mexico, 1894–1896," Part 2, *Alabama Review* 6 (January 1853): 31–58, 57.

5. James N. Leiker, "Racial Borders: Black Soldiers and Race Relations along the Rio Grande, 1866–1916" (Ph.D. diss., University of Kansas, 1999), 109, 138, 146, 155.

6. Ibid., 70, 72.

7. Louis R. Harlan et al., eds., *The Booker T. Washington Papers, Volume 8, 1904–1906* (Urbana: University of Illinois Press, 1978), 405; and Edwin S. Redkey, *Black Exodus: Black Nationalist and Back-to-Africa Movements, 1890–1910* (New Haven, Conn.: Yale University Press, 1969), 187, 188.

8. Clipping, November 19, 1889, C192, *Charles Turner Scrapbook,* Missouri Historical Society, St. Louis.

9. *El Paso Evening Tribune* (October 9, 1893); and *El Paso Evening Tribune* (October 18, 1893).

10. Alva M. Stevenson to Gerald Horne, May 23, 2001 (in possession of coauthor, Gerald Horne).

11. Maceo C. Dailey and Kristine Navarno, *Wheresoever My People Chance to Dwell: Oral Interviews with African American Women of El Paso* (Baltimore: Black Classics Press, 2000), 13.

12. Franklin Folsom, *Black Cowboy: The Life and Legend of George McJunkin* (Niwot, Colorodo: Roberts Rinehart, 1992), 12, 16, 21, 84, 108, 136.

13. Oral History, Clarence I. Harris, January 10, 1989, San Diego Historical Society, San Diego, California.

14. Mexican Consul in Laredo, Texas, to Hon. C. G. Brewster, U.S. Marshal, Laredo, November 14, 1911, L–E–849, Secretario de Relaciones Exteriores, Archivo Histórico, Mexico City; Memorandum, March 3, 1911, L–E–862, Secretario de Relaciones *Exteriores, Mexico City;* Memorandum from Mexican Consul, September 8, 1919, 17–18–143, Secretario de Relaciones Exteriores, Archivo Histórico, Mexico City.

15. *The Crisis* 8 (July 1914): 114.

16. Undated memorandum from Henry O. Flipper, Box 0, Folder 20, *Albert Fall Papers,* Huntington Library, San Marino, California.

17. See Letter from Henry O. Flipper, May 4, 1916, in Appendix, Theodore D. Harris, "Henry Flipper and Pancho Villa," *Password* 6 (Spring 1961): 39–46, 44, Vertical Files, Henry O. Flipper, El Paso Public Library.

18. *Albuquerque Journal* (April 26, 1997). See also Garna L. Christian, *Black Soldiers in Jim Crow Texas, 1899–1917* (College Station: Texas A&M University Press, 1995); and "Buffalo Thunder," undated leaflet from Buffalo Soldiers Society of New Mexico, PSC East Unit 376, 2050 Second Street SE, Kirtland, AFB, New Mex., 87117–5563, Vertical Files, "Afro-Americans-Military-Buffalo Soldiers," Center for Southwest Research, University of New Mexico, Albuquerque.

19. Bernard C. Nalty, *Strength for the Fight: A History of Black Americans in the Military* (New York: Free Press, 1986), 83; Richard O'Connor, "'Black Jack' of the 10th," *American Heritage* 18 (February 1967): 14–15, 102–107, 107; and Affidavit of Lem H. Spilbury, circa 1916, Box 71, Record Group 395, *Carrizal Encounter,* National Archives and Records Administration, Washington, D.C.

20. *The Crisis* 12 (August 1916): 163, 174, 184.

21. Mark Ellis, *Race, War and Surveillance: African Americans and the United States Government during World War I* (Bloomington: Indiana University Press, 2001), 214.

22. National Association for the Advancement of Colored People (NAACP) pamphlet, 1916, in Herbert Aptheker, *A Documentary History of the Negro People in the United States,* vol. 3 (New York: Citadel, 1973), 142.

23. Adam Fairclough, *Better Day Coming: Blacks and Equality, 1890–2000* (New York: Viking, 2000), 130–131; and Raymond Wolters, *Du Bois and His Rivals* (Columbia: University of Missouri Press, 2002), 103.

24. Frank Matthews to William Hanson, August 12, 1919, vol. 21, *Walter Prescott Webb Papers;* L. M. Henry to Bureau of Investigation, January 7, 1919, Reel 10, no. 10, *Surveillance Papers; The Crisis* 14 (October 1917): 307–308.

25. Roderick B. Patten, "Santo Flores: A Case of Mistaken Identity," *Chronicles of Oklahoma* 48 (Winter 1970–1971): 467–74.

26. Ibid.

27. Captain Hanson of Texas Rangers to Director of Military Intelligence, October 15, 1919, Reel 21, no. 824, *Surveillance Papers.*

28. Larmar L. Kirven, "A Century of Warfare: Black Texans" (Ph.D. diss., Indiana University, 1974), 100.

29. *New York Sun* (February 17, 1913).

30. *The Favorite Magazine* (Chicago), circa November 1919; "George" to Lanier Winslow, Esq., to U.S. State Department, no date, Reel 17, no. 832; and Theodore Kornweible, *Federal Surveillance of Afro-Americans (1917–1925): The First World War, the Red Scare and the Garvey Movement* (Chapel Hill: University of North Carolina, 1985).

31. William M. Hanson to Judge Kearful, October 11, 1919, Folder 177, *William F. Buckley Papers,* University of Texas at Austin.

32. Alan M. Wald, *Exiles from a Future Time: The Forging of the Mid-Twentieth Century Left* (Chapel Hill: University of North Carolina Press, 2002), 51.

33. Randy Roberts, *Papa Jack: Jack Johnson and the Era of White Hope* (London: Robston, 1986), 209; and Memorandum, October 15, 1919, Reel 109, M1194, *Name Index to Correspondence of the Military Intelligence Division of the War Department General Staff, 1917–1941,* National Archives and Records Administration, College Park, Md.

Understanding Greater Revolutionary Mexico
The Case for a Transnational Border History

RAÚL A. RAMOS

As Mexico commemorates the centennial of the Mexican Revolution and historians look back to understand that turbulent time, renewed attention to the impact of the conflict on ethnic Mexicans living on the American side has connected with larger analytical and methodological questions.[1] The works by the authors in this volume and others remind readers of the need for approaches to research and writing that examine historical subjects through a transnational prism. People, families, ideas, capital, goods, and violence crossed back and forth across the border to the point that self-contained national narratives lose their power to explain and make sense of the past. The displacements and traumas experienced during the Revolution continue to reverberate across the continent. These essays serve as a jumping-off point to further explore those revolutionary threads and repeat the call for incorporating this period into American history.

The essays in this volume develop multiple themes around violence, migration, and the limits of state authority. Although historians have dealt with these subjects in Chicano/a studies, their full understanding necessitates a transnational approach. These essays teach us that subjects such as violence, when viewed in a broader manner, have the ability to change the way we look at well-known events and phenomena. The Mexican Revolution itself takes on a new appearance when the extent of its influence is examined beyond the border. It is worth further developing these three themes by reexamining the insights raised by the essays in this volume and connecting their efforts with the transnational approach.

Recent works by historians and social theorists have added the transnational view to the quiver of useful analytical perspectives.[2] Historians working in both Chicano/a history and Borderlands history have, to a certain degree, engaged in this project from the beginning. In this case, transnational history more appropriately describes a methodology for research and writing, whereas borderlands history encompasses a broad region and space in which groups and states come in contact. Borderlands and transnational history both rely on each other and have much to offer investigators interested in expanding their analytical views. Chicano/a history, as both a subject position and methodology, sheds new light on how we can develop a nuanced historical narrative that accounts for a broad range of experiences and relationships over time.

These thematic approaches aid in understanding identity formation in the complex borderland frontier where the Mexican Revolution's impact can be found. To understand the context and shifting ground where identity takes root requires historians to move beyond their comfort zones and training specialties into multiple languages, national histories, and historiographies. Historians taking a transnational approach to their work have pointed to methodologies and analytical approaches that make it possible to untangle the complex web of identities in borderlands and other places of cross-cultural contact. Taking a transnational approach means writing history from a starting point beyond a single nation, consciously seeking and including sources, ideologies, and frameworks from and across multiple nations. This approach stands in contrast to international or area studies that begin their analysis at the nation-state.[3] In their recent introductory essay, David G. Gutiérrez and Pierrette Hondagneu-Sotelo note that "transnational spaces are envisioned as multisited 'imagined communities' whose boundaries stretch across the borders of two or more nation-states."[4] They focus on concepts such as migration, circulation, and cultural pluralism as ways to introduce transnational processes into our understanding of nation and identity. These essays take the notion of multisite analysis one step further by situating transnational processes across the border region in Texas.

Transnational history recasts the meaning of national and international categories by examining their cultural relevance to daily life at the local level. Perhaps it is counterintuitive to focus on the local level rather than on the geopolitical to fully understand the extensive web of ideas, cultures, peoples, and commodities across nations. But the examination of historical memory and political identity in cities and towns across the state reveal as much about their connection to ideas, cultures, and politics outside the region and nation as about their internal social structure. Such is the case for understanding the interconnection between Mexican politics, local historical memory, and ethnic identity formation seen during the Revolution. These essays take this sort of transnational approach to suggest new directions and deeper understandings of the trauma of violence, the new social arrangements of migration and the power and limits of state authority at the border.

Violence

Many of the essays in this volume describe aspects of violence extending from the Revolution into Texas. This violence touched the lives of all border people, whether directly, as was the case for the Manríquez brothers described in Richard Ribb's essay, or through social organizing, as described by Juanita Luna Lawhn with the *Cruz Azul* relief efforts. As these cases show, violence had both an immediate and delayed effect on ethnic Mexicans in the United States. The violence of the Revolution period became a traumatic episode in the collective memory of ethnic Mexicans across the region. Forgetting or erasing trauma also impacts identity formation, in which case it should be seen as further evidence of the impact of violence.

Ethnic Mexicans living on both sides of the border endured the violence that comes with living in or near a nation at war. The Revolution mobilized and shifted people and arms across the border. The new commerce in weapons and the movements of migrants back and forth came as an expected result of the conflict. Both George T. Díaz and John Eusebio Klingemann detail the commercial gain that came with selling arms and providing other material support to combatants in Mexico. While the American side exported instruments of war, Mexicans crossed the border, attempting to escape the daily threats it entailed. Yet the boundaries of the nation-state failed to contain the extension of violence into Texas. Popular imagination of the violence in Mexico had the further effect of labeling ethnic Mexicans as violent people. Ribb reminds readers of the indiscriminate campaign of terror against Mexicans by the Texas Rangers in South Texas.

This violent label, though, appears most directly in Miguel A. Levario's retelling of the race riot that evolved in El Paso in 1916. The violence in Mexico amplified racial distrust on the American side and legitimized violence as an acceptable form of social conduct. Levario notes ethnic Mexican people did respond to these attacks, to the point that required outside intervention. The episodes that revolved around the *Plan de San Diego* discussed by Trinidad Gonzales and Ribb lay out the complex ways ethnic Mexicans, Anglos, and state authorities deployed violence to further their interests or stake in the border region. Despite ethnic Mexican responses to violence, they were more likely to be exposed to arbitrary acts of violence, including lynching. Aside from eliciting these forms of direct response, memories produced by violence have a lasting effect on social and ethnic relations in the border region.[5] The violence of this period undoubtedly continues to reverberate in Texas.

The focus on violence itself can lead to gendered ways of looking at social interaction during war. Social organizing by women described by Lawhn and Sonia Hernández indicates other forms of response to violence that did not involve more violence. These efforts also involved marshalling resources back and forth across the border in an effort to diminish the human cost of war. Silencing the past served as yet another option to survive this period, as Thomas H. Kreneck notes with the new narrative of Felix Tijerina's migration. Tijerina, like the Cruz Azul supporters, availed himself of the realities of living in a transnational zone to mitigate the trauma of violence. Unlike those living on the Mexican side of the border, ethnic Mexicans in the American side lacked political and cultural resolution to the trauma of the Revolution.

Migration

As Tijerina's story reveals, the Mexican Revolution more directly impacted Texas through a period of mass migration. Research on Tijerina reveals the deep social and cultural impact of this revolutionary era migration beyond demographics. Roberto R. Treviño's retelling of Gerónimo Treviño's own immigration story strengthens how the Revolution shaped the decision to cross the border. The movement of people and ideas across the border only intensified existing transnational social connections. Treviño moved to a familiar place he knew from years of working as a migrant laborer. Tijerina took advantage of social and business relationships in Houston to exploit ambiguity around his birth to shape a convenient narrative of his life. In both these cases, the relatively open border of the Revolution period allowed these men to shape their future. That border would quickly constrict and become more meaningful in the following years, due in some part to continued fears of violence.

Gerónimo Treviño not only entered Texas; he entered the Texas workforce and all the economic and social struggles that it entailed. As part of the generation born and raised in Mexico, he and others found ways to survive those conditions. Hernández reveals the transnational form some of those responses followed through the paths social links and ideas made their way across the border. The labor ideology of the *Partido Liberal Mexicano* and the organizing of Jovita Idar shaped social views around labor and gender for generations to follow. Generational differences did develop between those revolutionary era migrants and long-time ethnic Mexicans across communities in Texas. These differences influenced some forms of social organizing but quickly diminished as important factors as external ideas of race and ethnicity flattened Mexican identity in the American context.

These migrations, social connections, and self-styled narratives took form largely outside of state control or oversight. Recent scholarship has noted that the state has been involved in policing the border particularly around areas of public health.[6] Violence and migration both become impetus for state action to manage and control the movement of bodies and microbes. Further analysis about state oversight of childcare and births after the Revolution indicate the turning point for this type of enforcement during this era.

State Authority

More generally, these works on the history of the Mexican Revolution on the American side stress the need to trace the impact of the state, or the lack of state authority, during contested times. Transnational analysis decenters the nation as a self-contained unit, opening the state to examination and question. In terms of Mexico, the Revolution threatened the state while the violence and dislocation that defined the war extended into the American side. Although the American state responded to threats, the war did not produce a nation-wide militarized response. To the contrary, Díaz and Klingemann note the lack of enforcement of neutrality laws on the American side when Mexicans used the border to organize the war. The state did participate in militarizing the border, with a deleterious effect on Mexican people. Klingemann notes the repressive consequences of increased American troops in the Big Bend region, particularly on Tejanos. Likewise, Margaret Stevens and Gerald Horne lay out the racial element added to border enforcement through black troops. In this case, American demographics reached the border through representation in the Army.

As with migration and violence, a transnational view of state involvement casts the border as a place of contact rather than closure. Yet, the state is more limited in its reach when it comes to constructing and enshrining the memory of the Revolution. Although the thousands of ethnic Mexicans who migrated into Texas carried the trauma of war with them, they lacked a state to redeem the violence in popular culture. The Mexican Revolution resulted in a new state on the Mexican side that institutionalized the memory of the Revolution in schools and public landmarks. The Revolution served as a sort of national rebirth extolling the new beginning in the post–war era.[7] Without a state apparatus in place on the American side, the remnants of the Revolution lay in the restructured lives and communities confronting a new border and massive social relocation. Absent the state and the limits of national identity, historians are left with a transnational approach to piece together the fragments of lives and livelihoods shattered by the Revolution.

As noted above, the Revolution shaped interconnections among Mexican politics, local historical memory, and ethnic identity formation across Texas and the American Southwest. These essays develop the elements of the Revolution that forged Mexican identity in the greater borderlands. Although generations of ethnic Mexicans formed an identity based on the historic link to the pre–American expansion past in Texas, this era cemented a shift that added a new idea of the Mexican state and strengthened the bond with an immigrant identity. Violence, once common during the frontier era in conflicts with indigenous groups, surfaced once again. Anglo-American outsiders associated violence in Mexico with Mexican identity, legitimizing a wave of terror over ethnic Mexican communities. Refugees and exiles from the Revolution made their lives among and with long-standing Tejano communities. Finally, the borderlands cast a shadow on the Mexican government before and after the Revolution. The ethnic Mexican communities in greater Mexico would no longer be considered marginal to Mexican state-building projects.

Even with the end of the Revolution the effects of violence, migration and state formation continue to impact Mexican ethnic identity formation in the United States. Whether through the repatriation drives of the Depression era, or Zoot riots and the Bracero Program in World War II, the American state leveraged its monopoly over violence to shape ethnic Mexican communities throughout the Southwest. Although historians have documented these events, other effects of state authority and violence lay in the shadows. Detailed analysis of mortality statistics on the border by Karl Eschback and colleagues a decade ago revealed the human cost of border enforcement in migrant deaths.[8] They estimated sixteen hundred possible migrant deaths in the five-year period between 1993 and 1997. These border deaths remain out of the daily coverage of the border, whereas the drug wars on the Mexican side make front-page news. The American state recently deployed new strategies to militarize the border through fencing, troop relocations, drone flights, and computerized surveillance. Despite the economic recession of 2008, migrants continue to lose their lives attempting to evade these new technologies.[9]

In the year commemorating the centennial of the Mexican Revolution, ethnic Mexicans continue to feel the reverberations of violence, migration, and state control. Debates around free trade, border atrocities, and immigration status have now taken a central position in American political discourse. Once again, violence on the Mexican side serves as a pretext to mobilize the state to limit and constrict Mexican bodies.[10] Ethnic Mexican communities follow the spread of these anti-immigrant laws and sentiments across the nation with great interest, whether because of familial connections or simply the impact of the discourse on American identity. Although the actors and settings have shifted over time, Mexican people are intimately familiar with the processes and obstacles unfolding in the present. As disheartening as these most recent developments appear, the essays herein speak volumes about the resilience and strategic responses that can always be found in Mexican communities across Texas.

Notes

1. I use the term "ethnic Mexican" to emphasize a connection with being Mexican and Mexico and to deemphasize migrant generation, birth location, or citizenship status. The term has come into increased use as a way of moving away from labels and toward markers of difference.

2. Recent works have taken a transnational approach, especially in the nineteenth-

century American West and Mexican North. See Adam McKeown, *Chinese Migrant Networks and Cultural Change: Peru, Chicago, Hawaii, 1900–1936* (Chicago: University of Chicago Press, 2001); Elliott Young, *Catarino Garza's Revolution on the Texas–Mexico Border* (Durham: Duke University Press, 2004); Andrés Reséndez, *Changing National Identities at the Frontier: Texas and New Mexico, 1800–1850* (New York: Cambridge University Press, 2005); Sam Truett, *Fugitive Landscapes: The Forgotten History of the U.S.–Mexico Borderlands* (New Haven, Conn.: Yale University Press, 2006); Robert McKee Irwin, *Bandits, Captives, Heroines, and Saints: Cultural Icons of Mexico's Northwest Border-lands* (Minneapolis: University of Minnesota Press, 2007); and Omar Valerio-Jiménez, *River of Hope: Identity and Nation along the Rio Grande, 1749–1890* (Durham: Duke University Press, forthcoming).

3. Thomas Bender, "Historians, the Nation, and the Plenitude of Narratives," in *Rethinking American History in a Global Age,* ed. Thomas Bender (Berkeley: University of California, 2002); and Micol Seigel, "World History's Narrative Problem," *Hispanic American Historical Review* 84 (August 2004): 442.

4. David Gutiérrez and Pierrette Hondagneu-Sotelo, "Introduction: Nation and Migration," *American Quarterly* 60 (September 2008): 504.

5. The memory of violence in Chile during the Pinochet regime has been a recent subject for historians who have traced the ways these memories shape society. Lessie Jo Frazier, *Salt in the Sand: Memory, Violence, and the Nation-State in Chile, 1890 to the Present* (Durham: Duke University Press, 2007), 59–62.

6. John McKiernan-González, "Bodies of Evidence: Representation and Recognition on the Mexican Border," *Interpreting Latino Cultures: A Smithsonian Symposium,* November 21, 2002; and Alexandra Minna Stern, *Eugenic Nation: Faults and Frontiers of Better Breeding in Modern America* (Berkeley: University of California Press, 2005), 57–81.

7. Pierre Nora discusses the places where public memory is created, including the creation of a new framework for time. Pierra Nora, "Between Memory and History: Les Lieux de Mémoire," *Representations,* No. 26, Special Issue: Memory and Counter-Memory (Spring 1989): 19.

8. Karl Eschbach, Jacqueline Hagan, Nestor Rodríguez, Rubén Hernández-León, and Stanley Bailey, "Death at the Border," *International Migration Review* 33 (Summer 1999): 430–454.

9. "Border deaths in Arizona may break record," *Los Angeles Times* (August 24, 2010), accessed December 8, 2010, from http://articles.latimes.com/2010/aug/24/nation/la-na-border-deaths-20100824.

10. Dana Milbank, "Headless bodies and other immigration tall tales in Arizona," *The Washington Post* (July 11, 2010), accessed December 8, 2010, at http://www.washingtonpost.com/wp-dyn/content/article/2010/07/09/AR2010070902342.html.

Anders, Evan. *Boss Rule in South Texas: The Progressive Era*. Austin: University of Texas Press, 1982.

Coerver, Don M., and Linda B. Hall. *Texas and the Mexican Revolution: A Study in State and National Border Policy*. San Antonio: Trinity University Press, 1984.

Cumberland, Charles C. "Border Raids in the Lower Rio Grande Valley—1915," 57 *Southwestern Historical Quarterly* (January 1954): 285–311.

Dameron, Chip. "The Bloody Bandit War of 1915." In *Still More Studies in Brownsville History,* edited by Milo Kearney. Brownsville, Tex.: The University of Texas at Brownsville, 1991.

Darrah, Jason T. "Anglos, Mexicans, and the San Ysabel Massacre: A Study of Changing Ethnic Relations in El Paso, Texas, 1910–1916." M.A. thesis, Texas Tech University, 2003.

De la Garza-Treviño, Ciro R. *El Plan de San Diego*. Ciudad Victoria, Tamps.: Universidad de Tamaulipas, 1970.

De León, Arnoldo. "Mexicans and Mexican Americans in Texas, 1910–1920." M.A. thesis: Texas Christian University, 1971.

Espinoza, Michelle Margot. "Las Mexicanas del Valle: Revolution, Power and Identity, 1910–1920." M.A. thesis, University of Texas at El Paso, 1994.

Estrada, Richard. "The Mexican Revolution in the Ciudad Juárez–El Paso Area, 1910–1920," *Password* (Summer 1979): 55–69.

García, Mario T. *Desert Immigrants: The Mexicans of El Paso, 1880–1910*. New Haven, Conn.: Yale University Press, 1979.

Garza, James Alex. "On the Edge of a Storm: Laredo and the Mexican Revolution, 1910–1917." M.A. thesis, Texas A&M International University, 1996.

Gerlach, Allen. "Conditions Along the Border–1915: The Plan de San Diego," *New Mexico Historical Review* 43 (July 1968): 195–212.

Gómez-Quiñones, Juan. "Plan of San Diego Reviewed," *Aztlán* 1 (Spring 1970): 124–32.

Gomilla, Michelle Lorraine. "Los Refugiados y los Comerciantes: Mexican Refugees and Businessmen in Downtown El Paso, 1910–1920." M.A. thesis, University of Texas at El Paso, 1990.

Gonzales, Trinidad. "The World of México Texanos, Mexicanos and México Americanos: Transnational and National Identities in the Lower Rio Grande Valley During the Last Phase of United States Colonization, 1900–1930." Ph.D. diss., University of Houston, 2008.

González, Gabriela, "Two Flags Entwined: Transborder Activists and the Politics of Race, Ethnicity, Class and Gender in South Texas, 1900–1950." Ph.D. diss., Stanford University, 2005.

Griswold del Castillo, Richard. "The Mexican Revolution and the Spanish-Language Press in the Borderlands." *Journalism History* 4 (Summer 1977): 42–47.

Hager, William A. "The Plan of San Diego: Unrest on the Texas Border in 1915," *Arizona and the West* 5 (Winter 1963): 327–36.

Harris, Charles H. and Louis R. Sadler. "The Plan of San Diego and the Mexican-United States War Crisis of 1916: A Reexamination," *Hispanic American Historical 58 Review* (August 1978): 381–408.

Harris, Charles H. and Louis R. Sadler. *The Texas Rangers and the Mexican Revolution: The Bloodiest Decade, 1910–1920.* Albuquerque: University of New Mexico Press, 2004.

Hedgpeth, Donald R. "The Plan de San Diego: A Border Conflict." M.A. thesis, Southwest Texas State University, 1969.

Henderson, Peter V. *Mexican Exiles in the Borderlands. 1901–1913.* El Paso: Texas Western Press, 1979.

Hernández, Mary Ester. "Some Connections between San Antonio and the Mexican Revolution." M.A. thesis, University of Texas at Austin, 1973.

Johnson, Benjamin H. *Revolution in Texas: How a Forgotten Rebellion and Its Bloody Suppression Turned Mexicans into Americans.* New Haven, Conn.: Yale University Press, 2003.

Johnson, David Nathan. *Madero in Texas: Prelude to a Revolution, 1910–1911,* edited by Félix D. Almaráz. San Antonio, Tex.: Corona Publishing, 2001.

Justice, Glenn. *Revolution on the Rio Grande: Mexican Raids and Army Pursuits, 1916–1919.* El Paso: Texas Western Press, 1992.

Lay, Shawn. *War, Revolution, and the Ku Klux Klan: A Study of Intolerance in a Border City.* El Paso: Texas Western Press, 1985.

Levario, Miguel Antonio. "Cuando vino la mexicanada: Authority, Race, and Conflict in West Texas, 1895–1924." Ph.D. diss., University of Texas at Austin, 2007.

Longoria, Mario D. "Revolution, Visionary Plan, and Marketplace: A San Antonio Incident." *Aztlan* 12 (Autumn 1981): 211–26.

Macías-González, Victor M. "Mexicans of the Better Class: The Exile of Chihuahuan Upper Classes in El Paso, 1913–1930." *Password* 45 (Winter 2000): 175–195.

Martínez, Oscar. *Fragments of the Mexican Revolution: Personal Accounts from the Border.* Albuquerque: University of New Mexico Press, 1983.

Martínez, Oscar. "The Mexicano Experience along the Texas–Chihuahua Border: Oral Recollections of the Period 1910–1920." *The Texas Humanist* 2 (February 1980): 4–5.

Martínez, Oscar J. "Pedro González Remembers the Revolution." *Password* 25 (Spring 1980): 29–37.

Meed, Douglas. *Bloody Border: Riots, Battles, and Adventures Along the Turbulent U.S.–Mexican Borderlands.* Tucson: Westernlore Press, 1992.

Meyer, Michael. "The Mexican-German Conspiracy of 1915," *The Americas* 23 (July 1966): 76.

Orozco, Cynthia. *No Mexicans, Women, or Dogs Allowed: The Rise of the Mexican American Civil Rights Movement.* Austin: University of Texas Press, 2009.

Raat, W. Dirk. *Revoltosos: Mexico's Rebels in the United States, 1903–1923.* College Station: Texas A&M University Press, 1981.

Reyes, Raúl R. "The Santa Isabel Episode, January 10, 1916: Ethnic Repercussions in El Paso and Ciudad Juárez." *Password* 42 (Summer 1997): 55–75.

Richmond, Douglas W. "La guerra en Tejas se renova: Mexican Insurrection and Carranzista Ambitions, 1900–1920." *Aztlán* 1 (Spring 1980): 1–32.

Ribb, Richard. "José Tomás Canales and the Texas Rangers: Myth, Identity, and Power in South Texas, 1900–1920." Ph.D. diss., University of Texas at Austin, 2001.

Rocha, Rodolfo. "The Influence of the Mexican Revolution on the Mexico–Texas Border, 1910–1916." Ph.D. diss., Texas Tech University, 1981.

Rocha, Rodolfo. "The Tejano Revolt of 1915." In *Mexican Americans in Texas History,* edited by Emilio Zamora, Cynthia Orozco, and Rodolfo Rocha, 103–119. Austin: Texas State Historical Association, 2000.

Romo, David D. *Ringside to a Revolution: An Underground Cultural History of El Paso and Juarez, 1893–1923.* El Paso: Cinco Puntos Press, 2005.

Samponaro, Frank N., and Paul J. Vanderwood. *War Scare on the Rio Grande: Robert Runyon's Photographs of the Border Conflict, 1913–1916.* Austin: Texas State Historical Association, 1992.

Sandos, James A. *Rebellion in the Borderlands: Anarchism and the Plan of San Diego, 1904–1923.* Norman: University of Oklahoma Press, 1992.

——— "The Plan of San Diego: War and Diplomacy on the Texas Border, 1915–1916." *Arizona and the West* 14 (Spring 1972): 5–24.

Tanner, Eric Carroll. "The Texas Border and the Mexican Revolution." M.A. thesis, Texas Tech University, 1970.

Taylor, Paul S. "The Mexican Invaders of El Paso." *Survey* 36 (July 8, 1916): 380–81.

Utley, Robert M. *Lone Star Lawmen: The Second Century of the Texas Rangers.* Oxford: Oxford University Press, 2007.

Watts, Jake. "The Plan of San Diego and the Lower Rio Grande Valley." In *More Stud-*

ies in Brownsville History, edited by Milo Kearney. Brownsville, Tex.: Pan American University at Brownsville, 1989.

Warburton, L.H. "The Plan de San Diego: Background and Selected Documents." *Journal of South Texas* 12 (1999): 125–155.

Wilkinson, William V. "The Mexican Revolution and the Bandit Wars: The Lower Grande Valley in 1915." In *Still More Studies in Brownsville History,* edited by Milo Kearney. Brownsville, Tex.: Pan American University at Brownsville, 1991.

ARNOLDO DE LEÓN is the C.J. "Red" Davidson Professor of History at Angelo State University. He is the author of several works on Texas, among them *Mexican Americans in Texas: A Brief History,* 3rd ed. (Wheeling, Il.; Harlan Davidson Inc., 2009); and with Robert A. Calvert and Gregg Cantrell, *The History of Texas,* 4th ed. (Wheeling, Il.; Harlan Davidson Inc., 2007).

GEORGE T. DÍAZ is a graduate of Southern Methodist University, where he received his PhD in 2010. His publications include "Twilight of the *Tequileros:* Prohibition Era Smuggling in the South Texas Borderlands, 1919–1933," in *Transnational Vice and Contraband in North America,* eds. Elaine Carey and Andrae M. Marak. (Tucson: University of Arizona Press, forthcoming 2011). He has taught at South Texas College.

TRINIDAD GONZALES, a PhD graduate from the University of Houston, is a history instructor at South Texas College. His research focuses on the history of the Lower Rio Grande Valley during the early twentieth century. Currently, he is researching and writing a book about the *revolución de tejas* and the *matanza.*

PAUL HART is associate professor of history at Texas State University and currently the Jesse Jones Professor of Southwestern Studies at the Center for the Study of the Southwest at Texas State. He is also the current President of the Southwest Council of Latin American Studies. Dr. Hart received his B.A. from the University of Texas at Austin, and his PhD from the University of California, San Diego. His first book, *Bitter Harvest: The Social Transformation of Morelos, Mexico and the Origins of the Zapatista Revolution, 1840–1910* (Albuquerque: University of New Mexico Press, 2005), received the Harvey L. Johnson Book Award from the Southwest Council of Latin American Studies in 2007. He is now working on a book that is tentatively titled *Empire and Immigra-*

tion, which will explore the causes and consequences of Mexican immigration into the United States from the beginning of the twentieth century to the present.

SONIA HERNÁNDEZ is an assistant professor in the Department of History and Philosophy at the University of Texas–Pan American. She is a founding member of the Mexican American Studies program and serves as the coordinator of the History Graduate Program. She is the author of "Malinche in Cross-Border Historical Memory," in *José Limón and La Malinche,* ed. Patricia Seed (Austin: University of Texas Press, 2008); "Mujeres, Género y Revolución en Tamaulipas," in *Tamaulipas y La Revolución Mexicana* (Gobierno del estado de Tamaulipas, 2010); and coeditor of *The Mexican American Experience in Texas: A Primary Source Reader* with Charles Waite (Dubuque, Iowa: Kendall Hunt, 2009). She is currently working on her book manuscript, *Negotiating the Making of a Borderlands: Gender and Labor in the Mexican Northeast, 1880–1940.*

GERALD HORNE holds the John and Rebecca Moores Chair of History and African American Studies at the University of Houston. He earned his PhD from Columbia University and his J.D. from the University of California, Berkeley. Selected publications include *The End of Empires: African-Americans and India* (Philadelphia: Temple University Press, 2008); *The Final Victim of the Blacklist: John Howard Lawson, Dean of the Hollywood Ten* (Berkeley: University of California Press, 2005); and *Black & Brown: Africans and the Mexican Revolution, 1910–1920* (New York: University Press, 2005)

JOHN EUSEBIO KLINGEMANN is an assistant professor in the Department of History at Angelo State University. He earned his PhD from the University of Arizona. He is a recipient of the García Robles Fulbright Fellowship for Mexico. His dissertation, "Triumph of the Vanquished: Pancho Villa's Army in Revolutionary Mexico," documents the history of *villismo* after 1920.

THOMAS H. KRENECK is Associate Director for Special Collections and Archives of the Mary and Jeff Bell Library and Graduate Lecturer in Public History at Texas A&M University–Corpus Christi. He founded and developed the Mexican American archival component at the Houston Metropolitan Research Center between 1978 and 1990. He also published *Del Pueblo: A Pictorial History of Houston's Hispanic Community* (Houston: Houston International University, 1989). Since 1990, among his other responsibilities at Texas A&M–Corpus Christi he has been curator of the Dr. Hector P. García Papers. Kreneck is a 2006 Fellow of the Texas State Historical Association.

JUANITA LUNA LAWHN is a professor of English at San Antonio College. Currently, she is one of the editors of the San Antonio College Multicultural Journal titled *Voices.* Her field of research includes the study of the women of *El México de Afuera* and the labor movement of the *mexicanas* in San Antonio in the 1930s. Her publications include a translation *Memorias De Mi Viaje/Recollections of My Trip,* by Beatriz Torres (Albuquerque: University of New Mexico Press, 1994); "*El Regidor* and *La Prensa:* Impediments to Women's Self-Definition," *Third Woman: The Sexuality of Latinas* 4 (1989); and "Victorian Attitudes Affecting the Mexican Woman in *La Prensa* during the Early 1900s and the Chicana of 1980s," in *Missions in Conflict: Essays on U.S.–Mexican Relations and Chicano Culture,* eds. Renate Von Bardeleben, Dietrich Briesmeister and Juan Bruce Novoa (Tubingen Gunter Narr Verlag, 1986).

MIGUEL A. LEVARIO is an assistant professor of history at Texas Tech University. He specializes in U.S.–Mexico borderlands. His research focuses on the transnational context of immigration, militarization, and race in the U.S. West and Northern Mexico. His dissertation, "Cuando vino la mexicanada: Authority, Race, and Conflict in West Texas, 1895–1924," focused on complex racial divisions enforced by militarization in the West Texas region at the turn of the twentieth century. He is currently working on his book manuscript "When They Came: Militarization and the Rise of the Mexican Nemesis, 1895–1933." He continues to teach a variety of courses including Texas history, Mexican American history and culture, U.S.–Mexico borderlands, diaspora, and race.

RAÚL A. RAMOS is an associate professor of history at the University of Houston. He received his PhD in history from Yale University and his A.B. from Princeton University. Ramos has previously taught at the University of Utah, Williams College, and Yale University. He was a fellow at the Clements Center for Southwest Studies at SMU during 2000–2001. He is the author of *Beyond the Alamo: Forging Mexican Ethnicity in San Antonio, 1821–1861* (Chapel Hill: University of North Carolina Press, 2008). The book received the 2008 T. R. Fehrenbach Book Award from the Texas Historical Commission. *Beyond the Alamo* also earned the 2010 NACCS–Tejas Book Award from the National Association for Chicana and Chicano Studies–Tejas Foco. More recently, Ramos coedited a volume on the Hispanic history of Texas, published by Arte Público Press, and is writing a new book on Mexican centennial parades across the American Southwest in 1910.

RICHARD HENRY RIBB is a Senior Academic Advisor in the Dean's Office of the College of Liberal Arts at The University of Texas at Austin. Since earning the PhD in American Studies from The University of Texas at Austin, he has taught at Texas A&M–College Station, The University of Texas at Austin, and Austin Community College. He continues to ready his dissertation, "José Tomás Canales and the Texas Rangers: Myth, Ideology, and Power in South Texas 1910–1920," for publication. His essay "Patrician as Redeemer: José Tomás Canales and the Salvation of South Texas" appeared in the *Journal of South Texas* 14 (Fall 2001). He appeared as commentator in the PBS-aired documentary "Border Bandits" (2004) and has been an invited speaker before historical societies throughout South Texas.

MARGARET STEVENS is an associate history professor and Director of the Urban Issues Institute at Essex County College in Newark, New Jersey. In 2010, she received her PhD from Brown University in the Department of American Civilization. Her doctoral work documents the history of transnational Communist organizations in New York City and the Caribbean during the interwar period.

ROBERTO R. TREVIÑO is associate professor of history at the University of Texas at Arlington. He is the author of *The Church in the Barrio: Mexican American Ethno-Catholicism in Houston;* coeditor (with Richard Francaviglia) of *Catholicism in the American West: A Rosary of Hidden Voices;* and the author of other writings about religion and American culture.

Books in the University of Houston Series in Mexican American Studies:

Música Tejana, Manuel Peña
Mexican American Odyssey, Thomas H. Kreneck
Ethnicity in the Sunbelt, Arnoldo De León
Brown, Not White, Guadalupe San Miguel
Cemeteries of Ambivalent Desire, Marie Theresa Hernández